Ready
when you are

Ready
when you are

a compendium of

comforting one-dish meals

MARTHA ROSE SHULMAN

clarkson potter/publishers
new york

Published by Clarkson Potter/Publishers, New York, New York
Member of the Crown Publishing Group, a division of Random House, Inc.
www.randomhouse.com

CLARKSON N. POTTER is a trademark and POTTER and colophon are registered trademarks of Random House, Inc.

Printed in the United States of America

Design by Jan Derevjanik

Library of Congress Cataloging-in-Publication Data
Shulman, Martha Rose.
    Ready when you are / Martha Rose Shulman; photographs by Luca Trovato
Clarkson.   1. Casserole cookery.   I. Title.
TX693.S38   2003
641.8'21—dc21   2002156671

ISBN 0-609-61084-8

10 9 8 7 6 5 4 3 2 1

First Edition

For my mum, Mary,

and my sis, Melchic,

who are a great comfort to me

acknowledgments

Like the recipes inside, this book simmered for a long time before taking shape. Several friends and colleagues helped to stir the pot. In particular, I'd like to express my gratitude to Susan Friedland, Fran McCullough, Russ Parsons, and my stalwart agent, Molly Friedrich, for their support and their ideas. And particularly to my editor extraordinaire, Roy Finamore, for making the project a beautiful reality. Thanks also to Adina Steiman.

My husband, Bill Grantham, continues to be my biggest fan and my best eater, and I'm grateful to my son, Liam, for being such a good eater and for saying to me so often during the course of my work on the book, "You're a great cooker, Mom."

Thanks also to photographer Luca Trovato and stylist Rori Trovato for the gorgeous photographs; to designer Jan Derevjanik, production manager Linnea Knollmueller, and production editor Trisha Howell; and to copy editor Janet McDonald. You've all helped make this the book I wanted it to be.

contents

Ready
when you are

introduction

One-dish meals, crowd-pleasers with big flavors—that's the kind of dish I like best to cook. This book fulfills my longtime desire to devote a big collection of recipes to them.

When I look back on my thirty-year career as a cook, I see that I've focused on this kind of food from my earliest days as a cook and caterer. That's because a passionate element of my work has always been entertaining, often on a large scale. I regularly served meals to twenty-five to thirty-five friends and guests at my private "supper clubs," both in Austin, Texas, where I began cooking, and in Paris, where I lived for twelve years. It was essential that I choose menus with main dishes that I could cook ahead, at least partially.

Even when I give a small dinner party I like to be with my guests, so I choose menus that accommodate sociability. Although the average number at my dinner parties has shrunk to a mere eight, I still entertain all the time. But now I have a young child and my schedule is as hectic as the next busy American's, so it's even more imperative that my meals, whether they're for the three of us or for company, not be fussy.

With a few exceptions, the dishes in this book don't have to be served as soon as they're done; often, they benefit from a day in the refrigerator. Those that are served right away are likely to be dishes made spontaneously with pantry ingredients, like rice and eggs. They work as well for family meals as they do for dinner parties. Most of them, in fact, are based on traditional recipes for home-cooked meals, what the French would call *cuisine bourgeoise* (but many other cuisines are represented here).

One friend of mine sets aside time most weekends to make two or three of the dishes, so that her family of four can sit down to a good meal every night through the week, despite their demanding schedules. She and her husband enjoy cooking this way together; it's relaxing for them, as well as reassuring: They know that everyone will be happy with the food, and that they'll all be well nourished, too.

the new comfort food

Today comfort food has gone beyond tuna casseroles and mashed potatoes. While it doesn't have to be rich, it does have to be big. Big meaning big flavors, like beef stewed in red wine; chicken braised with lots of peppers, onions, and garlic, or roasted with a ton of vegetables; chick peas stewed with sausage and tomatoes; a double-crusted torte filled with greens, potatoes, eggs, and cheese; a creamy risotto; a lasagne bursting with wild mushrooms; a minestrone that makes a meal; a vegetable ragout hiding under a shiny biscuit crust. This food is stylish but not fancy, sophisticated yet simple. It's enjoyable to cook, and even more so to eat. It fills you up, but doesn't make you full.

The new comfort food is comforting to the cook as well as to the eater. You will be calm when you serve this, and you'll know it's good. Chances are you made the dish yesterday, in a leisurely sort of way, and tasted it toward the end of its long stovetop simmer. Today it's even more delicious. Or maybe you assembled its fragrant components in a gratin dish or Dutch oven a few hours ago and have had time to relax and savor the aromas—or work or fetch your kids from school or play with your toddler or help your daughter with homework—while the dish simmers, braises, or browns in a hot oven. Serving it requires no fancy plating skills; just a big spoon, ladle, or spatula, and a wide bowl or plate. You could add a salad or a starter, but you don't have to.

When dinner is over, there will be no extra serving dishes to wash, because the food is served from the vessel in which it was cooked. The pot doesn't even require washing tonight, because there's enough left over in it for tomorrow's dinner. Its cover replaced, into the refrigerator it goes. Tomorrow the leftovers may take on a new form or be served up exactly as they were tonight. Yesterday's chicken bouillabaisse may become tomorrow's pilaf; the remains of a stew will make a delicious sauce for pasta. A favorite salad of mine is made with diced beef left over from pot-au-feu; I combine it with arugula in a mustardy vinaigrette. Minestrone becomes ribollita, chicken in green mole fills enchiladas; mushroom ragout enhances an omelet. One way or another, the family will be very happy to eat this food again.

When you do cook, it's incredibly satisfying to prepare one dish that constitutes an entire meal. All of the elements of a balanced meal come together in that one dish, producing a dinner with flavors that are familiar, yet so vivid that they surprise the palate. This is the best possible kind of comfort food: it delights eaters and inspires the cook with confidence.

Those who are familiar with my other work may be surprised to find so many meaty dishes here. If you don't eat meat, rest assured, this book won't be lost on you. Well over half the recipes here are meatless. Just skip Chapters 2 and 3, and you'll find a treasure chest of comforting vegetarian one-dish meals. They are easy to spot, because they're all marked with this symbol .

My passion is still for vegetables, and most of the meat dishes here pair the two together. Wonderful things happen when winter squash is stewed with beef or lamb (see the Argentinian Beef Stew with Winter Squash and Corn on page 60 and the Persian Meat Stew with Butternut Squash and Prunes, page 82), when lamb is cooked with tender spring vegetables (see page 86), or when chicken is cooked in a Catalan ratatouille of eggplant, peppers, and tomatoes (see page 114).

I've also lightened traditional recipes, not to the detriment of flavor, but because it's possible to make these recipes taste great without using vast quantities of oil and butter. Today's heavy nonstick cookware allows me to do this; I can brown a cut-up chicken in 2 tablespoons of oil in my nonstick pan, whereas a classic recipe from another era might instruct me to brown the chicken in twice that amount. The recipes also achieve lighter results because I usually use a separate pan to brown the meat, and pour off the fat rather than allow it to go into my stew. And because most of the meat and poultry recipes are even better if they're cooked a day ahead, when you chill them you can skim off a great deal of the fat from the surface before you reheat the dish.

But I'm also happy to announce that there are some indulgences here, such as Macaroni and Cheese (page 190) and, for dessert, Bill's Irish Trifle (page 362). This is, after all, a book of comforting recipes, and like jokes, the old ones are sometimes the best.

how to use this book

These recipes are meant to be liberating. You don't have to cook them when most people cook (right before dinner after a stressful day at work), although you're certainly free to. You can cook them over the weekend; or during the week make one part of a dish at midnight, if it suits you. Put it in the refrigerator and do another part of the recipe before you take your kids to school, then finish it after work. The dish won't suffer. When I was testing recipes for this book, that's exactly the way I had to work. Here's one of my typical cooking schedules:

❖ Recipe to Cook: Basque-Style Chicken (page 110)

❖ Sunday: Buy ingredients for dish.

❖ Monday night, late: Cut up onions and peppers. Refrigerate in plastic bags. Go to bed.

❖ Tuesday morning: Take Liam to preschool, swim, finish an article that's due.

❖ Tuesday afternoon: Cook onions, peppers, and tomato sauce for chicken dish. Take off the heat and cover. Pick up Liam.

❖ Tuesday late afternoon: Brown chicken while bringing pepper and tomato mixture back to a simmer. Put chicken into sauce and cook until done, following recipe. Take off heat.

I could have served the dish that night, or refrigerated it and served it the next day.

I have made advance preparation notes throughout the body of the recipes, so that you'll be able to see as you read a recipe what can be done ahead. I've also noted in many of the recipes what steps can be taken out of order. Even where this isn't noted, as you make preparations to cook a particular dish, read through the recipe carefully, and with the help of the advance preparation notes you'll be able to tell if it might be more convenient to do the steps in a different order. For example, if you look at the recipe for Basque-Style Chicken, you'll notice that in the recipe the cook is instructed to brown the chicken first. This works if you're going to cook the whole dish at once, but when I was doing it piecemeal, it was better to reverse the steps.

This also goes for mise en place, that is, the preparation of the ingredients. Recipes are usually written with the preparation advice in the list of ingredients. However, you can often prepare one ingredient while another one is cooking. It's amazing how much prep you can accomplish while you're waiting for a big pot of water to come to a boil. But it's *vital* that you *read the recipe through* to see where that's possible. If, for example, you have to add a pepper to an onion after the onion has cooked for only 3 minutes, cut up the pepper before you begin cooking the onion. If, on the other hand, you're instructed to brown the onions slowly for 10 minutes, stirring occasionally, before adding the pepper, you can cut up the pepper while the onions are cooking. Often an element of a recipe, such as blanched greens, will keep well in the refrigerator for 3 or 4 days. If, for example, you were making the Lasagne with Greens and Ricotta on page 196, you might want to clean and blanch the greens as soon as you got them home from the Sunday farmers' market (to save space in your refrigerator as well as time), even if you didn't plan to use them in a dish until later that week.

I've also noted recipes that can be finished a day (or sometimes two) ahead, or at least can be assembled up to the baking point. Many of the meat stews, for example, improve overnight. This takes a lot of the heat off both entertaining and feeding your family.

A GUIDE TO THE ICONS

You'll find many of the recipes in the book marked with symbols. Here's your key.

🕐 indicates a recipe that can be made a day or two ahead and that will likely benefit from that advance preparation.

🌿 indicates a vegetarian recipe, or one that can easily be made vegetarian.

increasing quantities

The dishes in this book lend themselves to quantity cooking. Because they hold so well, they're perfect for big buffets and dinner parties. I have never had trouble increasing the volumes by two for a sit-down dinner for twelve, say, or by up to four or five for a crowd. The only thing that you have to remember is that increasing a recipe means increasing the time that you'll have to set aside for making it. Chopping two onions instead of one takes twice as long. You'll also have to allow more time for the cooking—not so much for the final simmering of a dish, but definitely for the initial cooking of aromatics and browning of meat. I can't gauge precisely the amount of time that a large pan of onions will take to cook, but I know it will take more time than it takes to cook only one onion.

equipment

When I tested the recipes for this book, I used the same pots and pans over and over. Here are the items that you will grow to cherish as you cook your way through the recipes. This is by no means an exhaustive list for the beginning cook, but it does pertain to the recipes in this book.

NONSTICK COOKWARE

Because I use less fat in these recipes than is called for in many of the traditional versions, good nonstick cookware is essential. The quality of nonstick cookware has improved tremendously. As restaurants have begun to choose nonstick pans for their high-volume line cooking, manufacturers have had to come up with nonstick cookware that can withstand restaurant wear and tear and the high heat of restaurant stoves. You can find this heavy-duty cookware in a range of stores, from fancy cookware stores, to hardware stores, to restaurant supply outlets. Make sure to look for the heavy restaurant pans. I have great, moderately priced pans made by Wearever and by Nordic Ware. Here are the sizes I most used for the recipes.

❖ Heavy 12-inch skillet

   I use this pan more than any other single item in my *batterie de cuisine*.

- Heavy 12-inch, straight-sided, lidded pan (5.3-quart/5-liter capacity)

    This is known as a sauté pan or *sauteuse* in traditional French cooking. I use mine quite often for braises and stews, in which the ingredients must first be browned. It doubles as a casserole or Dutch oven and is very useful because of its nonstick surface.

- 10-inch skillet

    I use this much less often than my 12-inch, but it's useful for cooking smaller amounts and for making frittatas with leftovers.

- 8-inch omelet pan

    I often make omelets when I have a small amount of leftovers.

CARE OF NONSTICK COOKWARE

Nonstick cookware has come a long way since the days of peeling Teflon. But you still have to take precautions so the pots and pans won't scratch.

- Always use wooden spoons or heatproof plastic utensils when stirring food.

- Wash nonstick cookware carefully in warm water, and avoid using rough surfaces to clean. The cookware will last longer if you avoid the dishwasher.

- If you have to stack the pans to store, place paper towels between them, or stack in reverse order of size so that the bottom of one pan doesn't scratch the inside of another.

CASSEROLES AND DUTCH OVENS

- 5-quart, heavy casserole: For stews, ragouts, and soups. I like a heavy flameproof and ovenproof casserole or Dutch oven that can be used both on top of the stove and in the oven. Many recipes for casseroles begin with browning on a burner and end up simmering in the oven. The cookware that I have been using ever since I began to cook, and that I still swear by, is Le Creuset enameled cast iron. Every recipe in this book that called for a large, heavy casserole or Dutch oven was made in my 5.3-quart (5-liter) round lidded casserole. These are expensive, but they will last more than a lifetime (I still use some of my mother's enameled cast iron, which she bought in the 1940s). They hold the heat beautifully and are attractive enough to double as serving dishes.

- Daubière: These are heavy, oval Dutch ovens (mine is also an enameled cast-iron pot made by Le Creuset) whose lids have a depression that was traditionally filled with a little water. The long-simmering daubes were said to stay moist from the steam created on the inside and the outside of the pan. I think you can achieve an excellent daube without one of these pans, but I find mine useful because it's so large (it has a 6- or 7-quart capacity), and especially if I'm doubling or tripling a recipe, it is put to good use.

SAUCEPANS AND OTHER POTS

❖ Heavy nonaluminum saucepans: I use my heavy Le Creuset 2½-quart, 2-quart, and 1-quart saucepans the most, for making rice and sauces. I am specifying nonaluminum here, because aluminum reacts with certain foods and changes their flavor.

❖ Light saucepans: A set of light enameled or nonstick saucepans, inexpensive ones that you can find in a supermarket, is useful for steaming and blanching vegetables, and for boiling eggs.

❖ 8-quart (or larger) pasta pot: A pasta pot with a basket insert can be very useful. I use the pot as often to blanch vegetables as I do for cooking pasta. The pot can double as a stockpot.

❖ Stockpot: You should have one with an 8-quart capacity or greater. You can use a pasta pot, but you might wish to use a heavier pot for slow-simmering stocks.

BAKING DISHES

❖ 2-quart and 3-quart gratin dish or rectangular baking dishes. I have both earthenware and Le Creuset and use them interchangeably, both for savory baked dishes and desserts.

❖ Lasagne pan: I didn't buy one until I was in the midst of work on this book. My rectangular no-boil lasagne noodles didn't fit my oval gratin dishes well, so one evening I stopped in at a local kitchen store and bought a rectangular, 3-quart ceramic CorningWare lasagne dish. I never looked back. I use it for crumbles and cobblers as well as for lasagne.

❖ Tart pan and pie pan: I use my 10½-inch fluted white porcelain tart pan the most. But a regular pie pan will do fine for most of the pies in this book, and is recommended for the dessert pies. I recommend that you have two, so that you can keep a crust on hand in the freezer.

❖ Baking sheets: You'll use them for all sorts of tasks, including roasting peppers and tomatoes and cooking free-form galettes.

❖ 14-inch pizza pan: For pizzas and galettes. Mine doubles as a cover for my 12-inch non-stick frying pan.

❖ 10-inch springform pan: I use this as often for savory pies as I do for cakes. There are now a number of excellent nonstick springform pans available.

TOOLS AND GADGETS

❖ Chef's knife: Your most important tool. I use a sturdy, stainless-steel 8-inch knife. Keep it sharp by honing it and sharpening it regularly; a dull knife can be more dangerous than a sharp one. Some cooks prefer a longer blade.

❖ Paring knife: The other essential knife is a good, sturdy paring knife.

❖ Knife steel: For regular honing of your knives. Get into the habit of honing before and after each use.

❖ Large cutting board (or boards): It's important to have a large, heavy cutting board. You'll be amazed by how much space two chopped onions can take up, and it's so convenient to have them all in front of you and not spilling onto the floor. I and my knives prefer wood, though I have some small plastic ones for the odd job. I like to use a wooden or plastic cutting board with a lip for tomatoes and other juicy foods like stone fruit and citrus, so that the juice runs into the canal and not onto my floor.

❖ Mortar and pestle: This is still not a common item in most American kitchens, but having one will open up a new world to you. I have a small marble one for crushing small amounts of spices or garlic, and a larger, olive-wood mortar for larger quantities.

❖ Kitchen scale: I find it much easier to weigh certain items, like cheese, flour, and vegetables, than to measure. I have a mechanical scale with a large wide bowl, and a digital one. You don't need both. Just choose a scale with a surface large enough to rest a medium-size bowl on.

❖ Kitchen timer: I am totally dependent on my digital kitchen timers. I find them especially important for long-simmering dishes, when I need to be reminded to check them as I go about the rest of my day's business. Using a timer can be a great stress-reducer when it comes to cooking; you don't have to be watching your own watch. I like the digital timers because they will ring for a minute, and I can hear mine from two rooms away; and once they stop ringing they begin to count up, so you will know exactly how much more time has elapsed if you didn't get to the timer right away.

❖ Wooden spoons and spatulas: Look for a large, wide, long-handled spoon. If you travel, always look for wooden spoons in markets. Some of my best, widest spoons, with really useful long handles, came from markets in Brazil and Mexico. Wooden implements will last much longer if you don't wash them in the dishwasher or soak them in water.

❖ Chinese wire-mesh deep-fry skimmer (or basket): I use this wire-mesh implement all the time, and not for deep-frying. Mostly I use it to transfer blanched greens and other vegetables from boiling water to a bowl of cold water, or pasta to a serving bowl. It's one of my most useful tools.

❖ Skimmer: These are flat, round spatula-like implements with holes in them. Great for skimming scum off stock and lifting fat off cooled stock.

❖ Cheese grater: The one I use most often is the little rotary Mouli that I've had since I began to cook.

❖ Zester: Very useful for those recipes that call for thin strands of lemon or orange zest. A microplane makes a great zester.

❖ Strainer: A medium-size strainer, the kind you can find in a supermarket, is an item I could not be without.

- Lettuce spinner: Another essential. I find it as useful for cleaning greens and herbs as I do for washing lettuce.

- Heavy rolling pin: Essential for rolling out crusts, and it also comes in handy for crushing spices.

- Stainless-steel bowls: Have as many as you have room for. Great big ones are very useful for mixing up ingredients for tarts, gratins, casseroles, and for all sorts of food prep.

- Pyrex measuring cups: Have a 2-cup and a 4-cup to use for liquids.

- Nesting measuring cups: A set of stainless or plastic measuring cups is essential for measuring dry ingredients.

- Two sets of metal measuring spoons: One for dry ingredients and one for wet. Metal spoons are more accurate than plastic.

ELECTRIC GADGETS

- Electric spice mill: It's worth investing in an extra coffee mill so that you can grind spices in seconds. Put a piece of tape on the top that says SPICES ONLY! And label your coffee mill with COFFEE ONLY! That way your spices won't end up smelling like coffee and your coffee like spices.

- Food processor: Worth the investment for pie crusts alone. The food processor is not absolutely necessary for tasks in many of the recipes in this book, but it is a terrific option.

- Mini processor: I use this miniature food processor whenever I need more than one minced garlic clove, and for minced ginger. For that alone, it's worthwhile.

- Hand blender: This blender on a stick is terrific for puréeing soups right in the pot.

- Blender: Some of the dishes in this book, specifically some of the Mexican dishes, require a blended mixture that is seared before being simmered with other ingredients. To get the right texture, a blender does the job much better than a food processor.

- Electric mixer: If you don't bake a lot, then a hand-held mixer will fulfill most of your needs.

a note about serving sizes

The number of servings indicated for these dishes assumes that you will be serving them as a main dish. The servings are large. If you're making these dishes as part of a bigger menu, you'll get more out of them. For example, a soup or a tart that serves 6 as a main dish will serve 8 to 10 as a starter. A gratin that serves 4 as a main dish will serve 6 to 8 as a side dish.

hearty soups

Say the words *one-dish meal*, and I think of a hearty minestrone, robust with beans and pasta, bejeweled with vegetables, requiring only a thick slice of country bread and a nice glass of red wine as accompaniments. But then soup is what comes to mind when many of us think of comfort food. Its presence, simmering there on the stove, is reassuring. Chicken soup is what we want when we're sick and when we're stressed.

I would often serve the Provençal version of minestrone, Provençal Soupe au Pistou (page 16), at my Paris supper club, especially in the springtime, when the markets were filled with wonderful new vegetables. Guests always loved it, and I loved the fact that I had done most of the actual work the day before my dinner party.

Throughout the world soups are signature peasant dishes. They feed workers heartily after—or before—long days in the fields (in Vietnam the noodle soups called *pho* are typically eaten for breakfast, and the Tunisian chick pea soup called *leblebi* is also a breakfast staple). In Morocco, the substantial mixed bean soup called *harira* is eaten to break the daily fast during

Ramadan. Borscht is so common throughout Russia and Ukraine that there are more than thirty versions. And who hasn't enjoyed a substantial lunch in a Japanese noodle shop, where noodles, broth, vegetables, and meat, fish, or tofu come together in one bowl?

Many of these soups benefit from being made a day ahead of time. Sometimes the entire soup can be finished, whereas with other soups you'll want to add ingredients like pasta and green vegetables close to serving time. The recipes will let you know.

Not all of these soups, though, require long simmers. The Japanese "meals in a bowl" on pages 29–31 are not only one-dish meals, but also very quick.

Most of the soups here are vegetarian. Those that call for an ounce or two of pancetta or smoked bacon for flavoring can be rendered vegetarian simply by omitting that ingredient. If you don't eat meat, you won't miss the flavor, and the soup will be marvelously rich with other seasonings. I've indicated where this can be done.

provençal soupe au pistou
16

portuguese potato and greens soup
18

minestrone
20

lentil minestrone with greens
23

tomato, egg, and bread soup
25

tuscan bean and farro soup with cabbage
and winter squash
26

japanese noodle meals
29

WITH SALMON AND SPINACH 30

WITH SMOKED TROUT AND SPINACH OR DAIKON RADISH 30

WITH CHICKEN AND SPINACH 31

WITH SALMON OR TOFU, MUSHROOMS, AND SPINACH 31

WITH BEEF, MUSHROOMS, AND SPINACH 31

provençal soupe au pistou

This big spring vegetable soup from Provence is much like an Italian minestrone, but the enrich-
ment comes at the end rather than at the beginning. Instead of cooking aromatics in oil before
adding water and vegetables, everything is thrown into the pot here and cooked until the vegeta-
bles are tender and the broth fragrant. Then, just before the soup is served, a rich Provençal
pesto (pistou) is stirred in. The difference between pistou and pesto is the consistency: There
are no pine nuts in pistou. Sometimes a tomato is added. It's a heady mixture. Beans are another
important component of Soupe au Pistou. If you're lucky enough to find fresh cranberry beans at
your farmers' market, substitute them for half of the dried white beans. If you make this a day
ahead (it will be best if you do), don't add the pasta or bright green vegetables until shortly
before serving. ❖ **serves 8 generously**

for the soup

2 cups white beans, soaked for 6 hours in 2 quarts water and drained

1 large onion, chopped

6 to 8 large garlic cloves, minced or pressed

Bouquet garni made with a few sprigs each of fresh thyme and flat-leaf parsley, a Parmesan rind, and a bay leaf

½ pound green beans, or ¼ pound green beans and ¼ pound yellow wax beans, trimmed and broken into 1-inch pieces (about 2 cups)

2 medium zucchini (about ½ pound), scrubbed and diced

2 large carrots, chopped

2 celery stalks, chopped

2 leeks, white and light green part only, cleaned and sliced

2 medium turnips, peeled and diced

1 pound red-skinned potatoes, diced

1 pound tomatoes, peeled, seeded, and chopped, or 1 (14-ounce) can, with liquid

Salt

½ cup soup pasta, such as macaroni or small shells

Freshly ground black pepper

for the pistou

2 to 4 large garlic cloves (to taste), peeled

2 cups tightly packed fresh basil leaves

Salt

⅓ cup extra-virgin olive oil

1 small tomato, peeled, seeded, and chopped (optional)

1 cup freshly grated Parmesan, or a mixture of Gruyère and Parmesan

½ cup grated Parmesan or Gruyère, for sprinkling

combine the white beans and 2 quarts water in a large, heavy soup pot or Dutch oven, and bring to a boil. Skim off any foam, then add the onion, 2 of the garlic cloves, and the bouquet garni. Reduce the heat, cover, and simmer for 1 hour.

advance preparation
The soup can be made through this step up to 3 days ahead. Refrigerate, then bring back to a simmer and proceed with the recipe.

Set aside half the green beans and half the zucchini. Add 2 quarts water to the pot, and all of the remaining garlic and vegetables, except the reserved zucchini and green beans. Bring to a boil. Add salt (be generous), reduce the heat, cover, and simmer for 1 hour. Taste and adjust the seasonings.

advance preparation
The blanched zucchini and green beans will keep for 2 or 3 days in a covered bowl in the refrigerator.

While the soup is simmering, blanch the reserved beans and zucchini, and make the pistou. Bring a large or medium pot of water to a boil, add a teaspoon of salt and the zucchini, and cook for 3 or 4 minutes, just until the zucchini is bright on the outside and translucent.

Remove from the pot with a slotted spoon or skimmer and transfer to a bowl of ice-cold water. Drain and set aside. Bring the water back to a boil and drop in the green beans. Cook for 5 minutes, or until tender and bright. Transfer to a bowl of ice-cold water. Drain and set aside.

To make the pistou, turn on a food processor fitted with the steel blade and drop in the garlic. Scrape down the sides of the bowl, add the basil and salt, and process until finely chopped. Scrape down the sides once more and turn on the machine. Drizzle in the olive oil with the machine running, then drop in the tomato if using. Process to a paste. Stir in the Parmesan, and taste for salt.

Add the pasta to the simmering soup about 10 minutes before serving, and cook it al dente, 5 to 10 minutes. Add pepper, then taste and adjust the salt. Stir the blanched or steamed green vegetables into the soup and heat through.

To serve, either stir the pistou into the pot, place a dollop on each bowl and stir in, or pass the pistou in a bowl and let people stir in their own. Pass additional Parmesan or Gruyère for sprinkling.

leftovers : Like all soups of this nature, Soupe au Pistou gets better overnight, and it will keep for about 5 days. You'll lose the brightness of the vegetables, and the soup will thicken because of the pasta. If you wish to transform it into something else, see the recipe for Ribollita on page 22.

portuguese potato and greens soup

This is caldo verde, the national soup of Portugal, and it couldn't be more comforting. In Portugal turnip greens, Galician cabbage, and kale are all used, but I think any greens will work. The last time I was inspired to make the soup, it was because I had some blanched beet greens in the refrigerator and had to use them up. If you are going to use beet greens, it's best to blanch them first so that their color won't infuse the soup, which should be light green.

What gives this soup its real character is the sausage, which is added to the soup toward the end of cooking and imbues the dish with a marvelous flavor. Obviously the most authentic choice would be Portuguese chouriço, but that's not easy to come by. Spanish chorizo will also work, and I have made it with great success using mild Italian sausage. The one thing that definitely will not work is Mexican chorizo; there's too much chile in it. ❖ **serves 4**

2 tablespoons olive oil

1 medium onion, chopped

1 large garlic clove, minced

1¾ to 2 pounds floury potatoes, peeled and thinly sliced

Salt (about 2½ teaspoons or more)

1 pound turnip greens, kale, or other greens such as beet greens or chard, stems trimmed

6 ounces Portuguese *chouriço*, Spanish chorizo, or mild cooked Italian sausage, thinly sliced

Freshly ground black pepper

advance preparation
You can do this step a day ahead, and refrigerate overnight.

heat 1 tablespoon of the oil over medium heat in a large, heavy soup pot and add the onion. Cook, stirring, until tender, about 5 minutes, and add the garlic. Cook, stirring, until fragrant, about 30 seconds to 1 minute, and stir in the potatoes and 2 quarts of water. Bring to a boil, add salt, reduce the heat, cover, and simmer for 30 minutes, or until the potatoes are falling apart.

advance preparation
The blanched greens will keep for about 3 days in a covered bowl in the refrigerator.

Meanwhile, prepare the greens and the sausage. If using turnip greens, chard, or kale, stack the leaves, about six or eight to a stack, roll them up tightly, and slice crosswise into very thin strips. If using beet greens or red chard, blanch for 2 minutes, drain, squeeze dry, and finely chop.

Sauté the sliced sausage gently over medium-low heat in a medium skillet for about 10 minutes, until the fat runs out. Discard the fat.

Mash the potatoes in the pot with a potato masher or a hand blender. Stir the sausage and the greens into the soup and simmer 10 to 15 minutes (5 minutes for previously blanched greens), until the greens turn bright green and tender. Taste, adjust the salt, and add pepper. Stir in the remaining olive oil and serve, with crusty bread.

leftovers Although the vivid green color will pale, the soup will taste great for a few days. Whisk it briskly to get it back to its original texture when you reheat.

minestrone

There are many versions of minestrone. Some call for meat stock; others, like this, rely on plain old water. Like all "big soups," this one will taste even better the day after you make it; but don't add the pasta or bright green vegetables until shortly before serving. ❖ **serves 6**

2 tablespoons olive oil

2 medium onions, chopped

2 large or 3 medium leeks, white and light green part only, cleaned and sliced

2 medium carrots, peeled and chopped

2 celery stalks, chopped

Salt

6 large garlic cloves, minced

½ small head of green cabbage, shredded (about 4 cups)

2 medium potatoes, scrubbed and diced

2 medium turnips, peeled and diced

1 (14-ounce) can tomatoes, with juice, seeded and chopped

1 teaspoon chopped fresh oregano, or ½ teaspoon dried

1 Parmesan rind

A few sprigs each of fresh thyme and flat-leaf parsley

1 bay leaf

1 (15-ounce) can cannellini or borlotti beans, drained and rinsed

1 pound fresh fava beans, shelled

1 cup fresh peas (about 1 pound unshelled) or frozen peas, thawed

½ pound green beans, cut into 1-inch lengths (about 2 cups)

¼ pound Tuscan kale (cavolo nero), turnip greens, or Swiss chard, stemmed, washed well, and chopped (about 2 cups)

½ cup soup pasta, such as elbow macaroni, small shells, or broken spaghetti

Freshly ground black pepper to taste

¼ cup chopped fresh flat-leaf parsley

⅓ cup freshly grated Parmesan

advance preparation
The soup can be made through this
step a day or two ahead. It
improves overnight.

heat the olive oil over medium-low heat in a large, heavy soup pot or Dutch oven and add the onions. Cook, stirring, until they begin to soften, and add the leeks. Cook, stirring, for 5 minutes, until tender and translucent but not browned. Add the carrots and celery and a generous pinch of salt, and continue to cook, stirring often, for about 5 to 10 minutes, until the vegetables are tender and fragrant. Stir in the garlic and the cabbage, add a little more salt, and cook for about 5 minutes, until the cabbage has wilted. Add 2 quarts water, the potatoes, turnips, canned tomatoes with liquid, and oregano, and bring to a boil. Tie the Parmesan rind, thyme and parsley sprigs, and bay leaf together with kitchen string, or tie in cheesecloth, and add to the pot. Add salt (at least 2 teaspoons), reduce the heat to low, cover, and simmer for 45 minutes. Stir in the canned beans.

advance preparation
The green vegetables can be
blanched a day or two ahead and
kept in the refrigerator in a
covered bowl.

While the soup is simmering, bring a pot of water to a boil, drop in the shelled favas, and boil for 1 minute. Remove from the water with a slotted spoon or skimmer and transfer to a bowl of cold water. Drain and slip off the skins. Set aside. Bring the water in the pot back to a boil and add a teaspoon of salt and the fresh peas and green beans. Boil for 5 minutes, until just tender but still bright green. Remove from the water using a slotted spoon, refresh with cold water, and set aside. Retain the cooking water in case you want to thin out the soup later.

To finish, add the kale and the pasta to the soup and simmer for another 10 minutes, or until the pasta is cooked al dente. Stir the cooked peas, favas, and green beans into the soup. Grind in some pepper and taste. Does the soup taste vivid? Does it need more salt? (Probably.) Or garlic? It should be savory and rich-tasting. Adjust the seasonings as necessary. If it seems too thick, thin out with a little cooking water from the green vegetables.

Remove the bouquet garni from the soup, stir in the chopped parsley, and remove from the heat. Serve in wide soup bowls with a tablespoon of Parmesan sprinkled over the top.

(continued on next page)

leftovers ⋮ The soup will keep for 3 or 4 days in the refrigerator, and it benefits from being cooked a day ahead of time. However, the pasta will absorb more liquid, so the soup will require thinning out. If you're making the soup ahead, add the pasta and green vegetables to the soup on the day you are serving it. If you want to turn the leftovers into another dish, make ribollita, below.

leftovers ribollita variation

In Tuscany, the typical way to transform leftover bean and vegetable soup into a new, thoroughly enjoyable meal—and one that is the ultimate comfort food—is to heat it with dry or toasted bread, and blend this up to make something between a pap and a soup, much like a Portuguese açorda (page 244). This is called ribollita, *which means "reboiled." You can make ribollita with other types of vegetable or bean and vegetable soups. This one is based on Faith Willinger's formula in* Red, White & Greens *(HarperCollins, 1996), though hers is made with a winter bean and vegetable soup.*

For every 2½ cups soup, have 3 to 4 thick slices of good-quality artisanal country bread

Salt and freshly ground black pepper

Olive oil, for garnish

Heat the oven to 325°F. Place the bread on the rack and toast it until dry but not browned, 20 to 25 minutes. Remove from the oven.

Heat the soup in a saucepan or soup pot. Remove a generous spoonful of the beans and vegetables (⅓ cup for each 2 cups of soup). Bring the remaining soup to a simmer and add the bread. Submerge in the soup and remove the soup from the heat. Let stand for 20 minutes, until the bread is soft. Blend, using a hand immersion blender or the pulse action of a food processor. Return to the pot, add the beans and vegetables you set aside, and heat through. The ribollita should have the consistency of oatmeal. Dilute with water as necessary. Taste and adjust the salt and pepper. Spoon the ribollita into bowls or onto soup plates, drizzle olive oil over each serving, and serve.

lentil minestrone with greens

This is as warming, filling, and comforting a winter soup as you can get. The greens, added toward the end of cooking, make a great partner for the lentils, and you really have every nutrient I can think of in one bowl. If you make this soup a day ahead, don't add the pasta or rice, or the greens, until you reheat before serving. ❖ **serves 4 to 6**

1 tablespoon olive oil

4 pieces of smoked bacon, chopped (about 4 ounces)

1 small onion, chopped

1 large or 2 small carrots, minced (about ¾ cup)

4 large garlic cloves, minced

1 (14-ounce) can tomatoes, seeded and chopped, with juice

½ teaspoon dried thyme (1 teaspoon fresh leaves)

½ teaspoon dried oregano (1 teaspoon fresh leaves)

¾ pound lentils (about 1½ cups), picked over and rinsed

1 Parmesan rind

A few sprigs each of fresh flat-leaf parsley and fresh thyme

1 bay leaf

A few pinches of cayenne pepper (to taste)

Salt

Freshly ground black pepper to taste

½ pound Swiss chard, stalks removed, leaves washed and chopped (2 cups, tightly packed)

½ cup small pasta, such as elbows, small shells, or tubetti, or Arborio rice

2 tablespoons chopped fresh flat-leaf parsley

¼ cup freshly grated Parmesan, for serving

heat the oil over medium-low heat in a heavy soup pot or Dutch oven, and add the bacon, onion, and carrot. Cook, stirring, until the vegetables are tender, about 5 minutes or a little longer, and stir in the garlic. Cook, stirring, just until the garlic smells fragrant and is beginning to color, about 1 minute, and stir in the tomatoes, dried thyme, and dried oregano. Turn the heat to medium and bring the tomatoes to a simmer. Cook, stirring often, for about 10 minutes, until the tomatoes have cooked down somewhat and smell fragrant. Stir in the lentils and 8 cups of water and bring to a boil.

advance preparation
The soup can be made to this point up to 4 days before you serve. It will thicken. You can thin it out with water to taste. Bring back to a simmer and proceed with the recipe.

Tie the Parmesan rind, parsley and thyme sprigs, and bay leaf together with kitchen twine, or tie in a piece of cheesecloth. Add to the soup. Add the cayenne, reduce the heat, cover, and simmer for 30 minutes. Add salt, about 2 teaspoons to begin with (you will probably add more), and simmer another 15 to 30 minutes, until the lentils are tender and the broth fragrant.

Add pepper to the soup, and stir in the chard and pasta. Continue to simmer for another 10 to 15 minutes, until the pasta is cooked through. Taste. Is there enough salt? Garlic? Adjust the seasonings, and remove the Parmesan rind bundle. Stir in the chopped parsley. Serve, topping each bowlful with a generous sprinkle of Parmesan cheese.

leftovers Although the soup will thicken and the pasta will soften, it will taste great for 4 or 5 days, and it can be frozen for a few months. The thickened soup makes a delicious topping for bruschetta. Cut thick slices of good, crusty country bread, toast them, and rub the toast with a cut clove of garlic. Warm the leftover lentils, top the bread, sprinkle on a little Parmesan, and serve.

variation vegetarian version

Omit the smoked bacon and proceed with the recipe as directed. It'll taste wonderful without it.

tomato, egg, and bread soup

Bread and broth are comforting in and of themselves, and this amazing Mediterranean soup—a simple one with few ingredients, yet ample and filling—defines comfort food. Bread is sustenance throughout the Mediterranean, and stale bread has many delicious uses. Both Portugal, where it's called Stone Soup, and Provence have versions of this. And if you looked, you'd probably find something similar in Spain, Greece, and Italy, wherever there are good ripe tomatoes, olive oil, potatoes, eggs, and crusty country bread.

Saffron and garlic infuse the broth and give the potatoes a beautiful hue. The eggs, poached right in the soup and served up in each bowlful, enrich the dish and make each serving all the more sustaining. Use large, wide soup bowls for this. The bread will soak up much of the broth, and the bowl should be filled with the vegetables. ❖ **makes 4 generous servings**

2 tablespoons olive oil

1 medium or large onion, thinly sliced

2 large garlic cloves (more to taste), minced, plus 1 garlic clove, cut in half

1 pound ripe tomatoes, peeled, seeded, and chopped

Salt

2 tablespoons chopped fresh flat-leaf parsley, plus additional for garnish

1 bay leaf

¼ teaspoon sweet or hot paprika

1 pound waxy potatoes, peeled if desired and sliced

A generous pinch of saffron

Freshly ground black pepper to taste

4 large eggs

4 to 8 thick slices of stale or lightly toasted country bread

advance preparation
The soup can be made through this
step a day ahead and refrigerated.
Bring back to a simmer and proceed
with the recipe.

heat the olive oil in a large, heavy soup pot over medium heat and add the onion. Cook, stirring, until tender, about 5 minutes. Add the minced garlic and stir for about a minute, until fragrant. Add the tomatoes, salt to taste, parsley, bay leaf, and paprika and cook, stirring from time to time, for 10 minutes, or until the tomatoes have cooked down a bit and smell fragrant. Add 1 quart of water and the potatoes, and bring to a boil. Add more salt and the saffron, reduce the heat, cover, and simmer for 20 to 25 minutes, until the potatoes are tender. Taste, adjust the salt, and add pepper.

Make sure that the soup is at a bare simmer. Carefully break the eggs into a bowl or teacup and tip into the soup one by one. Cover (you can turn off the heat at this point) and cook for 4 to 6 minutes, or until the eggs are set. Rub each slice of bread on both sides with the cut clove of garlic and place in large, wide soup bowls. Ladle in the soup with an egg for each portion. Sprinkle on parsley and serve.

leftovers You will have eaten the eggs, but the rest of the soup will be good for 3 or 4 days. You can add more broth and eat it as soup, or pour off any remaining broth and use it as a filling for a frittata (see page 392).

tuscan bean and farro soup with cabbage and winter squash

This big soup, based on a Lynne Rossetto Kasper recipe from The Italian Country Table *(Scribner, 1999), is multidimensional, with layers of sweet and savory, earthy and herbal and vegetal flavors, and chewy and soft textures. Farro is an ancient whole-wheat grain that is still popular in Tuscany. It's a softer, gentler, and quicker-cooking wheat than our domestic whole-wheat berries, and it has a sweet flavor that Kasper aptly describes as tasting "like barley and hazelnuts." This soup was my introduction to the grain, and it sold me on it.* ❖ serves 6

for the soup

½ cup imported Italian farro, or domestic wheat berries

Salt

1 ounce pancetta, minced

1 tablespoon olive oil

1 medium onion, finely chopped

1 medium carrot, finely chopped

1 small celery stalk, with leaves, finely chopped

2 teaspoons chopped fresh sage

3 large garlic cloves, minced

1 pound green cabbage, cored and shredded

½ pound (1¼ cups) borlotti or pinto beans, soaked for 6 hours or overnight in 1 quart water, then drained

1 pound butternut squash, peeled, seeded, and diced (about 2 cups)

1 Parmesan rind, tied in cheesecloth

for the sofrito

1 tablespoon olive oil

1 ounce pancetta, minced

2 large garlic cloves, minced or pressed

Generous ½ teaspoon dried rosemary, crumbled

1 (14-ounce) can tomatoes, with liquid, chopped

Salt and freshly ground black pepper

Freshly grated Parmesan, for serving

THE SOFRITO

Sofrito is a mixture of aromatic ingredients cooked in oil or fat, and added to a dish. Sometimes cooking the sofrito can be the beginning step in a recipe, but here the sofrito is stirred into the soup after the beans have cooked, and simmered with it for another 30 minutes, with incredibly heady results.

---

advance preparation
The farro or wheat berries can be cooked a day or two ahead and held in the refrigerator.

combine the farro or wheat berries and 2 cups water in a medium saucepan and bring to a boil. Reduce the heat, cover, and simmer until tender, 30 to 40 minutes for farro (wheat berries will take 1 to 1½ hours). Stir in ¼ teaspoon salt and remove from the heat. If there is water left in the pan, drain.

Meanwhile, make the soup. Heat the pancetta and olive oil together over medium heat in a large, heavy soup pot or Dutch oven and add the onion. Cook until it begins to soften, about 3 minutes. Add the carrot, celery, and sage and continue to cook, stirring, until tender, about 5 minutes. Add the garlic and cook, stirring, until fragrant, about 1 minute, then add the cabbage and ½ teaspoon salt and cook, stirring often, until limp, about 10 minutes. Add the beans, squash, Parmesan rind, and 2 quarts of water, or enough to cover by 2 inches. Bring to a boil, reduce the heat, and simmer for 1 hour. Add salt and simmer for another 30 minutes, or until the beans are tender.

advance preparation You can make the soup through this step up to 3 days ahead. Refrigerate, then bring back to a simmer and proceed with the recipe.

Remove the Parmesan rind and discard. Ladle out 2 cups of the beans and vegetables, with a small amount of broth, and purée in a blender or food processor fitted with the steel blade (if using a blender, do this in batches to avoid hot soup splashing). Return to the pot.

advance preparation You can make the sofrito 1 to 3 days ahead and keep it in the refrigerator.

While the soup is simmering, make the sofrito. Heat the oil and pancetta over medium heat in a medium nonstick skillet. When the pancetta is sizzling, add the garlic and rosemary. Cook for 30 seconds to 1 minute, until fragrant, and stir in the tomatoes. Add salt and cook, stirring often, until the tomatoes have cooked down and the mixture is thick, beginning to stick to the pan, and delicious, 10 to 15 minutes.

Stir the sofrito into the soup. Continue to simmer for another 30 minutes. By now it should be incredibly aromatic. Stir in the farro or wheat berries. Taste and adjust the salt, and add lots of freshly ground pepper. Serve with freshly grated Parmesan.

leftovers The finished soup keeps well and gets even better over 2 or 3 days.

variation
vegetarian version
Omit the pancetta.

japanese noodle meals

These meals in a bowl are typical of Japanese noodle shops; they consist of a warming broth, which could be dashi, chicken stock, or vegetable stock; Japanese noodles (either soba or udon); a protein, which can be meat, fish, or tofu; and a vegetable, sometimes two. They're light and extremely warming, attractive, and satisfying. These are just some of the combinations you can make.

japanese noodles

One portion of Japanese noodles is about 1½ ounces—usually the quantity in a bundle, if your package of soba or udon has the noodles tied in individual bundles.

Bring 4 quarts of water to a boil in a large pot. Add soba or udon noodles gradually, so that the water doesn't go off the boil. Stir with a long-handled spoon or pasta spoon to prevent the noodles from sticking to each other. When all of the noodles have been added and the water is at a rolling boil, add a cup of *cold* water. Allow the water to come back to a boil and add another cup of cold water. Let the water come back to a boil one more time, then add a third cup of water. When the water comes back to a boil again, test a noodle, and if it is cooked through (it should be), drain the noodles and rinse briefly with cold water. If keeping for more than a few hours, toss with a teaspoon of sesame or canola oil so they won't stick together, and refrigerate in a covered bowl or in a plastic bag.

advance preparation
The noodles will keep for 3 days in the refrigerator.

Traditionally, the noodles are cooked without salt. However if you find them too bland, add a tablespoon of salt to the boiling water.

(continued on next page)

japanese noodle meal with salmon and spinach ❖ serves 4

6 cups Japanese stock (page 382), chicken stock (page 378), or Simple Vegetable Stock (page 377)

2 slices of peeled fresh ginger

1 to 1½ pounds skinless salmon fillet, cut in 4 equal pieces

1 pound fresh spinach, stemmed, washed, and coarsely chopped, or 1 pound of shelled fresh peas, sugar snap peas, or trimmed green beans

Salt or soy sauce to taste

6 ounces soba or udon noodles, cooked (see page 29) .

¼ cup chopped scallion greens or chives

bring the stock to a simmer and add the ginger. Cover and simmer for 15 minutes. Add the peas or green beans, if using, during the last 2 minutes. Remove the ginger from the broth and, making sure that the broth is at a simmer, add the salmon and spinach, if using. Cover tightly and turn off the heat. Let sit for 8 minutes without removing the lid. Check the salmon to make sure it is cooked through. Taste the broth and add soy sauce or salt as desired.

Distribute the noodles evenly among 4 wide or deep bowls. Using tongs, place a piece of salmon and a serving of spinach in each bowl alongside or on top of the noodles. Ladle in the broth and sprinkle the scallion tops or chives over the top. Serve hot.

leftovers ⋮ This won't get better with time, but if you have more stock and noodles than you need for the number of people that you're serving, hold back some stock so that you can make the dish again tomorrow.

variations with smoked trout and spinach or daikon radish

Substitute ½ pound smoked trout fillets, skin removed, for the salmon, and if you wish, 2 cups grated daikon radish for the spinach. Proceed as directed.

with chicken and spinach

Substitute 1 pound boneless, skinless chicken breasts for the salmon. Cut the chicken breasts crosswise into thin slivers, about ¼ inch wide. Add them to the simmering broth before adding the spinach and simmer 5 minutes, or until there is no trace of pink left. Stir in the spinach, cover tightly and turn off the heat, and let sit for a couple of minutes, until the spinach is wilted. Taste and adjust the seasonings. Sprinkle the bowls with scallion tops or chives (or substitute 2 tablespoons chopped cilantro) and serve as directed previously.

with salmon or tofu, mushrooms, and spinach

Place 2 ounces of dried shiitake mushrooms in a heatproof bowl or measuring cup and pour on 2 cups boiling water. Let sit for 30 minutes, or until tender. Drain through a strainer lined with cheesecloth or paper towels set over a bowl. Reserve the mushroom liquid, which will replace 2 cups of stock. Squeeze the mushrooms above the strainer, then rinse in several changes of water. Cut away the tough stems and discard, and cut the mushrooms into slivers. Combine the mushroom liquid and 4 cups of stock and proceed with the recipe, adding the mushrooms with the salmon and spinach. You can replace the salmon with 1 pound silken tofu, cut into 1-inch squares, if you wish.

with beef, mushrooms, and spinach

Substitute 1 pound lean beef, thinly cut across the grain in 1-inch slices, for the fish, chicken, or tofu. Use 2 ounces dried shiitake mushrooms and prepare as instructed above, straining the soaking water and combining that with 4 cups of stock (you can use beef stock or one of the others listed). Simmer the beef and mushrooms for 5 minutes before adding the spinach and turning off the heat. Proceed as directed above.

vegetarian borscht

This recipe is from my book The Best Vegetarian Recipes *(William Morrow, 2001),*
but it belongs in this collection too, as it makes such a satisfying winter one-dish meal.

❖ serves 4 generously

1 ounce dried mushrooms (about 1 cup)

1 bunch of beets (4 medium or 3 large), with greens, the
beets peeled and quartered, the greens stemmed, washed,
coarsely chopped, and set aside

2 garlic cloves, peeled and thinly sliced

Salt

1 to 2 teaspoons sugar, to taste

1 tablespoon mild vinegar, such as unseasoned rice wine
vinegar or champagne vinegar

1 tablespoon canola oil

2 medium onions, chopped

2 small turnips or 1 medium turnip, peeled and chopped

2 medium or large carrots, peeled and sliced

2 ounces fresh mushrooms (about 4 medium or 3 large),
trimmed and chopped

10 fresh flat-leaf parsley stems

2 bay leaves

3 allspice berries

6 black peppercorns

¼ cup chopped fresh flat-leaf parsley

1 cup thickened nonfat plain yogurt (see Yogurt Cheese,
page 387) or sour cream

place the dried mushrooms in a heatproof bowl and pour on 1 quart boiling water. Let sit for 30 minutes, then strain through a cheesecloth-lined strainer set
over a bowl. Squeeze the mushrooms over the strainer to extract any remaining flavorful liquid. Reserve the mushroom liquid. Rinse the mushrooms thoroughly, in several
changes of water, and chop.

advance preparation
You can reconstitute the mushrooms and cook the beets a day or two ahead, either before or after straining. Keep in the refrigerator with the broth.

While the mushrooms are soaking, combine the beets, garlic, and 1 quart of water in a saucepan and bring to a boil. Add a teaspoon of salt and the sugar, reduce the heat, and simmer, uncovered, for 30 minutes. Stir in the vinegar. Remove the beets from the water using a slotted spoon and rinse with cold water; allow to cool until you can handle them. Cut the beets into julienne slices, about ¼ inch wide by 1 inch long. Set the cooking water aside.

advance preparation
You can make this soup a few days ahead, and it freezes well for a couple of months. Don't add the parsley until serving.

Heat the oil over medium heat in a large, heavy soup pot and add the onions. Cook, stirring, until just tender, 3 to 5 minutes, and add the turnips, carrots, julienned beets, the chopped dried and fresh mushrooms, the mushroom stock, and 1 cup water. Tie the parsley stems, bay leaves, allspice berries, and peppercorns together in a cheesecloth bag and add to the pot, along with about 1 teaspoon salt, or more to taste. Bring to a boil, reduce the heat, cover, and simmer for 40 minutes. Add the chopped beet greens and simmer for another 10 minutes. Stir in the cooking water from the beets. Stir together and taste. Is there enough salt? Adjust the seasonings. Remove the cheesecloth bag, heat the soup through, sprinkle on the parsley, and serve, garnishing each bowl with a generous dollop of thickened yogurt or sour cream.

leftovers This soup benefits from being made a day ahead, and will taste good for 3 or 4 days. If it becomes too thick, thin it out with a little broth.

classic meaty borscht

I'm not sure that "classic" is the right word to use here, as there are more than 30 varieties of borscht (also spelled borshch), and I'm sure there are many variations on those varieties. This one uses a meat stock. It's best to make the beef stock at least a day ahead, and the soup improves overnight as well. ❖ **serves 8 generously**

for the stock

2 pounds beef shin or chuck, with bone

1 onion, quartered

2 large carrots, sliced

for the soup

1 bunch of beets (about 4 medium), with greens, the beets peeled and quartered, the greens stemmed, washed, coarsely chopped, and set aside

2 garlic cloves, peeled and thinly sliced

Salt

2 teaspoons sugar

1 tablespoon mild vinegar, such as rice wine vinegar or champagne vinegar

1 tablespoon vegetable oil

2 medium onions, chopped

½ medium cabbage, cored and shredded

2 small turnips or 1 medium turnip, peeled and chopped

2 medium or large carrots, peeled and chopped

2 ounces fresh mushrooms (about 4 medium or 2 or 3 large), trimmed and chopped

1 pound waxy potatoes, scrubbed and diced

2 bay leaves

10 fresh flat-leaf parsley stems

3 allspice berries

6 black peppercorns

¼ cup chopped fresh flat-leaf parsley

1 cup sour cream or thickened nonfat plain yogurt (see Yogurt Cheese, page 387)

make the stock a day ahead. Combine the meat with 3 quarts water, the onion, and the carrots; bring to a boil and skim off any foam. Reduce the heat, cover partially, and simmer for 2 hours. Remove the meat from the broth, wrap in foil, and refrigerate. Strain the broth through a strainer lined with cheesecloth. Refrigerate overnight and skim off the fat.

advance preparation
This can be done a day or two before making the soup and refrigerated, either before or after you drain and julienne the beets.

The next day, combine the beets with the sliced garlic and 1 quart of the stock. Bring to a boil and add a teaspoon of salt and the sugar. Reduce the heat, cover, and simmer for 30 minutes. Remove from the heat and stir in the vinegar. Allow the beets to cool for 30 minutes in the broth, then remove and when cool enough to handle, cut in julienne, about ¼ inch wide by 1 inch long. Strain the broth and set aside both broth and beets.

advance preparation
This can be done a day or two ahead, and benefits from it.

Heat the oil in a large, heavy soup pot over medium heat and add the onions. Cook, stirring, until just tender, 3 to 5 minutes, and add the cabbage, turnips, carrots, and mushrooms. Turn the heat to medium-low, cover, and cook, stirring often, until the vegetables are wilted and fragrant, about 10 minutes. Add the reserved beef broth and the potatoes. Tie the bay leaves, parsley stems, allspice berries, and peppercorns together in a cheesecloth bag and add to the pot, along with salt to taste (about 2 teaspoons). Bring to a boil, reduce the heat, cover, and simmer for 40 minutes. Remove the cheesecloth bag and stir in the julienned beets.

Bring the soup back to a simmer. Remove the cooked beef from the refrigerator. Cut away any fat and slice the meat thin, then cut it into dice and add to the simmering soup, along with the beet greens. Simmer for 10 minutes. Stir in the broth from the beets. Stir together, taste, and adjust the seasonings. You will probably want to add more salt. Heat the soup through, sprinkle on the parsley, and serve, garnishing each bowl with a generous dollop of thickened yogurt or sour cream and passing more of it at the table.

leftovers The soup will keep for 4 or 5 days in the refrigerator and frozen for 3 months. You will enjoy it for as long as it lasts.

mexican vegetable—chipotle soup

This soup, from the Mexican state of Veracruz, is known as a chilpachol, *because of the chipotle chiles. Although chilpachol is traditionally made with fish or shellfish, the heady broth lends itself to this vegetarian rendition.*

I'm always astounded by the complexity of flavors when I make chilpachol. Two things contribute to this: the mixture of spicy ingredients, and the roasting and searing of these ingredients. Roasting vegetables and aromatics, then blending them together and searing the purée is a traditional technique that accounts for much of the character of great Mexican food. Once these steps are accomplished—and you are free to do them long before you finish the soup—the rest of this main-dish soup goes very quickly. Don't forget to tell your guests to squeeze in the lime juice. It's an important finishing touch.

Note: Epazote is a Mexican herb with a distinctive, somewhat astringent flavor. Some herb purveyors at farmers' markets sell it. I've made it optional here, as it is not that easy to find.

❖ serves 6

2   pounds plum tomatoes

1   large onion, cut in half

4   large garlic cloves, skin left on

1   jalapeño pepper

4   small or 2 to 3 larger dried chipotle chilies, or 2 canned chipotles, rinsed and seeded

1   strip of Mexican cinnamon, or ½ teaspoon ground cinnamon

6   whole black peppercorns

2   toasted corn tortillas (see page 391), ground in a spice mill (about ¼ cup ground)

2   tablespoons olive oil

¾   pound red-skinned potatoes, cut in ¾-inch dice

1 small butternut squash (about 1½ pounds), peeled, seeded, and cut in ¾-inch dice

Salt (2 to 3 teaspoons)

1 large sprig of epazote (optional)

1½ cups fresh or frozen corn kernels (2 ears of corn)

1 (15-ounce) can chick peas, drained and rinsed

¼ pound green beans, trimmed, cut in 1-inch lengths, and blanched for 5 minutes in boiling salted water

¼ cup chopped fresh cilantro

3 or 4 corn tortillas, cut in wedges and toasted (page 391), for serving

2 or 3 limes, cut in wedges

heat the broiler. Line a baking sheet with foil. Place the tomatoes on the baking sheet, and set under the broiler, 2 to 3 inches from the heat (on the top rack setting). When the tomatoes are charred on one side, about 2 to 5 minutes, turn them over and char the other side. Transfer the tomatoes to a bowl to cool. Place the onion halves on the foil, cut side down. Broil for about 5 minutes, until the top layer is charred. Turn the onion halves over and char the other side, about 5 minutes. When cool enough to handle, remove and discard the charred black layer and coarsely chop the rest. Transfer to a blender. Peel and core the tomatoes and add to the blender, along with any juices that may have accumulated.

advance preparation You could prepare the recipe through this step and go out for a few hours, leaving the purée at room temperature. Then come home and make the soup base.

Heat a griddle or heavy frying pan over medium heat and toast the garlic and jalapeño, turning often until softened and brown in several spots. Remove from the heat and allow to cool. Skin the garlic, stem the jalapeño (seed for a less picante soup), and add to the blender with the tomatoes and onion. If using dried chipotles, open them out flat and remove the seeds and veins (use plastic gloves as they are extremely picante), and toast on the griddle or pan, pressing down with a spatula for a few seconds, just until you see the chili blister and puff, then turn and repeat on the other side. Add to the blender. (If using canned chipotle chiles, rinse and seed them, then add to the blender.) Toast the cinnamon strip and peppercorns for a few seconds, just until the strip of cinnamon browns slightly and the peppercorns begin to smell a bit toasty. Grind the cinnamon and peppercorns in a spice mill and add to the blender. Blend until smooth, and strain through a medium mesh strainer into a bowl. Combine 1 cup of water with the ground toasted tortillas in the blender and blend together for a few seconds, then add to the purée. Stir well to combine.

Heat the oil for a few minutes over medium-high heat in a large, heavy soup pot or Dutch oven until your hand feels the heat when you hold it over the pot. Drizzle in a small amount of the purée and if it sizzles loudly, add the rest (wait a few minutes if it doesn't). Stir the mixture, and turn the heat to medium. Cook, stirring often, for 10 to 15 minutes, until the mixture is thick. If the mixture splatters all over your stove, cover the pot partially with a lid.

advance preparation The soup can be prepared through this step up to 3 days ahead and kept in the refrigerator or frozen. Bring back to a simmer and proceed with the recipe.

Add 1½ quarts water to the tomato mixture and stir well. Add the potatoes and squash, and salt (be generous), and bring to a boil, stirring often. Reduce the heat, cover, and simmer, stirring occasionally, for 20 to 30 minutes, or until the vegetables are tender.

Add the epazote, if using, to the simmering broth, along with the corn and the chick peas, and simmer for another 5 minutes. Taste and adjust the salt.

Stir the blanched green beans and cilantro into the soup, heat through for a minute, and serve, distributing the vegetables evenly among the bowls. Top each serving with a few crumbled wedges of toasted tortillas. Pass cut limes for people to squeeze into their soup.

leftovers The broth for this soup will keep well for a couple of days in the refrigerator, and it can be frozen for a couple of months. You can continue to enjoy it as a vegetable soup by adding new vegetables to it.

hearty vietnamese chicken noodle soup *(pho ga)*

Often called Saigon Soup, this is a classic Southeast Asian chicken and noodle soup, a simple one-dish meal, and as soothing as any chicken soup can be. Passing the tray full of condiments makes for a convivial meal. ❖ **serves 4 to 6**

1 smallish chicken, about 3 to 3½ pounds, cut up and skinned, or the equivalent of chicken pieces, skinned

6 ounces boneless pork loin (optional)

1 onion, quartered

2 (2- to 3-ounce) pieces of unpeeled fresh ginger (2 to 3 inches long)

1 teaspoon black peppercorns

Salt to taste

1 teaspoon vegetable oil

2 eggs, beaten

Freshly ground black pepper

2 cups bean sprouts, rinsed

½ pound rice noodles

2 tablespoons Vietnamese or Thai fish sauce

1 bunch of scallions, white and green parts (or 2 to 3 shallots), thinly sliced

1 cup loosely packed chopped fresh cilantro

½ cup loosely packed chopped Thai basil or fresh mint

2 limes, cut into wedges

combine the chicken, pork, and 3 quarts water in a large, heavy soup pot and bring to a boil. While the water is heating, scorch the onion and one of the pieces of ginger by holding the pieces above a flame in tongs, or in a dry frying pan if using an electric stove. Turn the pieces of onion and the ginger until scorched black on all sides, and add to the pot with the chicken and pork.

advance preparation
The broth can (and should) be made the day before you serve the soup. It can be made, and the meat shredded, up to 2 or 3 days ahead.

When the broth comes to a boil, skim off any foam that rises, add the peppercorns, reduce the heat, and simmer, uncovered, for 30 minutes. Skim occasionally. Remove the white meat pieces of chicken and simmer for another 10 minutes. Remove the remaining chicken pieces and the pork from the broth and allow to cool. Line a strainer with cheesecloth and strain the broth, discarding the solids. When the chicken and pork are cool enough to handle, shred coarsely, and refrigerate in a covered container. Refrigerate the broth for at least 3 hours or, preferably, overnight. Skim off the fat from the surface.

Scorch the remaining piece of ginger following the instructions above. Peel, chop coarsely, combine with a generous pinch of salt in a mortar and pestle, and pound to a paste. Set aside.

Heat the oil in a small or medium nonstick skillet. Beat the eggs in a bowl, add a bit of salt and pepper, and add to the skillet. Swirl the pan so that the eggs spread out like a pancake. When cooked through, roll up like a crepe or omelet and remove from the pan. Cut in thin slivers.

advance preparation
These condiments can all be prepared a few hours or even a day ahead. The bean sprouts can be blanched, drained, and refrigerated and the noodles cooked. The omelet can be cooked and cut up a day ahead. Keep in a covered bowl in the refrigerator. The ginger paste will hold for several hours out of the refrigerator, and for a day in the refrigerator.

Bring a large pot of water to a boil. Blanch the bean sprouts for 20 seconds and transfer immediately to a bowl of cold water, using a strainer or skimmer. Drain and set aside. Bring the water back to a boil, add the noodles, and cook just until tender, 30 seconds to 3 minutes, depending on the noodles. Drain and rinse with cold water. Set aside.

About 30 minutes before you wish to serve, remove the chicken, pork, and broth from the refrigerator. Bring the broth to a simmer and add the fish sauce and salt to taste (about 2 teaspoons or more). Taste and adjust the seasonings.

To serve the soup, distribute the noodles among 4 to 6 bowls. Top with shredded chicken, pork, egg, and a sprinkling of the scallions or shallot. Ladle in the broth, add a dollop of the ginger paste, and sprinkle on the cilantro and Thai basil or mint. Serve at once, passing the limes for guests to squeeze on as they wish, and any remaining condiments. Alternatively, distribute the noodles, chicken, and pork among the bowls, ladle on the broth, and pass all of the other condiments on a tray, for guests to add themselves. This is the most fun. And just so you don't forget any of the condiments (as I have done), here's a list of the ingredients that should be on your tray:

Ginger paste

Blanched bean sprouts

Chopped cilantro

Chopped Thai basil or mint

Slivered omelet

Lime wedges

Thinly sliced scallions or shallots

leftovers The broth and the meat will keep for 3 or 4 days in the refrigerator, and can be frozen. If you run out of broth but still have chicken, noodles, and herbs, make lettuce roll-ups, spring rolls using rice wrappers, or a salad with the following Asian dressing.

asian chicken salad dressing

leftovers variation

1 tablespoon fresh lime juice

1 tablespoon seasoned rice wine vinegar or balsamic vinegar

1 small garlic clove, minced or put through a press

1 to 2 teaspoons (to taste) finely minced fresh ginger

1 tablespoon soy sauce

2 tablespoons dark Chinese sesame oil

4 to 5 tablespoons low-fat buttermilk or plain nonfat yogurt

Mix together the above ingredients in a bowl or measuring cup. Use for Asian noodle and chicken salads.

provençal wheatberry soup

This is my version of soupe d'épeautre, *a Provençal harvest soup made with the wheat grown in Provence. Epeautre is closer in texture and flavor to farro than to our harder-husked wheatberries, but you can still make the soup with the latter if farro is not available (épeautre is even hard to find now in France!). In traditional* soupe d'épeautre *the grain is simmered with a mutton, prosciutto, or ham bone. I dispense with this rather fatty flavoring and opt for a wealth of aromatics, including wild and fresh mushrooms, onion, garlic, rosemary, and thyme. If you want a bit of meaty flavor, there is the option of a little pancetta. Farro, which I used most recently for this recipe, is quite reminiscent of barley in flavor and texture, but sweeter, and because of that the soup is much like the classic mushroom-barley soup, with a little more Mediterranean soul. Give it a day for the sweetness of the grain to really penetrate the broth. The sprinkle of Gruyère that each bowl gets contributes a wonderful finish to this thick potage.*

❖ serves 6

2 cups whole wheatberries or farro, rinsed

1 ounce (about 1 cup) dried porcini mushrooms

1 tablespoon olive oil

1 ounce pancetta, diced (omit for vegetarian dish)

1 onion, chopped

1 pound carrots, chopped

1 celery stalk with leaves, chopped

1 large leek, white and light green parts only, cleaned and sliced

6 ounces fresh mushrooms, trimmed and sliced

1 teaspoon *each* chopped fresh rosemary and thyme, or ½ teaspoon crumbled dried

Salt

4 large garlic cloves, minced or pressed

½ pound turnips, peeled and diced

Bouquet garni made with a bay leaf, a few sprigs of fresh thyme and flat-leaf parsley, and a Parmesan rind

Freshly ground black pepper

1 (15-ounce) can white or red beans, drained and rinsed

¼ cup chopped fresh flat-leaf parsley

2 ounces Gruyère cheese, grated (½ cup)

soak the wheatberries or farro in water to cover for 1 hour or longer. Drain.

Meanwhile, place the dried mushrooms in a heatproof bowl or measuring cup and pour on 2 cups boiling water. Let sit for 15 to 30 minutes, until softened. Place a strainer lined with cheesecloth or paper towels over a bowl and drain the mushrooms. Squeeze over the strainer, then rinse the mushrooms in several changes of water to rid them of sand. Chop coarsely and set aside with the strained mushroom liquid.

advance preparation The soup can be made a day or two ahead, but don't add the parsley. If it thickens too much overnight, add a little water and reheat. Adjust the seasonings. Add parsley just before serving.

Heat the oil over medium heat in a large, heavy soup pot and add the pancetta (or the onion if not using the pancetta). When the pancetta begins to sizzle, add the onion and cook, stirring, for 3 to 5 minutes, until it begins to soften. Add half the chopped carrots, the celery, leek, sliced fresh mushrooms, rosemary, and thyme, and a generous pinch of salt. Cook, stirring, until the mushrooms begin to release liquid, then cover, turn the heat to medium-low, and cook, stirring often, for 5 to 10 minutes, until the mixture is tender and fragrant. Add the garlic and cook, stirring, for 30 seconds to 1 minute, until fragrant, and add the soaked mushrooms and their liquid, the remaining carrots, the turnips, wheatberries, bouquet garni, and 2 quarts water. Bring to a boil, add salt (at least 2 teaspoons), reduce the heat, cover, and simmer for 1 hour, until the wheatberries are tender and the soup fragrant. Add pepper and adjust the salt. Remove the bouquet garni and stir in the beans and parsley. Serve, passing the cheese for sprinkling.

leftovers The soup keeps for 3 or 4 days in the refrigerator. If it thickens you may want to add a little water. Or, if there's hardly any liquid, serve it as a grain side dish, pilaf-style.

tunisian chick pea breakfast soup

In Tunisia this hearty soup, called leblebi, *is traditionally eaten for breakfast. The soup itself is a spicy bowl of chick peas flavored with onion, garlic, harissa, olive oil, and lemon juice, but it's embellished with any number of garnishes. You could call it a Tunisian gazpacho. The garnishes can look beautiful on a buffet, and the whole combination makes for a fun meal.* ❖ **serves 4**

for the soup

1 pound chick peas, washed, picked over, and soaked in 2 quarts water for 6 hours or overnight

1 tablespoon olive oil

1 onion, chopped

4 large garlic cloves, minced or pressed

2 heaped teaspoons cumin seeds, ground

1 to 2 tablespoons harissa, to taste (commercial, or page 388)

Salt

2 to 4 tablespoons fresh lemon juice, to taste

for the garnishes *(for quantities, enough to fill small bowls or ramekins that you can set on a tray)*

Lemon wedges

Coarse sea salt

Harissa

Chopped fresh tomatoes

Chopped green and red bell peppers

Hard-cooked eggs, chopped

Rinsed capers

Sliced pickled turnips

Flaked canned tuna fish

Freshly ground cumin

Finely chopped fresh flat-leaf parsley

Finely chopped cilantro

Sliced Preserved Lemons (page 389)

Croutons or sliced stale bread

Thinly sliced scallions, both white and green parts

Olive oil

drain the chick peas and combine with 2 quarts water in a large, heavy soup pot. Bring to a boil, reduce the heat, cover, and simmer for 1 hour.

advance preparation The soup can be made through this step a day or two ahead.

Meanwhile, heat the oil over medium heat in a medium, heavy skillet and add the onion. Cook, stirring, until tender, about 5 minutes. Stir in the garlic and cumin and stir together for 30 seconds to a minute, until the garlic smells fragrant. Add to the beans.

advance preparation The finished soup will taste great for another 3 to 4 days. Keep in the refrigerator. If you plan to serve it the day after you cook the beans, do not add the lemon juice until you reheat.

After the beans have cooked for an hour, stir in the harissa and salt to taste (2 teaspoons or more). Cover and continue to cook for another 30 minutes to an hour, until the beans are very tender and the broth fragrant. Add lemon juice, taste, and adjust the salt.

Serve the soup, passing your choice of condiments on a large tray, or have them laid out on a buffet. Sprinkle the condiments over the soup and enjoy.

leftovers The cooked chick peas will keep for 4 to 5 days in the refrigerator. You will want to refresh the condiments each time you serve. You can also make a salad by draining the beans, then tossing with condiments of your choice. Season to taste with lemon juice, olive oil, garlic, salt, pepper, and cumin.

moroccan mixed bean soup with beef or lamb *(harira)*

Throughout Morocco the fast of Ramadan is traditionally broken with this hearty, incredibly fragrant bean soup (some would call it a stew). Many textures and sweet spicy flavors are at play here. I've seen vegetarian versions of harira and versions calling for beef or lamb. Harira is also eaten for breakfast in rural areas. It would definitely get a farmer through the day.

❖ serves 6 to 8

for the flour enrichment *(tadoura)*

1½ cups water

½ cup unbleached all-purpose flour

1 teaspoon lemon juice or cider vinegar

for the soup

2 tablespoons olive oil

2 onions, chopped

1 pound lean beef or lamb, cut in ½-inch cubes

½ pound chick peas, washed, picked over, and soaked for 6 hours or overnight, or 1 (15-ounce) can, drained and rinsed

1 celery rib, with leaves, chopped

1 cinnamon stick

1 teaspoon ground ginger

1 teaspoon freshly ground black pepper

1 teaspoon sweet paprika

1 teaspoon ground cumin

½ teaspoon ground turmeric

1 cup brown lentils, washed and picked over

1 cup dried split and peeled fava beans, if available

1 (28-ounce) can tomatoes, finely chopped or puréed, with liquid

2 tablespoons tomato paste

1 to 2 teaspoons (to taste) caraway seeds, crushed (optional)

Salt

½ cup finely chopped fresh cilantro

½ cup finely chopped fresh flat-leaf parsley

Generous pinch of saffron threads

for the flour enrichment, place the water in a bowl and gradually stir in the flour and lemon juice or vinegar until smooth. Cover and set aside at room temperature. Stir from time to time. For a tangy flavor, make this a couple days ahead.

Make the soup: Heat the oil over medium heat in a large, heavy soup pot and add the onions and meat. Cook, stirring, until the onions are golden and the meat browned, 15 to 20 minutes.

advance preparation The soup can be made a day ahead through this step and will benefit from sitting overnight. Bring back to a simmer and proceed with the recipe.

If using dried chick peas, drain them and add to the pot, along with 3 quarts water, the celery, and the spices. Bring to a boil, reduce the heat, and simmer for 1 hour. (If using canned chick peas, simply simmer the water, celery, and spices for 30 minutes.) Add the lentils, fava beans, tomatoes, tomato paste, and caraway and continue to simmer, covered, for 30 minutes. Add salt to taste, about a tablespoon, and simmer for another 30 minutes, or until all of the beans are nice and tender. If using canned chick peas, stir them in now. Remove the cinnamon stick.

Add the cilantro, parsley, and saffron to the simmering soup. Simmer for another 5 or 10 minutes, uncovered. Taste and adjust the salt.

Off the heat, stir in the flour and water mixture. Mix well, and return the pot to the heat. Simmer, stirring, for 5 to 10 minutes, until the soup is thick, with no floury taste.

leftovers This is one of those soups that keeps well and keeps tasting great, even better, for 3 or 4 days. Because of the flour and water thickener, it might need thinning out when you reheat. Stir vigorously to restore a smooth texture.

variation vegetarian harira

This soup is equally lovely without the meat. Simply omit it and proceed as directed, but only cook the onions for 5 to 10 minutes, until very tender and beginning to color.

two

meat stews
and braises

I'm not a big meat eater, but I do love a meat stew or braise that has simmered for so long that the meat can be pulled apart with a fork. I love the texture of the meat, and the way the aromatics, vegetables, and liquid in which it cooks become the sauce that defines the stew, and the way the flavors continue to deepen and ripen overnight. The stews and braises here include lots of vegetables, and sometimes fruit. These ingredients add color to what are normally brown dishes, and also texture, nutrients, flavors, and the license to call the dish a one-dish meal.

The collection of dishes in this chapter consists of many Old World favorites, like Burgundian beef stew and beef daube, French lamb stew with spring vegetables *(navarin)*, pot-au-feu, veal paprikash, and beef goulash. There's a brisket to die for as well as an Italian pot roast, and good old chili con carne from this side of the Atlantic. But there are also some surprising dishes that may be new to you, such as the sweet and savory Iranian stews called *koreshe* (the singular is *koresh*), in which meat and fruit are stewed together, and the Vietnamese beef and noodle soup called *pho bo,* that is really their version of pot-au-feu.

Don't be daunted by the long simmering times here. If you can't imagine being around the house for three or four hours while a daube cooks, then turn it off and stop your timer every time you have to go out. When you come back, bring the dish back to a simmer and restart your timer. I don't mind leaving the house if I have a heavy casserole on a very low flame on top of a flame tamer, and I've checked to make sure there's plenty of liquid in the pot. Many of these dishes, after all, were traditionally set on the embers of a dying fire to cook slowly through the day, while workers went to the fields. But you might not feel comfortable leaving the house with a burner on, and I don't blame you. What's nice about these stews is that they can cook partially, sit a while, then cook more to finish, without suffering. Time is on their side in every way.

Although crusty bread will suffice as an accompaniment to the dishes in this chapter, most of them will be best if you serve them with rice, noodles, or potatoes.

burgundian beef stew *(boeuf à la bourguignonne)*
52

beef daube
55

flemish beef and beer stew
(carbonnade à la flamande)
58

argentinian beef stew with winter squash and corn
60

ragù from emilia-romagna
62

french boiled beef dinner *(pot-au-feu)*
64

persian meat stew with peaches
67

chili con carne
68

vietnamese beef and noodle soup *(pho bo)*
72

brisket smothered in onions,
with vegetables and prunes
74

italian brisket or pot roast
76

veal paprikash (*paprikás*)
79

persian meat stew with quince or asian pears
81

curried lamb with cucumber raita
83

french lamb stew with spring vegetables
86

braised pork with red cabbage,
apples, and chestnuts
89

burgundian beef stew
(boeuf à la bourguignonne)

This classic French beef stew requires little more than time to come into its own. There's nothing difficult in the execution; you mince onion and carrots, cut the meat into large pieces, toss everything together in a bowl with a bottle of burgundy or pinot noir, and marinate the mixture for a day. Then you brown the meat with salt pork, add a little flour, and add the marinade to the pot. A three-hour simmer will bring the meat to a fork-tender state. But it's not until you add a pound of mushrooms and simmer for another 30 minutes (or longer) that the flavors come together. Before I add the mushrooms, I taste, adjust the salt, and think "this needs something." A half-hour later it's perfect. If you really want to serve this stew at its best, give it another day, or at least eight hours or so in the refrigerator. The protein-rich juices will gel, and the fat will float to the top. You can skim off this fat before you reheat the beef burgundy, and the dish will be all the better.

The only thing I think a traditional boeuf à la bourgignonne lacks is brightness; I long for a bright green vegetable somewhere. But how to work it into the dish? I do it just before I serve the stew: I stir in blanched green beans or peas (thawed frozen peas are fine). It's traditional to serve beef burgundy with boiled potatoes, but I prefer rice, because of the luscious way it soaks up the juices. ❖ serves 4 to 6

3 pounds beef chuck, cut into 2-inch pieces

1 large yellow onion, finely chopped

2 carrots, finely chopped

2 large garlic cloves, peeled and crushed

Bouquet garni (a few sprigs each of fresh thyme and flat-leaf parsley, 1 or 2 bay leaves, and about 6 black peppercorns, tied together in cheesecloth)

1 bottle good red burgundy or California, Washington, or Oregon pinot noir

4 ounces lean salt pork, diced

Salt and freshly ground black pepper

¼ cup all-purpose flour

1 pound mushrooms, stems trimmed, halved or quartered if large, caps left whole if small

1 heaped cup fresh or thawed frozen peas, or green beans, trimmed and broken into 2-inch pieces

Rice, noodles, or potatoes, for serving

combine the meat, onion, carrots, garlic, and bouquet garni in a large bowl. Pour in the wine and mix together well. This is most easily done with the hands. Cover the bowl with plastic wrap, or transfer to a resealable plastic bag, and refrigerate overnight, preferably for about 24 hours.

Remove the pieces of meat from the marinade and lay on a double thickness of paper towels. Pick off pieces of onion and carrot, and pat the meat dry. Heat a large, heavy pot or Dutch oven over medium heat and add the salt pork. Cook, stirring often, until the pork renders some fat and begins to look crisp, about 7 minutes. Sprinkle the meat all over with salt and pepper. Add to the pot, in batches if necessary, and brown on all sides, stirring, 7 to 10 minutes. When all of the meat has been browned, with all of it in the pot, slowly sprinkle in the flour through a strainer. Cook, stirring constantly, for 3 to 5 minutes, until all of the meat is well coated and you can smell the flour beginning to brown.

advance preparation
You can make the stew through this step a day or two ahead. It improves overnight.

Add the marinade with all of the vegetables and the bouquet garni, along with 2 cups water, and turn the heat to high. Using a wooden spoon, stir the bottom and sides of the pan to bring up any browned bits of flour or meat that may have stuck. Bring to a boil, reduce the heat to very low, cover, and simmer, stirring occasionally, for 3 hours, or until the meat is fork-tender. Taste and add salt as desired (I recommend a scant teaspoon). Stir in the mushrooms, cover, and simmer for another 30 minutes, or until the mushrooms are tender and the broth aromatic.

Meanwhile, bring a pot of water to a boil, add a couple of teaspoons of salt, and add the peas or beans. Cook for 3 to 5 minutes, until tender and bright. Drain and refresh with cold water. Simply allow frozen peas to thaw. If you just pulled them from the freezer, cover with very hot or boiling water and drain when softened.

Taste the stew, adjust the salt and add pepper to taste, and if serving right away, stir in the peas or beans. If serving the following day, refrigerate. When the dish has chilled, skim off visible fat from the top. If you have trouble skimming the fat without taking off a layer of other solid ingredients, place the skimmed ingredients in a strainer and rinse with cold water to wash off the fat, then return the solids to the pot. Reheat, stir in the peas or beans, and serve, with rice, noodles, or steamed or boiled potatoes.

leftovers : This gets better over time. You can keep it for 3 or 4 days in the refrigerator, and it freezes well for a few months.

There are some great things you can do with leftovers, depending on how much you have. The French might mince up the *restes* and fill ravioli with it. I see no reason for going to so much trouble, so I just shred the pieces of meat that are left, heat up everything, and toss with pasta, either perciatelli, penne, or rigatoni—something hollow and/or ridged, to catch the juices.

Another thing to make is a gratin of potatoes, if you have a lot of juice. Or a polenta gratin. Make polenta according to the recipe on page 396. Pour on leftover beef burgundy, and shred any big pieces of meat. Sprinkle on a handful of Gruyère cheese. Bake for 20 minutes at 400°F., or until bubbling and browned.

potato gratin à la bourguignonne

leftovers variation

1 garlic clove, cut in half

2 pounds russet or Yukon gold potatoes, peeled

Salt and freshly ground black pepper

2 cups Burgundian Beef Stew (or leftovers plus milk to make 2 cups

¼ cup grated Gruyère cheese

Heat the oven to 375°F. Rub a 2-quart gratin dish with the cut side of the garlic clove. Shred any meat that is left in the stew. Heat the stew gently to a simmer. Slice the potatoes about ¼ inch thick. Season with salt and pepper, then toss with the beef stew. Transfer to the gratin dish. Bake for 1 hour, stirring and breaking up the potatoes from time to time. Sprinkle the cheese over the top and continue to bake for another 15 minutes, or until the potatoes are tender and the top is brown.

beef daube

Beef daube is a Provençal beef stew, longer-cooking and more earthy, winey, and vegetal than beef burgundy. Like any good beef stew, it should be a three-day affair—one day for marinating, one for cooking, and one for resting. Don't use beef that is too lean, or it will become dry with all the simmering. And if possible, buy the beef in a whole piece, so that you can cut larger pieces than butchers usually cut for stew meat. In France, the cooking pot par excellence for daube is called a daubière. *It's a heavy pot with an indentation in the lid, which the cook fills with water or wine during the cooking. This is supposed to help create steam within the pot (does it really? I don't know) so that the dish will be all the moister after its long simmer.* ❖ **serves 4 to 6**

3 pounds stewing beef, preferably equal portions of bottom round and either chuck, shoulder blade, short rib meat, or shank

1 onion, cut in half and stuck with 4 cloves

2 onions, halved and thinly sliced

1 pound carrots, thinly sliced

2 bouquets garnis, each consisting of 2 bay leaves, several sprigs of fresh thyme (a small handful), and a couple of sprigs of fresh flat-leaf parsley tied together or in cheesecloth

2 strips of dried orange peel

½ teaspoon freshly grated nutmeg

4 crushed juniper berries

1 bottle dark tannic red wine, such as Côtes du Rhône

1 tablespoon red wine vinegar or sherry vinegar

2 tablespoons olive oil

2 ounces salt pork, cut in small dice (or omit and use 4 tablespoons olive oil in all)

Salt and freshly ground black pepper

2 to 4 large garlic cloves (to taste), minced or pressed

2 tablespoons tomato paste (see Note)

Noodles, rice, or potatoes, for serving

day 1. Cut the meat into 2- or 3-inch pieces. Place in a bowl and add the halved onion with the cloves, 1 of the sliced onions, half the carrots, 1 bouquet garni, 1 strip of orange peel, the nutmeg, juniper berries, wine, and vinegar. Toss everything together and cover. Marinate in the refrigerator for 8 to 24 hours. Stir the mixture two or three times.

advance preparation
You can brown the onions hours
before you brown the meat, and keep
covered on a plate.

Day 2: Drain the mixture into a colander set over a bowl. Remove the pieces of meat, blot thoroughly dry with paper towels, and set aside. Discard the bouquet garni, the onion stuck with clove, and the orange peel. Heat 1 tablespoon of the olive oil and the salt pork in a large, heavy flameproof casserole or daubière over medium heat until the salt pork renders its fat. Remove the pieces of salt pork with a slotted spoon, and add the sliced onion that was not included in the marinade. Cook, stirring, until the onion softens, about 5 minutes, then add the sliced onion and carrots from the marinade. Turn the heat to medium-low and cook the onions and carrots together slowly, stirring often, until golden brown, 10 to 15 minutes. Remove from the heat using a slotted spoon and transfer to a plate.

Add the remaining tablespoon of olive oil, then add the meat to the pot, in batches, and brown slowly on all sides, taking about 10 minutes for each batch. Do not crowd the pot. Transfer to a platter or bowl and immediately sprinkle with salt and pepper. Pour off the fat from the pot.

advance preparation
Once you've made the daube, it will
keep for at least 5 days in the
refrigerator and freezes well for a
few months.

When all of the meat has been browned, return to the pot along with the browned onions and carrots (not the remaining raw carrots), the marinade and its vegetables, the garlic, tomato paste, and the remaining bouquet garni. Bring slowly to a gentle simmer, skimming off any foam. Cover the pot and simmer for 3 hours. Add the remaining carrots, cover, and simmer for another hour. Taste and season with salt and pepper. Continue to simmer for another hour, or for up to 3 more hours. The meat

---

TOMATO PASTE

I try to find tomato paste in tubes. If I can't, when I open a can and only use a tablespoon or two, I freeze the remaining tomato paste in 1-tablespoon quantities. Then I pull them out of the freezer as needed.

should be fork-tender. Cover and allow to cool, add the remaining orange peel to the pot, then refrigerate overnight.

Day 3: Skim all of the visible fat off the top of the daube. Bring slowly to a simmer. Simmer for 30 minutes to an hour. Taste, adjust the seasonings, and serve with pasta, rice, or potatoes.

leftovers Many classic Provençal dishes are traditionally made with leftover beef daube. Niçoise ravioli and stuffed vegetables are probably the most famous. But both of those dishes are time-consuming to make—and let's face it, you worked hard enough on the daube. But *macaronade,* which is macaroni and cheese in which the béchamel is replaced by the daube sauce, is another story. And scrumptious—maybe as delicious as the beef daube itself!

macaronade

leftovers variation

Salt

½ pound penne or other macaroni noodles

1 cup beef daube sauce, with a few pieces of the meat, shredded

2 ounces Gruyère cheese, grated (½ cup)

¼ cup bread crumbs

1 tablespoon olive oil

other leftover ideas
Spaghetti tossed with daube (break up the meat)

Rice with daube

Polenta topped with daube and Gruyère

Heat the oven to 400°F. Butter or oil a 2-quart baking dish. Bring a large pot of water to a boil and add a tablespoon of salt. Cook the noodles a few minutes less than the package instructions say, so that they're al dente but still a little hard in the middle. Drain the noodles and toss with the daube and the cheese. Turn into the baking dish. Toss the bread crumbs with the olive oil and spread in an even layer over the top. Bake for 20 minutes, or until the top is browned. Serve hot or warm.

flemish beef and beer
stew *(carbonnade à la flamande)*

This stew gets double takes, so amazing are the flavors. People want to keep eating the gravy long after the meat is gone—with rice, with potatoes or bread, even plain with a spoon. It's all those onions and the little bit of brown sugar and the beer. The ingredients caramelize as they cook, and there's a sweet edge, but the stew isn't sweet, it's savory. This is incredibly easy to make; just make sure you cook it long enough, so the meat becomes fork-tender. ❖ serves 4

3 tablespoons all-purpose flour

Salt and freshly ground black pepper

2 pounds boneless chuck or round steak, cut in 1-inch cubes

4 ounces bacon, trimmed of some of its fat and diced

2 tablespoons unsalted butter

2 large onions, thinly sliced

1 tablespoon brown sugar (light or dark)

1 tablespoon cider vinegar

1½ cups dark beer

Bouquet garni made with 1 bay leaf and a few sprigs of fresh flat-leaf parsley and thyme tied in cheesecloth

2 thick slices of country bread

Dijon mustard

Potatoes, mashed potatoes, or rice, for serving

combine the flour, about ¼ teaspoon salt, and a few grinds of pepper, and lightly dredge the meat in it. Set aside.

advance preparation
You can cook the onions several hours before browning the meat and finishing the stew. Keep covered, at room temperature.

Heat half the bacon over medium-low heat in a large, heavy Dutch oven or flame-proof casserole until it renders its fat. Add 1 tablespoon of the butter and all of the onions and cook, stirring often, until the onions are tender and light brown, 10 to 15 minutes. Add the sugar and stir together. Remove from the heat.

advance preparation
The stew can be made through this
step 1 or 2 days ahead. Refrigerate,
and when ready to serve skim off the
fat and reheat gently, then proceed
with the recipe.

Meanwhile, heat the remaining bacon over medium heat in a large, heavy nonstick skillet. When it is cooked, remove from the skillet and transfer to the casserole with the onions. Add the remaining tablespoon of butter to the skillet, and when the foam subsides brown the meat, in batches, on all sides. Transfer the meat to the casserole with the onions. Pour off any fat from the frying pan and discard, then add the vinegar to the pan and deglaze, scraping all the caramelized meat juices from the bottom of the pan. Pour the scrapings into the casserole. Add the beer and bouquet garni to the casserole, and bring to a simmer. Reduce the heat to very low, cover, and simmer gently, stirring from time to time, for 3 hours, or until the meat is fork-tender. Taste and adjust the salt.

Spread the slices of bread thickly with mustard and cut in half. Place, mustard side down, on the surface of the stew. Cover and continue to simmer for another 30 minutes. Serve with steamed or mashed potatoes, or rice, and accompany with beer.

leftovers This will keep for 5 days in the refrigerator and freezes well for a few months. Like all stews it's better the day after you make it. The gravy, with bits of meat if there are any, is good with rice, with pasta, or on top of bread, the ultimate "gravy bread."

argentinian beef stew with winter squash and corn

This heavenly, cumin- and paprika-scented stew is based on a classic Argentinian dish called Carbonada Criolla. Like most classic dishes, it has many different interpretations and versions. Some include both winter and summer squash, others call for sweet peppers, some are baked in a pumpkin. What most have in common is the beef, the winter squash, and the corn.

❖ serves 6

3	tablespoons olive oil
2	onions, thinly sliced
4	large garlic cloves, minced or pressed
2	teaspoons cumin seeds, crushed
2	tablespoons all-purpose flour
	Salt and freshly ground black pepper
1	tablespoon sweet paprika
2	pounds beef stewing meat, such as chuck, cut in 2-inch pieces
2	tablespoons red wine or sherry vinegar
2	cups red wine
1	(14-ounce) can tomatoes, with liquid, chopped
2	carrots, peeled and sliced
1	teaspoon sugar
1	large or 2 small bay leaves
1	teaspoon dried oregano
¾	pound waxy potatoes, peeled and cut into ½-inch cubes
1	medium butternut squash (about 1½ pounds), peeled, seeded, and cut into ½-inch cubes
2	ears of corn, either cut in 1-inch rounds or kernels removed (or 1½ cups frozen corn, thawed)

advance preparation
You can do this step hours before
you brown the meat. Keep covered,
at room temperature.

heat 1 tablespoon of the oil in a large, heavy, flameproof casserole over medium heat and add the onions. Cook, stirring, until tender, 5 to 8 minutes, then add the garlic and cumin seeds. Cook, stirring, for about a minute, until the garlic is fragrant, and remove from the heat.

Season the flour with salt (¼ to ½ teaspoon) and pepper, mix with 1 teaspoon of the paprika, and lightly dredge the meat in it. Heat the remaining 2 tablespoons of olive oil in a large, heavy nonstick skillet over medium-high heat and brown the meat on all sides, in batches if necessary. This should take about 10 minutes per batch. As the meat is done, transfer to the casserole with the onions. When all of the meat has been browned, pour off any fat remaining in the pan and discard. Then add the vinegar and stir constantly with a wooden spoon to deglaze the bottom of the pan. Pour into the casserole with the meat.

advance preparation
Both this step and the next can be
completed a day or two ahead of
completing the stew. Refrigerate
overnight. Skim off the fat and
reheat to a simmer before proceeding
with the recipe.

Add the red wine to the pan and bring to a boil. Boil for a minute, stirring the bottom of the pan with a wooden spoon, then pour into the pan with the meat. Add to the casserole the tomatoes, the remaining 2 teaspoons of paprika, one of the carrots, the sugar, bay leaf, and oregano. Add 1½ to 2 cups water, enough to cover the meat, and a heaped teaspoon of salt. Bring to a simmer, cover, and simmer gently for 2 hours.

Add the remaining carrot, the potatoes, and the squash. Simmer for another hour, or until the meat and squash are fork-tender. Taste and add salt and pepper as desired.

Stir in the corn and simmer for another 10 minutes. Correct the seasonings again before serving, preferably the next day.

leftovers Like all beef stews this is best the day after it's made and even better a day after that. It will keep for about 4 days in the refrigerator and freezes well for a few months. Shred leftover cubes of beef, then toss, with the sauce and vegetables, with rice or pasta.

ragù from emilia-romagna

Although ragù is not served alone as a stew, but as a sauce, it belongs in the meat stew chapter, because it's cooked like a stew, and that's what it essentially is. There are probably as many recipes for it as there are families in Emilia-Romagna. The classic ragù from Bologna is made with beef only. Others include sausage, and still others are made with a mixture of beef, veal, and pork. No matter what meats you use, ragù should be like a thick meat gravy or stew. The sauce is a component of classic lasagne and is served with pasta, such as tagliatelle, spaghetti, or macaroni (see page 193). I also use it in a delicious Polenta and Ragù Gratin (page 207). It's one of those dishes to make one day when you just feel like cooking and making your house smell wonderful. Freeze it if you don't have a plan, and be confident that an extraordinary dinner is always at hand. ❖ **makes about 5 cups**

¾	pound lean beef, such as chuck blade or chuck center
¼	pound mild Italian sausage, bulk or link (removed from its casing)
1	ounce prosciutto di Parma
2	tablespoons olive oil
2	ounces pancetta, finely chopped
1	medium onion, minced
1	medium celery stalk, with leaves, minced
1	small carrot, minced
2	garlic cloves, minced or pressed
¾	cup dry red wine
1½	cups chicken stock (page 378) or meat stock
1	cup milk
1	(28-ounce) can plum tomatoes, with about half the juice, crushed or coarsely chopped
	Salt and freshly ground black pepper to taste

coarsely grind together the beef, sausage, and prosciutto, using a food processor or a meat grinder. Set aside.

Heat the oil in a large, heavy nonstick skillet over medium-high heat, and have a heavy 4- or 5-quart saucepan ready next to it. Add the pancetta, onion, celery, and carrot to the skillet and cook, stirring, until the onion is just beginning to color, 5 to 10 minutes.

Stir the garlic and ground meats into the pan and turn the heat to medium. Cook, stirring and breaking up the meats, until all the pink has been cooked out, 10 to 15 minutes. The meat should not be browned, just cooked through. Transfer the mixture to a strainer set over a bowl or sink and give the strainer a shake to drain some of the fat. Transfer the mixture to the saucepan.

Add the wine to the skillet and reduce over medium-low heat, stirring any glaze from the bottom of the pan up into the bubbling wine. Reduce by half, which should take from 3 to 5 minutes. Stir into the meat mixture in the saucepan and set over medium heat.

advance preparation
You can make this up to 5 days before you use it. It definitely benefits from being made one day ahead.

Add ½ cup of the stock to the saucepan and bring to a simmer. Cook over medium-low heat, stirring often, until the stock evaporates, 8 to 10 minutes. Add another ½ cup of the stock and repeat. Stir in the remaining stock and the milk. Turn the heat to low, partially cover, and simmer for 45 minutes to an hour, stirring often, until the milk is no longer visible. Add the tomatoes and their juice, and salt to taste (at least ½ teaspoon), and stir together. Turn the heat very low, so that the mixture is cooking at a bare simmer. Cook very slowly, partially covered, for 1½ to 2 hours. Stir often. The sauce should be thick and meaty when done. Season to taste with salt and pepper.

leftovers This will keep for 5 days in the refrigerator and freezes well for a few months.

french boiled beef
dinner *(pot-au-feu)*

This is considered by some to be the national dish of France. Pot-au-feu has many renditions; some cooks include only beef, as in this recipe, whereas others include chicken and other meats. The original probably called for cooking the meat and vegetables in the same pot, but today many cooks cook their vegetables separately, and all agree that the cabbage must be cooked separately so as not to give the broth a sulfuric flavor. The dish is a simple one whose success depends on the cuts of meat used and the proper skimming and seasoning of the broth. Although it isn't labor-intensive, it is time-consuming, because the meat must be brought to a simmer very slowly and then cooked slowly for a long time. It is definitely a dish to do a day ahead, both because it will taste better and because you can separate the fat from the broth so easily after chilling it. ❖ **serves 8 to 10**

1½ to 2 pounds beef short ribs, on or off the bone

3½ to 4 pounds beef brisket

1 teaspoon coarse sea salt for every quart of water (more to taste)

Bouquet garni made with 1 bay leaf, 5 sprigs of fresh flat-leaf parsley, 8 peppercorns, 2 sprigs of fresh thyme, and ¼ teaspoon fennel seeds, tied in a double thickness of cheesecloth

4 leeks, white and green parts separated, trimmed, cut in half lengthwise, and cleaned

1 garlic bulb, cut in half horizontally

2 onions, each peeled and studded with a whole clove

2 pounds carrots, peeled and quartered

8 marrow bones (about 1½ to 2 pounds), cut in 1- or 2-inch lengths

4 turnips, peeled and quartered

1 small celery root, peeled and cut in cubes

12 medium waxy potatoes, scrubbed and cut in half (optional)

1 medium cabbage, cut in 8 wedges

for serving

Cornichons (or a selection of pickles)

French Dijon mustard (classic, grainy, or both)

Coarse sea salt

the day before you wish to serve, cook the meat. If using short ribs on the bone, tie them into bundles. Arrange the meat in a large, heavy stockpot or Dutch oven. Cover with water, making sure to measure the water so that you can determine how much salt to add (you will need approximately 3 quarts). Place over medium-high heat and bring to a bare simmer, being careful not to allow the liquid to boil; this will take some time. Skim off any foam that rises to the top. Turn the heat to low, and continue to cook and skim, keeping the mixture at a bare simmer—the water should be moving and bubbles will be rising up from the bottom, but the surface of the water should not break as it does when water is boiling rapidly—for 30 minutes. Add the salt, the bouquet garni, the leek greens, the garlic bulb, the onions, and ¾ pound of the carrots. Continue to simmer gently, skimming often, for 3 to 4 hours, until the meat is fork-tender. Add the marrow bones and continue to simmer for another 30 minutes.

advance preparation Make the pot-au-feu through this step at least a day ahead and up to 3 days ahead.

Remove the meats and marrow bones from the stock and transfer to a bowl. Remove the short-rib meat from the bones (the meat should be falling off the bone), and discard the fatty parts. Cover the meat and marrow bones tightly with foil and refrigerate. Strain the stock into a bowl through a strainer lined with a double thickness of cheesecloth, and refrigerate.

Remove the stock from the refrigerator and lift off the fat. Return the meat and marrow bones to the pot and pour in the stock. Bring slowly to just below a simmer.

Meanwhile, place the remaining carrots, the turnips, the white part of the leeks, the celery root and the potatoes (if using) in a pot. Cover with water and bring to a boil. Add salt, and boil gently until tender, 20 to 30 minutes. Place the cabbage in another pot, cover with water, and bring to a boil. Add salt and simmer for 15 to 20 minutes, until tender.

advance preparation You can cook all of the vegetables a few hours ahead; reduce the cooking time by 5 minutes, turn off the heat, then reheat in their broth.

Drain the cabbage, discarding the broth. When ready to serve, place the warm vegetables on a large platter and keep warm in a low oven. Taste the vegetable broth and adjust the seasoning.

When the meat has been reheated, remove it from the liquid and slice or cut it into chunks. Place on a separate platter with the marrow bones, or on the platter with the vegetables if there's room. Taste the stock and adjust the seasonings. If you wish, serve this as a first course.

Spoon some of the vegetable poaching liquid as well as some of the meat stock over the meat and vegetables. Serve hot, with cornichons, French mustards, coarse salt, and additional broth passed in a gravy boat or tureen.

leftovers You are bound to have them. The cooked meats and meat broth will keep for up to 4 days in the refrigerator, and the broths freeze well for several months. This salad is one of my favorite ways to use the leftovers.

beef and arugula salad ❖ serves 4

for the dressing

2 tablespoons wine or sherry vinegar

1 teaspoon balsamic vinegar

1 tablespoon Dijon mustard

Salt and freshly ground black pepper

1 small garlic clove, minced or pressed

⅓ to ½ cup olive oil or a combination of olive and canola oils, to taste

for the salad

2 cups cubes or thin strips of cooked beef

2 cups arugula

1 ounce shaved Parmesan cheese

2 to 4 tablespoons chopped fresh herbs, such as flat-leaf parsley, tarragon, chervil

1 tablespoon chopped fresh chives

Salt and freshly ground black pepper

Mix together the vinegars and the mustard. Add salt, pepper, and the garlic, and whisk in the oil. Toss half the dressing with the beef and let sit for 30 minutes to 1 hour. Add the remaining ingredients and the rest of the dressing, toss together, and serve.

persian meat stew with peaches

This is a typical Iranian koresh, a luscious, easy meat stew that combines savory, sweet, and acidic flavors in just the right balance. The broth is infused with cinnamon and saffron. I have made the stew using veal, beef, and lamb. Let your taste in meat determine which you choose. For best results, make the stew in summer or early fall so that you can use fresh peaches. ❖ serves 4

3 tablespoons unsalted butter or vegetable oil

2 medium onions, thinly sliced

1 pound veal, beef, or lamb, trimmed of fat and cut in 1-inch cubes

1 teaspoon salt, or to taste

¼ teaspoon freshly ground black pepper (or to taste)

½ teaspoon ground cinnamon

¼ cup fresh lemon juice

3 to 4 tablespoons sugar (to taste)

1 tablespoon all-purpose flour

¼ teaspoon ground saffron dissolved in 1 tablespoon hot water, or a generous pinch of saffron threads, pounded in a mortar and pestle and mixed with a tablespoon of hot water

1¼ to 1½ pounds firm, not-quite-ripe peaches (3 large or 6 small), peeled and thinly sliced, or 2 cups canned peaches, drained

Rice, for serving

advance preparation
The stew can be made through this step a few hours or a day ahead. Refrigerate, then skim off the fat, reheat, and proceed as directed.

heat 2 tablespoons of the butter or oil over medium heat in a large, heavy casserole and add the onions. Cook, stirring, until translucent, 3 to 5 minutes, and add the meat. Cook gently, stirring often, until the meat and onions are browned, about 10 minutes. Add the salt, pepper, cinnamon, and enough water to cover the meat by an inch, about 2½ cups. Bring to a simmer, reduce the heat to low, cover, and simmer for 2 to 3 hours, until the meat is fork-tender.

Mix together the lemon juice, sugar, flour, and saffron. Stir into the meat. Cover and simmer for another 20 minutes.

Meanwhile, heat the remaining tablespoon of butter or oil in a large nonstick skillet over medium-high heat. Add the peaches and cook, stirring, until lightly browned, about 3 minutes. Add to the meat, cover, and simmer for another 10 to 20 minutes (10 minutes for canned peaches), or until the peaches and meat are tender. Taste and correct the seasonings. Serve with basmati rice or Iranian rice (page 386).

leftovers ⋮ This will keep for 4 days in the refrigerator, and it benefits from being made a day ahead. I make pilaf with leftovers, tossing whatever stew I have with basmati rice and heating gently.

chili con carne

Texans and even some non-Texans I know feel strongly about what a real bowl of chili should be. They would disapprove of the tomatoes in this chili, and of the option of adding beans, and they would also expect the meat to be cut up into small cubes instead of coarsely ground.

I have made chili the classic Texan way, but I prefer this one—a gorgeous red, the deep red burgundy of the ancho chilies adding their color and sweetness to the more orange and acrid pure ground chili powder. I prefer the texture of the coarsely ground meat, and the way the ground meat absorbs the flavors of the stew. The one thing I do insist on is that you use pure chili powder, and not commercial chili powder, which contains garlic powder and other spices. Any grocery store that sells Mexican ingredients—which is most these days—will usually have ground chili in plastic packages. They will also have the ancho chilies, a dried poblano chili that is sometimes referred to as pasilla. *The powder is most often made with California or New Mexico chilies, probably anaheims, and is quite mild, so the chili con carne does require the addition of cayenne or other hot chili powder. You can make it more or less hot according to your taste. This one is medium hot. Make this a day ahead if you can; the flavors will really develop overnight.* ❖ serves 4 to 6

3 tablespoons canola or vegetable oil

2 pounds beef round or chuck steak, coarsely ground in a food processor

Salt and freshly ground black pepper

2 medium onions, chopped

4 garlic cloves, minced or put through a press

2 tablespoons all-purpose flour

4 to 6 tablespoons pure ground chili powder

1 tablespoon ground cumin

1 (28-ounce) can crushed tomatoes

¼ teaspoon sugar

1 quart beef broth, water, or a combination of the two

3 ancho (or pasilla) chilies, seeded

1 teaspoon dried oregano

½ teaspoon cayenne pepper (more or less to taste)

2 (15-ounce) cans red or pinto beans, drained and rinsed (optional)

¼ cup chopped fresh cilantro (optional)

Corn bread, biscuits, or corn tortillas, for serving

heat 1 tablespoon of the oil over medium-high heat in a large, heavy nonstick skillet and brown the meat in 2 or 3 batches, stirring and breaking up the meat. Transfer the meat as it is done to a bowl and season with salt and pepper.

When all of the meat has been browned, pour off the fat, add another tablespoon of oil to the pan, turn the heat down to medium, and add the onions. Cook, stirring often to prevent the onions from scorching, until light brown, about 15 minutes. Add the garlic and stir together for 30 seconds to a minute, until fragrant. Sprinkle on the flour, stir together, and cook for a minute or two longer. Transfer to the bowl with the beef.

Heat the remaining tablespoon of oil over medium-high heat in a large, heavy casserole. Add the chili powder and cumin to the oil and stir for about 30 seconds to a minute, until you smell the spices beginning to toast, and pour in the tomatoes. They should sizzle and sear at once. Add the sugar and cook, stirring often, for 5 to 10 minutes, until the mixture has cooked down and is beginning to stick to the pan.

advance preparation
The chili can and should be made a
day or two ahead through this step.
Keep in the refrigerator.

Stir in the meat mixture, combine well, and add the stock or water, the ancho chilies, the oregano, cayenne, and about 2 teaspoons salt. Bring to a simmer over medium heat. Stir well, turn the heat to low, cover, and simmer for 1½ to 2 hours, until the stew is thick and fragrant. Stir often to make sure the chili isn't sticking to the bottom of the pot. Taste and adjust the salt. Add more cayenne if desired. Remove and discard the ancho chilies. If serving the same day, spoon grease off from the surface of the chili. If serving the following day, which is recommended, refrigerate overnight, then lift the fat off from the top of the pot.

Bring back to a simmer and stir in the beans if you want them. Heat through and serve, sprinkling each serving with chopped cilantro. Serve with corn bread, biscuits, or tortillas.

leftovers Chili has excellent staying power and will keep for up to 5 days. It freezes well too, for a few months. Leftovers make great fillings for soft tacos: Just heat tortillas in a dry pan or in the oven, wrapped in foil, fill with chili and a little Mexican crumbling cheese such as queso fresco, and serve. Or try either of the recipes below.

chili enchiladas ❖ serves 4

4 cups Chili con Carne

12 corn tortillas

1 white or red onion, chopped and rinsed with cold water (optional)

3 to 4 ounces Mexican queso fresco, or grated Monterey Jack

Heat the chili in a large saucepan or nonstick skillet.

Soften the tortillas: Wrap in a clean, heavy dish towel and place in a steamer basket above 1 inch of boiling water. Cover and steam for 1 minute. Remove from the heat and let sit, covered, for 10 to 15 minutes. Alternatively, wrap 3 or 4 at a time in a dish towel and heat in the microwave at full power for 30 seconds.

The enchiladas can be assembled on serving plates and served at once, or placed in a baking dish and heated through, in which case heat the oven to 325°F. Heat 4 to 6 dinner plates, or lightly oil a baking dish large enough to accommodate 12 enchiladas in a single row. Place a small amount of sauce in the baking dish, or spoon the sauce over each plate. One at a time, top the tortillas with 2 to 3 tablespoons of the chili, sprinkle on some onion, if using, and some cheese, and roll up. Place on the plates, top with more chili, sprinkle on more onion and cheese, and serve at once, or if using the baking dish, pour the chili over the top, sprinkle on the cheese, and heat through for 15 minutes in the oven. Sprinkle on the onions and serve.

chili cobbler with cornmeal biscuit topping ❖ serves 4 to 6

4	cups Chili con Carne
1	(15-ounce) can kidney beans or pintos, drained and rinsed
½	cup stone-ground cornmeal
1	cup unbleached all-purpose flour
2	teaspoons baking powder
½	teaspoon baking soda
½	teaspoon salt
6	tablespoons cold unsalted butter, cut into small pieces
⅔	cup plain yogurt (nonfat, low-fat, or whole milk)
1	egg, beaten

Heat the oven to 375°F. Butter or oil a 2-quart gratin or baking dish. Mix together the chili and beans and place in the dish.

Combine the cornmeal, flour, baking powder, baking soda, and salt in a food processor and pulse. Cut in the butter, pulsing with the food processor until the mixture has a coarse, mealy texture. Add the yogurt and process until the mixture is homogenous. Either gently roll or press out on a lightly floured surface and then place over the chili, or spoon heaped tablespoons over the chili. Lightly moisten your fingertips and press and smooth the topping so that it covers the chili. Brush with the beaten egg. Bake for 30 to 35 minutes, until the top is golden brown. Serve hot.

Note: If you have only 2 cups of leftover chili, make the dish in a 1-quart baking dish, and use half the biscuit dough. Make biscuits with the remaining dough, and bake them for 15 to 20 minutes at 375°F.

vietnamese beef and noodle soup *(pho bo)*

Even though this is a soup, I've put it in this chapter, because it is really Vietnam's version of pot-au-feu. Indeed, the name pho, *pronounced like the French* feu, *may have evolved from the French colonial days. This signature Vietnamese dish, traditionally eaten for breakfast in its country of origin, is served in Vietnamese restaurants all over the world.* ❖ **serves 6**

5 to 6 pounds oxtails or beef short ribs on the bone, or meaty beef bones

1 pound bottom-round beef roast, in one piece, trimmed of fat

1 (3-inch) piece of fresh ginger, unpeeled

1 large or 2 medium onions, quartered

2 to 4 tablespoons fish sauce (nuoc nam), to taste

1 tablespoon sugar

6 star anise pods

5 whole cloves

1 tablespoon black peppercorns

1 (2- to 3-inch) cinnamon stick

1 tablespoon coarse sea salt, or to taste

1 pound thin or medium-width rice noodles, cooked al dente

½ pound beef sirloin, very thinly sliced across the grain (freeze slightly first to make cutting easier)

1 cup chopped fresh cilantro

3 shallots, sliced paper-thin and separated into rings, soaked if desired (see page 375)

½ cup basil leaves, preferably Thai basil

4 scallions, chopped

2 cups bean sprouts

2 to 4 Asian or serrano chilies, finely chopped (to taste)

3 limes, cut in wedges

place the bones and beef roast in a very large stockpot and cover with water. Bring to a boil and boil for 5 minutes. Drain and rinse the meat and bones thoroughly. Clean the pot, then return the bones and roast to the pot and add 6 quarts of water, or enough to cover. Bring slowly to a gentle boil. Skim off any foam. Simmer gently for 30 minutes, skimming often.

Meanwhile, scorch the ginger and onion quarters by holding them directly over a gas flame with tongs and turning until charred on all sides. The onions can be only slightly charred; the ginger will quickly turn black. (If using an electric burner, heat in a dry heavy skillet or on a griddle until charred.) Rinse briefly, then add to the pot.

Add the fish sauce and sugar to the pot, skim, and simmer over low heat, partially covered and skimming often, for 2 to 3 hours, until the meat is very tender. Remove the meat from the pot and transfer to a bowl. Cover with water and let sit for 15 minutes. This will prevent the meat from drying out and darkening. Drain, wrap tightly in plastic, and refrigerate until shortly before serving.

Tie the spices in a cheesecloth bag and add to the soup, along with the salt (about 1 rounded teaspoon coarse sea salt per quart of water). Continue to simmer for another 2 hours, skimming often and adding water as necessary to keep the bones covered.

advance preparation The recipe can and should be made through this step a day or up to 4 days ahead so that the fat can be skimmed off. Remove the bones from the pot, using tongs, and discard. Line a strainer with a double thickness of cheesecloth, and place over a large bowl. Ladle in the broth. Allow to cool slightly, then refrigerate for at least 2 hours, or preferably overnight.

Cut the cooked beef across the grain into very thin slices. Set aside.

Skim off all the fat from the top of the broth and discard. Return the broth to a soup pot and bring to a simmer. Taste and adjust the seasonings.

Divide the noodles among 6 large soup bowls. Place a few slices each of raw sirloin and cooked beef on top of the noodles in each bowl, and ladle in a generous amount of simmering broth, which will cook the raw beef. Sprinkle on half the cilantro, the shallots, half the basil leaves, and the scallions. Pass the bean sprouts, chopped chilies, the remaining cilantro and basil, and the lime wedges. Serve with chopsticks and soup spoons.

leftovers The wonderful, spicy beef stock will keep for 5 days in the refrigerator and freezes well. You can keep making pho with the leftover beef, or make Beef and Arugula Salad (page 66).

brisket smothered in onions, with vegetables and prunes

This brisket is simply incredible. The onions—2 pounds of them—get sweeter and sweeter as the brisket braises, infusing the meat and the gravy. If you choose to add the prunes, and I recommend it, an even deeper, richer sauce will result. This will be great if you serve it the day you make it, but even better the next day. ❖ serves 6

3 tablespoons canola oil

4 medium to large onions (about 2 pounds), thinly sliced

1 tablespoon dark brown sugar

1 (3½- to 4-pound) beef brisket, trimmed

Salt and freshly ground black pepper

2 cups dry red wine, such as a Côtes du Rhône

1½ pounds carrots, peeled and quartered

1 head of garlic, cut in half crosswise

¾ pound parsnips, quartered and cored

¼ pound pitted prunes (optional)

1 pound Yukon gold potatoes, scrubbed and quartered

advance preparation
This step can be completed several hours before you brown the meat. Cover and let sit at room temperature.

heat the oven to 350°F. Heat 2 tablespoons of the oil over medium heat in a large, heavy nonstick skillet and add the onions. Cook, stirring, until softened, 5 to 10 minutes. Transfer to a large Dutch oven, one that can accommodate the meat, and toss with the brown sugar.

Add the remaining tablespoon of oil to the pan, turn up the heat to medium-high, and add the brisket. Brown well, being careful not to scorch, on both sides, about 10 minutes per side. Transfer to the pot with the onions, and season generously on both sides with salt and pepper. Place the meat with the fat side up and scatter most of the onions on top of the brisket.

Pour the fat off from the pan and discard. Add the wine to the pan and bring to a boil, scraping with a wooden spoon to deglaze the pan. Boil for a few minutes, then pour the wine into the pot with the meat. Lift the meat to be sure that the liquid flows underneath. Add 1 pound of the carrots to the pot, and the garlic. Cover and place in the oven for 2½ hours.

Add the remaining carrots, the parsnips, prunes, and potatoes to the pot, sprinkling them generously with coarse salt. Try to push them down into the liquid in the pot so that they simmer in the fragrant broth. Cover the pot and cook for another hour, or until the meat and vegetables are fork-tender. Remove from the heat.

Carefully transfer the vegetables to a bowl or platter, and transfer the meat to a cutting board if serving right away, to a smaller dish if serving the next day (which is preferable). Strain the liquid left in the pot. If serving the next day, refrigerate.

If there's a thick layer of fat on the top of the meat, trim it away. If serving right away, slice the meat thinly across the grain, and place on a platter. Spoon the pan juices over, and top with the onions, or put the onions on the side. Serve with the vegetables and prunes.

If serving the next day, wrap the meat tightly in foil and refrigerate. Place the onions in a bowl, cover, and refrigerate. To serve, slice the meat, cover with the juices and onions, and reheat gently in a 325°F. oven for 20 minutes.

l e f t o v e r s ⋮ The meat will keep for 4 or 5 days in the refrigerator and will taste great until you finish it. Use leftovers for sandwiches, or make the Beef and Arugula Salad on page 66.

italian brisket
or pot roast

When I was working on the brisket recipe on page 74, I kept thinking that an Italian sauce would also make a great complement to this type of slowly simmered, tender beef. I did a little research and found that indeed, in Italy pot roast, called stracotto, *is much loved. The sauce that results here is deep and rich-tasting, like a ragù, infused with the meat juices, but deeply vegetal as well, with the textures of the mushrooms and tomatoes. Spoon it onto the pasta or polenta you will serve on the side. You'll also have lots left over for pasta or lasagne during the week.* ❖ serves 6 to 8

1 ounce dried porcini mushrooms (about 1 cup)

2 cups boiling water

3 tablespoons olive oil

2 large onions, chopped

2 large carrots, chopped

1 celery stalk, with leaves, chopped

6 large garlic cloves, minced

¼ cup chopped fresh flat-leaf parsley

1 teaspoon chopped fresh sage

1 teaspoon chopped fresh rosemary, or ½ teaspoon crumbled dried

1 bay leaf, broken into pieces

1 (3½- to 4-pound) beef brisket or rump roast

Salt and freshly ground black pepper

1 cup dry red wine

2 tablespoons tomato paste

1 (28-ounce) can tomatoes, with liquid, chopped or crushed

Pasta or polenta (see page 396), for serving

place the dried mushrooms in a heatproof measuring cup or a bowl and pour in the boiling water. Let sit for 30 minutes. Set a strainer lined with cheesecloth or paper towels over a bowl and drain the mushrooms. Squeeze the mushrooms over the strainer, and measure out 1 cup of the soaking liquid. Rinse the mushrooms in several changes of water to remove all grit.

advance preparation
You can make the dish through this step several hours before browning the meat. Cover the casserole and set aside at room temperature.

Meanwhile, heat the oven to 350°F. Heat 2 tablespoons of the oil over medium heat in a large, heavy nonstick skillet and add the onions. Cook, stirring, until slightly softened, about 5 minutes. Add the carrots, celery, half of the garlic, the parsley, sage, rosemary, and bay leaf. Cook, stirring often, until the vegetables are tender and fragrant, about another 5 minutes. Transfer to a large Dutch oven, one that can accommodate the meat. Stir in the reconstituted mushrooms and set aside.

Add the remaining 1 tablespoon oil to the pan, turn up the heat to medium-high, and add the meat. Brown well, taking care not to scorch the meat, on all sides, about 20 minutes. Transfer to the pot with the aromatics, and season generously on all sides with salt and pepper. The meat should be placed with the fat side up.

Pour the fat off from the pan and discard. Add the wine and the tomato paste to the pan and bring to a boil, scraping with a wooden spoon to deglaze the pan. Boil for a minute or two, then pour the wine into the pot with the meat. Lift the meat to be sure that the liquid flows underneath. Stir in the mushroom soaking liquid, the tomatoes, and more salt. Cover tightly and place in the oven on a low rack. Cook for 3 to 4 hours (if using rump roast, turn every 30 minutes or so). Add the remaining garlic after the first 2 hours. When the meat is done it should be fork-tender. Remove the meat from the pot and transfer to a platter or cutting board. Cover with foil if not serving right away. If serving the next day, wrap in foil and refrigerate.

Skim off any fat from the top of the sauce. Taste and adjust the seasonings. If serving the next day, refrigerate in a covered bowl. Lift off the fat the next day and reheat.

When ready to serve the meat, slice it thinly, across the grain. If it is cold, reheat in a 325°F. oven for about 20 minutes. Serve with pasta or polenta, with the sauce topping both the meat and the accompaniment.

leftovers The meat will keep for 4 or 5 days in the refrigerator and will taste great until you finish it. There will be lots of sauce left over, and it's great with pasta or polenta. Or you can make the lasagne on the following page.

lasagne with italian
brisket sauce ❖ serves 4

2 tablespoons butter

2 cups milk

2 tablespoons flour

Salt and freshly ground black or white pepper to taste

½ pound no-cook lasagne noodles

2 cups sauce from the Italian Brisket, with meat shredded
into it if desired

3 ounces Parmesan cheese, grated (¾ cup, tightly packed)

1 to 2 tablespoons butter, for the top of the lasagne (optional)

Melt the butter over medium-low heat in a heavy saucepan, and heat the milk in
another saucepan or in the microwave. Add the flour to the melted butter and cook,
stirring, for about 3 minutes, until smooth and bubbling. Whisk in the milk and bring
to a simmer. Simmer, stirring, for 5 to 8 minutes, until the sauce has thickened and lost
its raw flour taste. Season with salt and pepper. The béchamel isn't meant to be very
thick.

Assemble the lasagne. Oil or butter a 2-quart baking dish. Heat the oven to 350°F.
Reserve about 6 tablespoons each of béchamel and cheese for the top layer of the
lasagne. Spread a thin layer of béchamel over the bottom of the baking dish. Arrange a
layer of pasta over the béchamel and spread about 4 tablespoons béchamel over the
noodles. Top with a thin layer of sauce (4 to 5 tablespoons) and a sprinkling of cheese.
Repeat the layers—pasta, béchamel, sauce, Parmesan—until all but one layer of pasta
and the béchamel and cheese that you set aside is used up. Add a last layer of pasta,
cover the top with the reserved béchamel, and finally, sprinkle on the remaining
cheese. Dot with butter if you wish. Cover the lasagne with foil (if you have not
buttered the top of the pasta, lightly oil or butter the dull side of the foil).

Bake the lasagne for 30 minutes, or until it's beginning to bubble and the pasta is al
dente. Remove the foil and allow to brown lightly on the top, another 10 minutes.
Remove from the heat and allow to sit for 10 minutes before serving.

veal paprikash *(paprikás)*

Not long before I became a vegetarian, my parents hosted a large, catered party at their beauti-
ful home in Connecticut. It was summertime, and we sat outside at candlelit tables set under
tents. The main dish was a delicious veal stew. I never did know what the stew was; perhaps I
never asked. In any case I soon became quite uninterested in meat. Thirty years later, after
testing this recipe, I now know what that dish was: veal paprikash. Veal so lends itself to this
savory medium, whose depth comes from the slow cooking of a quantity of onions, sweet Hungar-
ian peppers, garlic, and paprika. ❖ serves 6

3 tablespoons lard or olive oil

2 pounds veal stew meat, cut into 1½-inch pieces

2 medium onions, minced

3 large garlic cloves, minced or pressed

1 large, ripe tomato, peeled, seeded, and chopped, or 1 cup
   drained and chopped canned tomatoes

½ pound green Hungarian peppers, Italian peppers, or bell
   pepper, seeded and thinly sliced

1 heaped tablespoon sweet Hungarian paprika

1 tablespoon tomato paste dissolved in ½ cup chicken stock or
   water

1 teaspoon salt (or more to taste)

2 tablespoons sour cream (may use low-fat)

2 teaspoons all-purpose flour

   Freshly ground black pepper

2 tablespoons heavy cream

   Wide egg noodles or rice, for serving

melt 1 tablespoon of the lard over medium-high heat in a large, heavy,
lidded nonstick skillet and brown the veal, in batches, about 10 minutes per batch.
Transfer to a bowl and pour the fat off from the pan.

Turn the heat to medium-low, heat the remaining 2 tablespoons lard, and add the
onions. Cover and cook, stirring often, for about 5 minutes, or until they are soft. Add

The dish can be made through this step and held on top of the stove for several hours, or in the refrigerator overnight. Skim fat from the top, reheat gently, and proceed with the last steps. | the garlic and cook, stirring, for 1 minute, or until fragrant. Add the tomato and green peppers, stir together, and return the veal to the pan, along with any juices in the bowl. Cover and cook over low heat for 10 minutes. Stir in the paprika, the dissolved tomato paste, and the salt. Cook, covered, over very low heat for 1½ hours, or until the meat is fork-tender, stirring from time to time.

Mix together the sour cream, flour, and 1 tablespoon of cold water. Move the meat to one side of the pan and stir the sour cream mixture into the sauce. Stir together until smooth. Taste and adjust the salt, add pepper, and simmer for another 15 minutes. Taste and adjust the salt. Stir in the cream, combine well, and serve, with egg noodles or rice.

leftovers This keeps well for 4 days in the refrigerator. The leftovers are great with egg noodles, and a little will go a long way to sauce the noodles. Or make the savory kugel below.

savory noodle and paprikash kugel ❖ serves 4

1 to 2 cups Veal Paprikash

Salt

5 ounces egg noodles

2 ounces Gruyère cheese, grated (½ cup)

3 large eggs

¾ cup milk (whole, reduced-fat, or low-fat)

Freshly ground black pepper

Heat the oven to 350°F. Oil or butter a 2-quart baking or gratin dish. Using a fork or your fingers, shred the remaining meat pieces in the stew. Meanwhile, bring a large pot of water to a boil, add 2 to 3 teaspoons salt, and add the noodles. Cook al dente, about 5 to 6 minutes, drain, and toss with the leftover stew and the cheese.

Beat together the eggs and milk. Add salt (¼ teaspoon or more, to taste) and pepper, and toss with the noodles. Turn into the baking dish and bake for 20 to 30 minutes, until the top is browned. The noodles will be crispy on the top. Remove from the oven and serve hot or warm.

persian meat stew with quince or asian pears

This koresh is traditionally made with quince. But quinces are not always easy to find, and the first time I tested the recipe, they were not to be had. So I tried the dish with Asian pears, that crunchy/juicy fruit that tastes and looks like a cross between an apple and a pear. They worked just fine here. I think lamb lends itself better than beef to this dish. Its gamy flavor contrasts nicely with the tart, sweet, and sour elements of the stew. ❖ **serves 6**

4 tablespoons canola or vegetable oil

2 onions, thinly sliced

1 pound beef or lamb stew meat, cut into ¾-inch pieces (if using lamb shoulder meat, add the bones to the stew)

3 cups stock (chicken or beef) or water

1 teaspoon salt, or to taste

¼ teaspoon freshly ground black pepper

1 teaspoon ground cinnamon

2 large quinces or 3 Asian pears, peeled, quartered, cored, and cut into wedges

2 tablespoons sugar

¼ cup balsamic vinegar

¼ cup fresh lime juice

¼ teaspoon ground saffron dissolved in 1 tablespoon hot water

⅓ cup yellow split peas (available in Iranian and Indian markets)

Iranian Rice (page 386), or plain rice for serving

advance preparation
You can cook the onions a few hours before cooking the meat and stew.

heat 2 tablespoons of the oil over medium heat in a large, heavy Dutch oven or casserole and add the onions. Cook, stirring often, until the onions are golden, about 15 minutes.

advance preparation You can make the recipe through this step, take a break and turn off the heat for several hours, then bring back to a simmer and proceed with the next step.

Heat the remaining 2 tablespoons oil over medium-high heat in a large, heavy nonstick skillet and brown the meat, in batches, on all sides, about 10 minutes. Transfer to the casserole with the onions. Pour the fat off from the pan. Add 1 cup of stock to the pan and bring to a boil, scraping up any bits from the bottom of the pan. Pour into the casserole and add the remaining 2 cups of stock.

Add the salt, pepper, and cinnamon and bring to a simmer over low heat. Cover and simmer for 1 hour.

advance preparation The recipe can be made a day or two before serving. Refrigerate, then skim off the fat from the top before reheating.

Add the quinces or Asian pears, the sugar, balsamic vinegar, lime juice, saffron with its water, and yellow split peas. Bring back to a simmer, cover, and simmer for another hour or two, until the meat is fork-tender and the yellow peas are soft; the longer the better. Taste and adjust the seasonings, adding salt, lime juice, or sugar as desired. Serve with Iranian Rice (page 386) or regular rice.

variation

persian meat stew with butternut squash and prunes

I adapted this luscious, sweet and savory dish from a recipe in *New Food of Life,* by Najmieh Khalili Batmanglij (Mage Publishers,1997). Lamb beautifully offsets the sweetness of the squash and prunes. Cook the dish for a long time, and the squash will become infused with the sweet stew juices. This dish serves 6.

Follow the instructions in the above recipe, replacing the quince, balsamic vinegar, and yellow split peas with 1 large (about 2 pounds) butternut squash, peeled, seeded, and cut into large chunks, ¼ cup lime juice, and 2 cups pitted prunes or dried golden plums (which are available in Iranian markets). Serve with saffron rice.

leftovers Both dishes will keep for 3 or 4 days in the refrigerator and get better with time. The best thing to do with leftovers is to mix whatever you have with basmati rice or Iranian rice, for a delicious pilaf.

curried lamb with cucumber raita

Lamb really lends itself to curry. Its gamy flavor complements all of the spicy seasonings. I looked at a number of curries while I was developing this one, drawing on Julie Sahni's spice mix but using oil instead of ghee, and a minimum at that. Serve this with plain basmati rice and a cucumber raita. ❖ serves 4 to 6

for the curried lamb

4 tablespoons vegetable oil or canola oil

3 pounds boneless leg of lamb, cut into 1½-inch cubes

Salt and freshly ground black pepper

3 medium onions, chopped

4 large garlic cloves, minced or pressed

3 tablespoons minced fresh ginger

1 tablespoon ground cumin seeds

1 tablespoon ground coriander seeds

2 teaspoons ground turmeric

½ teaspoon ground cayenne (or more to taste)

1 teaspoon ground cinnamon

1 (14-ounce) can tomatoes, with juice, chopped

3 or 4 meaty beef bones or the bone from the leg of lamb (optional)

1 cup plain yogurt (whole or low-fat)

2 cups thawed frozen peas or blanched fresh peas

3 to 4 teaspoons chopped fresh cilantro

Basmati rice, for serving

(ingredients continued on following page)

for the cucumber raita

1   cucumber or ½ European cucumber, peeled, seeded,
    and finely chopped

    Salt

1½ cups plain yogurt (whole, low-fat, or nonfat)

    Freshly ground black pepper, chopped fresh mint, or
    chopped fresh cilantro (optional)

heat 2 tablespoons of the oil over medium-high heat in a large, lidded nonstick skillet and brown the meat in batches so that you don't overcrowd the pan. Each batch should take about 10 minutes. Transfer to a bowl as the meat is done and season generously with salt and pepper. When you have finished browning all the meat and it has all been removed from the pan, pour in ½ cup water and scrape the bottom of the pan with a wooden spoon to deglaze. Pour the water with the scrapings into the bowl with the meat, and dry the pan.

Shortly before serving, stir in the peas and heat through. Stir in the cilantro and serve with basmati rice and cucumber raita.

advance preparation
The dish can be prepared a few hours to a day ahead to this point. It can sit on top of the stove for a few hours.

Add the remaining 2 tablespoons oil to the pan, turn the heat down to medium, and add the onions. Cook, stirring, until the onions are very tender and tawny brown, about 15 minutes. Stir in the garlic and ginger and cook for about a minute, until fragrant. Stir in the cumin, coriander, turmeric, ½ teaspoon black pepper, cayenne, and cinnamon and cook, stirring, for a minute or two, until the spices smell fragrant. Add the tomatoes and about ½ teaspoon salt and cook, stirring often, for about 10 minutes, until the tomatoes cook down and the mixture has an almost pastelike consistency. It should be very aromatic. Return the meat and all the liquid from the bowl to the pan, along with the meat bones, the yogurt, salt to taste, and 1 cup hot water. Bring to a simmer, reduce the heat, and simmer for 1½ hours, until the meat is very tender and the sauce thick. Taste and adjust the seasonings. Remove and discard the meat bones.

For the cucumber raita: Sprinkle the cucumber generously with salt and place in a strainer set above a bowl. Let drain for 30 minutes. Toss with the remaining ingredients. Taste and adjust the seasonings. Chill until ready to serve. This should not be assembled too far ahead because the cucumbers will continue to release water into the yogurt.

Shortly before serving, stir the peas into the curried lamb and heat through. Stir in the cilantro and serve with basmati rice and cucumber raita.

leftovers ⋮ The lamb curry only gets better overnight and will keep for a good 3 or 4 days in the refrigerator. You can get another meal out of a heaped 1 to 1½ cups of leftovers if you make the following delicious pilaf.

curried lamb pilaf ❖ serves 4

1 cup basmati rice

¾ teaspoon salt

1 to 1½ cups leftover lamb curry, heated

1 tablespoon butter

2 tablespoons chopped fresh cilantro (or more to taste)

Wash the rice in several changes of water, until the water runs clear. Combine with 2 cups water in a 2-quart saucepan and bring to a boil. Add the salt, reduce the heat, cover, and simmer for 15 to 20 minutes, until all the water in the pan has evaporated. Turn off the heat, remove the lid, and place a clean dish towel over the top of the pan. Return the lid to the pan and let sit, undisturbed, for 10 minutes or longer. Stir in the curry (you can break up the pieces of meat with a fork prior to stirring it in, to distribute more meat throughout the pilaf), the butter, and cilantro, and serve.

french lamb stew with spring vegetables

This is known as a navarin in France, where it is often made with less expensive cuts of lamb. Here I'm using a pricier boneless leg of lamb, because it's leaner and easier to work with (not as much bone and fat to cut away). The stew is a very straightforward one, whose virtues come from the quality of the lamb and the vegetables. I tend to go crazy in the springtime farmers' markets here in California, and I have given you some options for the vegetables. I like to begin this a day ahead, browning and stewing the lamb with the onions. I refrigerate it overnight, skim off any visible fat, then bring back to a simmer and add the vegetables. This is great to make in April, when it can still be quite cool but those sweet spring vegetables have begun to arrive in the markets. ❖ **serves 6**

2½ to 3 pounds boneless leg of lamb or lamb neck or shoulder, trimmed and cut into 1½-inch cubes

Salt and freshly ground black pepper

10 ounces (1 packet) small boiling onions (pearl onions or pickling onions)

3 tablespoons canola oil, olive oil, or a combination of butter and oil

1 large onion, finely chopped

2 tablespoons all-purpose flour

1 cup dry white wine

3 cups beef or chicken stock

1 cup canned tomatoes, finely chopped, with liquid

Bouquet garni made with 1 bay leaf, a few sprigs of thyme, and about 6 sprigs of flat-leaf parsley

1 head of garlic, separated into cloves and peeled

¾ pound baby carrots, peeled and trimmed, or larger carrots, peeled, quartered, and cut into 2-inch pieces

¾ pound baby turnips, peeled, trimmed, and cut in half, or small turnips, peeled and cut into wedges

¾ pound small new potatoes, scrubbed, or larger new potatoes, scrubbed and quartered

4 baby artichokes, trimmed, tough leaves broken off, quartered and chokes removed (optional)

1 pound fava beans (optional)

¾ pound sugar snap peas, ends and strings removed, or green beans, trimmed and cut in half

2 to 4 tablespoons chopped fresh flat-leaf parsley or chives

Rice or noodles, for serving

season the lamb with salt and pepper.

advance preparation
You can prepare the onions up to a day before making the stew.

Bring a small pan of water to a boil, add the pearl onions, boil for 3 minutes, drain, and transfer to a bowl of cold water. Drain, cut off the ends, and peel. Set aside.

Heat 2 tablespoons of the oil over medium-high heat in a large, heavy casserole or Dutch oven and add the pearl onions. Cook, stirring, until browned, about 7 minutes. Remove from the casserole with a slotted spoon and set aside.

Add the lamb, in batches, and brown on all sides, being careful not to crowd the pan, about 10 minutes. As it is done, transfer to a plate.

When all of the lamb has been browned, add the remaining tablespoon of oil and the onion to the casserole and cook, stirring, until tender and golden, 5 to 8 minutes. Stir in the flour and cook for another minute, then add the wine, bring to a boil, and stir for a few minutes to deglaze the bottom of the casserole.

Return the lamb to the casserole with any juices that may have accumulated on the plate. Add the stock, tomatoes, bouquet garni, and garlic, and bring to a simmer. Cover the pot, reduce the heat, and simmer for 1 hour. Taste and adjust the seasonings.

advance preparation
The dish can be made a day or two ahead through this step. Refrigerate overnight. Skim off any visible fat before returning to the heat, and bring back to a simmer.

Add the pearl onions, carrots, turnips, potatoes, and artichokes to the pot, cover, and continue to simmer for another 30 minutes, or until the vegetables and meat are both tender. Taste and adjust the salt and pepper.

While the stew is simmering, remove the favas from the pods while you bring a large pot of salted water to a boil.

Drop in the favas, boil for 1 minute, and transfer to a bowl of cold water. Drain and slip off the skins. Set aside in a bowl. Bring the water back to a boil and add the sugar snap peas or green beans. Cook for 2 to 4 minutes, until bright green and just tender. Drain and rinse with cold water.

Shortly before serving the stew, stir in the favas and sugar snap peas or beans. Heat through. Sprinkle with parsley or chives and serve with rice or noodles.

leftovers This stew tastes marvelous for a couple of days, though the vegetables will not be as vivid as they were when freshly cooked. You could serve the leftovers over rice or with pasta, or make this fabulous gratin, which I like almost as much as (maybe even more than) the navarin.

gratin of lamb and spring vegetable stew ❖ serves 4

3   cups leftover French Lamb Stew with Spring Vegetables

3   large eggs

1   to 1½ cups cooked rice

2   ounces Gruyère cheese, grated (½ cup)

Salt and freshly ground black pepper

Heat the oven to 375°F. Butter or oil a 2-quart gratin or baking dish. If you wish, cut up the meat and vegetables into smaller pieces.

Beat the eggs in a medium bowl, and stir in the stew, rice, and cheese. Season with salt and pepper if you feel the mixture needs additional seasoning. Scrape into the gratin dish and place in the oven. Bake for 30 to 40 minutes, until lightly browned on the top. Serve hot or warm.

braised pork with red cabbage, apples, and chestnuts

This is a classic European dish. I found something very much like it in the first volume of Julia Child's Mastering the Art of French Cooking *when I was searching around for a recipe for roast pork with red cabbage. Hers had the added bonus of chestnuts with the cabbage, which I have made optional (you may not want to go to the trouble of peeling all those chestnuts; but they are good). Begin this dish a day ahead: Season the pork and, if you wish, braise the cabbage for an hour. It tastes even better if cooked ahead.*

In the classic dish, the pork is set on top of the cabbage to braise. This adds a great deal of flavor to the cabbage, but it also adds a lot of fat, even after you skim. To keep the dish light, I roast the pork separately and serve the two together, with plenty of crusty white bread for sopping up the juices. ❖ serves 6

PEELING CHESTNUTS

Peel chestnuts using either of these methods:

❖ Cut a ⅛-inch strip down the side of each chestnut with a sharp paring knife. Place in a saucepan, cover with water, and bring to a boil. Boil for 1 minute. Remove from the heat. Transfer the chestnuts a few at a time from the pot to a bowl of cold water, and peel. Return all of the chestnuts to the water, bring to a boil again, drain, rinse with cold water, and peel off any inner papery peel.

❖ Heat the oven to 425°F. Using a sharp paring knife, make an incision in the shape of an X on the flat side of the chestnuts. Place the chestnuts on a baking sheet and bake for 10 to 15 minutes, until browned. Remove from the heat, transfer to a bowl, and when they are cool enough to handle, peel, making sure to remove the papery inner peel. Set aside.

for the pork

1½ teaspoons salt

¼ teaspoon freshly ground black pepper

¼ teaspoon ground dried thyme or sage

1 small bay leaf, ground

½ teaspoon ground allspice

2 tablespoons vegetable oil

3- to 3 ½-pound boneless roast of pork (loin or shoulder; loin is leaner)

for the cabbage

1 large red cabbage, 2 to 2½ pounds, quartered, cored, and shredded crosswise

2 to 2½ ounces bacon (2 thick slices or a chunk), diced

1 tablespoon butter or vegetable oil

1 small onion, thinly sliced

1 tablespoon sugar

2 tart apples, such as Winesap or Granny Smith, peeled, cored, and sliced

⅛ teaspoon ground cloves or allspice

⅛ teaspoon ground nutmeg

¼ cup red wine vinegar

Salt and freshly ground black pepper to taste

1¼ cups chicken stock (page 378), beef stock, or water

24 chestnuts, peeled (see sidebar on page 89), or use canned chestnuts (optional)

the day before you wish to make this, mix together the salt, pepper, thyme, bay leaf, allspice, and oil and rub into the surface of the pork. Place in a resealable plastic bag or on a plate, cover, and refrigerate for 12 to 24 hours.

Begin braising the cabbage. Cover the shredded cabbage with cold water while you heat the bacon with the butter or oil in a large, heavy ovenproof casserole or Dutch oven over medium-low heat. When the bacon begins to render its fat, add the onion. Cook, stirring, until just about tender, about 5 minutes. Add the sugar and cook, stirring, until the mixture is golden, 5 to 8 minutes, then stir in the apples. Cover and cook, stirring from time to time, for 3 to 4 minutes.

advance preparation Drain the cabbage and add to the pot. Toss to coat thor-
The cabbage can be cooked ahead to oughly, then stir in the cloves or allspice, nutmeg, and
this point and refrigerated for vinegar, and toss together. Cover the pot and cook over
up to 2 days. low heat for 10 to 15 minutes, stirring from time to time, until the cabbage has wilted and is bright pinkish-purple.

Add the salt, pepper, and stock or water and bring to a simmer. Cover and simmer over low heat for 1 hour, stirring from time to time. Add more water if necessary. Meanwhile, peel the chestnuts if using, and heat the oven to 325°F.

If you have made the cabbage a day ahead, remove the casserole from the refrigerator and bring the cabbage back to a simmer on top of the stove while you heat the oven to 325°F. Continue to cook the cabbage gently on top of the stove for another hour while you roast the pork. Turn off after an hour and let sit, covered, on top of the stove.

Remove the pork from the refrigerator and pat it dry with a paper towel. Place the pork on a rack in a roasting pan. Roast until a meat thermometer inserted in the thickest part registers 150° to 155°F., about 1½ to 2 hours. Remove from the oven and transfer the pork to a warm platter. Tent with foil and let sit for 20 to 30 minutes.

Pour the fat off from the roasting pan. Transfer the cabbage to the platter with the pork, using a slotted spoon. Pour the juices from the cabbage into the roasting pan and bring to a boil on top of the stove. Cook, stirring and scraping up the solids from the bottom of the pan, until slightly thickened. Slice the pork, pour the pan juices over the pork and cabbage, and serve.

leftovers Both the cabbage and the pork are very good keepers, keeping well in the refrigerator for at least 3 or 4 days. Cold sliced pork is excellent. You can gently reheat the cabbage on top of the stove.

three

chicken and rabbit

What could be more reassuring or satisfying than a good roast chicken? And what could be easier for a cook? No matter how many soccer games you have to drive to, you can almost always find an hour or two to roast a chicken; and cold roast chicken can be every bit as good as it is hot.

Chicken is the fallback meal for many a cook, and in these pages, when it is roasted or stewed with vegetables, so that the rest of the meal is cooked along with the bird, it really is a comfort. When I'm thinking about an easy dinner and don't have anything in particular that I have to test, I will buy chicken if I want meat, and make pasta if I don't. A chicken stew is one of the best types of dishes I can think of if I'm entertaining, because I always do at least part of the work a day or more ahead. That way I can get a jump start on my dinner party; and there's the added benefit of being able to skim fat off the broth if the chicken has been cooked ahead.

Chicken and rabbit stews make great leftovers. If little meat is left, it doesn't matter. You can pull what there is off the bone, mix it into the broth with the vegetables, and make a great rice or pasta dish out of the mix. Sometimes I get even bigger raves from my husband and son over the leftovers pilaf than I did for the original masterpiece.

Everything I've said about chicken applies to rabbit. But we've had little exposure to rabbit in America, except in restaurants, where chefs tend to roast it rather than stew it. For home cooking I have always had my greatest successes with rabbit when I stew or braise it. The meat has a deep, rich, satisfying flavor, and because it's so lean I prefer to cook it in a liquid medium to be sure that it will be moist. Rabbit stews always improve overnight, becoming complex and deeply flavorful. The Rabbit Daube on page 126 is one of my all-time favorite recipes.

Rabbit is not as readily available in supermarkets as poultry, but if you look in the freezer section, you might find frozen vacuum-packed rabbits, which can be thawed in the refrigerator (it will take a day). However, it's been my experience that fresh rabbit is much tastier, with better texture, than frozen. Good poultry butchers almost always carry them and will obligingly cut them up for you, as they will chicken. For instructions on jointing rabbit and cutting up chicken, see page 97.

roast lemon chicken with honey glaze and sweet potatoes

Every once in a while my friend Tina Davis sends me a recipe, and it inevitably becomes a mainstay in my kitchen. This chicken, which marinates for a day in lemon juice and is brushed lavishly with honey while it roasts, is one such dish, sent by E-mail from Jerusalem with a note that said, merely, "This is really good." What an understatement. I've added the sweet potatoes to Tina's recipe; they're the perfect accompaniment to the chicken. The lemon juice tenderizes the meat, and the honey caramelizes on the skin. The chicken sort of collapses in the marinade, so that it's slightly splayed, like chicken cooked under a brick. ❖ **serves 4 to 6**

1 (3½- to 4½-pound) chicken

1 cup fresh lemon juice

Salt and freshly ground black pepper

4 to 6 medium or large sweet potatoes, scrubbed and pierced several times with a sharp knife or skewer

¼ cup mild honey, such as clover or acacia

the morning of or the night before you wish to serve this, place the chicken in a resealable plastic bag and pour in the lemon juice. Refrigerate for 12 to 24 hours (I've marinated the chicken for as few as 6 hours with good results).

Heat the oven to 450°F. Drain the chicken and season with salt and pepper. Place in a large roasting pan (big enough to accommodate both the chicken and the sweet potatoes), breast side down, and roast for 10 minutes. Turn the heat down to 350°F. and add the sweet potatoes to the roasting pan. Roast for 45 minutes.

Heat the honey for 12 to 15 seconds in the microwave, to facilitate brushing. Brush the chicken all over with the honey, and turn it over so that the breast is up. Roast for another 45 minutes to an hour, basting often and brushing with any honey left over in the cup, until the chicken is beautifully browned and the sweet potatoes are tender all the way through.

Remove from the heat and transfer the chicken and sweet potatoes to a platter. Let sit for 15 to 20 minutes. Carve the chicken and cut the sweet potatoes into chunks. Peel if desired. Serve some of the juices from the pan on the side.

leftovers : This is not a dish to do a day ahead; but a roast chicken will not lose too much if it sits for up to an hour. Leftovers are great as is, or put into sandwiches. Reheat the sweet potatoes in the microwave. They get better and better.

JOINTING A RABBIT

Using a large, heavy chef's knife or a cleaver, disjoint the forelegs from the body at the shoulder joint and the hind legs at the hip. Separate the rib section from the loin, and cut the loin and the rib sections in two crosswise. Cut the hind legs into two pieces at the knee if you want 10 pieces, or leave them intact if you want 8. Using scissors, trim off the lower bony parts of the ribs and discard.

CUTTING UP A CHICKEN

If you buy a whole chicken for roasting but decide you want to make a stew instead, here's what you do.

To cut the legs off, pull and press the leg away and down from the body and slice through the skin between the body and the leg with a sharp chef's knife or boning knife. Cut the flesh close to the body, until you reach the joint, then bend the thigh back from the body and cut the joint to separate it. To cut the drumstick away from the thigh, bend it at the joint and cut through the skin, then find the joint and finish cutting through the joint with your knife.

Cut the wings off in the same manner you cut off the legs, by pulling them away from the body and cutting the skin, then cut the flesh until you find the joint, and cut through the joint. Remove the backbone with poultry shears, and cut the breast in half through the breastbone.

roast chicken with a ton of vegetables

This is sometimes my clean-out-the-refrigerator dish. I buy a chicken, take all the carrots, celery, potatoes, and onions that have been hanging around waiting for me to do something with them, and throw everything together in a big roasting pan with some garlic, rosemary sprigs, and bay leaves. Other times, I go out and buy the vegetables for it, because I think that parsnips and turnips would be nice too, and I don't have them on hand. I recently made the dish for a Beaujolais nouveau dinner—Beaujolais nouveau is a perfect wine to serve with roast chicken—and the turnips and parsnips were adored by all. Whatever vegetables you use, the resulting dish is deeply satisfying. Consider the quantities listed as suggestions. You can add more or less, whatever will fit in the pan; or you can choose the pan to fit the vegetables. The more the merrier. ❖ serves 4 to 6

1 medium chicken, about 4 pounds

1 large or 2 medium onions, peeled and cut in wedges

4 large carrots, peeled, cut in half crosswise, and halved lengthwise

1 to 1½ pounds potatoes, scrubbed and left whole if small, quartered if medium, peeled and cut in sixths if large russets

2 or 3 celery stalks, cut in 3-inch lengths

¾ pound turnips, peeled and quartered

¾ pound parsnips, peeled, cored, and quartered

1 head of garlic, cut in half crosswise

Salt and freshly ground black pepper

3 tablespoons olive oil

6 sprigs of fresh rosemary

2 bay leaves

heat the oven to 450°F. Rinse the chicken inside and out, pat dry, and set aside.

Toss together all of the vegetables and the garlic with salt, pepper, and 2 tablespoons of the olive oil. Transfer to a baking dish or roasting pan large enough to accommodate

advance preparation
This can be assembled and ready to roast, then refrigerated, tightly covered, for a day. Uncover, bring to room temperature, and proceed with the recipe.

all of the vegetables and the chicken. Make a little nest in the center and place the chicken in it. Rub the chicken with the remaining tablespoon of olive oil, season with salt and pepper, and stick sprigs of rosemary under its wings and legs. Turn the chicken over so that the back is facing up, and sprinkle with salt and pepper. Put a few garlic cloves, rosemary sprigs, and a bay leaf in the chicken's cavity. Bury the remaining bay leaf and sprigs of rosemary in the vegetables.

advance preparation
I have made this an hour or so ahead; if the chicken sits for an hour it'll still be good, and the vegetables can be warmed in a medium oven or a microwave.

Place the pan in the oven. Roast for 10 minutes and turn the heat down to 350°F. Roast for 30 minutes, and turn the chicken over so the breast is up. Baste lightly. Stir the vegetables. Roast for another 30 to 40 minutes, or until the chicken is golden brown and the juice runs clear when pierced with a knife (the temperature at the thickest part of the thigh should be at least 165°F.). Remove from the heat, transfer the chicken to a carving board, stir the vegetables, and return them to the oven for another 15 minutes if necessary, until they're browned and tender. Transfer everything to a platter and serve.

leftovers The chicken will keep for 4 or 5 days in the refrigerator. Everyone loves leftover chicken, for sandwiches, salads, and tacos. As for the vegetables, I suggest you make this scrumptious French-style soup. You can use the chicken carcass to make stock.

leftovers variation
puréed vegetable soup ❖ serves 2 to 4

2 to 2½ cups of the cooked vegetables

2 cups chicken stock (page 378) or water (preferably stock)

½ to 1 cup milk

Salt and freshly ground black pepper to taste

Process the vegetables coarsely in a food processor. Combine with the stock and bring to a simmer. Add the milk and heat through. Season to taste with salt and lots of freshly ground pepper, and serve.

chicken bouillabaisse with pastis

This saffron-scented, saffron-hued, soupy chicken dish is unforgettable because of the slight anise flavor resulting from the pastis. It is Provençal through and through, and it's so good, sometimes I've noticed that nobody says anything for a while when they're eating it, so focused are they on what is going on with the flavors. Serve it in wide bowls, and set the table with soup spoons, forks, and knives. ❖ **serves 4 to 5**

1   (3½- to 4½-pound) chicken, cut up and skinned

½   cup pastis

3   tablespoons olive oil

2   generous pinches of saffron

½   teaspooon crushed fennel seeds, or 1 dried fennel branch

2   medium onions, thinly sliced

2   carrots, chopped

1   celery stalk, chopped

6   garlic cloves, minced or pressed, plus 1 garlic clove, cut in half

½   cup chopped fresh flat-leaf parsley

1½ pounds tomatoes, peeled, seeded, and chopped, or 1 (28-ounce) can, with liquid, chopped

    Salt and freshly ground black pepper

3   cups chicken stock (page 378)

1   pound potatoes, such as Yukon golds or red-skinned, scrubbed and sliced

1   baguette, thinly sliced

½   cup Rouille (page 390)

several hours before beginning the stew, combine the chicken with the pastis, 1 tablespoon of the olive oil, 1 pinch of the saffron, and the fennel seeds or branch. Transfer to a resealable plastic bag and refrigerate for several hours or overnight.

advance preparation
You can do this step several
hours before adding the remaining
ingredients, and allow it to sit at
room temperature, or overnight in
the refrigerator.

Heat the remaining 2 tablespoons oil over medium heat in a large, heavy casserole or Dutch oven and add the onions. Cook, stirring, until just tender, about 5 minutes, then add the carrots and celery. Cook, stirring often, for about 5 to 8 minutes, until all of the vegetables are tender and fragrant. Stir in the minced garlic and 2 tablespoons of the parsley and cook, stirring, until the garlic begins to smell fragrant, 1 to 2 minutes. Add the tomatoes and salt and pepper to taste. Turn the heat up to medium-high and cook, stirring often, for 10 to 15 minutes, until the tomatoes are cooked down and smell fragrant.

advance preparation
This is one of those dishes that is
better the next day and even better
two days later. Make it to this point,
refrigerate for up to 3 days, and bring
back to a simmer before proceeding.

Add the chicken with its marinade, 3 tablespoons of the remaining parsley, and the chicken stock. Bring to a simmer. Cover and simmer for 15 minutes. Add the potatoes and simmer for another 15 to 30 minutes, until the chicken and potatoes are tender. Taste and adjust the salt.

Turn up the heat, and when the broth is boiling, add the second pinch of saffron. Cook for another 5 minutes, remove from the heat, and stir in the remaining 3 tablespoons of parsley and more salt and pepper to taste.

Lightly toast the bread and rub with the cut clove of garlic. Spread slices with rouille and place 3 or 4 in each wide soup bowl. Serve the chicken and the potatoes with the broth ladled over. Pass the rouille and additional bread.

leftovers This will keep for about 5 days in the refrigerator. You can serve leftovers as is, or make them into a simple rice or noodle dish. Pull the chicken off the bones and toss, with the leftover sauce, with cooked rice or wide noodles. Warm in a 350°F. oven or in the microwave.

rich flemish chicken stew (waterzooi)

This is richer than most of my dishes, but a creamy dish like this classic Belgian stew is an indulgence that can hit the spot on a cold winter night. Chicken, with lots of carrots and leeks, is poached in wine and chicken stock, and the resulting broth is enriched with egg yolks and cream. Serve it with rice or steamed potatoes, and make sure everybody has a soup spoon for the sauce, as well as a knife and fork. ❖ **serves 4 to 5**

Salt

1 (3½- to 4-pound) chicken, cut up and skinned

1 medium onion, thinly sliced

2 large leeks, white and light green parts only, cut in half lengthwise, cleaned, and sliced

2 large carrots, sliced

3 medium celery stalks, trimmed and sliced

2 cups dry white wine

3 cups chicken stock

Bouquet garni made with 1 bay leaf and a few sprigs each of thyme and flat-leaf parsley

½ pound green beans, trimmed and cut in 1-inch lengths

6 egg yolks

⅔ cup heavy cream or crème fraîche

2 tablespoons chopped fresh flat-leaf parsley

1 tablespoon chopped fresh tarragon

Freshly ground black pepper

Rice or potatoes, for serving

salt the chicken lightly and place in a large flameproof casserole or Dutch oven. Add the onion, leeks, carrots, celery, white wine, chicken stock, and bouquet garni and bring to a simmer. Reduce the heat to very low, cover, and cook at a bare simmer for 45 minutes, or until the chicken is tender. Taste the broth and adjust the salt. Using tongs, transfer the chicken to a bowl. Strain the broth through a cheesecloth-lined strainer into another bowl. Discard the bouquet garni and transfer the vegetables to the bowl with the chicken. Refrigerate the broth for several hours or overnight (refrigerate the chicken and vegetables if not serving within a few hours).

advance preparation Everything through this step can be done up to 3 days ahead. Just be sure to bring the chicken to room temperature and the broth to a simmer before proceeding with the recipe.

Bring another, medium pan of water to a boil and add a teaspoon or two of salt and the green beans. Cook for 5 minutes, transfer to a bowl of ice-cold water, and drain. Set aside.

Remove the chicken with the vegetables and the broth from the refrigerator. Skim the fat from the surface of the broth and transfer to a heavy casserole or soup pot. Allow the chicken to come to room temperature.

advance preparation The thickened stew can be completed a few hours before serving. Reheat very gently, taking care not to boil.

Shortly before serving, bring the broth to a simmer. Beat the egg yolks and cream together in a bowl. Have the broth at a bare simmer, and slowly drizzle about 1 cup, a little bit at a time, into the egg and cream mixture, beating all the while with a whisk. Remove the casserole from the heat and stir in the tempered egg and cream mixture. Then return to the heat and heat over medium-low, stirring all the while, until the mixture thickens. Be careful not to let it boil or the eggs will curdle. Remove from the heat as soon as the sauce thickens and add the chicken pieces and vegetables, along with the cooked green beans.

Just before serving, heat through, being careful not to let the liquid boil. Stir in the parsley and tarragon, add some pepper, taste, and adjust the seasonings. Serve in wide soup bowls, with rice or steamed or boiled potatoes.

leftovers The dish will keep for a day or two in the refrigerator. Make a pot of rice, preferably basmati. Shred any leftover chicken and warm it in the sauce. Stir into the rice, heat through, and serve. I think this leftover dish is even more comforting than the stew itself!

greek braised chicken with onions, olives, and feta

*This recipe is based on a traditional Greek dish. I've seen a couple of versions of the stew in Diane Kochilas's books (*The Glorious Foods of Greece *and* The Food and Wine of Greece*). The traditional dish is made with much more olive oil, and with green olives. My lighter version is still marvelously rich. The onions and their juice, which serves as a cooking medium for the chicken, give the dish an enduring sweet flavor. When I use canned tomatoes for this, I don't need the water.*

Since the onions cook for such a long time before you add the other ingredients, you can begin cooking them before you prep the tomatoes and chicken. Peel, seed, and chop the tomatoes and rinse and dredge the chicken while the onions cook. ❖ **serves 4 to 5**

3 tablespoons olive oil

2 large red onions, chopped

2 to 4 garlic cloves (to taste), minced or pressed

1 (3½- to 4½-pound) chicken, cut up and skinned

About ¼ cup flour, seasoned with salt and pepper, for dredging

2 tablespoons red wine vinegar

6 plum tomatoes (1½ pounds), peeled, seeded, and chopped, or 1 (28-ounce) can tomatoes

Salt and freshly ground black pepper

½ teaspoon dried thyme, or 1 teaspoon fresh thyme leaves

½ cup Greek olives (such as kalamatas or amphisas), rinsed and pitted

¼ pound feta cheese, cut into thin slices, or crumbled if very soft

Rice or country bread, for serving

heat 1 tablespoon of the olive oil over medium heat in a large, deep, heavy, lidded nonstick skillet. Add the onions and cook, stirring, until they begin to soften. Turn the heat to low, cover, and let the onions cook for 15 to 20 minutes, stirring from time to time, until they are very soft and have released a fair amount of water. Add the garlic and stir together for a minute or two more, until the garlic is fragrant, then transfer to a bowl. Rinse the pan and wipe dry.

advance preparation
The dish can be made through this step hours or even a few days before serving. Reheat gently, then proceed with the recipe.

Dredge the chicken lightly in the seasoned flour. Heat the remaining 2 tablespoons oil in the skillet, turn the heat to medium-high, and brown the chicken, in batches if necessary, about 5 minutes on each side. Remove the pieces to a plate as they're browned. When all the chicken has been browned, pour off the fat from the pan.

Add the vinegar to the pan and scrape up all the bits from the bottom. Return the onions and garlic to the pan along with the chicken, tomatoes, and enough water to barely cover the chicken. Add salt, pepper, and the thyme. Bring to a simmer, reduce the heat, cover, and simmer for about 40 minutes, until the chicken is very tender, just about falling off the bone. Stir in the olives, taste, and adjust the seasonings.

Lay the feta slices over the top, cover the pan partially, and simmer for another 10 minutes, or until the feta softens. Serve with rice or over thick slices of toasted country bread.

leftovers The stew keeps for 3 or 4 days in the refrigerator. With leftovers, make a delicious rice casserole by spreading rice over the bottom of a baking dish and topping with the chicken, pulled off the bones, and sauce. Add more feta if you wish. Heat through for 20 minutes at 325°F.

stewed chicken with chipotles and prunes

An earlier version of this Veracruzana chicken stew is in Mexican Light (Bantam, 1996). It remains one of my favorite chicken stews, one that always wows company, mainly because they've never tasted anything like it. This version is easier to shop for at the supermarket, as I've used canned chipotles instead of the dried peppers in the original version. ❖ serves 4 to 5

12 prunes, pitted

1 large onion, cut in half crosswise

2 pounds tomatoes

4 large garlic cloves, 2 whole and unpeeled, 2 minced or pressed

4 black peppercorns

1 whole clove

2 to 3 canned chipotle chilies in adobo, rinsed, stemmed, and seeded (to taste)

3 tablespoons vegetable or canola oil

1 (3½- or 4½-pound) chicken, cut up and skinned if desired

Salt and freshly ground black pepper

3 cups chicken stock (page 378) or water

3 inches cinnamon stick

Rice, for serving

place 2 of the prunes in a heatproof bowl and pour on boiling water to cover. Let sit for 15 minutes, and drain.

advance preparation
The vegetables can be roasted up to a day ahead and kept in the bowl in the refrigerator.

Cover a baking sheet with foil and heat the broiler. Place the onion and tomatoes on it (you may have to do this in batches) and set under the broiler, about 2 to 3 inches from the heat. Turn after 3 to 5 minutes, when the tomatoes have charred on one side, and repeat on the other side. As the tomatoes are done, transfer them, using tongs, to a large bowl. The onion will take longer than the tomatoes and will have to be flipped over several times so it chars rather than burns to a cinder. (It should be charred and softened in 5 to 10 minutes.) Transfer to the bowl with the tomatoes. When the tomatoes are cool enough to handle, core and peel.

Toast the whole garlic cloves in their skin in a dry skillet or on a griddle over medium-high heat. Turn the cloves often, until they are blackened in a few spots and smell toasty, about 10 minutes. Remove from the heat and peel.

advance preparation
The strained purée will keep for a day in the refrigerator.

Grind the peppercorns and clove in a spice mill. Transfer the tomatoes, along with any juices from the bowl, the roasted onion, the garlic, ground pepper and clove, the 2 soaked prunes, and the chipotles to a blender. Blend until smooth, and pour into a bowl through a medium strainer. Push the purée through with the back of a spoon and tap the strainer against the bowl to get all of the purée through.

Heat 2 tablespoons of the oil over medium-high heat in a large, heavy nonstick skillet and brown the chicken on both sides until golden, about 5 minutes per side. Season each side with salt and pepper after you flip the chicken over. Transfer to a plate or bowl as the chicken is done. When all of the chicken has been browned, pour off the fat from the pan and discard.

advance preparation
I made this a day ahead, right through to the end, for a dinner party recently, and it was fabulous—and maybe even better, as all of those flavors settled and ripened overnight—reheated the next day. I was able to skim off some fat from the top before reheating.

Heat the remaining 1 tablespoon oil in the pan over medium-high heat, and add a drop of the puréed tomato mixture. If it sizzles loudly, add the rest (wait a minute or two if it doesn't). Add the purée and cook, stirring, until it thickens slightly, about 5 minutes. Stir in ½ cup of the chicken stock or water and ½ teaspoon salt. Bring to a simmer, turn the heat to low, and simmer, uncovered, stirring often with a long-handled spoon, until the sauce is fragrant and thick, about 20 minutes. (Be careful not to stand too close to the pan when you're not stirring, because the sauce will splutter a lot. Have a damp dish towel handy for wiping the stove.) Add the chicken pieces, the remaining 10 prunes, the cinnamon, the remaining 2½ cups of stock or water, and salt to taste. Bring to a simmer, reduce the heat, and simmer for 30 to 40 minutes, until the chicken is tender. Taste and adjust the seasonings. Serve hot, with rice.

(continued on next page)

leftovers : You are bound to have quite a bit of sauce left over here. If you have any chicken, shred it into the sauce. Then heat the sauce and add to it stale corn tortillas, broken up into pieces. Simmer until they soften and break up in the sauce. This makes a fabulous enchilada casserole-like dish, truly comforting. We enjoyed it two nights in a row.

chicken paprikás

Chicken Paprikás is all about peppers—the melting together of paprika, sweet green Hungarian or Italian peppers (or, if those aren't available, bell pepper), and onions. This is what gives a paprikás, be it chicken or veal (see page 79), such wonderful depth of flavor.

Authentic paprika chicken begins with lard, and any good Hungarian would dismiss my suggestion that you use olive oil. But olive oil is where my taste resides, and this is still a marvelous dish. Also, I have made the dish with light sour cream, the only "light" product I use, and it works just fine. ❖ **serves 4 to 5**

3 tablespoons lard or olive oil

1 (3½- to 4½-pound) chicken, cut up, skinned, rinsed and patted dry

2 medium onions, minced

2 large garlic cloves, minced or pressed

1 large ripe tomato, peeled, seeded, and chopped, or 1 cup drained and chopped canned tomatoes

½ pound green Hungarian peppers, Italian peppers, or bell pepper, seeded and thinly sliced

1 heaped tablespoon sweet Hungarian paprika

1 tablespoon tomato paste dissolved in ½ cup chicken stock or water

1 teaspoon salt (or more to taste)

2 tablespoons sour cream (may use low-fat)

2 teaspoons flour

Freshly ground black pepper

2 tablespoons heavy cream

Egg noodles or rice, for serving

heat 1 tablespoon of the lard or olive oil over medium-high heat in a large, heavy, lidded nonstick skillet and brown the chicken, in batches, about 5 minutes per side. Transfer to a plate and pour the fat off from the pan.

Turn the heat to medium-low, heat the remaining 2 tablespoons lard or oil, and add the onions. Cover and cook, stirring often, for about 5 minutes, until the onions are soft. Add the garlic and cook, stirring, for 1 minute, or until fragrant. Add the tomato and green peppers, stir together, return the chicken to the pan, cover, and cook over low heat for 10 minutes. Stir in the paprika, the diluted tomato paste, and the salt. Cook, covered, over very low heat for 30 minutes, stirring from time to time. Remove the lid and cook, turning the chicken from time to time, for another 10 minutes. Remove the chicken pieces from the pot.

advance preparation The dish can be made through this step and held on top of the stove for several hours, or refrigerated overnight. Reheat gently and proceed with the last step.

Mix together the sour cream, flour, and 1 teaspoon cold water. Stir into the sauce until smooth. Taste and adjust the salt, add pepper, return the chicken to the pot, cover, and simmer for another 10 to 15 minutes, until the chicken is tender. Taste and adjust the salt. Stir in the heavy cream and serve with egg noodles or rice.

leftovers The dish keeps well for 4 days in the refrigerator. The best thing to do with the leftovers is to toss the sauce, and whatever chicken you have—off the bone and shredded if there isn't much of it—with egg noodles. You can also make the Savory Noodle and Paprikash Kugel on page 80.

basque-style chicken

Poulet basquaise is a classic French bistro dish that is always received with cheers. The chicken is cooked in a pipérade of onion, garlic, hot and sweet peppers, cured ham (it would be Bayonne ham in France; prosciutto will do fine), and tomatoes. There's a lot of peppers and tomatoes in relation to chicken here, but all the better for the pipérade with scrambled eggs that you'll make with the leftovers (see below). Serve this dish with rice or noodles. ❖ **serves 4 to 5**

1 (3½- to 4-pound) chicken, cut up, skinned if desired

Salt and freshly ground black pepper

2 tablespoons canola or vegetable oil

1 tablespoon olive oil

2 large onions, chopped

2 to 4 mildly hot chilies, such as anaheims or New Mexico chilies, cored, seeded, and cut in very thin strips, or ¼ to ½ teaspoon hot red pepper flakes

2 pounds mixed green and red bell peppers, cored, seeded, and thinly sliced

6 garlic cloves, thinly sliced

2 pounds tomatoes or 1 (28-ounce) can, peeled, seeded, and chopped

¼ pound (thickly sliced if possible) cured ham, such as prosciutto or Bayonne, cubed

Pinch of sugar

advance preparation
You can brown the chicken and refrigerate it for a few hours. If all of your ingredients are prepped, when you proceed with the recipe, it will be done in an hour and a half.

rinse the chicken pieces and pat dry. Season liberally with salt and pepper. Heat the canola or vegetable oil in a large, heavy nonstick frying pan over medium-high heat and brown the chicken pieces, in batches, on each side for about 5 minutes, until the pieces turn golden brown. Transfer to a bowl or plate. Pour off the fat from the pan.

Turn the heat down to medium. Add the olive oil and the onions. Cook, stirring, until tender, 5 to 10 minutes. Add the hot and sweet peppers, a bit of salt, and the garlic, and cook, stirring, until the peppers begin to soften, about 10 minutes. Add the tomatoes, ham, and sugar and stir together. Cook until the tomatoes begin to bubble and smell fragrant, about 5 minutes.

advance preparation
Since the dish keeps well in the refrigerator, you could also make the entire dish a day ahead of time as directed, and refrigerate overnight. Reheat gently on top of the stove.

Return the chicken to the pan. Cook for 45 minutes to 1 hour over medium-low heat, stirring at regular intervals and turning the chicken pieces over so that the ingredients don't scorch and the chicken cooks evenly. The peppers should be very soft and the chicken quite tender. Add freshly ground pepper, taste and adjust the salt, and serve with rice or noodles.

leftovers The dish will keep well in the refrigerator for 3 or 4 days. You might use up the chicken and have lots of the sauce left, in which case there's no more appropriate dish than pipérade, in which eggs are scrambled in the wonderful pepper mixture.

leftovers variation
pipérade

The proportions of sauce to egg can be variable here. I've made the dish for my husband and myself using as much as 1½ cups sauce for 4 eggs, but it's also great with less sauce— a cup or so. ❖ serves 2 to 4

1 to 3 cups leftover sauce from Basque-style Chicken

4 to 8 large eggs

Salt and freshly ground black pepper

Bring the sauce to a simmer over medium-low heat in a large nonstick frying pan. Beat the eggs in a bowl, add salt and pepper, and stir into the sauce. Cook, stirring often, until the eggs have scrambled in the sauce. This should take some time—about 10 minutes if the heat is low. Serve with or over crusty country bread.

chicken alla cacciatora with mushrooms, tomatoes, and wine

This classic Italian dish must have hundreds of versions, all resulting in a rustic braise of chicken, aromatic vegetables, and tomatoes. My version includes lots of mushrooms, both dried and fresh. Alla cacciatora means "hunter's style," which says to me that mushrooms should be included in the dish, as they are in similar French preparations (such as sauce chasseur). I can't say I've seen Italian versions of this dish that call for mushrooms, but I love their meaty presence here. ❖ serves 4 to 5

½ ounce dried mushrooms, such as porcini (½ cup)

3 tablespoons olive oil

1 (3- to 4½-pound) chicken, cut up into 8 pieces and skinned if desired

Salt and freshly ground black pepper

1 small onion, minced

1 small carrot, minced

1 celery stalk, minced

2 large garlic cloves, minced or pressed

2 tablespoons minced fresh flat-leaf parsley

1 heaped teaspoon minced fresh rosemary, or ½ teaspoon crumbled dried

¼ teaspoon red pepper flakes

½ pound fresh mushrooms, trimmed and sliced

½ cup red wine

1 (28-ounce) can crushed tomatoes in purée

place the dried mushrooms in a heatproof bowl or measuring cup and pour on boiling water to cover. Let sit for 15 to 30 minutes, until softened. Drain through a cheesecloth- or paper-towel-lined strainer set over a bowl. Rinse the mushrooms in several changes of water, squeeze out excess water, and chop coarsely. Set aside. Measure out ¼ cup of the soaking liquid and set aside.

advance preparation If you want to make the sauce a day ahead, that's fine. Proceed with the recipe, but don't brown the chicken until the day you wish to finish the dish. Brown the chicken as directed, bring the sauce to a simmer, stir in the chicken, and cook in the sauce as directed.

Heat 2 tablespoons of the olive oil over medium-high heat in a large, heavy nonstick skillet. Season the chicken with salt and pepper and brown, in batches, for 5 minutes on each side, until golden. Transfer the chicken pieces to a bowl or plate as they are done. Pour the fat off from the pan and discard. (You can prep the vegetables while you're browning the chicken.)

Turn the heat to medium and add the remaining 1 tablespoon oil, the onion, carrot, and celery. Cook, stirring, until the vegetables begin to soften, about 5 minutes. Add the garlic, parsley, rosemary, red pepper flakes, and ¼ teaspoon salt, cover, turn the heat to low, and cook, stirring often, for 5 to 10 minutes, until the mixture is soft and aromatic. Stir in the fresh and dried mushrooms and a little more salt, turn the heat back up to medium, and cook, stirring, until the mushrooms are just tender, about 5 minutes. Stir in the wine and bring to a boil. Cook, stirring, for a few minutes, until the wine has reduced by about half. Add the tomatoes and salt and pepper to taste.

advance preparation The dish can be made through this step and held on top of the stove for several hours (refrigerate the chicken).

Cook over medium heat, stirring often, for 5 to 10 minutes, or until the tomatoes have cooked down a little and smell fragrant. Stir in the reserved mushroom soaking liquid; taste and adjust the salt and pepper.

Return the chicken pieces to the pan, stir so that they are well submerged in the tomato mixture, and simmer over medium heat, partially covered, for 30 minutes, or until the chicken is tender. Taste the sauce, adjust the seasoning, and serve, with pasta or rice.

leftovers The dish can be made a day or two ahead and reheated. It will keep for about 4 days in the refrigerator. When you run out of chicken, but still have that luscious, gutsy sauce, use it as a sauce for pasta or a topping for bruschetta.

catalan chicken with eggplant, peppers, and tomatoes

This fragrant Catalan dish is essentially chicken smothered in ratatouille, minus the squash.
Make the eggplant and pepper mixture the day before you wish to serve this, then you can come
home from work, brown the chicken, and finish it off in no time. ❖ serves 4 to 5

3 tablespoons olive oil, plus more for the baking sheet

1 pound red bell peppers (2 large)

Salt

1½ pounds eggplant, cut in half lengthwise

1½ pounds tomatoes, peeled, seeded, and chopped

1 large onion, very thinly sliced

4 large garlic cloves, minced

Freshly ground black pepper to taste

1 (3½- to 4½-pound) chicken, cut into 10 pieces and skinned

½ cup chicken stock (page 378)

Crusty bread or rice, for serving

heat the oven to 450°F. Cover a baking sheet with foil, brush the foil with olive oil, and place the peppers on it. Roast in the hot oven for 30 minutes, turning every 10 minutes, until brown and puffed. Remove from the oven and transfer the peppers to a bowl. Place a plate over the bowl or cover with plastic wrap, and allow the peppers to cool.

While the peppers are roasting, prepare the eggplant. Score it down the middle on the cut side, being careful not to cut through the skin. Sprinkle generously with salt and let sit for 15 to 30 minutes. Rinse and pat dry. Add a little more olive oil to the foil on the baking sheet, and lay the eggplant on it, cut side down. Roast in the oven for 20 to 30 minutes, until the skins are shriveled and the eggplant has softened. Remove from the heat and transfer the eggplant halves to a colander in the sink. Let them drain and cool, cut side down.

advance preparation
You can roast the eggplant and
peppers several hours before
proceeding with the recipe.
Refrigerate the pepper (or pepper
and tomato) juice in a separate bowl
or glass, covered tightly.

Core, skin, and seed the peppers, holding them over a bowl to catch their juice. Cut into strips, and cut the strips in half crosswise. Strain the liquid in the bowl and set aside. If you have chopped your tomatoes and transferred them to a bowl, and there is a lot of juice in the bowl, add it to the pepper juice. Dice the eggplant. It should be quite soft.

advance preparation
This can (and should) be done a day
ahead and held overnight in the
refrigerator. Bring everything back
to room temperature or warmer, and
proceed with the recipe.

Heat 1 tablespoon of the olive oil over medium heat in a large, heavy nonstick skillet and add the onion. Cook, stirring, until tender and beginning to color, about 10 minutes. Stir in the garlic and cook, stirring, until fragrant, 30 seconds to a minute. Add the eggplant, peppers, and salt to taste. Cook, stirring, for 5 to 10 minutes, until the eggplant is thoroughly soft and beginning to fall apart. Stir in the tomatoes, add more salt, and cook over medium heat for about 15 minutes, until the tomatoes have cooked down and the mixture smells and tastes very fragrant. Season to taste with salt and pepper. Set aside, or refrigerate overnight.

Heat the remaining 2 tablespoons oil over medium-high heat in a large, deep, heavy, lidded nonstick frying pan. Salt the chicken on both sides, and brown, in batches, for 5 minutes on each side, or until golden. Transfer to a plate or bowl lined with paper towels. Pour the fat out of the frying pan and discard, then add the pepper liquid (or pepper and tomato liquid) to the pan. Stir to deglaze the bottom of the pan. Return the chicken to the pan and cover with the eggplant mixture. Pour in the chicken stock, bring to a simmer, cover, and cook over medium-low heat, stirring from time to time, for 30 minutes, or until the chicken shows no sign of pink and pulls away from the bone easily. Taste and adjust the seasonings. If there is a lot of liquid in the pan, remove the lid and turn up the heat to boil some of it off. Add pepper, taste, and adjust the salt. Serve with thick crusty slices of bread, or with rice.

leftovers This will keep for 3 or 4 days—if you should happen to have any left over. You can make a delicious pilaf with scant leftovers by shredding the chicken and mixing with the sauce and rice. Or shred the chicken, stir into the sauce, and fill crêpes or sauce pasta with it.

chicken pot pie

My father and stepmother had a beautiful June wedding at the home of friends in Westport, Connecticut. I was fourteen at the time, and I still remember the main dish, which was a chicken pot pie. I asked my stepmother why they had chosen it, and she said, "Because it's a dish that everybody likes." And she's right . . . if it's a good one.

This version is a revelation, and my husband can't get enough of it. The poached chicken yields up a comforting broth that is combined with milk to make the light, velvety sauce that bathes the chicken and vegetables—carrots, onions, celery, dried mushrooms, peas, and asparagus, all enhanced with tarragon and thyme—and then this bounty is covered with a classic French pâte brisée. I prefer the lighter pie crust to the biscuit crust that many traditional pot pies call for.

You should definitely make this in two stages (or even three; see the advanced preparation notes). Poach the chicken to make the broth on one day, then refrigerate the broth to facilitate skimming the fat off the top. The next day prepare the vegetables and the crust, make the sauce, assemble, and bake.

Here's the order in which I recently made this, for a dinner party that was to be on a Saturday when I knew I wouldn't be home for most of that day:

1. Poach chicken, strain broth, cool and shred chicken, and refrigerate everything (I did this on Thursday, but could have done it on Friday).

2. Prepare vegetables and combine with chicken (I did this on Friday).

3. Make béchamel and prepare dough for crust (I did this late Saturday afternoon).

4. Combine béchamel and chicken mixture, transfer to baking dish, roll out pastry, and cover. Refrigerate until time to bake. ❖ **serves 6 generously**

for the poached chicken

1 (3½- to 4½-pound) chicken, cut up and skinned

1 large onion, quartered

2 large carrots, peeled and thickly sliced

1 celery stalk, thickly sliced

4 garlic cloves, crushed and peeled

Bouquet garni made with a few sprigs of thyme
and flat-leaf parsley and 1 bay leaf

6 black peppercorns

1½ teaspoons salt (more to taste)

for the chicken filling

½ ounce dried porcini mushrooms (½ cup)

2 tablespoons unsalted butter or olive oil

1 medium onion, chopped

2 medium carrots, peeled and finely chopped

2 celery stalks, finely chopped

3 tablespoons chopped fresh flat-leaf parsley

2 garlic cloves, minced or pressed

Salt and freshly ground black pepper

1 cup frozen peas, thawed

½ pound asparagus, steamed 4 minutes and cut into
1-inch lengths

2 tablespoons chopped fresh tarragon leaves

1 teaspoon fresh thyme leaves

for the sauce and topping

3 tablespoons unsalted butter

4 tablespoons all-purpose flour

2 cups hot chicken stock (page 378)

½ cup mushroom soaking liquid (see page 118)

1 cup hot milk

Pinch of grated nutmeg (optional)

2 tablespoons sherry (optional; personally, I don't think it
needs it, but you might like it)

Salt and freshly ground black pepper

1 recipe Classic French Pastry (page 265)

2 tablespoons beaten egg

to poach the chicken: Combine the ingredients with 2 quarts water in a large soup pot. Bring to a boil. Reduce the heat, cover partially, and simmer over low heat for 20 minutes. Remove the breasts. Simmer for another 10 minutes. Remove the legs and thighs. Leave the wings in and simmer for another 30 minutes for a richer broth. Remove the wings. Allow the meat to cool, then skin any pieces that still have the skin on, and shred the meat, but not too small. You should have about 4 cups. Cover and refrigerate.

advance preparation
The poached chicken and stock will keep for 3 or 4 days in the refrigerator.

Strain the chicken stock through a strainer lined with cheesecloth. Refrigerate overnight, or for several hours, until a layer of fat can easily be skimmed or lifted off the top. Skim off the fat and measure out 2 cups of stock. Freeze the remaining stock for another purpose.

To prepare the filling: Put the mushrooms in a heatproof bowl or measuring cup and pour on boiling water to cover. Let sit for 15 to 30 minutes, while you prepare the other ingredients. Drain through a cheesecloth-lined strainer set over a bowl, rinse the mushrooms thoroughly to remove grit, then squeeze dry and coarsely chop. Set aside ½ cup of the soaking liquid.

advance preparation
The vegetables can be prepared and tossed with the chicken a day or two ahead.

Heat the butter or oil over medium heat in a heavy saucepan or nonstick skillet and add the onion, carrots, celery, and 1 tablespoon of the parsley. Cook, stirring, until the onion begins to soften, about 3 minutes, then turn the heat down to low, cover, and cook, stirring often, for another 5 to 10 minutes, until the mixture is tender and aromatic. Stir in the garlic and cook for another minute or so, until the garlic is fragrant. Stir in the mushrooms and season to taste with salt and pepper. Remove from the heat and toss with the chicken in a large bowl, along with the peas, asparagus, tarragon, thyme, and the remaining 2 tablespoons parsley. Combine everything well, taste, and adjust the seasoning. Set aside, in the refrigerator if not using within a few hours.

To make the sauce: Melt the butter over medium-low heat in a large, heavy saucepan. Stir in the flour and cook, stirring, for 1 minute; the mixture should bubble but not brown. Combine the chicken stock and mushroom soaking liquid, and whisk into the roux. Whisk vigorously until the mixture is smooth, then whisk in the milk. Stir constantly over medium heat until the mixture comes to a simmer. Scrape the sides and bottom with a wooden spoon or heatproof spatula to make sure all of the roux is

advance preparation
The béchamel can be made a day ahead, but you should place plastic wrap or wax paper directly on the surface before refrigerating, to keep it from forming a skin. Whisk thoroughly over low heat before proceeding with the recipe.

advance preparation
The pie can be assembled and held in the refrigerator for a few hours before baking.

incorporated into the sauce, then turn the heat to low and simmer, stirring often, for 5 to 10 minutes. The sauce should be smooth and velvety, with no trace of a floury taste. It should be medium-thick, but not at all gummy. Add the nutmeg and sherry, if using; add salt to taste and grind in a small amount of pepper. Remove from the heat. Stir into the chicken mixture and combine well.

To assemble the pie: Heat the oven to 375°F. Butter or oil a 3-quart gratin or baking dish. Stir the filling, taste one more time to verify the seasonings, and turn into the baking dish. Roll out the pastry dough to fit the dish, with some overlap, and cover the filling, tucking the edges deep down into the sides of the dish. Make a few slashes in the crust, and brush with the beaten egg.

Place the pie on a baking sheet to catch drips. Bake for 40 to 50 minutes, until the crust is golden and the filling is bubbly. Remove from the heat and allow to sit for 10 minutes or longer before serving.

leftovers You can keep eating this until there's no more, for 3 or 4 days. Reheat in a low oven or a microwave.

oaxacan chicken and egg soup

This is a Oaxacan wedding dish called higaditos, *an eggy chicken soup that I tasted at a celebration in the village of Teotitlan del Valle during the summer of 1971. I've put it in this chapter, rather than the soup chapter, because I think of it primarily as a chicken dish. Eggs are beaten and slowly added to an aromatic chicken broth filled with shredded chicken, chicken livers, and sometimes pork. The eggs gently set in billowing curds, settling into the broth and enveloping some of the poultry shreds. The combination of the meat, broth, and pillows of egg is incredibly sensuous. I remember how, when I first ate it at the party in the village, it excited and startled me as much as my first taste of soufflé had years earlier. For years, until I actually looked at a recipe for* higaditos, *I imagined the hard-working women of Teotitlan carefully dipping each shred of meat into the egg before adding it to the soup. The dish made such an impression on me that I staged a wedding just so that I could have it again. But that's another story. . . .* ❖ serves 6

for the chicken and broth

1 (4-pound) chicken, cut up and skinned, with the gizzards

1 onion, quartered

¼ pound chicken livers

4 garlic cloves, crushed

1 carrot, sliced

Salt and freshly ground black pepper

for the soup

½ pound tomatillos, or 1 (13-ounce) can, drained

½ pound ripe tomatoes, peeled and seeded

1½ teaspoons cumin seeds

4 black peppercorns

2 whole cloves

1 tablespoon olive or canola oil

1 small onion, chopped

4 large garlic cloves, minced or pressed

6 cups reserved chicken broth (see above)

1 serrano pepper, minced (optional)

12 large eggs

½ teaspoon salt, plus more to taste

¼ cup chopped fresh cilantro

Red or green salsa, for serving (optional)

advance preparation
You can poach and shred the chicken
up to 3 days before you finish
the dish.

for the chicken and broth: Combine all the ingredients in a large pot with 2 quarts of water and bring to a boil. Reduce the heat and skim any foam that rises to the surface. Cover, turn the heat to low, and simmer for 30 minutes. Remove the chicken livers and set aside.

Continue to simmer the chicken for 15 minutes, or until the chicken is tender and the broth fragrant. Turn off the heat and allow the chicken pieces to cool for about 30 minutes in the broth. Remove the chicken pieces and livers from the broth and set aside, then strain the broth through a cheesecloth-lined strainer. Discard the vegetables and the gizzards. Bone and shred the chicken when it's cool enough to handle, and chop the chicken livers. Refrigerate the broth and meat separately, preferably overnight. In the morning, or several hours later, skim the fat off the broth, and measure out 6 cups (freeze extra or use for another purpose). Season to taste with salt and pepper.

For the soup: If using fresh tomatillos, husk them and simmer them in a pot of water for 10 minutes, until soft. Drain and purée the fresh or canned tomatillos, along with the tomatoes, in a blender or food processor fitted with the steel blade. Grind the cumin seeds, peppercorns, and cloves together in a spice mill.

Heat the oil over medium heat in a large, heavy casserole (in Mexico earthenware would be used; I use enameled cast iron) and add the onion. Cook, stirring, until tender, about 5 minutes, and stir in the garlic. Stir together until fragrant, 30 seconds to 1 minute, turn up the heat to medium-high, and add the tomatoes and tomatillos and the ground spices. Cook, stirring, for about 5 minutes, until the mixture has cooked down and smells fragrant.

advance preparation The dish can be made through this step up to 3 days ahead and held in the refrigerator. Bring back to a simmer before proceeding.

Add the chicken broth. Bring to a boil and add the shredded chicken, chopped chicken livers, and serrano peppers, if using. Reduce the heat and simmer for 10 minutes. Taste and adjust the seasonings.

Shortly before serving, beat the eggs with ½ teaspoon salt. Have the soup at a bare simmer, and very slowly pour in the eggs, pouring them around the edge of the pot. Turn off the heat and cover the pot. Let sit for 5 to 10 minutes. The eggs should set. Sprinkle with the cilantro and serve in wide bowls, with salsa on the side, if desired.

leftovers I can't think of anything more comforting than a big bowl of rice mixed with this leftover soup. You can make this soupy, or more like a pilaf. I prefer it soupy. To make a really balanced meal out of it, steam some broccoli and add to the mix.

green mole

This is an almost-classic Mexican mole verde, a little lighter than most but scrumptious and richly flavored and textured nonetheless. I like it with chicken or rabbit (see the following recipe), and with salmon. The color alone is reason enough to make it. If pumpkin seeds are not to be found, substitute hulled sunflower seeds. The mole will still be green. ❖ **serves 6**

½ cup hulled pumpkin seeds (see above)

3 cups chicken stock (page 378)

1 pound tomatillos, husked and rinsed, or 2 (13-ounce) cans, drained

2 to 4 serrano or jalapeño chilies, to taste, seeded

5 large leaves of romaine or leaf lettuce, washed and dried

½ medium onion, roughly chopped and soaked for 10 minutes in water to cover, then drained

3 large garlic cloves, roughly chopped

10 sprigs of fresh cilantro

¼ teaspoon ground cumin

2   cloves, ground

¾   teaspoon ground cinnamon

1   corn tortilla, toasted (see page 391), then crumbled and
    ground in a spice mill (see page 375)

2   tablespoons vegetable or canola oil

    Salt

heat a dry skillet over medium-high heat and add the pumpkin seeds.
Toast, shaking the pan or stirring constantly, until they have browned and popped,
5 to 8 minutes. Remove from the heat and transfer to a bowl. When they have cooled,
pulverize in a spice mill and sift into a bowl. Stir in ¾ cup of the stock and mix well.
Set aside.

If you're using fresh tomatillos, bring a medium pot of water to a simmer, add the
tomatillos, and simmer for 10 minutes, or until soft, flipping them over in the water
halfway through. Drain and place in a blender. If using canned tomatillos, drain and
place them in a blender. Add the chilies, lettuce, onion, garlic, cilantro, and spices.
Blend at high speed until smooth (use a blender, not a food processor, for the best
texture). Add the ground tortilla and blend again to mix it in well. If necessary, stop
the blender from time to time and stir, then blend again until the mixture is smooth.

Heat the oil over medium-high heat in a large, heavy saucepan, casserole, Dutch oven,
or nonstick skillet until it ripples. Drizzle in a bit of the pumpkin seed mixture, and if it
sizzles immediately, add the rest. (Wait for a minute or two if it doesn't.) Cook, stirring
constantly, until the mixture thickens, about 5 minutes. Add the tomatillo mixture
and cook, stirring often, for 5 to 10 minutes, until the mixture thickens. To know if it is
properly thickened, run your wooden spoon down the center of the pan. It should
make a canal that doesn't fill in quickly.

advance preparation
This will keep for 3 days in the
refrigerator and can be frozen. Whisk
well after defrosting to restore the
texture. Bring to a simmer and
proceed with the recipe.

Stir in the remaining 2¼ cups stock, stir together
well, and bring to a simmer. Cover partially and
cook, stirring from time to time, for 20 minutes,
or until the sauce is thick enough to coat the front
and back of a spoon like cream. Add salt to taste.
Remove from the heat.

(continued on next page)

chicken or rabbit with green mole ❖ serves 6

2 tablespoons vegetable or canola oil

1 (4-pound) chicken, cut into 10 pieces and skinned if desired, or 3 whole breasts, split and skinned if desired

or

1 rabbit, cut into 8 or 10 pieces

Salt and freshly ground black pepper

1 recipe Green Mole

Rice and corn tortillas, for serving

1 bunch of red radishes, made into roses, or sliced

Sprigs of fresh cilantro, for garnish

Heat the oil over medium-high heat in a large, heavy, deep nonstick skillet or a casserole and brown the chicken or rabbit, in batches, for about 5 minutes per side. Season with salt and pepper. Transfer to a plate or bowl and pour off the fat from the pan, then return the chicken or rabbit to the pan and add the green mole sauce. Bring to a simmer, cover, and simmer for 20 minutes for chicken breasts, 30 minutes for a cut-up whole chicken, and 45 minutes to an hour for rabbit, until the meat is very tender when tested with a fork. Taste, adjust the seasonings, and serve the chicken or rabbit, napped with plenty of sauce, with rice and corn tortillas. Garnish with radishes and cilantro.

leftovers ⁞ Both the chicken and rabbit with mole keep well, for 3 or 4 days, in the refrigerator. This makes great tacos and enchiladas.

green mole tacos

Remove leftover chicken or rabbit from the bones and shred. Mix with leftover sauce.

Heat corn tortillas in a dry skillet until flexible. Fill with the mole, and place on a plate. Garnish with a bit more sauce if desired, and crumble on some queso fresco or queso añejo. Serve warm.

green mole enchiladas

Remove the chicken or rabbit pieces from the sauce and shred. Nap with a spoonful or two of sauce. Bring the remaining sauce to a simmer in a wide saucepan or frying pan. Dip tortillas into the sauce, and using tongs, flip them over. When heated through and flexible, transfer to a plate or a large serving dish. Top with a spoonful or two of the shredded meat and roll up. Continue with the remaining tortillas, then pour on any remaining mole. Garnish the enchiladas with crumbled queso fresco or queso añejo, or with sour cream, and with radishes and cilantro, and serve.

oven-steamed salmon
with mole sauce

If you have some sauce left over but not much meat, try it with this wonderful, easy salmon. I learned this technique from my friend and colleague Russ Parsons. Now I rarely cook salmon any other way. ❖ serves 6

> 2 pounds salmon fillet, in 1 piece
>
> Salt and freshly ground black pepper
>
> Leftover Green Mole

Heat the oven to 300°F. Fill a roasting pan with boiling water and place it on the floor of the oven. Remove any visible bones from the salmon fillet using a tweezers. Salt and pepper the fish generously. Place on a lightly oiled baking sheet.

Place in the oven and bake until the fish flakes, 15 to 25 minutes. If the fillet is not very thick, check after 10 minutes. The fish should pull apart with a fork but should still look (and be) moist. Scrape off the white bubbles of fat that will accumulate on top of the fish. Transfer to a platter, nap with the mole sauce, and serve hot. Or, allow to cool without the sauce, and serve warm or at room temperature, topped with warm mole.

rabbit daube

My husband, Bill, and I ate this dish for three nights running and loved it more each night. The fourth night, we still had some of the sauce, so we cooked up some pappardelle and had it with that (that was a huge hit with Liam, then 3½ years old). It's the kind of sauce you just want to sop up with anything you can find, or even eat with a spoon. One thing that contributes to the flavor here is the salt pork. But you don't need the salt pork for the fat, so I trim that away. It's the flavor of the meat that enriches the stew. I highly recommend polenta as an accompaniment, but wide flat noodles, such as pappardelle, are also great. ❖ serves 4 to 6

1 fresh rabbit, cut into 8 to 10 pieces

1 bottle fruity, tannic red wine, such as a Côtes du Rhône

Bouquet garni made with a couple of bay leaves and a few sprigs each of thyme and flat-leaf parsley

2 onions, 1 quartered, 1 chopped

6 garlic cloves, 2 crushed, 4 minced or pressed

2 tablespoons unbleached all-purpose flour

Salt and freshly ground black pepper

3 tablespoons olive oil

2 ounces salt pork, trimmed of fat and diced

2 large carrots, peeled and chopped

2 celery stalks, chopped

Wide strip of fresh or dried orange zest

Polenta (see page 396), pasta, rice, potatoes, or thick slices of country bread for serving

combine the rabbit, wine, bouquet garni, the quartered onion, and the 2 crushed garlic cloves in a large bowl. Cover and refrigerate for anywhere from 4 hours to a day. Drain through a colander set over a bowl. Keep the bouquet garni and discard the quartered onion and garlic. Dry the rabbit pieces with paper towels.

Mix together the flour with some salt and pepper, and place in a wide bowl or on a plate. Lightly dredge the rabbit in the flour. Heat 2 tablespoons of the olive oil over medium-high heat in a large, heavy nonstick skillet and brown the rabbit on all sides,

advance preparation
This step can be done several hours
before finishing the daube. Don't let
the rabbit sit out of the refrigerator
for more than an hour.

in batches if necessary to avoid crowding the pan. This should take about 10 minutes per batch. Transfer the rabbit pieces to a bowl or plate lined with paper towels. When all of the rabbit has been browned, pour about ½ cup of the wine marinade into the pan and stir and scrape the bottom of the pan with a wooden spoon, to incorporate all of the solids that are stuck to the pan into the wine. Remove from the heat and set aside.

Heat the remaining tablespoon of olive oil with the trimmed salt pork over medium heat in a large, heavy casserole or Dutch oven. When the salt pork begins to sizzle, add the chopped onion and cook, stirring often, for about 5 minutes, until tender. Add the carrots and celery and cook, stirring often, for another 5 to 10 minutes, until the onion is slightly colored and the carrot and celery are tender and fragrant. Add the minced garlic and stir together for a minute or two, until fragrant. Add the wine marinade, including the ½ cup that you used to deglaze the rabbit pan, and bring to a boil. Turn the heat to medium and boil gently for 7 minutes, then add the rabbit pieces to the pan, along with the bouquet garni and salt. Cover, reduce the heat to low, and simmer for 30 minutes. Add the orange zest, cover again, and simmer for another 30 minutes, or until the rabbit is very tender. Add pepper, taste, and adjust the salt. Cover and refrigerate overnight if possible. The next day, scrape off the fat from the surface of the stew, and reheat gently.

Serve with polenta, pasta, rice, potatoes, or thick slices of toasted country bread.

leftovers This gets better with each day. It will keep for 4 days in the refrigerator. Pasta is the best vehicle for the leftovers. A half cup of sauce will suffice for two servings of pasta. You could also make a polenta gratin. Make polenta following the directions on page 396. Shred leftover meat, heat with the sauce, and spread over the top. Sprinkle on ¼ to ½ cup Gruyère cheese and bake in a 375°F. oven until the top browns, about 15 minutes.

rabbit in mustard sauce

This classic French lapin à la moutarde *has a number of interpretations. Mine is without cream; the sauce is instead thickened by the mustard itself and by a small amount of flour, then finally with an egg yolk, which gives it a velvety texture. Many layers of flavors work together here to create a truly extraordinary dish that only gets better with time.* ❖ **serves 4 to 6**

1 large fresh rabbit, cut into 8 serving pieces and trimmed of excess fat

1 bottle dry white wine

2 tablespoons olive oil or canola oil

2 tablespoons unsalted butter

2 medium onions, chopped

1½ tablespoons all-purpose flour

½ cup Dijon mustard

Salt and freshly ground black pepper

2 cups chicken stock (page 378)

2 teaspoons fresh thyme leaves, or 1 teaspoon crumbled dried thyme

1 bay leaf

1 large egg yolk, beaten

Handful of chopped fresh flat-leaf parsley

Wide egg noodles or rice, for serving

place the rabbit in a bowl, pour on the wine, and cover, or transfer to a heavy resealable plastic bag. Refrigerate for 6 hours or longer, shifting the pieces around from time to time.

Heat 1 tablespoon of the oil and 1 tablespoon of the butter over medium heat in a large, heavy nonstick skillet and add the onions. Cook, stirring, until golden brown, about 12 minutes. Transfer to a large, heavy casserole. Sprinkle on the flour through a strainer and stir the onions well. Set aside.

While the onions are cooking, remove the rabbit from the marinade, reserving the wine. Dry thoroughly with paper towels. Brush 1 side of each piece with a thick coating of mustard. Heat the remaining 1 tablespoon butter and 1 tablespoon oil over medium-high heat in the nonstick frying pan. Working in batches, brown the rabbit, mustard side down, a few pieces at a time, about 5 minutes. While browning on the first side, season the other side with salt and pepper and brush with the remaining mustard. Turn over and brown for another 5 minutes. Transfer to the casserole with the onions.

advance preparation The recipe can be made through this step up to 4 days ahead. Bring back to a simmer before proceeding with the recipe.

Add the wine to the pan and bring to a boil, scraping the bottom with a wooden spoon to deglaze. There will be a lot of mustard adhering to the pan. Boil for a minute or two, then pour over the rabbit and onions in the casserole. Add the chicken stock, plus any remaining mustard, the thyme, and the bay leaf. Return the pan to the stove, cover partially, and simmer over medium-low heat for 1 hour, or until the rabbit is very tender. Stir and turn the pieces of meat over from time to time so they don't dry out.

advance preparation The recipe can also be made through this step up to 4 days ahead. The final enrichment below is done just before serving.

Using tongs, remove the rabbit pieces from the sauce and place in a bowl or on a platter. Strain the sauce and return to the pot. Bring the sauce to a boil and reduce by about a third. Taste and adjust the seasonings. If you want a more pungent sauce, add more mustard.

Bring the sauce up or down to a bare simmer. Add a ladleful to the beaten egg yolk and combine well. Now transfer the egg mixture back to the sauce, and stir together until the sauce is velvety, being careful not to allow the sauce to boil. Return the rabbit pieces to the pot, sprinkle with chopped parsley, and serve over wide noodles or rice.

leftovers Leftovers will keep for about 4 days. The best leftovers dish is pasta or rice with the rabbit and sauce. Remove whatever rabbit is left and break up into small pieces. Toss with pasta or rice and the warm sauce.

my pozole: hominy stew with chicken and tomatillos

Hominy stew, or pozole, is a hearty, festive dish in Mexico and is traditionally made with pork. It can be either green, with a tomatillo base, or red, with a chili base. My pozoles tend to be lighter than the traditional ones, but no less delicious. The word pozole (in New Mexico it's spelled posole*) refers to the dried field corn—hominy—that is the staple ingredient in the dish. Pozole must be soaked in water treated with lime for the shells to soften sufficiently for the kernels to open out like a flower after their long simmer. The pozole that I buy in the Mexican markets in Los Angeles has already been treated and dried. You also have the option of using canned hominy, but if you can find the dried ingredient, you'll appreciate it for the savory broth that you can use in the stew. The garnishes are important here. They add texture, flavors, and fun to the dish.* ❖ **serves 10**

for the chicken and stock

1 (3½- to 4½-pound) chicken, cut up and skinned, plus 2 legs and 2 thighs, skinned

1 large onion, quartered

2 carrots, sliced

4 garlic cloves, crushed and peeled

1 bay leaf

2 sprigs of fresh flat-leaf parsley

for the pozole

1 pound dried pozole, or 2 (1-pound) cans

1 pound fresh tomatillos, husked and rinsed, or 2 (13-ounce) cans, drained

1 small bunch of sorrel, stemmed, washed, and coarsely chopped

8 sprigs of fresh cilantro, plus 1 cup chopped cilantro

6 serrano or 3 jalapeño chilies (or more to taste), stemmed and coarsely chopped

2 tablespoons vegetable or canola oil

1 large onion, chopped

6 large garlic cloves, minced or pressed

Salt to taste (be generous)

2 large sprigs of fresh epazote, chopped (optional)

for garnish

1 small red onion, minced and soaked (see page 375), then drained and rinsed

1 or 2 ripe but firm avocados, diced

10 tortillas, toasted (see page 391) and crumbled

8 leaves of romaine lettuce, cut crosswise into thin slivers (chiffonade)

Minced fresh green chilies

to prepare the chicken and stock: One or two days (or up to four days) before you wish to serve this dish, place the chicken in a large soup pot or Dutch oven with 3 quarts water and bring to a simmer. Skim off any foam, then add the onion, carrots, garlic, bay leaf, and parsley sprigs. Reduce the heat, cover, and simmer for 1 hour. Allow the chicken to cool in the broth. Remove the chicken from the broth and transfer to a bowl. Strain the broth into a bowl through a cheesecloth-lined strainer. Cover and refrigerate. The next day, lift the fat from the surface of the broth and discard.

advance preparation
The chicken and broth will keep for 4 days in the refrigerator. If keeping for more than a day, store in a covered bowl.

When the chicken is cool enough to handle, remove from the bones and shred. Keep in a covered bowl or a plastic bag in the refrigerator.

To make the pozole: If using dried pozole, combine with 4 quarts water in a large pot. Bring to a boil, cover, and simmer for 2 hours, or until the kernels are tender and have begun to splay. Drain over a bowl and measure out 1 quart of the cooking liquid.

While the pozole is simmering, simmer fresh tomatillos in water to cover for 10 to 15 minutes, flipping them over halfway through, until they are tender. Drain and place in a blender (transfer drained canned tomatillos directly to the blender). Add the sorrel, cilantro sprigs, and chilies and blend until smooth.

Measure out 3 quarts of the chicken stock if using canned hominy, or 2 quarts of the chicken stock combined with the quart of cooking liquid from the pozole if you cooked the pozole (freeze any remaining stock).

advance preparation
The dish can be made through this step a day or two ahead. The pozole will become even more tender and the flavors richer. Heat the oil over medium heat in a large, heavy soup pot or Dutch oven and add the onion. Cook, stirring often, until tender, about 5 minutes. Add half the garlic and stir together for about 30 seconds, until fragrant. Turn the heat to medium-high and pour in the tomatillo mixture. Cook, stirring with a long-handled spoon (to avoid splutters), until the mixture is thick and bright green, about 5 minutes. Add the remaining garlic, the pozole or the canned hominy, and the stock, and bring to a boil. Cover, reduce the heat, and simmer for 1 to 2 hours, until the pozole is very tender and opened out like a flower. Now add salt to taste. You will need at least a tablespoon and probably more.

About 20 minutes before you wish to serve, bring the pozole back to a simmer. Stir in the shredded chicken and the epazote. Simmer for 15 minutes, partially covered. Taste and adjust the seasonings. Stir in the chopped cilantro and serve, passing the garnishes for everyone to sprinkle on top.

leftovers Pozole keeps for about 5 days and can be frozen for a couple of months. Just keep reheating and serve with lots of corn tortillas.

braised chicken with wild mushrooms

You'll have to have seconds with this one. It's incredibly rich-tasting, though not particularly rich—okay, a little cream or crème fraîche if you want it, but not too much. The mushrooms and chicken together provide a great contrast of textures as well as flavors. The mushroom element of this dish is not much different from other mushroom ragouts in this book (see the Wild Mushroom Ragout and Cobbler on page 174). In the company of chicken they become a savory sauce. ❖ **serves 4 to 5**

1 ounce dried porcini mushrooms (about 1 cup)

3 tablespoons olive oil

1 (3½- to 4½-pound) chicken, cut up and skinned if desired

Salt and freshly ground black pepper

4 shallots, chopped, or 1 medium onion, chopped

4 garlic cloves, minced or pressed

1 pound mixed wild mushrooms, such as oyster mushrooms, shiitakes, morels, and chanterelles, trimmed and torn into pieces if very large, or if other wild mushrooms cannot be found, use all oyster mushrooms

2 teaspoons chopped fresh rosemary or 1 teaspoon crumbled dried

1 tablespoon all-purpose flour

1 tablespoon soy sauce

½ cup fruity red wine, such as a Côtes du Rhône

2 cups chicken stock (page 378)

¼ cup cream or crème fraîche (optional)

2 tablespoons chopped fresh flat-leaf parsley

Egg noodles or rice, for serving

place the dried mushrooms in a heatproof bowl or measuring cup and pour on 2 cups boiling water. Let soak for 30 minutes, while you prepare the other ingredients. Place a strainer over a bowl, line it with cheesecloth or paper towels, and drain the mushrooms. Squeeze the mushrooms over the strainer to extract all the flavorful juices. Then rinse the mushrooms, away from the bowl with the soaking liquid, until they are free of grit. Squeeze dry and set aside. If very large, chop coarsely. Measure out 1 cup of the soaking liquid and set aside.

Heat 2 tablespoons of the olive oil over medium-high heat in a large, deep, nonstick skillet and brown the chicken on both sides, in batches if necessary, about 5 minutes per side. Transfer to a plate or bowl and season with salt and pepper.

advance preparation This step can be done a day or two ahead. If you cook the mushrooms ahead, wait until the day you're serving to brown the chicken. Brown it in another pan while you reheat the mushrooms in the large deep pan, and proceed with the recipe.

Pour the fat out of the pan and discard. Lower the heat to medium and add the remaining 1 tablespoon olive oil and the shallots. Cook, stirring, until tender, about 5 minutes. Add the garlic, stir together for about 30 seconds, until fragrant, then add the wild mushrooms, rosemary, and about a teaspoon of salt. Cook, stirring often, until the mushrooms begin to soften and to sweat, about 5 minutes. Add the flour and continue to cook the mushrooms, stirring, until they have softened a little more and you can no longer see the flour, about 2 minutes. Add the reconstituted dried mushrooms, the soy sauce, and the wine and turn the heat to high. Cook, stirring, until the liquid boils down and glazes the mushrooms, 5 to 10 minutes. Season with pepper.

Stir in the chicken stock and the reserved mushroom soaking liquid and return the chicken to the pan. Bring to a simmer, add salt to taste, cover, and simmer for 45 minutes, or until the chicken is tender.

advance preparation You can make the dish, up to the point at which you add the cream, a day ahead and keep overnight in the refrigerator. Skim any fat off the top, reheat, and add the cream or crème fraîche and the parsley.

Remove the chicken from the pan using tongs, and place it in a bowl while you reduce the liquid in the pan. Turn the heat to high and boil until reduced by about a third, about 10 minutes. Turn the heat down to medium-low, stir in the cream or crème fraîche, return the chicken to the pan, and heat through. Taste and adjust the seasonings. Stir in the parsley and serve, either with egg noodles or rice.

leftovers : The dish will be good for 5 days in the refrigerator, though I can't imagine much will be left over. You can use leftovers for a splendid lasagne. Shred any remaining chicken and stir it into the remaining stew. Follow the recipe for mushroom lasagne on page 194, using the chicken and mushrooms for the filling.

If you only have a bit of chicken, and a cup or so of sauce, just serve it with pasta or rice. You can't go wrong.

Leftovers also make a great tart or gratin.

braised chicken and wild mushroom tart ❖ serves 4

1 unbaked pie crust, such as the Classic French Pastry (page 265) or a store bought crust

3 eggs, beaten

2 cups leftover Braised Chicken with Wild Mushrooms, with the chicken shredded

½ cup milk (low-fat is fine)

Salt and freshly ground black pepper

2 ounces Gruyère cheese, grated (½ cup)

Heat the oven to 375°F. Line a 9- or 10-inch pie pan with the dough. Brush with a bit of the beaten egg and bake for 7 minutes. Heat the leftover stew until warm.

Beat together the eggs, milk, and salt and pepper to taste. Stir in the chicken and mushrooms and the cheese. Scrape into the pie crust. Bake for 30 minutes, or until lightly browned and firm. Serve hot or warm.

four

vegetable and bean stews, cobblers, and pot pies

The summer I began assembling the recipes in this book, I filled this chapter very quickly. No surprise: I couldn't resist buying the beautiful eggplant, tomatoes, squash, and green beans at my local farmers' markets, and making endless variations on summer vegetable stew.

The onset of fall and winter (albeit California fall and winter) didn't stop me. Hearty bean stews and winter vegetable pot pies followed my summer dishes, and then came irresistible spring vegetable ragouts, made with artichokes and peppers, or peas and beans, new potatoes and baby carrots, favas and baby turnips.

Sometimes my stews lie beneath a cobbler topping; others can be served with pasta or rice. A ragout that includes potatoes, like the Artichoke, Mushroom, and Potato Ragout on page 144, can stand alone. Bean stews, whether or not they include sausages, are substantial enough to make a meal when accompanied by crusty bread.

This chapter will delight vegetarians. With the exception of a few stews that include sausage, most of these recipes are meatless. There may be some pancetta or bacon here and there, but you can omit those ingredients for vegetarian versions.

greek artichoke and potato stew

I think of this slightly lemony, dill- and mint-seasoned dish, based on a recipe from Diane Kochilas's The Greek Vegetarian (St. Martin's Press, 1996), as a summer stew, but in truth it's equally delicious made with canned or fresh tomatoes. Classic Greek vegetable stews like this are traditionally made with abundant olive oil, much more than I use in my cooking. The vegetables and aromatics simmer in up to ½ cup of olive oil, absorbing much of it. But my emphasis is on the pure flavors of the vegetables, aromatics, and herbs. ❖ **serves 4 to 6**

Juice of 2 lemons

12 small or 6 medium or large artichokes

2 tablespoons olive oil (or more to taste)

1 medium red onion, chopped

4 garlic cloves, minced or pressed

1½ pounds potatoes, preferably red-skinned, scrubbed and halved if small, quartered if large

1 pound plum tomatoes, peeled and chopped, or 1 (14-ounce) can, drained and chopped

Salt

1 bay leaf

1 generous bunch of fresh dill, chopped (about ½ cup, tightly packed)

¼ to ½ cup chopped fresh mint (to taste)

Freshly ground black pepper to taste

Country bread, for serving

Feta cheese, for serving

fill a bowl with water and add the juice of 1 lemon. Cut the stems off the artichokes, about ½ inch from the artichoke bottom, and using a sharp knife, cut away the tops, about ½ inch from the top. Dip the cut parts into the lemon water. Break off the tough outer leaves until you get to the lighter green leaves near the middle. Cut small artichokes in half, large artichokes into quarters, and cut away the chokes. Immediately place in the bowl of lemon water.

advance preparation You can make the dish through this step 2 or 3 days ahead. When I was testing this recipe the first time, I realized after I'd begun that I'd forgotten to get the dill and mint. I went ahead with the recipe through this step, and put it in the refrigerator. Events prevented me from getting to the market until the next day, and I didn't get around to finishing the recipe until the day after that. It was wonderful. Refrigerate and bring back to a simmer before proceeding.

advance preparation The finished dish can be made a day ahead and refrigerated.

Heat the oil over medium heat in a large, heavy casserole or lidded nonstick frying pan. Add the onion and cook, stirring, until just about tender, 3 to 5 minutes. Add the garlic, stir together for a minute, until fragrant, then add the potatoes. Drain the artichokes, add to the pan, and stir the vegetables together until coated with oil. Add the tomatoes and a little salt and cook, stirring often, until the tomatoes cook down slightly and smell fragrant. Add enough water to just cover the vegetables; add the bay leaf and more salt, and bring to a simmer. Cover and simmer for 30 minutes, until the vegetables are just tender.

Stir in the fresh herbs and continue to cook for another 10 minutes. If the broth seems too watery to you, uncover and cook over high heat until the liquid reduces somewhat (there should be some juice). Add pepper, taste, and adjust the salt. Stir in 1 to 3 tablespoons lemon juice, to taste. Remove the bay leaf. Serve hot or at room temperature, with thick slices of crusty country bread for soaking up the juice, and with a slice of feta cheese.

leftovers Leftovers are good for 3 or 4 days. Keep in the refrigerator, reheat, or serve at room temperature, or serve with pasta, rice, bulgur, or couscous.

provençal artichoke ragout with fresh fava beans

Artichokes à la barigoule, as this is called in Provence, is at the top of my list of favorite arti-choke recipes. The word barigoule *actually refers to a little wild mushroom that I've never once tasted or seen in this dish, which is garlicky and sweet with peppers and tomatoes—everything a Provençal dish should be. Because I had a pound of fava beans in the refrigerator when I was retesting this recipe, I added them, and it was a marriage made in heaven. This dish is for those who don't mind using fingers and getting them a little greasy in the process.* ❖ **serves 6**

1 lemon, cut in half

2 pounds small artichokes (or globe artichokes if small ones are not available)

2 tablespoons olive oil

1 large sweet onion, such as Vidalia or Maui, chopped, or 1 bunch of spring onions, chopped

1 large or 2 small red bell peppers, diced

Salt

4 large garlic cloves, minced or pressed

1½ pounds (6 medium) tomatoes, or 1 (14-ounce) can, drained, peeled, seeded, and chopped

1 teaspoon fresh thyme leaves, or ½ teaspoon dried thyme

1 bay leaf

Freshly ground black pepper

1 pound fresh fava beans

2 to 4 tablespoons chopped fresh basil or flat-leaf parsley

fill a bowl with water and add the juice of the lemon. Cut the stems off the artichokes, about ½ inch from the artichoke bottom, and, using a sharp knife, cut away the tops, about ½ inch from the top. Dip the cut parts into the lemon water. Break off the tough outer leaves until you get to the lighter green leaves near the middle. Cut small artichokes in half, large artichokes into quarters, and cut away the chokes. Immediately place in the bowl of lemon water.

Heat the oil in a large, heavy nonstick skillet or casserole over medium heat and add the onion. Cook, stirring, until tender, about 3 to 5 minutes. Add the red bell pepper and about ¼ teaspoon salt, and stir together for 3 to 5 minutes, until the pepper begins to soften. Add the garlic and stir together for another minute, until the garlic is fragrant. Add the tomatoes and a little more salt, and cook, stirring from time to time, for 5 to 10 minutes, until the tomatoes have cooked down slightly and smell fragrant.

advance preparation The dish can be made up to a day ahead through this step. Refrigerate and bring back to a simmer before proceeding.

Add the artichokes, thyme, bay leaf, and ¾ cup water, or enough so that the artichokes are halfway submerged in liquid, and bring to a simmer. Add salt and pepper, cover, and simmer for 30 to 40 minutes, until the artichokes are tender and the sauce is fragrant. Check from time to time and add water if necessary. Taste and adjust the salt and pepper.

advance preparation The favas can be skinned a day ahead and held in the refrigerator.

While the artichokes are simmering, shell the fava beans. Bring a small pot of water to a boil and drop in the fava beans. Boil for 1 minute, then transfer to a bowl of cold water. Drain and slip off the skins. Stir into the artichokes and simmer for 5 or 10 minutes, until tender but still bright green. Stir in the basil or parsley. Remove the bay leaf. Serve hot or at room temperature.

leftovers This keeps well for 3 or 4 days in the refrigerator. I usually toss leftovers with pasta. But it also makes a great omelet or quiche filling, or use to top a pizza.

artichoke, mushroom, and potato ragout

This is a more robust Provençal fall recipe, with mushrooms. ❖ serves 4 to 6

1½ ounces dried porcini mushrooms (about 1½ cups)

Juice of 2 lemons

12 small or 6 medium or large artichokes

2 tablespoons olive oil

1 large onion, thinly sliced

4 to 5 large garlic cloves, minced or pressed

2 pounds waxy potatoes or Yukon golds, scrubbed and quartered

½ cup dry white wine

1 bay leaf

1 teaspoon fresh thyme leaves or ½ teaspoon dried thyme

Salt and freshly ground black pepper

¼ cup chopped fresh flat-leaf parsley

place the mushrooms in a large heatproof bowl or measuring cup. Bring 3 cups water to a boil and pour over the mushrooms. Let sit for 30 minutes.

Meanwhile, fill a bowl with water and add the juice of 1 lemon. Cut the stems off the artichokes, about ½ inch from the artichoke bottom, and, using a sharp knife, cut away the tops, about ½ inch from the top. Dip the cut parts into the lemon water. Break off the tough outer leaves, until you get to the lighter green leaves near the middle. Cut small artichokes in half, large artichokes into quarters, and cut away the chokes. Immediately place in the bowl of lemon water.

Place a strainer lined with cheesecloth or paper towels over a bowl and drain the mushrooms. Squeeze out liquid over the strainer, then rinse the mushrooms in several changes of water to rid them of grit. Set aside. Add enough water to the soaking liquid to measure 3 cups.

advance preparation
The dish can be made a day or two
ahead and reheated.

Heat the olive oil over medium heat in a large, heavy casserole or lidded nonstick skillet. Add the onion and cook, stirring, until tender, about 5 minutes. Stir in the garlic and mushrooms and cook together, stirring, until fragrant, about 1 minute. Drain the artichokes and add with the potatoes, stir together for another minute, then stir in the wine. Bring to a boil, and cook until most of the liquid is gone, then add the soaking liquid from the mushrooms, the bay leaf, thyme, salt, and pepper. Bring to a simmer, reduce the heat, cover, and simmer for 40 minutes, or until the potatoes and artichokes are tender. Taste and adjust the salt. Stir in 1 to 3 tablespoons lemon juice, to taste, and the parsley. Simmer, uncovered, for another few minutes—longer if you want to reduce the liquid. Taste and adjust the seasonings. Serve hot or at room temperature.

leftovers Leftovers are good for 3 or 4 days. Keep in the refrigerator, reheat, and toss with pasta, or serve with couscous or rice.

two methods for one ratatouille

There can never be too much ratatouille, nor can there be too many recipes for it. For a long time I stuck to a recipe I'd spent a long time developing when I was working on my cookbook Provençal Light. This long-simmering version has a rich, intense flavor. Then my friend Russ Parsons brought a beautiful, bright ratatouille to a party, and I liked his as much as mine. And his was prettier. So I decided to include both methods here. The first cooks for 1 to 1½ hours in the oven, and you can intensify the flavors further by reducing the sauce. The second cooks on top of the stove, and only long enough to bring out the savory juices of the vegetables. For this reason the greens, reds, and yellows (I like to mix yellow and green squash, and yellow and red peppers, in season) stay brighter, and it's really a beautiful dish. No matter which method you use here, it's important that each separately cooked batch of vegetables be properly seasoned. Ratatouille is the sum of many tasty parts. I roast the eggplant, rather than cook it in the pan before adding it to the casserole; it requires less oil if you do this, and the flavor is intense. ❖ **serves 6**

1½ pounds eggplant

Salt

3 tablespoons olive oil

¾ pound (2 medium) onions, thinly sliced

¾ pound mixed red and yellow bell peppers, cored, seeded, and cut into slices about ¾ inch wide by 1½ inches long

4 to 6 large garlic cloves, minced or pressed

1½ pounds mixed yellow and green zucchini, sliced about ½ inch thick (if very thick, cut in half lengthwise)

Freshly ground black pepper

¾ pound tomatoes, peeled, seeded, and coarsely chopped

1 bay leaf

1 to 2 teaspoons fresh thyme leaves or ½ to 1 teaspoon dried thyme

½ teaspoon dried oregano

2 to 4 tablespoons slivered or chopped fresh basil, to taste

method 1: long-cooking ratatouille

Cut the eggplant into ½-inch cubes. Salt generously and place in a colander in the sink. Let sit for 30 minutes to an hour. Meanwhile, heat the oven to 500°F. Rinse the eggplant and pat dry, place in a large casserole, preferably an earthenware one, and toss with a tablespoon of the olive oil. Place in the hot oven and roast for 15 to 20 minutes, tossing from time to time, until the eggplant is lightly browned and fragrant. Remove the casserole from the oven and turn the oven down to 350°F.

advance preparation If you need to leave the house (or go to bed), you can make the recipe through this step and not put it in the oven until you have got an hour to an hour and a half at home. Leave it out for a few hours, or refrigerate it for a day.

Heat 1 tablespoon of oil over medium heat in a large, heavy nonstick skillet. Add the onions, and cook, stirring often, until just about tender, about 5 minutes. Stir in the peppers and a generous pinch of salt. Cook, stirring often, until the peppers have softened and smell fragrant, 5 to 10 minutes. Stir in half the garlic and cook for another minute, then season with salt and pepper and transfer to the casserole with the eggplant. Heat the remaining 1 tablespoon oil in the skillet and add the squash, more salt to taste, and some freshly ground pepper, and cook, stirring, until the squash begins to look translucent, 5 to 10 minutes. Stir in the remaining garlic, stir together for a minute, or until fragrant, and transfer to the casserole. Add half the tomatoes to the casserole along with the bay leaf, thyme, oregano, and more salt, to taste. Toss everything together, cover, and place in the oven.

advance preparation Your ratatouille will benefit from a day to mellow in the refrigerator.

Bake the ratatouille for 1 to 1½ hours, stirring every 30 minutes, until the vegetables are very soft and very fragrant. Stir in the remaining tomatoes during the last half hour. The ratatouille should be very soft and juicy. For a really intense flavor, transfer the ratatouille to a colander set over a bowl. Let drain for 15 minutes, then heat the juice in a pan to a boil, and reduce its volume by half. Stir back into the ratatouille. Taste and season with salt and pepper. Serve warm or cold, preferably the next day. Remove the bay leaf and stir in the basil shortly before serving.

(continued on next page)

method 2: quicker ratatouille

Cut the eggplant into ½-inch cubes. Salt well and place in a colander in the sink. Let sit for 30 minutes to an hour. Meanwhile, heat the oven to 500°F. Rinse the eggplant and pat dry, place in a large, heavy flameproof casserole, and toss with a tablespoon of the olive oil. Place in the oven and roast for 15 to 20 minutes, tossing occasionally, until the eggplant is lightly browned and fragrant. Remove the casserole from the oven.

Heat 1 tablespoon of oil over medium heat in a large, heavy nonstick skillet. Add the onions and cook, stirring often, until just about tender, about 5 minutes. Stir in the peppers and a generous pinch of salt. Cook, stirring often, until the peppers have softened and smell fragrant, 5 to 10 minutes. Stir in half the garlic and cook for another minute, then season with salt and pepper and transfer to the casserole with the eggplant. Heat the remaining 1 tablespoon oil in the skillet and add the squash, more salt to taste, and some freshly ground pepper, and cook, stirring, until the squash is tender but still bright, 5 to 10 minutes. Stir in the remaining garlic, stir together for a minute, or until fragrant, and transfer to the casserole. Add the tomatoes to the casserole along with the bay leaf, thyme, oregano, and more salt and pepper, to taste. Toss everything together and place the casserole over medium-low heat. When the vegetables begin to sizzle, cover the casserole and cook, stirring often, for about 15 minutes, until the mixture is juicy and fragrant, the vegetables tender but still bright. Taste and adjust the seasonings. Serve warm or cold, preferably the next day. Remove the bay leaf and stir in the basil shortly before serving.

leftovers ⋮ Ratatouille will keep for 5 days in the refrigerator, and it definitely benefits from being made a day ahead. I like to eat leftovers as a first course with a vinaigrette, in an omelet or tart, as a crêpe filling (see page 150), or in the gratin below.

ratatouille gratin ❖ serves 4 to 6

2 to 2½ cups ratatouille (or whatever you have left)

3 eggs

½ cup milk, as needed

¼ teaspoon salt

Freshly ground black pepper

2 ounces Gruyère cheese, grated (½ cup, tightly packed)

½ cup bread crumbs

1 tablespoon olive oil

1 ounce Parmesan cheese, grated (¼ cup)

Heat the oven to 375°F. Oil a 2-quart gratin dish. Place the ratatouille in a strainer or colander set over a bowl. Let drain for 5 minutes.

Beat the eggs. Measure out the liquid from the ratatouille with enough milk to make ¾ cup. Beat into the eggs, along with the salt and pepper. Stir in the ratatouille and the Gruyère cheese. Mix together well and place in the gratin dish. Toss together the bread crumbs, olive oil, and Parmesan, and sprinkle in an even layer over the top. Bake for 30 to 40 minutes, until the top is browned and the gratin is fairly firm. Remove from the oven and serve hot or warm.

ratatouille tart

Use the ingredients for Ratatouille Gratin (page 148), but omit the bread crumbs and olive oil. Mix everything together, including the Parmesan, as directed. Prebake a pie crust (see pages 263–265) for 7 minutes, allow to cool, then fill with the ratatouille mixture. Bake for 30 to 40 minutes, until the top is nicely browned.

large ratatouille frittata

You can make individual omelets filled with ratatouille, or you can make one large frittata.

❖ serves 4

1 cup, or more, leftover ratatouille

8 eggs

Salt and freshly ground black pepper

2 tablespoons milk

2 tablespoons olive oil

If the ratatouille has a lot of liquid, place in a colander set over a bowl and drain for 15 to 30 minutes. Beat the eggs well and stir in the salt, pepper, and milk. Stir in the ratatouille.

Heat the olive oil over medium-high heat in a heavy 10- or 12-inch nonstick skillet that can later be used under a broiler. Hold your hand above it; it should feel hot. Drop a bit of egg into the pan and if it sizzles and cooks at once, the pan is ready. Pour in the egg mixture. Swirl the pan to distribute the eggs and filling evenly over the surface. Shake the pan gently, tilting it slightly with one hand while lifting up the edges of the frittata with the spatula, in your other hand, to let the eggs run underneath during the first few minutes of cooking. Turn the heat down to low, cover (use a pizza pan if you don't have a lid that will fit your skillet), and cook for 10 minutes, shaking the pan gently every once in a while. From time to time remove the lid and loosen the bottom of the frittata with a wooden spatula, tilting the pan so that the bottom doesn't burn. It will, however, turn a deep golden brown. The eggs should be just about set; cook for a few minutes longer if they're not. Meanwhile, heat the broiler.

Finish the frittata under the broiler for 2 to 3 minutes, watching very carefully to make sure the top doesn't burn (it should brown slightly, and it will puff under the broiler). Remove from the heat, shake the pan to make sure the frittata isn't sticking (it will slide around a bit in the nonstick pan), and serve, or allow to cool for at least 5 minutes and up to 15, then loosen the edges with a wooden or plastic spatula. Carefully slide from the pan onto a large round platter. Serve hot, warm, or at room temperature.

ratatouille crêpes

The mixture also makes a delicious crêpe filling (see page 394 for a recipe for crêpes).

andalusian chick pea and cabbage stew

This recipe is adapted from one in Clifford Wright's A Mediterranean Feast *(William Morrow Publishers, 2000). It's a simple, soothing stew, one that's very easy to put together.* ❖ serves 6

1 pound dried chick peas, soaked overnight in 2 quarts water

1 large onion, chopped

4 large garlic cloves, minced or pressed

Salt

2 tablespoons olive oil

1 (14-ounce) can tomatoes, chopped, with juice

2 teaspoons freshly ground cumin seeds

4 ounces Canadian bacon, diced

1 medium head of green cabbage (about 1½ to 2 pounds), cored and chopped

Freshly ground black pepper

Cayenne pepper to taste

Slices of crusty bread, for serving

advance preparation
You may turn off the heat after this step and proceed with the next step several hours later.

advance preparation
At this point the beans may be removed from the heat and refrigerated overnight or for up to 3 days. Bring back to a simmer before proceeding with the recipe.

drain the chick peas and combine with 3 quarts water in a large soup pot or Dutch oven. Bring to a boil. Skim off any foam, then add the onion and half the garlic. Reduce the heat, cover, and simmer for 1 hour.

Add the salt, 1 tablespoon of the olive oil, tomatoes, cumin seeds, and bacon, and simmer for another hour, or until the chick peas are tender.

Add the cabbage, the remaining garlic, and olive oil to the beans, bring back to a simmer, and simmer, partially covered, for 30 minutes. Add the black pepper and cayenne pepper, taste, and adjust the salt. Serve with thick slices of crusty bread.

leftovers This keeps well for up to 5 days in the refrigerator. You can stretch leftovers by mixing with rice, which makes a very comforting and satisfying pilaf.

mixed bean and winter squash stew

This is based on a Chilean dish called Porotos Granados. *It's a hearty, comforting dish. In summer you can make it with fresh corn and tomatoes, but don't be deterred from making it at other times of the year, using frozen corn and canned tomatoes. One of the things that this has going for it is texture; there is so much of it here—the different beans (it's important to use the lima beans, even if you think you don't like limas; the stew really got me hooked on them), the crunchy corn kernels, the soft winter squash. Then there's the play of flavors, with the sweet winter squash and corn, the savory beans, the pungent paprika, and garlic and basil. The dish improves with time, so try to make it a day or two ahead.* ❖ serves 6

½ pound dried white beans, soaked in 1 quart water for 6 hours or overnight

½ pound dried cranberry, borlotti, or pinto beans, soaked in 1 quart water for 6 hours or overnight

Salt (you'll probably need a tablespoon)

2 tablespoons olive oil

1 medium onion, chopped

1 tablespoon sweet paprika

3 large garlic cloves, minced or pressed

1 pound tomatoes, peeled, seeded, and chopped, or 1 (14-ounce) can, with liquid

1 bay leaf

1½ pounds fresh pumpkin or winter squash, peeled, seeded, and cut into cubes

½ pound fresh or frozen lima beans

Kernels from 2 ears of fresh corn, or 1½ cups thawed frozen kernels

Freshly ground black pepper

2 tablespoons chopped fresh basil or flat-leaf parsley

drain the dried beans, combine with 2 quarts water in a large pot, and bring to a boil. Cover and simmer for 1 to 1½ hours, or until tender but intact. Add salt to taste and set aside 1½ cups of the beans.

advance preparation The recipe can be made through this step a day or two ahead of finishing.

Heat the oil over medium heat in a large, heavy soup pot or Dutch oven and add the onion. Cook, stirring, until the onion is tender, about 5 minutes, and add the paprika. Stir together for about a minute, and add the garlic. Cook, stirring, for a minute or two, until the garlic and onion are very fragrant but not brown, and stir in the tomatoes. Cook, stirring often, until the tomatoes are cooked down and fragrant, 5 to 10 minutes. Add the cooked beans, except for the 1½ cups you set aside, the bean broth, the bay leaf, pumpkin or winter squash, and lima beans. Bring to a boil, add a bit more salt, reduce the heat, and cover. Simmer for about 30 minutes, until the squash and beans are tender. Add the corn and simmer, uncovered, for about 5 minutes, until the corn is tender. Taste and adjust the salt, and add freshly ground pepper.

Blend the reserved 1½ cups of beans in a blender or food processor, or mash them in a mortar and pestle. Stir into the stew, along with the basil or parsley. Heat through. The mixture should be thick. Remove the bay leaf. Serve the stew hot, with corn bread or crusty French bread.

leftovers This will keep for at least 5 days in the refrigerator and is best eaten 2 days after making it. It freezes well. This stew is so good as is, just keep reheating it until it's gone.

tomato and bean ragout or gratin

I make this dish throughout the year, using fresh tomatoes in summer and canned in winter. White beans or borlottis are traditional, but I've made a marvelous rendition using pintos, which are not too different from borlottis. ❖ serves 6

1 pound (2 heaped cups) dried white beans, borlotti beans, or pinto beans, washed, picked over, and soaked in 2 quarts water for 6 hours or overnight

2 onions, 1 cut in half, both halves stuck with a whole clove, the other chopped

4 to 6 large garlic cloves (to taste), minced or pressed

Bouquet garni made with a few sprigs of thyme and flat-leaf parsley, 1 bay leaf, and a Parmesan rind

Salt

2 tablespoons olive oil

2 pounds fresh or canned tomatoes, peeled, seeded, and chopped

1 tablespoon tomato paste

⅛ teaspoon sugar

1 teaspoon fresh thyme leaves or ½ teaspoon dried thyme

Freshly ground black pepper

2 to 3 tablespoons slivered fresh basil or chopped fresh flat-leaf parsley

1½ to 2 ounces (⅓ to ½ cup) Gruyère or Parmesan cheese, grated (optional)

For a gratin: ½ cup fresh or dried bread crumbs

drain the soaked beans and combine with 2 quarts water in a large pot. Bring to a boil and skim off any foam, then add the halved onion, 2 of the garlic cloves, and the bouquet garni. Reduce the heat, cover, and simmer for 1 hour. Add salt to taste (2 teaspoons or more) and continue to simmer for another 30 to 60 minutes, until

advance preparation
The beans can be cooked a day or
two ahead through this step.

the beans are tender but not mushy. Remove from the heat, remove the bouquet garni and halved onion, and drain over a bowl. Measure out 2½ cups of the cooking liquid, taste, and adjust the salt. Set aside. (Refrigerate the rest of the cooking liquid if you are making this ahead; you may need it for thinning out the ragout.)

advance preparation
You can make the tomato sauce a day
or two before you cook the beans,
and vice versa.

advance preparation
The dish benefits from being made
1or 2 days ahead through this step.
Bring back to a simmer before
proceeding.

Heat 1 tablespoon of the oil over medium heat in a large, heavy soup pot or casserole and add the chopped onion. Cook, stirring, until tender, about 5 minutes. Stir in as much of the remaining garlic as you wish, stir together until fragrant, 30 seconds to a minute, and add the tomatoes, tomato paste, sugar, thyme, and salt to taste. Cook, stirring, for 10 to 15 minutes, until the tomatoes have cooked down somewhat and smell very fragrant. Stir in the beans and the 2½ cups of cooking liquid. Bring to a simmer, cover, and cook over low heat for 30 minutes, until the ragout is thick and fragrant. Stir often so that the mixture doesn't stick to the bottom of the pot. Add pepper, taste, and adjust the salt and garlic.

Stir in the basil or parsley and simmer for another minute. If serving as a ragout, drizzle on the remaining tablespoon of olive oil (hold the oil if serving as a gratin). Serve over thick garlic croutons, with cheese sprinkled over the top, if desired.

If serving as a gratin, heat the oven to 400°F. Oil a 3-quart gratin or baking dish. Spoon the ragout into the dish. Toss the bread crumbs with the remaining tablespoon of olive oil. Sprinkle in an even layer over the beans. Sprinkle on the cheese. Bake for 30 minutes, or until the top is browned and the gratin is bubbling. Serve hot or warm.

leftovers This will keep for 3 or 4 days in the refrigerator. You may need to thin it out with water or liquid from the beans if you're serving it as a ragout. You can serve the dish as a ragout the first night, and as a smaller gratin the second (reduce the amount of bread crumbs and cheese). You can also make pasta e fagioli (hearty pasta and bean stew) by adding cooked pasta—2 or 3 ounces per serving—to the leftovers.

italian beans with
pasta *(pasta e fagioli)*

This Italian classic is often listed as a soup on restaurant menus. It's really a thick stew, and one I've been making for many years. I tweak my recipe all the time, as this is a dish with many interpretations. But it always boils down to a gutsy, hearty, tomatoey mixture of pasta and beans. Skip the pancetta to make this vegetarian. ❖ **serves 4 generously**

½ pound dried white or borlotti beans, washed and picked over, soaked in 1 quart of water for 6 hours or overnight

1 tablespoon olive oil

1 medium or large onion, chopped

1 ounce pancetta, minced (optional)

Generous 1 teaspoon chopped fresh rosemary or ½ teaspoon crumbled dried rosemary

2 to 4 large garlic cloves (to taste), minced or pressed

1 (28-ounce) can tomatoes, with liquid, chopped

Salt and freshly ground black pepper

1 heaped tablespoon tomato paste

1 small dried hot red pepper, or ¼ to ½ teaspoon hot red pepper flakes

Bouquet garni made with 1 bay leaf, 1 Parmesan rind, and a few sprigs of thyme and flat-leaf parsley

½ pound uncooked macaroni, penne, or fusilli

2 to 3 tablespoons chopped fresh flat-leaf parsley

1 to 2 tablespoons chopped fresh basil (optional)

2 ounces Parmesan cheese, grated (½ cup)

advance preparation
This step can be done hours ahead and left to stand on top of the stove, covered.

drain the beans. Heat the oil over medium heat in a large, heavy casserole or Dutch oven and add the onion and pancetta. Cook, stirring, until just tender, about 5 minutes. Add the rosemary and garlic and stir together for another minute, until the garlic is fragrant.

Stir in the tomatoes, add some salt and pepper, and cook, partially covered, for 15 minutes, stirring often, until the tomatoes have cooked down and the mixture is very fragrant.

advance preparation You can make the dish through this step a day or two ahead. Refrigerate, then bring back to a simmer, stirring often, before continuing.

Add the beans, tomato paste, red pepper, bouquet garni, and 5 cups water. Bring to a boil, reduce the heat, cover, and simmer for 1 hour. Add salt to taste (1 to 2 teaspoons), cover, and simmer for another 30 minutes to an hour, until the beans are tender. Remove the bouquet garni.

About 10 to 15 minutes before serving, stir the pasta into the simmering beans. When it is cooked al dente, taste and adjust the seasonings, stir in the parsley and basil, and serve, passing the Parmesan in a bowl.

leftovers The dish will keep for about 4 days in the refrigerator, but the pasta will continue to soften and swell, reducing the amount of liquid in the stew. But that won't matter if you turn the dish into Macaroni and Beans and Cheese.

macaroni and beans and cheese

Heat the oven to 350°F. Oil a gratin or baking dish, the size of which will be determined by how much pasta e fagioli you have left over. Toss leftovers with ¼ to ½ cup freshly grated Parmesan cheese, or a mixture of Parmesan and Gruyère, and spoon into the dish. Sprinkle 2 tablespoons bread crumbs over the top, and drizzle on a tablespoon of olive oil. Bake for 25 to 35 minutes, until the top is browned and the mixture is sizzling.

catalan chick peas
with sausage

This combination of chick peas, tomatoes, peppers, lots of garlic, cured ham, and mild sausage makes a lusty dish that nobody forgets. Humble it may be, but I'd serve this to company any time. In Spain the sausage would be Catalan chorizo, but that isn't easy to come by here (it is not at all like Mexican chorizo), so I use mild Italian sausage for the dish. ❖ serves 4 to 6

1 pound dried chick peas, soaked in 2 quarts water for 6 hours or overnight and drained

1 bay leaf

Salt

¼ to ½ pound fresh mild Italian sausage, sliced or crumbled

1 tablespoon olive oil

1 medium onion, chopped

2 garlic cloves, minced

2 tablespoons diced cured ham, such as prosciutto

1 medium green bell pepper, cored, seeded, and chopped

1 pound fresh tomatoes, peeled, seeded, and chopped, or 1 (14-ounce) can, lightly drained

½ teaspoon dried thyme

Freshly ground black pepper

advance preparation
You can cook the chick peas up to 3 days before doing the next step. Keep in the refrigerator.

combine the chick peas with enough water to cover by 2 inches in a large soup pot or Dutch oven, add the bay leaf, and bring to a boil. Reduce the heat and skim off any foam. Cover and simmer for 1 hour. Add 2 teaspoons salt, or to taste, and simmer for another hour, or until tender. Drain over a bowl and retain 2 cups of the cooking liquid. Set aside.

advance preparation
You can make this right through to
the end a couple of days before you
wish to serve it. Time will only
improve it.

While the chick peas are cooking, heat a large, heavy casserole over medium heat and add the sausage. Cook, stirring, until the sausage has browned lightly and rendered its fat. Remove from the heat, remove the sausage from the pan, and pour off all but about 1 tablespoon of the fat. Add the olive oil to the casserole, heat for a moment, and add the onion. Cook, stirring, until it begins to soften, and add the garlic, sausage, ham, and green pepper. Cook, stirring often, until the onion and green pepper are tender, 5 to 10 minutes. Add the tomatoes, thyme, pepper, and salt to taste, cover, and cook over medium heat, stirring often, for 10 minutes, until the tomatoes have cooked down slightly. Add the chick peas and the reserved 2 cups of cooking liquid. Bring back to a simmer, stir together, turn the heat to very low, cover, and cook gently for 30 minutes to 1 hour, until the chick peas are very tender and the broth fantastically fragrant. Taste, adjust the seasonings, and serve.

leftovers The dish will keep for about 4 days in the refrigerator. With pasta, this becomes a scrumptious pasta e fagioli. It's also great with couscous.

tuscan white beans with sage and sausage

Fresh sage is the defining herb in this savory Italian bean and sausage dish. White beans tend to become mushy and fall apart if you cook them too quickly, so bring them to a boil slowly, and keep at a simmer. ❖ serves 6

1 pound dried cannellini beans or Great Northern beans, washed, picked over, and soaked for 6 hours or overnight

1 medium or large onion

1 whole clove

4 to 6 garlic cloves (to taste), minced or pressed

1 tablespoon chopped or slivered fresh sage (or more to taste)

1 bay leaf

Salt

½ pound mild Italian sausage, casings removed, sliced or crumbled

2 tablespoons olive oil

1 small carrot, peeled and finely chopped

1 celery stalk, finely chopped

2 tablespoons chopped fresh flat-leaf parsley

1 pound fresh or canned tomatoes, peeled and chopped, with juice

Freshly ground black pepper

drain the beans and combine with 2 quarts water in a large pot. Bring very slowly to a boil. Meanwhile, cut the onion in half and stick one half with the clove. Chop the other half and set aside. When the water reaches a boil, skim off any foam. Add the halved onion with the clove, 2 of the garlic cloves, half the sage, and the bay leaf. Turn the heat very low, cover, and simmer for 1 hour. Add salt to taste and

advance preparation
You can cook the beans 2 or 3 days before you wish to serve this. Keep in the refrigerator.

advance preparation
You can make this flavorful "sofrito" a day before finishing the dish. Keep in the refrigerator.

advance preparation
The tomato and sausage mixture can be made before you cook the beans and refrigerated for up to 2 days.

simmer for another 30 minutes, or until the beans are tender all the way through but still intact. Drain over a bowl and measure out 2½ cups of the broth (save the remaining broth for soups).

While the beans are cooking, heat a large, heavy flame-proof casserole over medium heat and add the sausage. Cook, stirring, until the sausage has browned lightly and rendered its fat. Remove from the heat, remove the sausage from the pan, and pour off the fat. Add the olive oil to the pan, heat for a moment, and add the chopped onion, carrot, celery, and parsley. Cook, stirring, until the vegetables are tender and fragrant, about 5 minutes, and add the remaining garlic. Stir together for 30 seconds to 1 minute, until the garlic is fragrant, and add the sausage, tomatoes, and the remaining sage. Season to taste with salt and cook over medium heat, stirring often, for 10 minutes, until the tomatoes have cooked down somewhat and smell fragrant. At this point, if the beans are not yet cooked through, turn off the heat and resume when the beans are ready.

Add the white beans and the reserved 2½ cups of their broth to the tomatoes. Bring back to a simmer, stir together, turn the heat to very low, cover, and cook gently for 30 minutes. Add pepper, taste, and adjust the seasonings. For the best flavor, refrigerate overnight and reheat. Add more fresh sage if desired.

leftovers This will keep for 3 or 4 days in the refrigerator and can be frozen for 3 months. Leftovers can be transformed into pasta e fagioli, if you have quite a bit left over, by stirring cooked pasta into the mixture. Or, if you don't have more than a cup or two, toss with a larger amount of pasta as a sauce. Alternatively, use as a topping for bruschetta, or make a gratin (see Tomato and Bean Ragout or Gratin, page 154).

variation
vegetarian version

Simply omit the sausage and follow the recipe as written. If you wish, add a Parmesan rind to the beans when you cook them (remove when done), and garnish with freshly grated Parmesan.

french lentils with
sausage and chard

This great lentil and greens combo is inspired by the classic preparation for the tasty French Le Puy lentils. Those little green lentils are usually served with salt pork and/or with sausage. For my dish I don't insist on Le Puy lentils (although I highly recommend them), and I dispense with the salt pork. I've also incorporated another food that goes well with lentils: greens. It makes a splendid meal. A salad would be nice, but it isn't required. ❖ serves 4

1 tablespoon olive oil

1 pound mild pork sausage, such as Italian sausage, cut in 2-inch pieces

4 ounces smoked bacon, trimmed of some of the fat and diced

1 onion, chopped

2 carrots, chopped

1 celery stalk, chopped

4 large garlic cloves, minced or pressed

1 pound dried lentils, preferably imported green lentils, washed and picked over

2 bay leaves

Salt and freshly ground black pepper

1 bunch of Swiss chard (¾ to 1 pound), stemmed, washed, and coarsely chopped

advance preparation
You can cook the lentils and sausage a few days before you wish to serve this. Keep in the refrigerator. Bring back to a simmer and proceed with the recipe.

heat the olive oil over medium-high heat in a heavy soup pot or Dutch oven and brown the sausage lightly on all sides. Transfer to a plate and pour off the fat from the pot. Add the bacon to the pot, turn the heat to medium, and cook, stirring, until it renders its fat and browns lightly. Add the onion and cook, stirring, until it begins to soften, 3 to 5 minutes. Add the carrots and

The dish keeps for about 5 days in the
refrigerator, but the color of the
chard will fade. If you want to make
it ahead for a dinner party, make it
up to the point of adding the chard,
then bring it back to a simmer and
add the chard shortly before serving.

celery and cook, stirring, until all the vegetables are tender, about 5 minutes. Add the garlic and continue to cook, stirring, until fragrant, 30 seconds to a minute, and add the lentils, 2 quarts water, and bay leaves. Bring to a boil, return the sausage to the pot, reduce the heat, and simmer for 40 minutes. Add salt and pepper to taste.

Stir the greens into the simmering lentils. Cook for another 10 minutes or so, until the lentils and greens are tender. The chard should be tender but still bright. Taste, adjust the seasonings, and serve.

leftovers Leftovers are great as they are. You could also toss the lentils and sausage with pasta, or use as a topping for bruschetta.

fava beans
and greens

This is based on a classic Southern Italian dish from Puglia, fava beans and chicory, which by many authoritative accounts is the region's signature dish. In Italy it would be eaten as a first course, light supper, or snack. But I think it makes a great one-dish meal—especially with the hefty quantities of greens I'm calling for. I find the sweet-tasting puréed beans to be a particularly comforting background for the bitter greens, which retain their crunch even after they're blanched and finished in the frying pan. Chicory, a long, dark green leaf that is similar in appearance, taste, and texture to dandelion greens, is not readily available here unless you know a gardener who's growing it. You can make just as fine a dish with chard or curly endive (frisée). You can find dried split fava beans in most markets that sell Middle Eastern products, as well as in some Mexican markets. The split beans require no soaking and fall apart conveniently as they cook. ❖ **serves 4**

1 pound dried, peeled, and split fava beans, rinsed

1 medium potato, peeled and diced

3 large garlic cloves, minced or pressed

Salt

1½ to 2 pounds Italian chicory, wild greens, Swiss chard, or curly endive

Freshly ground black pepper

¼ cup extra-virgin olive oil

Crusty bread, for serving

advance preparation
This step can be done a day or two ahead of serving. Refrigerate the beans in their broth.

combine the fava beans with 2 quarts water in a large soup pot and bring to a boil. Skim off any foam, then add the potato and 2 of the garlic cloves. Reduce the heat, cover, and simmer for 1 hour. Add salt to taste (about 2 teaspoons) and continue to simmer for another 30 minutes, or until the beans are falling apart. Drain over a bowl and set the broth aside.

advance preparation
The greens can be blanched up to a
few days ahead. They'll keep for 3 or
4 days in a bowl in the refrigerator.

While the beans are simmering, bring a large pot of water to a boil while you wash and stem the greens in several changes of water (for chicory, just break off the bottom of the stem). When the water comes to a rolling boil, add a tablespoon of salt and the greens. Cook for 2 minutes, or until tender, and transfer to a bowl of cold water. Drain and squeeze out most of the water. Chop coarsely and set aside.

Purée the beans and potato through the medium blade of a food mill or a potato ricer, or with the back of a large spoon in a bowl. Use some of the broth to moisten, and add broth as necessary to achieve a creamy consistency. Taste, adjust the salt, and add pepper. Keep warm in a low oven while you season the chicory.

Heat 1 tablespoon of the oil in a large, heavy nonstick skillet over medium heat. Add the remaining garlic and cook, stirring, until it begins to smell fragrant, 30 seconds to a minute. Stir in the greens, season to taste with salt and pepper, and remove from the heat.

Divide the favas among wide soup bowls and make a small depression in the middle. Spoon the greens into the depression. Drizzle on the remaining olive oil and serve, with crusty bread.

leftovers Both the favas and the greens will keep in the refrigerator for 3 to 5 days. I can't imagine you'll have leftovers, but if you do, serve the beans on bruschetta, topped with a small spoonful of greens if you wish. You can also toss the greens with hot pasta, olive oil, and Parmesan for a fabulous quick meal.

white bean and chard ragout

Like beans with sausage, beans with greens come in many, many configurations. I decided to make this recipe a vegetarian one, savory with tomatoes and garlic and Mediterranean herbs, particularly rosemary. ❖ **serves 6**

1 pound dried white beans, either Great Northern or cannellini, soaked in 2 quarts water for 6 hours or overnight

1 large onion, chopped

4 to 6 garlic cloves, to taste, minced or pressed

Bouquet garni made with 1 bay leaf, a few sprigs of flat-leaf parsley and thyme, and a Parmesan rind

Salt

2 tablespoons olive oil

1 teaspoon crumbled dried rosemary

1 teaspoon fresh thyme leaves, or ½ teaspoon dried thyme

1 (28-ounce) can tomatoes, with juice, chopped, or 1½ pounds fresh ripe tomatoes, peeled, seeded, and chopped

1 bunch of Swiss chard (¾ to 1 pound)

Freshly ground black pepper

Freshly grated Parmesan, for serving

drain the beans and combine with half the onion, half the garlic, 7 cups water, and the bouquet garni in a large soup pot or Dutch oven. Bring to a boil, skim off any foam, reduce the heat, cover, and simmer for 1 hour. Add salt to taste.

While the beans are simmering, heat the oil over medium heat in a large, heavy non-stick skillet and add the remaining onion. Cook, stirring, until tender, about 5 minutes, and stir in the remaining garlic, the rosemary, and the thyme. Cook for 30 seconds to a minute, until fragrant, and stir in the tomatoes. Add salt to taste and cook, stirring often, until the tomatoes have cooked down and the mixture is thick, beginning to stick to the pan, and delicious, 15 to 20 minutes. Stir into the beans.

advance preparation
You can make the recipe through this step 1 or 2 days ahead.

Simmer the beans and tomato mixture together for another 30 to 60 minutes, until the beans are tender and the broth very tasty.

advance preparation
The dish keeps well for 4 days, but for the best color you'd want to add the chard on the day you wish to serve.

Meanwhile, separate the chard leaves from the stems and wash both stems and leaves thoroughly. Slice the stems crosswise, about ¼ inch thick, and stir into the beans. Simmer for 10 minutes, or until tender. Stack the chard leaves and cut them crosswise into slivers. Shortly before serving, stir into the beans. Simmer 10 minutes, until tender but still bright. Add lots of fresh pepper, taste, adjust the salt, and serve, passing Parmesan to sprinkle on top.

leftovers You can make a delicious gratin with this. Turn into a lightly oiled baking dish, sprinkle the top with bread crumbs and Parmesan, and drizzle on a tablespoon or two of olive oil. Bake at 375°F. until the top browns, 20 to 30 minutes. You can also toss the leftovers with pasta.

soupy majorcan bread and vegetable stew

This is called a sopas in Majorca, a thick soup in which day-old bread soaks up much of the broth. The broth is so delicious, you might just want to eat the bread on the side. But with the bread this is definitely a one-dish meal. Add a poached egg to it if you want something even more substantial. ❖ **serves 4 generously**

3	tablespoons olive oil
1	bunch of scallions, white and light green parts, chopped
1	small onion, chopped
4	garlic cloves, minced, plus 1 additional clove, cut in half
1	green bell pepper, cored, seeded, and finely chopped
½	pound zucchini, scrubbed and chopped
2	tablespoons minced fresh flat-leaf parsley
½	pound tomatoes, skinned, seeded, and chopped
¾	pound cabbage, coarsely chopped
2	artichoke hearts, cut in sixths (optional; may use canned, in brine)
	Salt and freshly ground black pepper to taste
5	cups chicken stock (page 378)
½	pound green beans, trimmed and broken in half
12	slices country bread, stale or lightly toasted

advance preparation
The dish can be made through this step up to 3 days before serving, and kept in the refrigerator. The beans will lose color, but not flavor. The broth just gets better.

heat 2 tablespoons of the oil over medium heat in a large, flameproof casserole, and add the scallions and onion. When they begin to soften, after about 3 minutes, stir in the minced garlic, green pepper, zucchini, and parsley. Stir together for a minute or two, then cover and turn the heat to low. Cook for 15 minutes, stirring occasionally. Add the tomatoes, turn the heat to medium-high, and cook, stirring, for 5 minutes. Add the cabbage and artichoke hearts, salt, and pepper; cover, turn the heat to low, and cook slowly for 15 minutes.

Add the broth, bring to a boil, stir in the green beans, reduce the heat, cover, and simmer for 20 minutes. Taste and adjust the seasonings.

Heat the oven to 450°F. Rub both sides of the bread with the cut clove of garlic. Slide half the bread under the vegetables, ladling broth and vegetables over the slices so that they are submerged, and place the remaining bread on top. If you don't mind washing out another pot, you could place the first layer of bread in a large earthenware casserole, ladle in the soup, then top with the second layer of bread. Drizzle with the remaining tablespoon of olive oil, transfer to the oven, and bake for 10 minutes. Serve hot or warm.

leftovers : This keeps for 3 or 4 days in the refrigerator, but it's best if you remove any bread that is in the pot.

variation Five minutes before serving, carefully break 4 eggs into the soup. Cover and poach for 5 minutes, or until set, then serve.

spring vegetable ragout

For this heavenly, simple, pure vegetarian ragout I indulge my impulses to buy every beautiful spring vegetable in the farmers' market. And the dish does require the best—young, tender baby carrots and turnips, sweet sugar snap peas, bright fava beans, beautiful new potatoes, thin stalks of asparagus. The key to success is to simmer the carrots and turnips long enough with the cooked white beans for them to infuse their sweetness into the broth, but not so long that they lose their texture and become just like any other stewed vegetable. Twenty minutes is just about right, 30 at the most. The beans I use are Spanish giant kidney beans; I find them in most shops that sell imported foods. I like to serve this over couscous, but it's also good with wide noodles, a pasta like fusilli, or rice. ❖ serves 4 to 6

½ pound dried giant white beans, soaked for at least 6 hours in 1½ quarts water

1 medium onion, chopped

1 head of garlic, cut in half crosswise

Bouquet garni made with 1 bay leaf, a few sprigs of flat-leaf parsley and a few sprigs of thyme

Salt

2 tablespoons olive oil

2 medium leeks (½ to ¾ pound), white and light green parts only, cleaned and sliced

1 bunch of sweet spring onions (about ½ pound), bulbs only, chopped

2 garlic cloves, minced

¾ pound baby carrots, peeled and trimmed

1 pound baby turnips, peeled and halved or quartered

1 pound small new potatoes, scrubbed, cut in half if desired

1 pound fresh fava beans

¾ pound sugar snap peas, ends and strings removed

1   bunch (about ½ pound) tender young asparagus, trimmed

4   to 6 baby artichokes, trimmed, cut in half, chokes removed (optional)

    Freshly ground black pepper

2   to 3 tablespoons chopped fresh cilantro, plus a few sprigs, or 1 to 2 tablespoons chopped fresh tarragon

2   tablespoons chopped fresh chives (optional)

1   tablespoon unsalted butter

2   cups couscous, reconstituted and steamed (see page 335), for serving

advance preparation
This step can be done a day or two ahead. Refrigerate the beans in their broth, then continue with the next step.

drain the soaked beans and combine with 1½ quarts water in a large, heavy saucepan. Bring to a boil and skim off any foam, then add the onion, halved head of garlic, and bouquet garni. Cover, reduce the heat, and simmer for 1 hour. Add salt to taste and continue to simmer another hour or longer, until the beans are tender but still intact and the broth fragrant. Taste and adjust the seasoning. Discard the garlic and bouquet garni.

Drain the beans over a bowl. Measure out 4 cups of the broth.

Heat the olive oil in a large, heavy, flameproof casserole or Dutch oven over medium heat and add the leeks and chopped spring onions. Cook, stirring, until tender, about 5 minutes, then stir in the minced garlic. Cook, stirring, until the garlic smells fragrant, about 1 minute, then stir in the cooked beans and reserved broth, the carrots, turnips, and potatoes. Bring to a simmer, reduce the heat, cover, and simmer for 20 to 30 minutes, or until the vegetables are tender but not mushy.

advance preparation
These green vegetables can be blanched a day ahead and refrigerated.

Meanwhile, shell the favas while you bring a large pot of water to a boil. Drop the favas into the boiling water and boil for 1 minute, then immediately remove with a skimmer to a bowl of cold water and drain. Slip off the skins. Bring the water back to a boil, add a teaspoon or two of salt and add the sugar snap peas, the skinned favas, and asparagus. Boil for 2 to 4 minutes, until just tender, and transfer to a bowl of cold water. Drain and set aside.

Steam the artichokes until just tender, about 20 minutes. Remove from the heat.

Shortly before serving, stir the green vegetables and artichokes into the simmering ragout. Taste and adjust the salt, and add pepper to taste. Stir in the fresh herbs and the butter. Stir until the butter melts, then serve over couscous.

leftovers : The ragout keeps well for about 3 days, but because the green vegetables and herbs lose their vivid colors and fresh flavors, it's best to transform it into something else, like this wonderful cobbler.

leftovers variation
spring vegetable cobbler ❖ serves 4

3 to 4 cups leftover Spring Vegetable Ragout

Cobbler Topping (page 173)

Heat the oven to 375°F. Pour off the liquid from the ragout into a measuring cup. Butter a 2-quart baking or gratin dish and fill with the leftover vegetables. Stir a teaspoon of flour for each ¼ cup of liquid from the ragout into the liquid and mix well. Pour over the vegetables.

Press or roll out the cobbler topping to fit the baking dish; place over the vegetables. Alternatively, drop by spoonfuls over the top of the vegetable mixture. Brush the top with beaten egg, then bake until golden, about 30 minutes. Serve hot or warm.

Note: You can make a smaller cobbler, if you have a smaller quantity of leftovers. Use a smaller baking dish, and make the topping but only use what you need to cover the vegetables. Cut the remaining dough into circles or triangles and bake for 12 to 15 minutes at 375°F. for scrumptious scones.

cobbler topping

With this basic recipe—which you can use for biscuits and scones as well as cobblers—you can turn any stew or ragout into a cobbler. You'll find some recipes in the book that include slight variations on this topping.

1 cup whole wheat flour or whole wheat pastry flour

1 cup unbleached white flour

1 tablespoon baking powder

½ teaspoon baking soda

½ teaspoon salt

6 tablespoons cold unsalted butter

½ cup plain yogurt (nonfat is fine)

¼ to ½ cup milk

1 egg, beaten

heat the oven to 375°F. Mix together the flours, baking powder, baking soda, and salt, in either a bowl or a food processor fitted with the steel blade. Cut in the butter with forks, with your hands, or in the food processor. Stir together the yogurt and ¼ cup of the milk, and add to the flour mixture. If it seems dry add the remaining milk as needed. Gather gently into a ball, then press or roll out to fit the baking dish; alternatively, drop by spoonfuls over the top of the cobbler filling. Brush the top with beaten egg, then bake until golden, about 30 minutes.

For biscuits or scones: Roll or press out as instructed above, about ½ inch thick. Cut into triangles or rounds. Place on a lightly greased cookie sheet and bake for 12 to 15 minutes, or until the tops are just beginning to brown.

variation sage cobbler topping

Add 2 teaspoons chopped fresh sage to the dry ingredients.

wild mushroom ragout & cobbler

Mushrooms have been the vegetarian's meat stand-in for decades. They're hearty, savory, and, for a vegetable, well—meaty. This ragout has great depth of flavor and is terrific on its own, but it's put to brilliant use as the filling for a cobbler. Make the mushroom ragout a day or two before you bake the cobbler for the best results. And if you can't get oyster mushrooms, make the whole thing with button mushrooms, thickly sliced. ❖ **serves 6**

1 ounce dried porcini mushrooms (about 1 cup)

2 tablespoons olive oil

1 medium onion, chopped

4 garlic cloves, minced or pressed

1 pound button mushrooms, cleaned, trimmed, and sliced ½ inch thick

1 pound oyster mushrooms, trimmed and torn into pieces if very large

Salt

1 tablespoon all-purpose flour

1 tablespoon soy sauce

½ cup fruity red wine, such as a Côtes du Rhône

2 teaspoons chopped fresh rosemary or 1 teaspoon crumbled dried rosemary

2 teaspoons chopped fresh sage

Freshly ground black pepper

Cobbler Topping (page 173)

place the dried mushrooms in a heatproof bowl or measuring cup and pour on 2 cups boiling water. Let soak for 30 minutes while you prepare the other ingredients. Place a strainer over a bowl, line it with cheesecloth or paper towels, and drain the mushrooms. Squeeze the mushrooms over the strainer to extract all the flavorful juices. Then rinse the mushrooms, away from the bowl with the soaking liquid, until they are free of sand. Squeeze dry and set aside. If very large, chop coarsely. Reserve 1½ cups of the soaking liquid.

advance preparation The ragout can be made up to 3 or 4 days before you wish to serve it, either on its own or in the cobbler. Heat the olive oil in a large, heavy, nonstick skillet over medium heat and add the onion. Cook, stirring often, until tender, about 5 minutes. Add half the garlic, stir together for about 30 seconds, then add the button and oyster mushrooms and 1 teaspoon salt. Cook, stirring often, until the mushrooms begin to soften and to sweat, about 5 minutes. Add the flour and continue to cook the mushrooms, stirring, until they have softened a little more and you can no longer see the flour, about 2 minutes. Add the reconstituted dried mushrooms, the soy sauce, and the wine and turn the heat to high. Cook, stirring, until the liquid boils down and glazes the mushrooms, 5 to 10 minutes. Add the rosemary and sage, stir together, and stir in the mushroom soaking liquid. Bring to a simmer, add salt to taste, and cook over medium-high heat, stirring often, until the mushrooms are thoroughly tender and fragrant and the surrounding broth is thick and gravy-like, 10 to 15 minutes. Remove from the heat, stir in some freshly ground pepper, taste, and adjust the salt. Set aside, preferably in the refrigerator, overnight.

Oil or butter a 2-quart gratin or baking dish. Heat the oven to 375°F. Check the mushroom seasonings one more time and adjust if necessary. Transfer to the baking dish. Press or roll out the cobbler topping to fit the baking dish and cover the mushrooms; alternatively, drop by spoonfuls over the mushrooms. Slash in a few places with a sharp knife. Brush the top with beaten egg, then bake until golden, 30 to 40 minutes.

leftovers The ragout will be good for 5 days in the refrigerator and makes a great pasta or polenta topping. The cobbler will do fine as a leftover for a couple of days. Reheat in a low oven or microwave.

last of the summer vegetables stew
(or cobbler)

When I sense the end of my summer vegetable bounty approaching, I buy little else at the farmers' market. But there's never a shortage of meals that can be made out of corn, tomatoes, and squash. A cobbler topping turns this fragrant mixture into a beautiful and substantial main dish. ❖ serves 4 to 6

½ pound Romano beans or green beans, trimmed and broken into 2-inch lengths

2 tablespoons olive oil or butter

1 sweet or red onion, chopped

2 garlic cloves, minced or pressed

1 pound small tender zucchini, or mixed zucchini and yellow squash, scrubbed, trimmed, and sliced about ⅓ inch thick

Salt

1 pound plum tomatoes, peeled, seeded, and chopped

1 teaspoon fresh thyme leaves

Kernels from 2 ears of corn

¼ cup chopped mixed sweet fresh herbs, such as basil, flat-leaf parsley, tarragon, marjoram, chives

Freshly ground black pepper

Sage Cobbler Topping (page 173)

1 egg, beaten

advance preparation
The blanched beans will keep for 3 days in the refrigerator.

bring a large pot of salted water to a boil and add the beans. Blanch for 3 to 4 minutes, until crisp-tender, and transfer to a bowl of cold water. Drain and set aside.

advance preparation
The cooked vegetables will keep for
2 or 3 days in the refrigerator.

Heat the oil or butter in a large, heavy nonstick skillet over medium-low heat. Add the onion and cook, stirring, until tender, 5 to 8 minutes. Add the garlic, squash, and salt to taste; increase the heat to medium and cook, stirring, until the squash is bright and beginning to be translucent, about 4 minutes. Add 3 tablespoons water and continue to cook, stirring, until the water has evaporated and the squash is just tender but still bright. Stir in the tomatoes, raise the heat to medium-high, add the thyme and additional salt, and cook, stirring, until the tomatoes cook down and smell fragrant, about 5 to 10 minutes. Stir in the corn kernels and mixed herbs, add pepper and more salt to taste, and cook, stirring, for another 3 minutes, until the corn is just cooked through. Stir in the green beans. Taste and adjust the seasonings.

Heat the oven to 375°F. Butter a 2-quart gratin or baking dish, and turn the vegetables into the dish. Press or roll out the cobbler topping to fit the baking dish; place over the vegetables. Alternatively, drop by spoonfuls over the top of the vegetable mixture. Brush the top with the beaten egg, then bake until golden, about 30 minutes.

leftovers Although a cobbler doesn't improve with time, it will keep, and can certainly be enjoyed, for another 2 or 3 days. Reheat in a low oven or in the microwave.

turkish summer vegetable stew

This recipe is based on the summer vegetable stew in Ghillie Basan's Classic Turkish Cooking. The Turkish palate is unlike any other. While the vegetables in this dish are not unlike those in a Provençal ratatouille, the seasonings—coriander seeds, ground fenugreek, cinnamon, vinegar, sugar, parsley, mint, dill—are stunningly unique. Serve this over rice and sprinkle feta over the top, or top with thickened yogurt, for a sensational vegetarian meal. ❖ **serves 6**

Salt

1 large (1¼ pounds) eggplant, quartered lengthwise and thickly sliced

1 tablespoon tomato paste

1 tablespoon white wine vinegar or apple cider vinegar

1 teaspoon sugar

1 teaspoon ground cinnamon

1 teaspoon ground fenugreek

¼ cup *each* chopped fresh mint, flat-leaf parsley, and, if desired, dill

2 to 3 tablespoons olive oil, as needed

2 onions, sliced

5 large or 10 small garlic cloves, minced

1 tablespoon coriander seeds, crushed slightly in a mortar and pestle

2 red or green bell peppers (or 1 each), sliced

1½ pounds tomatoes, peeled, seeded, and sliced or coarsely chopped

3 bay leaves

¼ pound green beans, trimmed and cut in 2-inch lengths

3 artichoke hearts, quartered (may use canned; optional)

Freshly ground black pepper

Juice of ½ lemon

Rice or couscous, for serving

Feta cheese or Yogurt Cheese (page 387), for garnish

salt the eggplant and let it sit in a colander while you prepare the other
ingredients. Mix together 1 cup water, the tomato paste, vinegar, sugar, cinnamon,
fenugreek, and chopped herbs and set aside.

advance preparation
This benefits from being made a day
or two ahead.

Heat 2 tablespoons of the olive oil over medium heat in a
large, heavy nonstick lidded frying pan or casserole and
add the onions. Cook, stirring often, until tender, about
5 minutes. Add the garlic and coriander seeds and stir
together for another minute or two, until the garlic is fragrant. Rinse the eggplant,
shake or pat dry, and add to the pan along with the bell peppers and tomatoes. Stir
together well and add the herb and spice mixture, the bay leaves, and salt to taste
(about a teaspoon to start). Bring to a boil, reduce the heat to low, cover, and simmer
gently for 45 minutes, stirring from time to time. Add the green beans, artichoke
hearts, and freshly ground pepper to taste, cover, and simmer for another 30 minutes,
or until the vegetables are tender and fragrant.

Stir in the lemon juice and turn the heat to high. Boil for 5 minutes to concentrate the
flavors in the liquid. Taste and adjust the seasonings. Discard the bay leaves. Serve hot
or at room temperature, with rice or couscous. Garnish with feta cheese or thickened
yogurt.

leftovers This will keep for 5 days in the refrigerator. There are lots
of things you can do with the leftovers. See the suggestions following Two Methods for
One Ratatouille (page 146); anything that works for that will work for this stew.

variation

For a more substantial dish, toss in a can of chick peas, drained and rinsed, with the
lemon juice, and heat through with the mixture.

winter vegetable pot pie

For this generous pie I wanted to use mostly white and orange root vegetables and tubers. They're sweet and earthy, and they become even sweeter when they bake inside the pie. First the vegetables are parboiled in leek broth, and the resulting liquid is used for the sauce. Fresh thyme and parsley add character to this dish, which will make a winter vegetable eater out of any steak-and-potatoes person who wants a little comfort on his plate. As with other pot pies in this book, there are a few steps to accomplish here, but the recipe can be put together piecemeal. The first time I tested it there seemed to be many interruptions, so the resulting dish, which began on a Thursday, wasn't finished until Saturday. It was terrific. ❖ **serves 6 generously**

for the vegetables

3 medium leeks

Salt

¾ pound parsnips

4 medium carrots

3 turnips

½ pound Yukon gold potatoes, scrubbed

1 large sweet potato (about ¾ pound), peeled

6 ounces (1 small package) pearl onions, trimmed, peeled, and left whole

1 cup frozen peas, thawed

1 tablespoon fresh thyme leaves

Freshly ground black pepper

for the béchamel sauce

3 tablespoons unsalted butter

3 tablespoons all-purpose flour

1 cup hot milk

Salt and freshly ground black pepper

Pinch of freshly grated nutmeg

¼ cup chopped fresh flat-leaf parsley

❖

1 recipe Classic French Pastry (page 265), or the equivalent amount of frozen puff pastry, thawed

1 egg, beaten

cut the tops and dark green leaves off the leeks. Clean the dark green leaves and set aside. Cut the leeks in half lengthwise and run under cold water to rid them of sand, then slice thin.

Combine the dark leek greens with 4 quarts water in a large saucepan or pot and bring to a boil. Add 2 teaspoons of salt. Reduce the heat and simmer for 20 minutes. While the broth simmers, peel and dice the parsnips, carrots, and turnips. Cut the potatoes into ¾-inch dice.

advance preparation You can parboil the vegetables and hold them in a covered bowl in the refrigerator for 3 days.

Remove the greens from the water and discard. Bring back to a boil and drop in the pearl onions. Boil for 5 minutes and drop in the leeks, carrots, and turnips. Boil for 3 to 5 minutes, until just tender. Remove the vegetables from the water with a slotted spoon and transfer to a bowl. Bring back to a boil and add the potatoes. Boil for 5 to 8 minutes, until they can just be pierced with a knife or skewer but are still firm. Transfer with a slotted spoon to the bowl with the vegetables. Reserve 2 cups of the broth. Add the peas and the thyme to the bowl of vegetables. Season with salt and pepper.

advance preparation You can make the béchamel a day or two ahead, without adding the parsley, cover it well with plastic, and refrigerate. Whisk thoroughly over low heat before proceeding with the recipe.

Make the béchamel sauce. Melt the butter over medium-low heat in a large, heavy saucepan. Stir or whisk in the flour and continue to stir or whisk for 1 minute. The mixture should bubble but not brown. Whisk in the reserved 2 cups of vegetable broth. Whisk vigorously until the mixture is smooth, then whisk in the milk. Stir constantly over medium heat until the mixture comes to a simmer. Scrape the sides and bottom with a wooden spoon or spatula to make sure all of the roux is incorporated into the sauce, turn the heat to low, and simmer, stirring often, for 5 or 10 minutes. The sauce should be smooth and velvety, with no trace of a floury taste. It should be medium-thick, but not at all gummy. Add salt and pepper to taste and a small amount of nutmeg. Stir in the parsley. Remove from the heat. Stir into the vegetable mixture and combine well.

The pie can be assembled and held in the refrigerator for a few hours before baking. I have transported the baked pie to a party and taken no less pleasure in eating it hours later, after a 15-minute reheat in a 250°F. oven.

Heat the oven to 375°F. Butter or oil a 3-quart gratin or baking dish. Stir the filling, taste one more time to verify the seasonings, and turn into the baking dish. Roll out the dough to fit the dish, with some overlap, and cover the filling, tucking the edges deep down into the sides of the dish, or rolling it to make an attractive fluted edge around the sides of the dish. If you have extra dough, cut shapes with a cookie cutter and place on top. Make a few slashes in the crust, and brush with the beaten egg.

Place the pie on top of a baking sheet to catch drips and bake for 40 to 50 minutes, until the crust is golden and the sauce bubbly. Remove from the heat and allow to sit for at least 10 minutes before serving.

leftovers This doesn't really benefit from keeping, but it will taste good for a few days. Reheat in a low oven or in the microwave.

PROVENÇAL SOUPE AU PISTOU *(page 16)*

JAPANESE NOODLE MEAL
WITH SALMON AND SPINACH *(page 30)*

BEEF DAUBE *(page 55)*

ROAST CHICKEN WITH A TON OF VEGETABLES (*page 98*)

above: CHICKEN POT PIE *(page 116);*
right: CHICKEN BOUILLABAISSE WITH PASTIS *(page 100)*

PROVENÇAL ARTICHOKE RAGOUT WITH FRESH FAVA BEANS *(page 142)*

LAST OF THE SUMMER
VEGETABLES COBBLER *(page 176)*

RATATOUILLE CREPES *(page 150)*

above: STRATA WITH TOMATOES AND THYME *(page 223);*
left: TUSCAN WHITE BEANS WITH SAGE AND SAUSAGE *(page 160)*

BEET GREEN GRATIN
WITH GOLDEN BEET CRUST *(page 214)*

LASAGNE WITH GREENS AND
RICOTTA *(page 196)*

ZUCCHINI, POTATO, AND ARTICHOKE MOUSSAKA *(page 204)*

above: MACARONI AND CHEESE *(page 190);*
right: OPEN-FACED TUNA AND RED PEPPER SANDWICHES *(page 234)*

GREEK GREENS AND SWEET ONION PIE *(page 266)*

PROVENÇAL WINTER SQUASH TORTE

(made with pumkin as a galette)

(page 278)

YANGCHOW FRIED RICE *(page 314)*

HONEY-BAKED APPLES WITH CRÈME ANGLAISE *(page 369)*

veracruz-style black bean stew with greens

This spicy stew is based on a classic black bean and greens stew called xonequi, *or* sopa de xonequi, *from the highlands of the Mexican state of Veracruz.* Xonequi *is the word for a type of wild green that looks a little like lamb's quarters and tastes more like a cross between chard and something a bit stronger. Just about any green will work here—Swiss chard, turnip greens, spinach, or something stronger like collards or kale. My first choice would be Swiss chard. The traditional stew includes masa dumplings, but for those you need fresh masa or dried masa harina, which you may not be able to get. Crisp corn tortillas crumbled over the top make a fine alternative. For the best flavor, cook the beans a day ahead.* ❖ serves 6

1 pound (about 2½ cups) dried black beans, washed, picked over, and soaked for 6 hours or overnight in 2 quarts water (do not drain)

1 medium onion, chopped

5 large garlic cloves, 2 minced or pressed, 3 peeled

Salt

2 dried chipotle chilies, or 2 canned chipotles in *adobo* (or more to taste)

2 or 3 ancho chilies (about 1½ ounces)

2 tablespoons olive oil or canola oil

¾ pound Swiss chard, lamb's quarters, kale, or turnip greens, stemmed and sliced in ribbons about ½ inch wide (about 6 cups stemmed sliced greens)

½ cup chopped cilantro

6 corn tortillas, cut into strips and toasted (see page 391)

bring the beans to a boil in their soaking water in a large, heavy soup pot or Dutch oven. Skim off any foam, then add half of the chopped onion and the 2 minced garlic cloves. Cover and simmer for 1 hour. Add salt (about 2 teaspoons) and continue to simmer for another 30 minutes to an hour, until tender.

Meanwhile, stem and seed the chilies and open them out flat. Heat a griddle or heavy frying pan over medium heat and toast the chilies, pressing them on the hot griddle just for a few seconds, until they begin to blister and smell toasty. Turn over and repeat on the other side, then transfer to a bowl. Cover with hot water and rehydrate for 30 minutes, turning the chilies often. If using canned chipotles, seed, stem, and rinse them.

Drain the chilies and purée in a blender or food processor with the remaining onion and garlic and about ½ cup water, or as needed. Strain into a bowl through a medium strainer.

Heat the olive oil over medium-high heat in a heavy nonstick skillet and add a little of the purée. If it sizzles, add all of the purée and cook, stirring constantly, for about 5 minutes, until seared and thickened. Stir into the beans and simmer for 30 minutes, stirring from time to time to make sure the thickened broth doesn't stick to the bottom of the pan. Taste and adjust the salt.

Have the beans at a simmer. Taste and adjust the salt. The broth will be thick, but there should be enough of it so that you can cook the greens. If it seems too thick, add a little water. On the other hand, if it seems thin to you, purée a cup of the beans and stir back into the pot.

Stir the greens, a handful at a time, into the simmering beans. They will wilt into the beans after a few minutes, even if the stew is a thick one. Simmer for 5 to 10 minutes, until tender but still bright. Stir often. Stir in the cilantro and serve with toasted tortilla strips sprinkled over each bowl.

leftovers : Leftovers can be enjoyed for a few days and frozen for a few months. You could transform leftovers into delicious tacos, enchiladas, or enfrijoladas.

enfrijoladas

For enfrijoladas: Fill a 10-inch frying pan with about 1 inch of the stew and heat to a simmer. Dip a corn tortilla into the simmering stew to soften, then transfer to a lightly oiled baking dish. Spoon a little more of the stew over the tortilla, then fold in quarters. Fill as many tortillas as you wish, sprinkle with queso fresco, and serve hot. Or cover and heat through in a 325°F. oven for 15 minutes, then sprinkle with the cheese and serve.

five

gratins and casseroles

All of the dishes in this chapter are baked, and at one point in the language of American cookery would have been called "casseroles." They bake until their contents are bubbling, and usually until the surface and sides are deliciously brown. It's this brown surface, the part that sticks to the sides of the baking dish, that gives the gratin—which is what I call most of these dishes—its name. *Gratin* comes from the French word *gratter,* which means to scratch or scrape, and that's what you do to get those delicious browned bits off the sides and bottom of the baking dish.

You will find some of your favorite meals here: macaroni and cheese with several variations, lasagnes, baked beans, potato gratins. They probably won't be the versions you grew up eating; they're better, lightened a little, vibrant, and brimming with flavors. You'll never go back to stodgy casseroles after you experience these. Then there are entirely new dishes, recipes for all sorts of vegetable gratins that will allow you to impulse buy all you want at farmers' markets.

This chapter is a vegetarian's dream. With the exception of a handful of recipes, these are meatless meals.

Although the dishes are usually served the day they're baked, most of them can be assembled the day before. When recipes in this chapter are accompanied with the symbol, it means they can be assembled ahead, but not necessarily baked. The recipe will let you know. The important thing is that the work can be done. Those that cannot be assembled ahead, like the macaronis, the stratas, and some of the vegetable gratins, make great impromptu dishes.

macaroni
and cheese

We think of this classic as kids' food, and it is, but it can be adult food, too. The gloppy familiar version is made with (too much, in my opinion) Cheddar cheese. I use Gruyère and Parmesan, and plenty of it so that the macaroni is indeed cheesy, but it isn't gooey. ❖ **serves 4**

Salt

½ pound penne or elbow macaroni

2 cups milk (low-fat or 2-percent is fine)

3 tablespoons unsalted butter

2 tablespoons all-purpose flour

Freshly ground black pepper

Pinch of sweet paprika

¼ pound imported Gruyère cheese, grated (1 cup, tightly packed)

2 ounces freshly grated Parmesan (½ cup, tightly packed)

½ cup fresh bread crumbs

heat the oven to 350°F. Butter or oil a 2-quart baking or gratin dish. Bring a large pot of water to a boil, add a tablespoon of salt, and cook the pasta for a couple minutes less than the package directions recommend, so that the pasta is still hard in the middle. Drain, rinse with cold water, and transfer to a bowl.

advance preparation
The béchamel can be made a day or two ahead and kept in the refrigerator. Don't add the cheese to it until you're ready to assemble the macaroni. Reheat, whisking, and stir in the cheese.

While waiting for the water to come to a boil, make the béchamel. Bring the milk just to the simmering point in a saucepan or in a measuring cup in the microwave. Melt 2 tablespoons of the butter over medium-low heat in another heavy saucepan. Stir in the flour using a wooden spoon or a whisk and cook over low heat, stirring constantly, for 3 to 5 minutes. The mixture should not bubble but brown. Remove from the heat and whisk in the hot milk. Return to the heat and bring to a simmer, whisking constantly. Whisk over medium heat until the sauce thickens, about 5 minutes. Season to taste with salt, pepper, and paprika. Remove from the heat and stir in the cheeses, then toss with the pasta. Scrape into the baking dish.

advance preparation
The assembled macaroni can be made a day ahead and refrigerated, tightly covered. Bake when you wish to serve.

Melt the remaining tablespoon of butter and toss with the bread crumbs. Sprinkle in an even layer over the pasta. Place in the heated oven and bake for 25 to 30 minutes, until the top is lightly browned. Let sit for 5 or 10 minutes before serving.

leftovers
The dish is always at its best when it comes out of the oven, but leftovers will keep for 3 or 4 days. The noodles will get softer.

variation macaroni with gorgonzola and walnuts

There's a French phrase, *péché mignon,* that means "little sin" and refers to the indulgences you can never resist. This luxurious macaroni could easily become one of those for me. Make sure to serve this hot; the sauce will become too stodgy if it cools.

Follow the above recipe, deleting the paprika and substituting 6 ounces Gorgonzola dolce (cut into chunks) for the Gruyère and Parmesan. Add ½ cup of the freshest walnut pieces you can find, finely chopped, when you toss the pasta with the cheese sauce.

If you really want to go over the top, peel, core, and dice a large ripe pear. Toss with the pasta and sauce and bake as directed.

macaroni with tomato sauce and goat cheese

Although I think of this dish as a summer macaroni, to make when tomatoes are at their peak, the truth is, it's equally delicious when you use canned tomatoes. The goat cheese gives it the creaminess that a béchamel gives a standard macaroni and cheese. ❖ serves 4 to 6

Salt

½ pound penne or elbow macaroni

2 tablespoons olive oil

2 to 3 large garlic cloves, minced or pressed (to taste)

2 pounds tomatoes, quartered, or 1½ (28-ounce) cans tomatoes, drained of all but about ½ cup of the juice

⅛ teaspoon sugar

4 ounces soft, mild goat cheese, cut into chunks

½ cup freshly grated Parmesan

2 tablespoons slivered fresh basil leaves

Freshly ground black pepper

½ cup bread crumbs

heat the oven to 350°F. and oil a 2-quart baking or gratin dish with olive oil.

Bring a large pot of water to a boil, add a tablespoon of salt, and toss in the pasta. Cook for a couple of minutes less than the package directions recommend, so that the pasta is still hard in the middle. Drain and transfer to a large bowl.

advance preparation
You can make the tomato sauce up to 3 days ahead and keep it in the refrigerator, or freeze it for several months. Reheat and stir in the cheese just before tossing with the pasta.

While waiting for the water to boil, prepare the sauce. Heat 1 tablespoon of the oil over medium heat in a large, heavy nonstick skillet and add the garlic. When the garlic just begins to color, after 30 seconds to 1 minute, add the tomatoes and their liquid, the sugar, and ½ teaspoon salt. Cook, stirring often, for 20 to 25 minutes, until the tomatoes are cooked down and fragrant. Remove from the heat

advance preparation
The assembled macaroni will keep
for several hours outside of the
refrigerator, and it can be covered
and refrigerated for a day
before baking.

and pass through the mediumblade of a food mill. Stir in the goat cheese and Parmesan and combine well. Add the fresh basil and a few grinds of the pepper mill. Taste and adjust the salt. Toss with the pasta in the bowl, then scrape into the baking dish.

Toss the bread crumbs with the remaining tablespoon of olive oil and sprinkle over the top of the macaroni. Bake until the bread crumbs are lightly browned, about 30 minutes. Let stand for 5 to 10 minutes before serving.

leftovers The dish is always at its best when it comes out of the oven, but leftovers will keep for 3 or 4 days. The noodles will get softer.

baked macaroni with ragù

I can think of many good reasons for making the Ragù from Emilia-Romagna on page 62, and having it on hand for this dish is one of the best. ❖ serves 6 to 8

1   tablespoon salt

1   pound penne or other macaroni noodles

3   to 3½ cups Ragù from Emilia-Romagna (page 62)

3   ounces Parmesan cheese, grated (¾ cup)

1   tablespoon olive oil

advance preparation
The casserole can be assembled
several hours, or even a day or two,
before you bake it. Keep in the
refrigerator.

heat the oven to 350°F. Butter or oil a 3- or 4-quart baking or gratin dish. Bring a large pot of water to a boil and add the salt and the pasta. Cook the noodles for a couple of minutes less than the package instructions say, so that they're still a little hard in the middle. Drain and toss with the ragù and the Parmesan. Turn into the baking dish. Drizzle on the olive oil. Cover and bake for 25 minutes. Uncover and bake for another 10 minutes, until lightly browned on the top and bubbling.

leftovers This will keep for 3 or 4 days in the refrigerator. Just keep reheating it in a low oven or microwave.

mushroom lasagne

Lasagne is definitely comfort food, but how often do we make it? My lasagne-making life changed forever when I discovered no-boil lasagne noodles. Before, it was an event, because I always made the pasta. Even when you don't make the pasta, having to cook the noodles can mean the difference between not making lasagne regularly and making it. This particular lasagne tastes very rich, even though it really isn't. It combines a béchamel with my standard mushroom ragout and Parmesan cheese. It's a true crowd pleaser. ❖ **serves 6**

Wild Mushroom Ragout & Cobbler (see page 174)

for the béchamel

3 tablespoons unsalted butter

3 cups milk (may use low-fat milk)

3 tablespoons sifted all-purpose flour

Salt and freshly ground black pepper

Freshly grated nutmeg to taste

for the lasagne

4 ounces Parmesan cheese, grated (1 cup)

½ pound no-bake lasagne noodles

1 tablespoon unsalted butter (optional)

advance preparation
The mushroom ragout can be made up to 4 days before assembling and baking the lasagne.

advance preparation
The béchamel can be made a day ahead. Whisk well and reheat gently before assembling the lasagne.

gently heat the ragout, then make the béchamel. Heat the butter over medium-low heat in a heavy saucepan, and heat the milk in another saucepan or in the microwave. Add the flour to the butter and cook, stirring, for a couple of minutes, until smooth and bubbling. Off heat, whisk in the milk, then return to the stove and simmer, stirring, for 5 to 10 minutes, until the sauce has thickened and lost its raw flour taste. Season with salt, pepper, and a pinch of nutmeg. The béchamel isn't meant to be very thick.

advance preparation
The assembled lasagne can be tightly
covered and refrigerated for a day
before baking.

Assemble the lasagne. Heat the oven to 350°F. Oil or butter a 2-quart rectangular baking dish. Reserve about 6 tablespoons each of béchamel and cheese for the top layer of the lasagne. Spread a thin layer of béchamel over the bottom of the baking dish. Arrange a layer of lasagne noodles over the béchamel and spread a thin layer of béchamel over the noodles. Top with a thin layer of mushroom ragout and a sprinkling of cheese. Repeat the layers until all but one layer of pasta and the reserved béchamel and cheese are used. Add a last layer of pasta, cover the top with the reserved béchamel, and finally, sprinkle with the reserved cheese. Dot with butter if you wish. Cover the pasta with foil (if you have not buttered the top of the pasta, lightly oil or butter the dull side of the foil).

Bake for 30 minutes in the heated oven. Remove the foil and bake for another 10 to 15 minutes, until the top begins to brown and the sauce is bubbling. Serve hot or warm.

leftovers Leftovers will keep for 3 or 4 days. Reheat in a low oven or in a microwave.

lasagne with greens and ricotta

The gift of several pounds of greens—chard, kale, and Italian chicory—ignited a desire to make a greens lasagne, with ricotta and Pecorino cheese, béchamel, and Parmesan. The only even slightly-time consuming step in this recipe is washing the greens, a task I find rather relaxing. This makes a hefty 5- or 6-layer lasagne. ❖ **serves 6 to 8**

2   pounds mixed greens, such as chard, chicory, dandelion greens, kale, and broccoli raab, stemmed and washed well

Salt

2   tablespoons olive oil

3   garlic cloves, minced or pressed

Freshly ground black pepper

8   ounces ricotta cheese

1   recipe béchamel sauce (see page 383)

1   pound no-boil lasagne noodles

3   ounces Pecorino Romano, grated (¾ cup)

2   ounces Parmesan, grated (½ cup)

Butter or olive oil for the top of the lasagne

advance preparation
The greens can be blanched up to 3 days ahead of making the lasagne. Keep in the refrigerator in a covered bowl.

bring a large pot of water to a boil while you stem and rinse the greens in at least two rinses of water, making sure to remove all of the dirt and sand. When the water comes to a boil, add 1 tablespoon salt and the greens (you may have to do this in two batches). After the water returns to the boil, boil for 1 to 2 minutes, until the greens are just tender, then transfer them, using a skimmer or slotted spoon, to a bowl of cold water. Drain and squeeze dry. Chop coarsely.

advance preparation
The cooked seasoned greens can sit at room temperature for a few hours.

Heat the oil over medium heat in a large, heavy nonstick skillet. Add the garlic, cook for about 1 minute, just until it begins to color, and stir in the greens. Toss in the hot pan for about 1 minute, just until the greens are lightly coated with oil and fragrant with garlic. Season with salt and pepper and remove from the heat.

Heat the oven to 350°F. Generously butter or oil a 3-quart baking or gratin dish. Place the ricotta in a bowl, mash with the back of a large spoon, and stir in the greens. Combine well.

advance preparation
The lasagne can be assembled and
refrigerated for a day Spread about ⅓ cup of the béchamel sauce over the bottom of the baking dish and top with a layer of lasagne noodles. Top with a thin layer of béchamel. Dot the béchamel with spoonfuls of ricotta and greens, and spread evenly. Mix together the two grated cheeses and sprinkle a thin layer over the ricotta. Repeat the layers, reserving a layer of pasta, a layer of béchamel, and a layer of grated cheese for the top. End with the grated cheese. Dot with butter or drizzle on a bit of olive oil. Cover with an oiled or buttered sheet of aluminum foil.

Bake for 30 to 40 minutes, until the noodles have softened. Remove the foil and continue to bake for another 5 to 10 minutes, until the top begins to brown and the sauce is bubbling. Serve hot or warm.

leftovers This will keep for 3 days in the refrigerator but the greens will become less bright and vivid tasting.

quicker free-form lasagne with greens

variation

Once, when I had one hour total to prepare a dinner for friends, and had that same gift of greens with which I wanted to make lasagne, I simply prepared the greens as directed above, blanching them and cooking them with garlic, dispensed with the béchamel, went to the movies, came home with my five friends, cooked the lasagne noodles (they only took 3 or 4 minutes) in boiling water, and tossed together the noodles, a little of their cooking water to melt the ricotta, the ricotta, greens, and grated cheeses. This, followed by an arugula and red pepper salad (same gift of greens) and a bowl of chocolate sorbet, made a luxurious late-night dinner. The greens remain brighter than in the assembled and baked lasagne, and for this reason you might like the free-form lasagne even better.

eggplant parmigiana

This classic gratin is often heavy and oily, but it needn't be. I think of it as a summer dish, to make when eggplants and fresh tomatoes are at their height. However, since eggplants are available year-round in supermarkets and you can make a perfectly good tomato sauce with canned tomatoes, you could make it at any time of year. ❖ **serves 4 generously**

Salt

1½ to 2 pounds eggplant, sliced in rounds about ⅓ inch thick

¼ cup olive oil

2 to 3 large garlic cloves, minced or pressed (to taste)

3 pounds tomatoes, quartered, or 2 (28-ounce) cans tomatoes, drained of all but about ½ cup of the juice

⅛ teaspoon sugar

2 to 3 tablespoons slivered fresh basil leaves

Freshly ground black pepper

6 ounces mozzarella, sliced if fresh, grated if hard

½ cup freshly grated Parmesan cheese

¼ cup bread crumbs

salt the eggplant slices generously and let stand for about 30 minutes, while you make the tomato sauce.

advance preparation
The tomato sauce will keep in the refrigerator for 3 days and freezes well for a couple of months.

Heat 1 tablespoon of the oil over medium heat in a large, heavy nonstick skillet and add the garlic. When the garlic just begins to color, after about 30 seconds, add the tomatoes and their liquid, sugar, and ¾ teaspoon salt. Cook, stirring often, for 20 to 25 minutes, until the tomatoes are cooked down and fragrant. Remove from the heat and pass through the medium blade of a food mill. Stir in the fresh basil and add a few grinds of the pepper mill. Taste and adjust the seasonings.

Blot the eggplant slices dry and place on an oiled baking sheet. Heat the oven to 500°F. Brush both sides of the eggplant rounds with olive oil and bake in the oven until browned on the bottom and tender, 10 to 15 minutes. Remove from the heat.

advance preparation
The gratin can be assembled a day or
two ahead of time and baked just
before serving. It also reheats well,
if you need to bake it a few
hours ahead.

Reduce the oven temperature to 375°F. Oil a 2-quart gratin dish. Spoon a third of the tomato sauce over the bottom of the dish. Layer half the eggplant slices over the tomato sauce. Top with the mozzarella and spoon on another third of the tomato sauce. Sprinkle on half the Parmesan. Add the remaining eggplant in a layer, top with the remaining tomato sauce, and sprinkle on the remaining Parmesan. Sprinkle the bread crumbs over the top and drizzle on a tablespoon of olive oil. Bake for 30 minutes, until bubbling and browned on the top.

leftovers This keeps for 4 or 5 days in the refrigerator and can be frozen for a couple of months. If you want to do something new with the leftovers, you could fill an omelet with spoonfuls of the gratin. It will be quite marvelous, almost decadent. You could also make vegetarian hero sandwiches.

bohémienne gratinée

This is like a Provençal version of eggplant Parmesan, but the eggplant and tomatoes are cooked together until they meld into a confit. In Provence, anchovies season the mixture. I like the depth of flavor that they contribute, but I have omitted them for a truly delicious vegetarian mixture with pure summer vegetable flavors. ❖ serves 4

2	pounds (2 large or 3 medium) eggplant
	Salt
3	tablespoons olive oil
2	medium onions, thinly sliced
3	to 4 large garlic cloves, to taste, minced or pressed
3	pounds fresh or canned tomatoes, peeled, seeded, and chopped
⅛	teaspoon sugar
1	teaspoon fresh thyme leaves or ½ teaspoon dried thyme
	Freshly ground black pepper
2	tablespoons slivered fresh basil leaves
1	heaped tablespoon all-purpose flour
2	eggs, beaten
¾	cup freshly grated Parmesan
2	tablespoons bread crumbs

slice the eggplant about ⅓ inch thick and sprinkle the slices with a generous amount of salt. Let sit for 30 minutes while you prepare the remaining ingredients and heat the oven to 500°F.

Blot the eggplant slices dry, and cut them into dice. Toss with 1 tablespoon of the oil, and place in the heated oven in a baking pan or on a baking sheet. Bake for 10 to 15 minutes, tossing every 5 minutes, until just about soft and beginning to brown. Remove from the oven.

advance preparation
You can make the dish through this
step up to 3 days ahead.

Heat 1 tablespoon of the oil over medium heat in a large, heavy nonstick skillet and add the onions. Cook, stirring, until tender, about 5 minutes. Add the garlic and stir together for another minute, or until the garlic begins to color and smell fragrant. Stir in the tomatoes, eggplant, sugar, thyme, salt, and pepper. Turn the heat to low, cover, and cook, stirring from time to time, for 1 to 1½ hours, until the vegetables have cooked down to a thick, fragrant mixture. Taste and adjust the seasonings.

Oil a 2-quart gratin dish and heat the oven to 400°F. Stir the basil, flour, eggs, and ½ cup of the Parmesan into the eggplant mixture, then scrape into the gratin dish and top with the remaining grated Parmesan and the bread crumbs. Drizzle on the remaining 1 tablespoon olive oil. Bake for 20 to 30 minutes, until the top browns and the mixture is bubbling.

leftovers Like eggplant parmigiana, this keeps for 4 or 5 days in the refrigerator and can be used as a filling for omelets or sandwiches.

balkan-style moussaka

Immodestly, I will tell you this is the best moussaka I've ever eaten. First of all, the eggplant isn't fried, it's roasted, so it isn't saturated with oil. The meat filling—spiced with a little cinnamon, a pinch of allspice, a few cloves—has complex, sweet and savory Eastern Mediterranean flavors that you won't soon forget. Finally, the topping isn't a traditional Greek béchamel, which can be heavy. Instead, it's a light mixture of yogurt and eggs, a topping that is often used in Balkan versions of this dish. You can spread the preparation of this dish over a couple of days, or put it together on a leisurely afternoon and bake it right before dinner.

Greek cheeses can be found in Greek markets and delicatessens specializing in Mediterranean and Middle Eastern foods. ❖ serves 6

for the eggplant

2 to 2½ pounds (3 medium or 2 large) eggplant

Salt

Olive oil

for the meat and tomato filling

1 pound minced or ground lamb or beef (leaner is better)

2 tablespoons olive oil

2 medium onions, chopped

2 large garlic cloves, minced or pressed

1 pound tomatoes, peeled and chopped, with juice, or 1 (14-ounce) can, with juice

1 heaped tablespoon tomato paste

½ teaspoon sweet paprika

¼ rounded teaspoon ground cinnamon

3 whole cloves, ground in a mortar

Pinch of ground allspice (or 2 or 3 berries, ground in a mortar)

½ teaspoon sugar

1 bay leaf

½ to 1 cup hot water

Salt and freshly ground black pepper

1 egg, beaten

½ cup chopped fresh flat-leaf parsley

for the topping

4 eggs, beaten

1¼ cups plain yogurt

Salt and freshly ground black pepper

Pinch of sweet paprika

½ cup freshly grated Parmesan, Kefalotiri, or Kashkaval cheese

for the eggplant: Slice the eggplants lengthwise, about ⅓ inch thick. Salt the slices generously and place in a large bowl or colander for 30 minutes to an hour, the longer the better. Meanwhile, heat the oven to 450°F. and oil baking sheets with olive oil.

advance preparation The sauce can be made a couple of days ahead and kept in the refrigerator in a covered bowl. Bring back to room temperature, then stir in the beaten egg and parsley.

While you are waiting for the eggplant you can make the meat and tomato filling: Heat a large nonstick skillet over medium-high heat and crumble in the minced meat. Cook, stirring and breaking up the meat, until it has browned and rendered its fat, 5 to 10 minutes. Remove from the heat and pour off the fat. Set the meat aside.

Add a couple of tablespoons of water to the pan and scrape up any bits sticking to the pan with a wooden spoon. Add to the meat. Heat the olive oil in the pan over medium heat and add the onions. Cook, stirring, until tender, about 5 minutes, then add the garlic. Cook, stirring, until fragrant, about 1 minute, and stir in the tomatoes, tomato paste, the browned meat, paprika, cinnamon, cloves, allspice, sugar, bay leaf, salt to taste, and enough of the hot water to cover the meat. Bring to a simmer, reduce the heat to low, cover, and simmer for 45 minutes to an hour, stirring occasionally. The mixture should be thick and very fragrant. Cook, uncovered for another 5 to 10 minutes, until the liquid in the pan is just about gone. Remove the bay leaf, stir in pepper to taste, and remove from the heat. Taste and adjust the salt (remember that the eggplant will be salty). When the mixture has cooled slightly, stir in the beaten egg and the parsley.

advance preparation
Eggplant can be salted and roasted
earlier in the day.

Rinse the eggplant slices and pat dry with paper towels. Place on the oiled baking sheets and brush the tops with olive oil. Bake for 10 to 15 minutes, until lightly browned and cooked through. Transfer to a bowl. Turn the oven down to 350°F.

advance preparation
The assembled casserole, without the
egg and yogurt topping, will keep for
a couple of days in the refrigerator,
or it can be frozen (without the
topping). Bring back to room
temperature before proceeding
with the recipe.

Oil a 3-quart baking or gratin dish. Make an even layer of half the eggplant over the bottom, and spread on all of the meat sauce in one layer. Top with a layer of the remaining eggplant. Place the moussaka in the 350°F. oven and bake for 30 minutes.

For the topping: Beat together the eggs and yogurt, season with salt (about ½ teaspoon), pepper, and paprika, and pour over the eggplant. Sprinkle the grated cheese evenly over the top. Return to the oven and bake for another 25 to 30 minutes, until golden. Serve warm.

leftovers The dish will be good for 3 or 4 days. Reheat in a low oven or a microwave.

zucchini, potato, and artichoke moussaka

Because there are many fasting days in the Greek Orthodox calendar, when no meat may be eaten, a number of wonderful vegetarian dishes have evolved throughout Greece and the Balkans. The egg and yogurt topping and the tomato sauce are the same as those used in the traditional recipe for Balkan-style Moussaka on page 202. Only the meat is missing, and layers of potato and zucchini slices stand in for eggplant. ❖ serves 6

3 tablespoons olive oil, plus more for oiling the baking sheets

1¾ pounds zucchini

1½ pounds potatoes, such as Yukon golds

Salt

2 medium onions, chopped

2 large garlic cloves, minced or pressed

2 pounds tomatoes, peeled and chopped, or
1 (28-ounce) can tomatoes, with juice

1 heaped tablespoon tomato paste

½ teaspoon sweet paprika

¼ rounded teaspoon ground cinnamon

3 whole cloves, ground in a mortar

Pinch of ground allspice (or 2 or 3 berries,
ground in a mortar)

½ teaspoon sugar

1 bay leaf

Freshly ground black pepper

½ cup chopped fresh flat-leaf parsley

1 jar of artichoke hearts packed in water, drained,
rinsed and sliced

4 eggs, beaten

1¼ cups plain yogurt

Pinch of paprika

½ cup freshly grated Parmesan, Kefalotiri,
or Kashkaval cheese

heat the oven to 425°F. Oil baking sheets with olive oil. Slice the zucchini in lengthwise slices, about ⅓ inch thick. Slice the potatoes lengthwise in oval slices about ¼ inch thick. Place the potatoes on the baking sheets, salt lightly, and bake for about 15 minutes, until they are just beginning to brown and can be easily pierced with a knife.

Heat 1 tablespoon of the olive oil over medium-high heat in a large nonstick skillet and add the zucchini in a single layer (you will have to do this in batches). Cook for about 3 minutes, until lightly browned, flip over, and cook for another 3 minutes, until lightly browned. Transfer to a bowl or baking sheet lined with paper towels.

advance preparation
The tomato sauce will keep for 4 days in the refrigerator.

advance preparation
You can bake the potato slices and/or brown the zucchini slices any time during the day. You can prep everything for the sauce while you're roasting the potatoes and browning the zucchini.

advance preparation
The moussaka can be assembled a day or two before baking and refrigerated (without the egg and yogurt topping). It can also be frozen. Bring to room temperature before proceeding.

Heat the remaining 2 tablespoons olive oil in the pan over medium heat and add the onions. Cook, stirring, until tender, about 5 minutes, and add the garlic. Cook, stirring, until fragrant, about a minute, then stir in the tomatoes, tomato paste, paprika, cinnamon, cloves, allspice, sugar, bay leaf, and salt to taste. Bring to a simmer, reduce the heat to low, cover, and simmer for 30 to 45 minutes, stirring occasionally. The mixture should be thick and very fragrant. Remove the bay leaf, stir in pepper to taste, and remove from the heat. Taste and adjust the salt. Remove from the heat and set aside. When the mixture has cooled slightly, stir in the parsley.

Heat the oven to 350°F. Oil a 3-quart baking or gratin dish. Make an even layer of half the potatoes over the bottom. Top with half the zucchini. Pour on the tomato sauce and spread in an even layer. Top with the artichoke hearts in a layer, then the remaining zucchini, and finally, the remaining potatoes.

Place the moussaka in the 350°F. oven and bake for 30 minutes. Beat together the eggs and yogurt, season with ½ teaspoon salt, pepper to taste, and the paprika, and pour over the moussaka. Sprinkle the grated cheese evenly over the top. Return to the oven and bake for another 25 to 30 minutes, until golden. Serve warm.

leftovers The dish will be good for 3 or 4 days. Reheat in a low oven or a microwave.

polenta and ragù gratin

It's worth making a ragù for this sensual dish. The textures of the creamy polenta and meaty ragù, and their savory and bland flavors, play against each other beautifully. ❖ **serves 4**

1 cup polenta

1¼ teaspoons salt

1 tablespoon unsalted butter

2 cups Ragù from Emilia-Romagna (page 62)

⅓ cup freshly grated Parmesan or Gruyère

advance preparation Ragù will keep for 5 days in the refrigerator and freezes well for 3 months. The polenta can be made a day or two ahead.

heat the oven to 350°F. Combine the polenta, 4 cups water, salt, and butter in a 2 quart baking dish. Stir together well so that the salt is evenly distributed, and place in the oven. Bake for 1 hour. Remove from the oven, stir with a fork, and return to the oven for 10 more minutes. Remove from the oven. Pour the ragù over the polenta, and top with the cheese. Turn the oven up to 375°F. and return the gratin to the oven. Bake for 20 minutes, or until the ragù is bubbling and the cheese is just beginning to brown. Cut into squares and serve.

variation If you make the polenta ahead, allow it to cool, then cut it into squares and remove from the baking dish. Oil the dish and return the polenta to it, with the squares slightly overlapping if you wish. Top with the ragù and cheese and bake as above.

leftovers Leftovers will keep for 3 or 4 days in the refrigerator. Reheat in a low oven or in a microwave.

potato and mushroom gratin

I've always had a weakness for potatoes and mushrooms in the same dish, and here they simmer together in the most savory of gratins. The potatoes become infused with that earthy mushroom flavor, all the more so if you use wild mushrooms, but with the dried porcini, even regular white mushrooms will produce a memorable dish. The robust flavors of this gratin make it taste and seem richer than it is. ❖ **serves 6**

1 ounce dried wild mushrooms, preferably porcini (about 1 cup)

1 pound fresh mushrooms, preferably wild, such as oyster mushrooms, shiitakes, or morels, cleaned, stems trimmed (remove stem if using shiitakes), and thinly sliced

Salt

2 tablespoons olive oil

3 large garlic cloves, minced or pressed

2 teaspoons fresh thyme or 1 teaspoon dried thyme

2 teaspoons chopped fresh sage (optional)

¼ cup dry white or red wine

Freshly ground black pepper

2½ pounds russet or Yukon gold potatoes, peeled and thinly sliced

2 ounces Gruyère cheese, grated (½ cup)

1 ounce Parmesan cheese, grated (¼ cup)

2 cups milk

advance preparation
This step can be done several hours, even a day or two ahead, of assembling the gratin. Keep the mushrooms and soaking liquid in the refrigerator if you are holding them for more than several hours.

place the dried mushrooms in a heatproof bowl or measuring cup and pour on 2 cups boiling water. Let sit for 30 minutes. Drain through a cheesecloth-lined strainer over a bowl and squeeze the mushrooms over the strainer. Rinse the mushrooms thoroughly to remove the grit, squeeze dry, and chop coarsely. Reserve 1 cup of the soaking liquid.

advance preparation
The mushrooms can be cooked several hours or even a day or two ahead. Refrigerate if holding for more than a couple of hours.

Meanwhile, heat a large nonstick skillet over medium-high heat and add the fresh mushrooms. Sprinkle them with salt and cook, stirring, until they begin to release liquid, in about 3 to 5 minutes. Cook in their own juices, stirring often, for 5 minutes, until just about tender.

Turn the heat to high to cook off the liquid in the pan, then turn it back down to medium and add the olive oil, garlic, the soaked dried mushrooms, thyme, and sage. Continue to cook for another minute or two, until the mixture is fragrant. Add the wine and cook until the liquid in the pan has evaporated. Remove from the heat. Season with additional salt if desired, and pepper.

advance preparation
You can assemble this a few hours before baking. The gratin can be baked ahead a couple of hours and reheated, either for 30 to 40 minutes in a low (warm or 250°F.) oven, or for 20 minutes at 350°F.

Heat the oven to 350°F. Cover the rack below the one you are baking on with aluminum foil. Butter a 3-quart baking or gratin dish, or rub with olive oil. Toss the sliced potatoes and mushrooms together in a large bowl. Season with salt and pepper. Add half of the cheeses and toss together. Transfer to the baking dish. Mix together the mushroom soaking liquid and the milk. Season with 1 teaspoon salt (more or less to taste) and grind in some pepper. Pour over the potatoes. Place in the oven and bake for 1 hour. Sprinkle the remaining cheese over the top and bake for another 30 to 45 minutes, until the top is nicely browned. Remove from the oven and let sit for 10 minutes before serving.

leftovers The gratin is terrific reheated the next day; it will keep in the refrigerator for 3 or 4 days. If you have a small amount left over and want to stretch it into another meal, stir the leftover gratin into beaten eggs and make a delicious frittata (see page 392).

summer potato gratin with tomatoes, peppers, and sausage

This gratin is pure Provence. The tomatoes shed their juice as they bake; some of the juice, now infused with garlic, peppers, sausage, and herbs, is absorbed by the potatoes, and enough is left in the baking dish to spoon over the finished gratin and sop up with bread. For a luscious vegetarian dish, omit the sausage and replace the chicken stock with vegetable stock. ❖ **serves 6 to 8**

4 large garlic cloves, minced or pressed, plus 1 clove, cut in half

3 tablespoons olive oil, plus more for brushing the gratin dish

2 medium onions, thinly sliced

3 tablespoons chopped fresh herbs, such as flat-leaf parsley, thyme, sage, rosemary

Salt and freshly ground black pepper

½ pound mild Italian sausage

2 pounds fresh ripe tomatoes, sliced

1 pound red bell peppers, quartered, seeded, and sliced crosswise in thin strips

1 teaspoon dried oregano

½ teaspoon sugar

2 pounds Yukon gold potatoes, peeled and thinly sliced

1 cup chicken stock (page 378)

2 bay leaves

½ cup grated Gruyère cheese

heat the oven to 350°F. Rub a 3-quart gratin or baking dish with the cut clove of garlic, then brush with olive oil.

advance preparation
This step can be done hours before
assembling the gratin. Hold it in the
pan on the stove, or if keeping for
more than a couple of hours,
refrigerate.

Heat 2 tablespoons of the olive oil over medium heat in a large skillet and add the onions. Cook, stirring, until tender, 5 to 10 minutes. Add 2 of the minced garlic cloves, 1 tablespoon of the fresh herbs, salt, and pepper and cook, stirring, until the garlic is fragrant, 30 seconds to a minute. Crumble in the sausage and cook, stirring and breaking up the sausage, until the sausage is sizzling and no longer pink. Remove from the heat. Taste and adjust the seasonings.

Toss together the tomatoes, peppers, the remaining garlic, the oregano, sugar, and a tablespoon of the herbs in a large bowl. Season generously with salt and pepper. Toss the sliced potatoes with the third tablespoon of herbs and season with salt and pepper.

advance preparation
The gratin can be assembled a few
hours before baking. Hold at room
temperature or in the refrigerator.

advance preparation
The gratin can be baked a few hours
ahead of serving, up to the adding of
the cheese. Reheat for 20 to 30 minutes at 350°F., adding the cheese at
this time.

Layer half the tomato mixture in the gratin dish. Layer half the potatoes over the tomatoes and sprinkle with salt and pepper. Top the potatoes with all of the onion and sausage mixture, then add another layer of potatoes, again seasoning with salt and pepper, and top with the remaining tomato and pepper mixture (so the layers go: tomatoes and peppers, potatoes, onions and sausage, potatoes, tomatoes and peppers). Pour in the stock and insert the bay leaves into the gratin. Drizzle on the remaining tablespoon of olive oil.

Bake for 1½ to 2 hours, until the potatoes are tender and the top is beginning to brown. From time to time press down on the top layer with a large spoon and baste the gratin with the juices. Sprinkle the cheese over the top of the gratin during the last 20 minutes of baking. Remove from the heat, discard the bay leaves, and let the gratin sit for 10 minutes before serving.

leftovers This gratin ripens and improves overnight. Reheat it at 350°F. for 20 minutes, or for 30 minutes or longer in a low oven (warm or 250°F.). It will keep for about 3 days. There will be a lot of juice in the pan, which you should spoon over the leftover gratin. Leftovers can be beaten into eggs for a frittata, or eaten warm with scrambled eggs for a wonderful hearty breakfast or brunch.

spinach and fish gratin

This dish, loosely based on the Provençal salt cod and spinach gratin called tian de morue aux épinards, *is about as comforting as they come: mild fish fillets baked under a blanket of spinach-laced béchamel. It's a dinner to make when you've found irresistible bunches of sturdy fresh spinach in the farmers' market; if you can't find excellent spinach, make the dish with Swiss chard. As for the fish, I made my most recent version with halibut, which I loved. But cod or snapper will also do just fine. You have to mess up more than one pot to put this dish together, but the cooking can be done and the gratin assembled long before dinner.*

Though the sauce here is quite thick, when the fish underneath it bakes, it will release quite a bit of liquid, which will dilute the sauce, deliciously. As an accompaniment to this gratin, there's nothing better than steamed new potatoes; a white creamer is particularly good. ❖ **serves 4**

1½ pounds fresh spinach or chard, stemmed and washed thoroughly

Salt

2 tablespoons olive oil, plus more for oiling the gratin dish

1 large or 2 medium garlic cloves, minced or pressed

Freshly ground black pepper

1 recipe Olive Oil Béchamel, using 3 tablespoons flour (page 383)

1 to 1½ pounds white fish fillets, such as halibut, snapper, or cod, pin bones removed

⅓ cup fresh or dry bread crumbs

advance preparation
Spinach and greens can be cleaned and blanched as soon as you get home from the market. Squeeze out water, place in a bowl (you can also chop it), cover with plastic, and refrigerate for up to 3 days.

bring a large pot of water to a boil over high heat while you wash and stem the spinach, using at least two changes of water to make sure all the sand and grit have been washed away. Add 1 tablespoon salt to the boiling water, and add the spinach. Cook just until the spinach is wilted, less than a minute (chard will take 1 to 2 minutes). Remove from the water with a slotted spoon or skimmer and transfer immediately to a bowl of cold water. Drain, squeeze dry, and chop.

Heat 1 tablespoon of the olive oil over medium heat in a large, heavy nonstick skillet and add the garlic. When it just begins to color and smell fragrant, in 30 seconds to a minute, stir in the spinach. Mix together to coat the spinach with the oil and garlic, season with salt and pepper, and remove from the heat. Set aside.

Make the béchamel if you haven't already, and stir in the chopped spinach or greens. Taste and adjust the seasonings.

Heat the oven to 425°F. Oil a 2-quart gratin or baking dish with olive oil. If your fish fillets are an inch or more thick, as halibut tends to be, cut them in half crosswise so they'll be thinner and cover the surface of the baking dish in one layer. Spoon about ⅓ cup of the sauce into the bottom of the baking dish and spread evenly. Make a layer of fish fillets and season them with salt and pepper. Cover with foil and place in the oven for 5 minutes, until the fish is just becoming opaque on the surface. Remove from the oven, uncover, and top the fish with the remaining sauce. Sprinkle the bread crumbs over the top and drizzle on the final tablespoon of oil.

Bake for 20 to 25 minutes, until the top is browned and the gratin is bubbling. Remove from the heat, check that the fish is cooked through (if it is not, return to the oven for 5 to 10 minutes), and serve hot.

leftovers Although this reheats nicely on the second day, it's a dish that does not get better with time.

beet green gratin with golden beet crust

Golden beets are particularly sweet, and their greens are sturdy and tangy. This gratin is packed with the greens; enriched with egg, cheese, and milk; and encrusted, top and bottom, in a beautiful golden layer of sliced beets. It's a gorgeous display of contrasting colors and rich flavors. If you roast your beets and blanch the greens when you get them home from the market, the gratin is quickly assembled.

Cook's note: You can often get beet greens for free at farmers' markets. Many shoppers ask the farmers to cut off the greens, and there is often a big box of them at the stalls that offer beets. If you don't want to buy extra beets to get the extra greens called for in this recipe, ask the vendors if they have them, or watch for them cutting off the bunches. ❖ serves 4

2 bunches (6 to 8) golden beets

2 pounds golden beet greens (from about 4 large bunches), stemmed and washed

   Salt

4 eggs, beaten

   Freshly ground black pepper

¾ cup milk

1 large garlic clove, minced or pressed

2 ounces Gruyère cheese, grated (½ cup)

1 ounce Parmesan cheese, grated (¼ cup)

1 tablespoon olive oil, plus more for oiling the gratin dish

advance preparation
Roasted beets will keep for about 5 days in the refrigerator in a covered bowl.

heat the oven to 425°F. Cut the greens off of the beets, leaving about ½ inch of the stems attached. Scrub the beets and place in a baking dish or ovenproof casserole. Add about ¼ inch water to the pot. Cover tightly with a lid or foil, and bake for 35 to 40 minutes, until the beets are tender. Remove from the heat and allow to cool. If not using right away, refrigerate in a covered bowl.

Bring a large pot of water to a boil while you stem and wash the greens. Add a tablespoon of salt to the water, and blanch the greens for a minute or two (you will probably need to do this in two batches). Transfer the greens to a bowl of cold water, then drain and squeeze out the water. Chop coarsely.

Heat the oven to 375°F. Oil a 2-quart gratin dish generously with olive oil. Slip the skins off the beets, and slice very thin across the equator. Line the bottom and sides of the gratin dish with sliced beets. Beat together the eggs, ¾ teaspoon salt, pepper to taste, the milk, garlic, and all but 2 tablespoons of the cheeses. Stir in the greens and turn into the gratin dish. Cover the top of the gratin with the remaining beet slices, overlapping them slightly. Sprinkle the remaining 2 tablespoons of cheese over the beets, and drizzle on the olive oil. Bake for 35 to 40 minutes, until set and lightly browned on the top. Allow to sit for 10 to 15 minutes before serving. Serve hot or warm.

The leftovers will keep for 3 or 4 days in the refrigerator and they're great hot or cold.

variation beet and beet green tart

You can put the same combination into a tart crust, single or double. Use any of the crusts on pages 263–265. Brush the inside of the crust with egg if using a single crust, and prebake for 7 minutes at 375°F. If covering with a double crust, or making a galette, brush the outside of the crust with beaten egg. Bake, following the directions for baking the gratin, above.

spring onion and greens tart or gratin

Packed to the brim with greens that are sweetened and complemented by gently cooked spring onions, this is something to make when you've bought bunches of beets and turnips with their tops on, or irresistibly generous bunches of Swiss chard, at the farmers' market. ❖ **serves 6**

2½ to 3 pounds greens (3 or 4 bunches), such as Swiss chard, beet greens, turnip greens, or chicory, stemmed and washed thoroughly

Salt

2 tablespoons olive oil

2 pounds spring onions, bulbs and light green parts only, chopped (2½ cups)

2 garlic cloves, minced or pressed

Freshly ground black pepper

3 large eggs, beaten

½ cup milk

2 ounces Gruyère cheese, grated (½ cup)

1 ounce Parmesan cheese, grated (¼ cup)

Pie crust of your choice (pages 263–265, or use a prepared crust; optional), prebaked

advance preparation
The greens can be blanched and chopped up to 3 days ahead and kept in a covered bowl in the refrigerator.

bring a large pot of water to a boil while you prepare the greens. When the water reaches a rolling boil, add a tablespoon of salt and the greens. Blanch for 2 minutes, or until just tender, and transfer to a bowl of cold water. Drain and squeeze out the water. Chop coarsely and set aside.

advance preparation
This step can be completed several
hours before you assemble the gratin
or tart, and the vegetables can be
held at room temperature.

Heat the oven to 375°F. Butter a 2-quart gratin dish or a
9½- or 10-inch tart pan. Heat the olive oil over medium
heat in a large, heavy nonstick frying pan and add the
spring onions. Cook, stirring often, until tender and fragrant, 5 to 8 minutes. Stir in the garlic and cook for
another minute or so, just until fragrant. Add the
chopped greens and stir together. Remove from the heat and set aside. Season with salt
and pepper.

Beat the eggs in a medium bowl. Beat in the milk and ½ teaspoon salt, and stir in the
greens and onions. Add plenty of freshly ground pepper, and stir in the cheeses. If making a tart, prebake the crust as directed, and pour in the filling. If making a gratin,
scrape into the gratin dish. Bake for 30 to 40 minutes, until firm and beginning to
brown on top. Remove from the heat and serve hot, warm, or at room temperature.

leftovers This keeps well for 3 to 5 days in the refrigerator, and it
can be frozen for a month. It's at its best the day you make it, or the day after, but left
overs make a nice lunch, and an even nicer lunchbox item, cut into squares.

pepper and tomato gratin with sausage

This bright summery gratin yields lots of savory juice as it bakes—how could it not, with all the fresh tomatoes and the sausage?—so make sure you have plenty of rice, couscous, bulgur, and/or crusty country bread to serve with it. ❖ serves 4 to 6

2 tablespoons olive oil

3 onions, chopped

4 large garlic cloves, minced or pressed

2 tablespoons minced fresh flat-leaf parsley

   Salt and freshly ground black pepper

¾ pound mild Italian sausage, chopped or crumbled

2½ pounds tomatoes, peeled and coarsely chopped

6 large red bell peppers, quartered lengthwise, seeds and membranes removed, then thinly sliced crosswise

2 tablespoons slivered fresh basil

3 ounces grated Gruyère cheese (¾ cup)

advance preparation
The onion and sausage filling can be made a day ahead and refrigerated.

heat the oven to 350°F. Oil a 3-quart gratin dish. Heat the oil over medium heat in a large skillet and add the onions. Cook, stirring, until tender, 5 to 10 minutes. Add 3 of the garlic cloves, the parsley, salt, and pepper and cook, stirring, until the garlic is fragrant, 30 seconds to a minute. Stir in the sausage, cook together for another couple of minutes, until the sausage is sizzling and no longer pink, and remove from the heat. Taste and adjust the seasonings.

advance preparation
The gratin can be assembled hours before baking and held in the refrigerator.

Toss together the tomatoes, peppers, the remaining garlic, and the basil in a large bowl. Season generously with salt and pepper. Layer half the tomato mixture in the gratin dish. Spread all of the onion–sausage mixture over the tomatoes, then top with the rest of the tomatoes and peppers. Sprinkle the cheese over the top.

Bake for 45 minutes, or until the top is golden and the gratin is bubbling. Serve hot or warm.

leftovers : The dish will keep for 3 or 4 days in the refrigerator. Reheat and toss leftovers with pasta, or use as a topping for polenta.

summer vegetable gratin with cumin

Studded with diced red bell peppers, corn kernels, and thin rounds of young, slender zucchini, this gratin is not as rich as it tastes. I blend the kernels from one of the ears of corn with the eggs and milk to achieve a sweet, rich custard that holds it all together. Cumin seeds give it a southwestern flavor. ❖ serves 4 to 6

Kernels from 2 ears of sweet corn (about 2 cups), divided

1 tablespoon olive oil

1 medium onion, finely chopped

1 medium red bell pepper, cored, seeded, and diced

1 large garlic clove, minced or pressed

½ pound young, slender zucchini, thinly sliced

Salt and freshly ground black pepper

3 large eggs

½ cup milk

½ rounded teaspoon cumin seeds, slightly crushed in a mortar

2 ounces Gruyère cheese, grated (½ cup)

advance preparation
This step can be done several hours or a day ahead. Keep on top of the stove for a few hours, or in a covered bowl in the refrigerator.

heat the oven to 375°F. Butter a 2-quart gratin dish. Set aside the kernels from one of the ears of corn. Heat the olive oil over medium heat in a large, heavy nonstick skillet and add the onion. Cook, stirring often, until it begins to soften, about 3 minutes, and add the red bell pepper. Cook, stirring often, until the onions and peppers are tender, 5 to 8 minutes. Add the garlic and the zucchini, stir together, and add a generous pinch of salt and some pepper. Cook, stirring often, until the zucchini is just beginning to look bright green and some of the slices are translucent, about 5 minutes. Stir in the kernels from one of the ears of corn. Stir together for a minute or two, and remove from the heat. Scrape into a large bowl.

Place the remaining corn kernels in a blender jar, and add the eggs, milk, and ½ teaspoon salt. Blend until smooth. Pour into the bowl with the vegetables. Add the cumin seeds and the cheese and stir everything together. Turn into the gratin dish. Use your fingers to redistribute the zucchini slices in an attractive layer on the top. Bake for 35 to 40 minutes, until the top is browned and the gratin is firm to the touch. Serve hot or warm.

leftovers : This will keep for 3 or 4 days in the refrigerator.

provençal summer squash, red pepper, and tomato gratin

Here's another gorgeous summer gratin, inspired by the gift of some wonderful round French summer squash called ronde de Nice. *Lush red bell peppers and red onions from the farmers' market, and tomatoes from my garden, complete the picture. This is like many Provençal gratins (called* tians*) and includes rice as a binder; any type of rice will do here, as will any type of green or yellow summer squash.* ❖ **serves 4 to 6**

3 tablespoons olive oil, plus more for oiling the gratin dish

1 large or 2 small red onions, chopped

1 large red bell pepper, cored, seeded, and cut in ¼-inch dice

3 large garlic cloves, minced or pressed

About 1¼ pounds summer squash, cut in ½-inch dice (4 cups diced squash)

Salt and freshly ground black pepper

2 teaspoons fresh thyme leaves, or 1 teaspoon crumbled dried thyme

1 cup cooked rice (½ cup raw)

3 eggs

½ cup milk (whole, reduced-fat, or low-fat)

3 ounces Gruyère cheese, grated (¾ cup)

¾ pound tomatoes, sliced

¼ cup fresh or dry bread crumbs

heat the oven to 375°F. Oil a 2- to 2 ½-quart gratin dish.

advance preparation The vegetables can be cooked several hours before you assemble the gratin and held in the pan on top of the stove. Or refrigerate overnight.

Heat 2 tablespoons of the olive oil in a large, heavy non-stick skillet over medium heat. Add the onion and cook, stirring often, until translucent, about 5 minutes. Add the bell pepper and continue to cook, stirring, until the pepper begins to soften, 3 to 5 minutes. Add the garlic, stir together for about 30 seconds, until it begins to smell fragrant, and stir in the squash. Cook, stirring often, until the squash is translucent but not mushy, 5 to 10 minutes. Season with salt and pepper. Stir in the thyme and rice, and remove from the heat.

Beat the eggs in a large bowl. Beat in the milk, ½ teaspoon salt, and the cheese. Stir in the cooked vegetables and combine well. Scrape into the gratin dish.

Cover the top of the gratin with the sliced tomatoes. Sprinkle the bread crumbs over the top. Drizzle on the remaining tablespoon of olive oil. Bake for 45 minutes, or until the top is browned and the gratin is sizzling.

Allow to sit for at least 10 minutes before serving. Serve hot, warm, or at room temperature.

leftovers These Mediterranean gratins keep well for 3 or 4 days. You can serve them cold for lunch, or eat as a main or a side dish for dinner.

savory bread
puddings *(stratas)*

There are many reasons I love stratas, not the least of which is the fact that I hate throwing out food. A loaf of bread that is too hard to slice is never destined for the garbage in our house; when I use it for a strata—plain or embellished—it becomes the most important ingredient in my main dish. There are many ways to make a strata; mine are not as rich as many. ❖ All of these stratas serve 4 to 6.

basic strata

½ pound bread, slightly stale if possible, sliced about ½ inch thick

1 large garlic clove, cut in half

3 ounces Gruyère cheese, grated (¾ cup)

4 large eggs

2 cups milk (may use 1-percent or 2-percent)

½ teaspoon salt

Freshly ground black pepper

advance preparation
The bread and cheese layers for this recipe and for all of the variations that follow can be assembled hours before beating together the eggs and milk and completing the casserole.

heat the oven oven to 350ºF. Oil or butter a 2-quart baking or gratin dish. If the bread is soft, toast it lightly and rub all the slices, front and back, with the cut clove of garlic. If it's stale, just rub with garlic; if it's so stale that it's difficult to cut, soak in 1 cup milk just until soft enough to slice (about a minute), then slice. Layer half of the slices in the baking dish. Top with half the cheese. Repeat the layers.

Beat together the eggs and milk. Add ½ teaspoon salt and a few grinds of pepper and pour over the bread. Bake for 40 to 50 minutes, until puffed and browned. Remove from the oven and serve hot or warm.

strata with mushrooms and sage

To the basic strata recipe add:

1 pound mushrooms, cleaned and sliced

Salt

1 tablespoon olive oil

2 garlic cloves, minced or pressed

2 to 3 tablespoons slivered or chopped fresh sage leaves

Freshly ground black pepper

Heat a large nonstick skillet over medium heat and add the mushrooms and a generous pinch of salt. Cook, stirring, until the mushrooms begin to release water. Continue to cook until they've softened and most of the liquid has evaporated, 5 to 8 minutes. Add the olive oil and garlic and cook, stirring, for another minute, until the garlic is fragrant. Add the sage, stir together, remove from the heat, and season with salt and pepper. Pour off any liquid remaining in the pan into a 2-cup heatproof measuring cup.

Proceed with the basic strata recipe, adding half the mushrooms to the first layer of bread before adding the cheese, and topping the second layer with the remaining mushrooms. Beat the eggs, add the salt and pepper, measure the milk into the cup with the mushroom liquid to make 2 cups, and beat together with the eggs. Pour over the bread and bake as directed.

cheddar and mushroom strata

Substitute Cheddar cheese for the Gruyère. Cheddar and sage make a very nice match.

strata with tomatoes and thyme

Red or yellow tomatoes, canned or fresh, make a fine addition to a strata.

To the basic recipe add 1 pound fresh tomatoes, sliced, or 1 (14-ounce) can tomatoes, drained and sliced, and 1 teaspoon fresh thyme or ½ teaspoon dried thyme. Substitute 1 ounce of grated Parmesan (¼ cup) for 1 ounce of the Gruyère (so you have 2 ounces Gruyère and 1 ounce Parmesan). If any garlic remains after rubbing the bread, press or mince and toss with the tomatoes.

Layer half of the bread slices in the baking dish. Top with half the tomato slices. Sprinkle the tomato slices with salt, pepper, and thyme and top with half the cheese. Repeat the layers.

Beat together the eggs, salt, pepper, and milk as directed, pour over the bread, and bake.

strata with greens, or with tomatoes and greens

To the basic recipe or to the strata with tomatoes and thyme add:

Salt

1 pound greens, such as Swiss chard, spinach, beet greens, or kale, stemmed and washed

1 tablespoon olive oil

1 or 2 garlic cloves (to taste), minced or pressed

Freshly ground black pepper

Bring a large pot of water to a boil and add 1 tablespoon salt and the greens. Blanch for 2 minutes, until just tender. Transfer immediately to a bowl of cold water, then drain, squeeze out the excess water, and coarsely chop. Heat the olive oil over medium heat in a large nonstick skillet and add the garlic. Cook, stirring, for about 30 seconds, just until it begins to color. Add the greens and toss together until coated with oil, about 30 seconds to a minute. Remove from the heat and season with salt and pepper. If adding to the basic recipe, divide in half and layer over the bread before adding the cheese. If using tomatoes, toss with the tomatoes, garlic, thyme, and salt and pepper before layering the tomatoes, and proceed with the recipe.

leftovers A strata is a dish that you can make *with* leftovers, so I've never tried to turn one into anything else. But I do like eating leftover strata, even cold. It slices nicely and can be warmed in a microwave or a medium oven. It keeps for 3 days in the refrigerator.

tomato, bread, and green bean strata with yogurt topping

This dish started one summer morning, when I decided to test the yogurt and egg topping for the Balkan-style Moussaka on page 202. I had some green beans in the refrigerator that needed to be used up, a half loaf of bread that was almost too stale to cut, and some beautiful fresh tomatoes. So I decided to make a sort of strata and test the topping on it. Little did I know how wonderful and beautiful the dish would be. The most surprising aspect of this is the intense flavor of the green beans, a result of roasting in the gratin. ❖ **serves 4 to 6**

6 to 8 ounces baguette, preferably stale, sliced about ¾ inch thick

1 garlic clove, cut in half

Salt

½ pound green beans, ends trimmed

1 pound tomatoes, sliced

Freshly ground black pepper

1 scant teaspoon sugar

4 large eggs, beaten

1 cup plain yogurt

Pinch of sweet paprika

2 ounces Parmesan, grated (½ cup)

heat the oven to 375°F. Oil a 2-quart gratin or baking dish with olive oil. If the bread isn't stale and hard, then toast the slices lightly. Rub the toasted or stale slices of bread on both sides with the cut clove of garlic, and layer them in a single layer in the bottom of the baking dish.

advance preparation
The blanched beans will keep for 3 days in the refrigerator.

Bring a large pot of water to a boil, add a couple of teaspoons of salt, and drop in the green beans. Blanch for 3 minutes and transfer to a bowl of cold water. Drain.

Layer the tomato slices, overlapping slightly, in a single layer over the bread. Sprinkle with salt, pepper, and sugar. Lay the green beans in a tight row down the center of the tomatoes. Salt lightly. Beat together the eggs and yogurt, and season to taste with salt (about ½ teaspoon), pepper, and paprika. Pour over the vegetables. Sprinkle the Parmesan over the top. Bake for 30 to 40 minutes, until the top is nicely browned. Remove from the oven and allow to sit for at least 15 minutes before serving. Serve warm or at room temperature.

leftovers : The dish will keep for 2 or 3 days. It'll taste good, but it's best on the day you assemble it.

balkan baked beans

It must be the long, slow, gentle cooking that makes these beans so tender and full of flavor. The beans never fall apart, but the broth becomes thick and heady with lots of onion and garlic, tomatoes and paprika, mint, and a hint of chili. ❖ serves 6

1 pound borlotti or pinto beans, rinsed, picked over, and soaked overnight or for 6 hours in 2 quarts water

1 dried or fresh hot red chili pepper

Salt

2 medium onions, chopped

3 large garlic cloves, minced or pressed

2 red bell peppers, 1 chopped, 1 sliced into strips or rounds

1 pound tomatoes, half chopped, half cut in rounds

2 tablespoons olive oil

1 teaspoon sweet paprika

Freshly ground black pepper

1 heaped tablespoon chopped fresh mint

Chopped fresh mint or flat-leaf parsley, for garnish

advance preparation
The beans can be cooked through
this step 1 or 2 days ahead.

drain the beans and combine with 5 cups water (or enough to cover by ½ inch) and the chili pepper in a large flameproof casserole or Dutch oven. Bring to a boil, reduce the heat, and simmer for 45 minutes to an hour, until the beans are tender but intact. Stir in a teaspoon of salt.

advance preparation
The beans can be prepared through
this step up to a day before you bake
them. Refrigerate overnight. Bring
back to a simmer on top of the stove
before proceeding.

While the beans are simmering, prepare the remaining vegetables and heat the oven to 325°F. Heat the oil over medium heat in a large nonstick frying pan and add the onions. Stir together, cover, and cook, stirring occasionally, for 15 minutes, or until lightly browned. Stir in the garlic and the chopped bell pepper and cook, stirring, for 5 minutes, until the pepper is just tender and the mixture is fragrant. Add the chopped tomatoes and some salt and cook, stirring often, until the tomatoes have cooked down a little, 5 to 10 minutes. Remove from the heat and stir in the paprika, salt (1 teaspoon or more), black pepper, and the tablespoon of mint. Stir into the beans. Taste and adjust the salt.

advance preparation
You can also bake the beans a day or
two ahead (they will benefit from it).
Refrigerate, then bring back to a
simmer on top of the stove before
proceeding with the next step.

Place the beans in the oven and bake, covered, for 1 hour, or until very tender. Check from time to time to make sure the beans are covered with liquid. Add hot water if necessary. Taste and adjust the salt.

If you wish, transfer the beans to a large gratin dish or baking dish. Arrange the sliced tomatoes and sliced bell peppers over the top of the beans. Return to the oven and bake, uncovered, for 1 more hour, or until the vegetables on the top are tender. The beans should remain submerged in the broth, but if necessary, add hot water. Sprinkle the additional mint or parsley over the top and serve, hot or warm.

leftovers The beans will keep for 3 to 5 days in the refrigerator. If you want to transform the beans into another dish, you can toss with pasta for a delicious pasta e fagioli. They'd also make a wonderful, earthy dish mixed with rice. Or toss with a vinaigrette for a hearty bean salad.

baked lentils
and red cabbage

This balsamic-sweetened dish tastes like a rendition of Boston baked beans. The sweetness also comes from the cabbage and onions, which caramelize during their long cooking. Your kitchen will smell heavenly as this wonderful, simple dish bakes. ❖ **serves 6**

2 ounces bacon (2 thick slices), diced, plus 3 or 4 slices

¾ pound lentils (about 1¾ cups), washed and picked over

1 bay leaf

3 tablespoons balsamic vinegar

Salt and freshly ground black pepper

1 tablespoon olive oil

1 small or medium onion, finely chopped

3 large garlic cloves, minced or pressed

1 medium red cabbage (1½ to 2 pounds), cored and finely chopped

combine half the diced bacon, the lentils, 4 cups water, the bay leaf, and 2 tablespoons of the balsamic vinegar in a large, ovenproof Dutch oven or flameproof casserole and bring to a boil. Reduce the heat, cover, and simmer for 30 minutes. After 30 minutes, remove from the heat and stir in 1 to 2 teaspoons salt (to taste), some pepper, and ¾ cup water, or enough to just barely cover the lentils.

Heat the oven to 350°F.

Meanwhile, heat the olive oil and the remaining diced bacon over medium heat in a large, heavy nonstick skillet and cook the bacon until it begins to render its fat. Add the onion and cook, stirring, until the onion begins to soften, about 3 minutes. Add the garlic and cabbage, and about ½ teaspoon salt, stir together, cover (use a pizza pan if your pan doesn't have a lid), and turn the heat to low. Cook, stirring occasionally, for 10 to 15 minutes, until the cabbage is tender and limp. Add 3 tablespoons of water and the remaining tablespoon of balsamic vinegar, cover, and continue to cook for another 15 minutes. Add salt and pepper.

advance preparation
You can assemble the dish a day
ahead of time and keep in the
refrigerator. Bake it on the day you
wish to serve.

Spoon the cabbage mixture over the top of the lentils in an even layer. Arrange a few slices of bacon over the cabbage and place in the oven. Bake for 1 hour, or until bits of the cabbage and bacon slices are charred around the edges. Serve hot or at room temperature.

leftovers The dish will keep for 3 or 4 days in the refrigerator, but the bacon won't look as attractive. Serve leftovers with rice.

fisherman's soups and stews

Fish soups and stews can be complicated affairs, like bouillabaisse, that require specific seafood from particular places. But most of these dishes—even bouillabaisse—have simple origins. They began as fisherman's soups, which were usually made with little more than water, sometimes aromatics, sometimes bread, and the unsold catch of the day that wasn't big enough to sell, wasn't good enough, or had came up in nets along with the desired fish destined for market. Given that fishermen around the world were working with the same basic ingredients, it's amazing how much variety there is in the world's menu of fisherman's stews.

The fish soups from the Mediterranean, my biggest inspiration when it comes to these dishes, benefited greatly from the tomato when it arrived from the Americas. Broths became increasingly aromatic, with stew bases that are delicious even before the fish is added.

The soups and stews I've chosen for this chapter are easy to make and don't require exotic or expensive fish or shellfish. I've omitted lobster stews, good as they are, because, frankly, I can't bring myself to cut up a live lobster. The dishes should be made in the spirit in which they evolved—with the freshest seafood possible. I've given you choices in most of the recipes, and you should always choose the fish that looks best to you. Unfortunately, the fish that is most available in this country is farmed salmon, but salmon is one fish that doesn't work in these stews; its flavor is too strong, its flesh too fatty. Halibut and snapper, cod and sea bass, and mahimahi are better.

Although a finished fish soup is best eaten on the day it's made, with seafood bought that morning, the real work that goes into these dishes, making the stew bases or broth, can be done ahead. The final preparations rarely take much time, because fish cooks in minutes in the simmering broth. And if you thought your dish tasted good before you added the fish, wait until you taste it now.

basque tuna ragout
(*marmitako*)

This recipe is based on the Basque tuna soup called Marmitako, a fisherman's dish with simple origins (it was originally made with bread and tuna), which was greatly enhanced when peppers, tomatoes, and potatoes arrived from the New World. Every Basque cook has a version of this dish, and I am no exception. I have never seen an authentic recipe that calls for red peppers as well as green peppers, but I like the combination. You needn't spend a fortune on sushi-quality tuna here; albacore, at half the price, will be just fine. ❖ serves 5 to 6

3 dried Anaheim or mild New Mexico chilies, or 1 teaspoon mild pure ground chili powder

2 tablespoons olive oil

2 medium onions, finely chopped

4 to 6 garlic cloves (to taste), minced, plus 1 clove, cut in half

2 large green bell peppers, cored, seeded, and chopped

2 large red bell peppers, cored, seeded, and chopped

¼ cup minced fresh flat-leaf parsley

1 tablespoon sweet paprika

1 pound tomatoes, skinned, seeded, and chopped, or 1 (14-ounce) can with juice, chopped

1½ pounds waxy potatoes, scrubbed and diced

5 cups fish broth or 4 cups clam juice diluted with 1 cup water

½ cup dry white wine

¼ to ½ teaspoon red pepper flakes

Salt and freshly ground black pepper

1½ pounds tuna or albacore steaks, skin and blood lines removed, cut in ¾-inch cubes

12 slices of baguette, toasted

place the chilies in a bowl and cover with hot water. Soak for 30 minutes. Meanwhile, heat the oil in a large, wide lidded pan or flameproof casserole over medium heat and cook the onions until they begin to soften, about 3 minutes. Add the minced garlic, the bell peppers, and 2 tablespoons of the parsley and cook, stirring, for about 5 minutes. Reduce the heat to very low, cover, and cook slowly, stirring from time to time, for 30 minutes.

advance preparation The dish can be cooked to this point and set aside for several hours at room temperature, or refrigerated overnight.

Using rubber gloves to protect your hands, seed and stem the soaked chili peppers, and either scrape the flesh away from the skins or mash to a purée in a mortar and pestle. Stir into the onion and pepper mixture (or stir in chili powder if using), along with the paprika, tomatoes, and potatoes. Stir everything together for a minute or two, then add the fish broth (or diluted clam juice), wine, and red pepper flakes. Season with salt and pepper, bring to a boil, reduce the heat, and simmer, partially covered, for 30 minutes, or until the mixture is fragrant and the potatoes tender. Taste and adjust the seasonings.

Bring the broth back to a simmer and add the tuna. Turn off the heat, cover, and let sit for 5 to 8 minutes, until the tuna is just cooked through but still moist. Taste, adjust the seasonings, and sprinkle on the remaining parsley. Rub the baguette slices with the cut clove of garlic and serve with the ragout.

leftovers Tuna makes better leftovers than other fish, and you can keep this for a couple of days in the refrigerator. Use it for a fabulous open-faced sandwich or risotto.

leftovers variations
open-faced tuna and
red pepper sandwiches

If you have just a little Marmitako left over, try topping crusty rolls or bruschetta with it.

Cut hard rolls in half, or toast thick slices of country bread and rub with garlic. Drain off any liquid from the stew, and top the bread with leftover fish and peppers. Serve with a glass of cool dry rosé.

marmitako risotto

This risotto is as exciting as the stew whose leftovers inspired it. I had quite a small amount of actual Marmitako to work with here, yet it was still incredibly fragrant. ❖ serves 2 to 4

1 to 2 cups leftover Marmitako

3 cups fish or chicken stock

2 tablespoons olive oil

1 bulb of fresh spring garlic, peeled and chopped,
  or 4 regular garlic cloves, peeled and chopped

1 cup Arborio rice

½ cup dry white wine

Salt and freshly ground black pepper

Set a strainer over a bowl and pour in the leftover Marmitako. Pour the strained liquid into a measuring cup and add stock to make 3 cups. Bring to a simmer in a saucepan.

Heat the oil over medium heat in a large, heavy nonstick frying pan and add the garlic. Cook, stirring, until translucent and fragrant, about a minute, and add the rice. Cook, stirring, until the grains of rice are separate and beginning to crackle.

Stir in the wine and cook over medium heat, stirring constantly. The wine should bubble, but not too quickly. You want some of the flavor to cook into the rice before it evaporates. When the wine has just about evaporated, stir in a ladleful or two of the simmering stock, enough to just cover the rice. The stock should bubble slowly. Cook, stirring often, until it is just about absorbed. Add another ladleful of the stock and continue to cook in this fashion, not too fast and not too slowly, adding more stock when the rice is almost dry, for 20 to 25 minutes. Taste a bit of the rice. It should taste chewy but not hard in the middle. If it is still hard, add another ladleful of stock and cook for another 5 minutes or so. Now is the time to ascertain if there is enough salt. Add if necessary.

Stir the leftover Marmitako into the rice. Add freshly ground pepper, taste one last time, and adjust the salt. The rice should be creamy. Stir for a couple of seconds, and serve.

Note: You can make a larger amount of risotto, using the same amount of Marmitako; use 1½ cups rice and 4½ cups stock.

provençal fish stew

You could call this a stew or a soup, but whatever it is, it's decidedly not a bouillabaisse, just a fragrant fish stew with the hallmark Provençal touches: saffron and garlic, orange zest and fennel. With the potatoes, there's a bit of Manhattan chowder as well. In fact, when I first developed the dish, years ago for my Paris Supper Club chez Martha Rose, I called it "Chowder à la Provençale." Because the dinners I prepared for the Supper Club were served to twenty-five people at one seating, I always made a main dish that was relatively easy to prepare in quantity and that I could get done, at least partially, ahead of time. Once my guests arrived, I was able to trade my chef's hat for that of hostess and leave the final touches to my able assistants. This particular dish has always been one of my favorites from those days. I never tire of making it, tweaking the recipe a bit here and there, using what looks best at the fish market, but essentially sticking to the same formula. ❖ **serves 6**

for the fish stock

1 pound fish trimmings (heads and bones) from a white-fleshed fish, or a whole white-fleshed fish, rinsed

1 onion, quartered

1 carrot, sliced

1 celery stalk, sliced

1 leek, white and light green part only, cleaned and sliced

2 garlic cloves, crushed

Bouquet garni made with 2 sprigs of flat-leaf parsley, 2 sprigs of thyme, and 1 bay leaf

1 cup dry white wine

2½ dozen mussels or clams, purged (see page 376)

Salt

for the soup

1 tablespoon olive oil

1 large onion, chopped

½ teaspoon fennel seeds, crushed in a mortar

4 garlic cloves, minced or pressed

2 (28-ounce) cans tomatoes, with their liquid, peeled, seeded, and chopped

Salt

2 tablespoons tomato paste

1 teaspoon fresh thyme leaves or ½ teaspoon dried thyme

Freshly ground black pepper

¾ pound waxy potatoes, cut in ½-inch cubes

1 pound winter squash, peeled and cut in ½-inch cubes, or zucchini, sliced or cut in ½-inch cubes

Pinch of cayenne pepper (or more to taste)

2 wide strips of orange zest

Generous pinch of saffron

2 pounds fish fillets or steaks, such as halibut, mahimahi, monkfish, snapper, swordfish, or shark (a combination is nice), cut in 2-inch pieces

3 tablespoons chopped fresh flat-leaf parsley

1 tablespoon slivered fresh basil (optional)

make the fish stock: Combine the fish trimmings or whole fish, the quartered onion, carrot, celery, leek, garlic, and bouquet garni with 1 quart of water in a large soup pot. Bring to a boil, skim off all foam, reduce the heat, and simmer for 15 minutes.

Meanwhile, place the wine and ½ cup of water in another large pot with the mussels or clams. Bring to a boil, cover tightly, and boil for 5 minutes, or until the mussels or clams have opened up. Remove the shellfish and set aside, in a covered bowl in the refrigerator if not using soon. Strain the broth through a strainer lined with cheesecloth or a double thickness of paper towel set over a bowl. Add this to the fish broth and simmer for another 15 minutes. Remove from the heat and strain through a fine sieve or a strainer lined with cheesecloth or paper towel into a bowl. Discard the fish bones and vegetables. Taste and add salt as desired. Set the stock aside.

For the soup, heat the olive oil over medium heat in a large, heavy soup pot or Dutch oven and add the onion. Cook, stirring, until tender, about 5 minutes, then add the fennel seeds and garlic. Cook, stirring, until the garlic is fragrant and just beginning to color, about 1 minute. Stir in the tomatoes and salt to taste. Cook over medium heat,

The tomato sauce, without the fish stock, could be made a day or two ahead and refrigerated. The fish stock and finished soup base can be made the morning of the evening you wish to serve this and held on the stove or in the refrigerator.

stirring from time to time, for about 15 minutes, until the tomatoes have cooked down and smell fragrant. Add the tomato paste, thyme, pepper, and the fish stock. Bring to a simmer and cook, uncovered, for 30 minutes. Add the potatoes, squash, and cayenne, cover, and cook until the vegetables are tender, about 20 minutes. Taste and adjust the salt.

Fifteen minutes before you wish to serve the soup, bring back to a simmer and add the orange zest and saffron. Add the fish and simmer for 5 to 10 minutes, until just cooked through. Taste and adjust the seasonings. Stir in the parsley and basil, and serve, garnishing each bowl with mussels and clams.

leftovers You might enjoy this the day after it's made, but fish stews and soups aren't great keepers. However, you can always use leftovers for a risotto (see Marmitako Risotto, page 235), or just toss with cooked rice for a sort of Mediterranean jambalaya.

italian fish stew with chick peas and green beans

This thick, hearty dish is based on a recipe from Emilia-Romagna by Lynne Rossetto Kasper. I've added green beans to the stew to brighten it up and add some texture to the wonderful mix.

❖ serves 6

for the chick peas

½ pound (1¼ cups) chick peas, soaked for 8 hours in 4 cups water, drained and rinsed

1 medium onion, chopped

2 large garlic cloves, minced

2 canned plum tomatoes, or 1 large vine-ripened tomato, peeled, seeded, and chopped

1 bay leaf

Salt

for the soup

Salt

½ pound green beans, trimmed and cut into 2-inch lengths

2 tablespoons olive oil

1 medium onion, chopped

1 small carrot, peeled and minced

3 tablespoons minced fresh flat-leaf parsley

2 large garlic cloves, minced or pressed

3 tablespoons chopped fresh basil, or 2 fresh sage leaves, chopped

1 tablespoon tomato paste

2 pounds canned tomatoes, with juice (1½ 28-ounce cans), or fresh tomatoes, peeled, seeded, and chopped

⅛ teaspoon sugar

Freshly ground black pepper

Pinch of cayenne pepper (optional)

¾ pound medium shrimp, shelled and halved

1 pound mixed fish fillets, such as snapper, sea bass, halibut, rockfish, mullet, or mahimahi, cut into 1-inch pieces

Additional chopped parsley or basil, for garnish

Olive oil, for drizzling

advance preparation
The cooked chick peas will hold for 3 days in the refrigerator. Keep them in the pot, in their liquid, and bring back to a simmer when proceeding with the recipe.

cook the chick peas. Place the chick peas in a large pot. Add 10 cups water and bring to a boil. Skim off any foam, then add the chopped onion, garlic, tomatoes, and bay leaf. Reduce the heat, cover, and simmer for 1 hour. Add 2 to 3 teaspoons salt and continue to simmer for 30 minutes to an hour, until the chick peas are tender.

advance preparation
Blanched green beans will keep for
3 or 4 days in a covered bowl in the
refrigerator.

Meanwhile, start the soup. Bring a medium pot of water to a boil and add 2 teaspoons salt and the green beans. Boil for 4 to 5 minutes, until tender and bright, and transfer to a bowl of ice-cold water. Drain and set aside.

advance preparation
You can make the tomato sauce up to
3 days ahead, and for best results, do
make it a day ahead.

Heat the olive oil over medium heat in a large, heavy nonstick frying pan or saucepan and add the onion, carrot, and parsley. Cook, stirring, until the onion and carrot are just about tender, about 5 minutes, then stir in the garlic. Cook, stirring, just until fragrant, 30 seconds to a minute. Add the basil or sage, tomato paste, tomatoes, and sugar. Season with salt to taste (½ teaspoon or more), and cook briskly, stirring often, until thickened, 10 to 15 minutes. Remove from the heat.

advance preparation
The entire soup can be made through
this step as far ahead as 2 or 3 days.
Keep in the refrigerator.

When the chick peas are tender, stir in the tomato sauce. Add a generous amount of pepper and if desired, a pinch of cayenne. Simmer together for 10 minutes. Taste and adjust the seasonings. Discard the bay leaf. Remove 1½ cups of the chick peas with some broth, and purée in a blender. Stir back into the soup.

Just before serving, with the soup at a simmer, stir in the shrimp and the fish. Cook, uncovered, for 3 to 5 minutes, or until the shrimp are pink and the fish opaque. Stir in the green beans and heat through. Add chopped parsley or basil if desired, taste one last time, and adjust the seasonings. Serve at once, passing olive oil for drizzling.

leftovers This reheats nicely, though, of course, the fish won't taste as fresh after the day you buy it. If there's not enough for actual soup servings, use it in a risotto (see Marmitako Risotto, page 235) or toss it with rice or pasta.

tuna daube

I first came upon a tuna daube in Patricia Wells's Patricia Wells at Home in Provence *and couldn't resist trying it, although I'm reluctant to cook any fish for an hour. But the thick steaks become succulent during that hour of simmering in a savory mixture of tomatoes, onions, capers, olives, wine, and herbs. I've made the dish with tuna steaks and with the less expensive alba-core, and I'm sorry to report that the albacore did dry out, too much for my taste—and that was the time I was serving it at a dinner party for nine! But nobody seemed to mind; the fish disap-peared, and the sauce was heavenly, almost like a tomato tapenade, with capers and anchovies, black olives, rosemary, thyme, tomatoes, and white wine. What could be more Provençal? Serve the dish with steamed potatoes, rice, or thick, garlic-rubbed slices of country bread.* ❖ serves 6

3 tablespoons olive oil

1 large onion, chopped

2 to 4 anchovy fillets (to taste), soaked for 15 to 30 minutes in water or milk, drained, and chopped

4 large garlic cloves, minced or pressed

¼ cup capers, rinsed and chopped

1 teaspoon chopped fresh rosemary or ½ teaspoon crumbled dried rosemary

½ cup imported black olives, pitted and cut in half

1 (28-ounce) can tomatoes, with juice, chopped

Salt and freshly ground black pepper

1 cup dry white wine, such as sauvignon blanc or pinot grigio

Bouquet garni made with 2 bay leaves and a few sprigs each of fresh thyme and flat-leaf parsley

2 pounds tuna, cut in 2-inch-thick steaks

Zest of ½ lemon

2 tablespoons slivered fresh basil or chopped fresh flat-leaf parsley

heat the oven to 350°F. Heat 1 tablespoon of the oil over medium heat in a large, heavy, flameproof casserole or Dutch oven and add the onion. Cook, stirring, until tender, 5 to 8 minutes. Stir in the anchovy fillets and mash with the back of the spoon. Cook for a minute or two, then add the garlic, capers, and rosemary.

Stir together for a minute, until the garlic smells fragrant, and add the olives, the tomatoes with their juice, and salt and pepper to taste (remembering that the capers, olives, and anchovies are salty). Cook, stirring often, until the tomatoes have cooked down a bit and smell fragrant, 10 to 15 minutes. Stir in the wine and bring the mixture to a boil. Boil for about 7 minutes, to cook off the alcohol; add the bouquet garni and reduce the heat to a simmer.

Meanwhile, heat the remaining 2 tablespoons oil over high heat in a large, heavy nonstick skillet and sear the fish fillets for about 2 minutes. Turn over, salt the seared side, and sear the remaining side. Remove from the heat, flip onto a plate, and salt the second side.

Submerge the steaks in the tomato mixture. Bring the liquid back to a simmer, cover tightly, and place in the oven. Bake for 45 minutes to 1 hour, until the tuna is very tender. Remove from the heat, cut the tuna steaks into serving portions and transfer to wide soup plates or dinner plates, or to an attractive gratin dish or deep platter. Stir the lemon zest and basil or parsley into the sauce. Simmer for a minute, taste and adjust the seasonings, spoon over the tuna, and serve.

leftovers This makes great leftovers and is terrific cold. You can keep the fish for a couple of days, and the sauce for up to 4 days. Slice the fish and serve cold with the sauce, or break up the fish and stir into the sauce, then toss with pasta. Or make bruschetta. The sauce alone makes a nice topping for pasta, rice, bruschetta, and polenta.

penne with tuna daube sauce and green beans ❖ serves 2

Salt

6 ounces penne or other pasta

1 cup (or more) sauce from Tuna Daube, with any leftover tuna broken up into the sauce

Generous handful of green beans, trimmed

Bring a large pot of water to a boil and add a generous amount of salt and the pasta. Cook for 8 minutes, or until al dente. Meanwhile, heat the sauce in a large microwave-safe bowl.

About 4 minutes into the cooking of the pasta, add the green beans to the boiling water. They should be tender and bright green when the pasta is done. Drain, toss with the sauce, and serve.

thick portuguese seafood and bread stew

This is a typical Portuguese açorda, *a cross between a soup and a bread pudding. In a word, a pap, and never has a pap tasted so wonderful. It's a great way to use up stale bread, and even if your bread isn't so stale, it's worth making, and easy.* ❖ **serves 6**

1 pound medium shrimp, in the shell

Salt

1 bay leaf

2 sprigs of fresh cilantro

2 sprigs of fresh flat-leaf parsley

2 tablespoons olive oil

2 medium onions, thinly sliced

4 large garlic cloves, minced or put through a press

1 pound, or 1 (14-ounce) can, tomatoes, peeled, seeded, and chopped

2 dozen clams, purged (see page 376)

1 cup dry white wine

½ to ¾ pound stale white country or French bread, cubed or thinly sliced

Freshly ground black pepper

6 eggs

¼ cup chopped fresh flat-leaf parsley or cilantro, to taste

advance preparation
The broth can be made several hours before you begin the rest of the soup. If holding for more than an hour, refrigerate.

shell and devein the shrimp, reserving the shells. Place the shrimp in a bowl, salt lightly, and refrigerate. Place the shells in a saucepan with 2 quarts water. Bring to a boil and add the bay leaf and the cilantro and parsley sprigs. Reduce the heat, cover, and simmer for 1 hour. Drain through a strainer lined with cheesecloth set over a bowl.

advance preparation
The onions and tomatoes can be
cooked up to a day ahead and held in
the refrigerator. Reheat gently and
proceed with the recipe.

Heat the oil over medium heat in a heavy soup pot or
Dutch oven and add the onions. Cook, stirring, until
tender, 5 to 10 minutes, and add the garlic. Cook
together for about 1 minute, just until the garlic begins
to smell fragrant, and stir in the tomatoes. Cook, stirring
often, for about 10 minutes, until the tomatoes have
cooked down slightly. Remove from the heat.

advance preparation
The clams can be cooked several
hours before you finish the soup.
Refrigerate if cooking more than an
hour ahead.

Meanwhile, combine the clams and wine in a large lidded
pot and bring to a boil. Cover and steam for 5 minutes,
until the clams have opened. Remove from the heat and
discard any clams that have not opened. Remove the
clams from their shells, rinse briefly to wash off any
lingering sand, and set aside. Strain the cooking liquid
through a strainer lined with cheesecloth into the bowl with the shrimp broth.
Measure the liquid, then, if necessary, bring to a boil and reduce to about 6 cups. Taste
and season with salt.

Stir the broth into the tomato mixture and heat to a simmer over medium heat. Add
the shrimp and simmer just until pink, about 3 minutes. Stir in the clams and bread
and continue to stir, using a long-handled wooden spoon, over low heat until the
mixture is quite thick. Taste and adjust the salt; add pepper. The mixture should be
like thick porridge. Break the eggs into the surface of the mixture, stir them in with
half the parsley or cilantro, sprinkle the rest of the parsley or cilantro over the top,
and serve.

leftovers While any seafood dish is best on the day you cook it,
I enjoyed leftovers just as much the next day. I transformed the dish slightly by
blanching a bunch of beet greens (chard or spinach would also work), squeezing dry,
chopping coarsely, and stirring them into the reheated açorda. It was pretty as well
as delicious.

squid ragout

My friend Lulu Peyraud, proprietress of the winery Domaine Tempier in Bandol, France, makes a similar ragout with either octopus or squid. When the squid cooks in the wine, it becomes incredibly tender, and the sauce has a deep, rich taste of the sea. Serve over rice or wide noodles. ❖ **serves 6**

2½ pounds squid, cleaned

3 tablespoons olive oil

2 onions, chopped

1 large carrot, chopped

4 large garlic cloves, minced or pressed

1 pound tomatoes, peeled, seeded, and chopped, or 1 (14-ounce) can tomatoes, with liquid

Salt

2 ounces bacon, trimmed of some of the fat and chopped

¼ cup Cognac or brandy

2 cups dry red wine

1 dried hot pepper, or a pinch of cayenne pepper

Freshly ground black pepper

2 teaspoons all-purpose flour

1 tablespoon unsalted butter, at room temperature

Handful of chopped fresh flat-leaf parsley

rinse the squid, pat dry with paper towels, and slice the bodies into 1-inch pieces; leave the tentacles in whole pieces.

advance preparation
You can make the recipe through this step, and set it aside for several hours or in the refrigerator overnight. Reheat before proceeding.

Heat 2 tablespoons of the oil over medium heat in a large, heavy, flameproof casserole or Dutch oven and add the onions. Cook, stirring, until tender and beginning to color, 8 to 10 minutes. Stir in the carrots and garlic and cook for about a minute, until fragrant. Add the tomatoes and a little salt and cook, stirring from time to time, for another 5 to 10 minutes, until the tomatoes have cooked down slightly. Remove from the heat and set aside.

Heat the bacon and the remaining 1 tablespoon olive oil over medium heat in a large, heavy nonstick skillet. Cook the bacon until it renders its fat and is just beginning to crisp. Transfer, using a slotted spoon or spatula, to the pot with the tomato sauce. Turn the heat to medium-high and add the squid, in batches if necessary. Cook, stirring occasionally, until the squid is opaque and pinkish, about 10 minutes. If there is a lot of liquid in the pan, carefully pour it off into the pot with the sauce. Add the Cognac to the squid, heat for a minute, stirring, then carefully light it with a match. When the flames die down, transfer the squid to the pot with the tomato sauce.

advance preparation The dish can be made to this point several hours or even a day ahead (refrigerate overnight). Bring back to a simmer and proceed with the recipe. Add the wine to the nonstick pan and bring to a boil, stirring and scraping the bottom of the pan with a wooden spoon. Boil for a minute or two, then carefully pour into the pot with the other ingredients. Add the hot pepper or cayenne, salt to taste, and, if necessary, water to cover the squid. Bring to a simmer, cover, and simmer for 45 minutes, or until the squid is very tender. Taste and correct the seasonings, adding salt, pepper, or cayenne as desired.

Mix together the flour and butter. Just before serving whisk the mixture, in little bits, into the stew. Simmer, stirring, until the stew thickens slightly. Taste and adjust the seasonings once more, add the parsley, and serve.

leftovers The dish will still taste good for a couple of days. It also freezes very well for 2 or 3 months. Stretch this into another delicious meal by mixing together 1 cup of cooked rice with each cup of leftover ragout to make squid jambalaya. Add a little more cayenne if you want it to taste spicier. I love it as is.

cioppino

Not too long ago I met a woman at a party and, as inevitably happens, we got to talking about food. She is a third-generation northern Californian from an Italian family, and naturally I wanted to know how she made cioppino, the San Francisco fish stew that was created by that city's Italian and Portuguese fishermen. "We always used a lot of garlic, a lot of red wine, and good tomatoes," she told me. "As for the fish, crab of course, then whatever looked good at the market." Alternatives to the snapper and halibut listed below might include shark, swordfish, and sea scallops. As always, I take advantage of the shrimp called for in the recipe, and use the shells for the stock. ❖ **serves 6**

24 hard-shelled clams, such as littlenecks, purged (see page 376)

1 pound large shrimp (16 to 20), shelled and deveined (reserve shells)

Salt

2 tablespoons olive oil

2 medium onions, chopped

1 green bell pepper, diced

4 large garlic cloves, minced or pressed

1 (28-ounce) can tomatoes, with juice, chopped

½ teaspoon red pepper flakes (or more to taste)

1 teaspoon dried oregano

1 bay leaf

1½ cups dry red wine

Freshly ground black pepper

1 whole dungeness crab, cooked and cracked, or 1 king crab leg, thawed, if frozen, and cracked

1½ pounds red snapper, halibut, or mahimahi fillets, cut into 1½-inch pieces, pin bones removed

¼ cup chopped fresh flat-leaf parsley

2 tablespoons chopped or slivered fresh basil

Crusty bread or focaccia, for serving

set the clams in a large, lidded pot with ½ cup water. Bring to a boil, cover, and cook for 5 to 8 minutes, or until the clams open, shaking the pan and checking the clams after 5 minutes. Remove the clams from the pot and set aside in a bowl. Strain the liquid through a cheesecloth- or paper-towel-lined strainer set over a bowl.

advance preparation The shrimp and clam broths can be made a few hours before you make the tomato base, below. Refrigerate if holding for more than a few hours.

Combine the shrimp shells and 3 cups water and bring to a boil. Reduce the heat, cover, and simmer for 30 minutes. Strain through a cheesecloth- or paper towel-lined strainer set over a bowl, and measure out 2 cups of the broth. Combine with the clam broth and season to taste with salt. Set aside.

advance preparation The cioppino can be made up to this point several hours or even a day ahead. You can hold it on top of the stove for a few hours, or refrigerate it.

Heat the oil over medium heat in a large, heavy soup pot or Dutch oven and add the onions. Cook, stirring often, until they begin to soften, about 5 minutes. Add the bell pepper, turn the heat to medium-low, cover, and cook for another 5 to 10 minutes, until tender. Stir in the garlic and cook together for another minute, until fragrant.

Add the tomatoes, red pepper flakes, oregano, and bay leaf and cook, stirring from time to time, until the tomatoes smell fragrant and have cooked down somewhat, about 10 minutes. Stir in the red wine and bring to a boil. Boil for about 5 minutes, until reduced by about half. Stir in the broth and simmer, covered, for 30 minutes. Add salt and pepper to taste.

Thirty minutes before you wish to serve, remove the fish and shrimp from the refrigerator and salt lightly. Remove the crabmeat from the shells. Bring the soup back to a simmer and adjust the seasonings. Five or ten minutes before you wish to serve, stir the fish, crab, and shrimp into the simmering stew. Cover and cook for 5 minutes, or until the fish is just cooked through and the shrimp is pink. Remove from the heat, discard the bay leaf, and stir in the clams, parsley, and basil. Serve, with crusty bread or focaccia.

Note: If the clams have detached from their shells, stir them into the soup without the shells, and use some of the shells for garnish.

leftovers A fish stew or soup should be eaten the day it's finished. However, leftovers can make a fine jambalaya. Stir cooked rice into the stew, heat through, and serve, adding more hot pepper if you wish.

seafood *chilpachol* from veracruz

Guests will never forget this unique soup. The chilpachol is one of the defining dishes of the Mexican state of Veracruz. It is a masa-thickened soup (here I use toasted tortillas instead of masa) that is seasoned with toasted chipotle chilies, toasted garlic and spices, roasted tomatoes and onions, and epazote that is added shortly before serving the soup. The soup base can be made hours or days ahead of adding the seafood, and here you have a choice of shrimp, fish, or crabmeat, or a combination. See also the vegetarian version, Mexican Vegetable–Chipotle Soup, on page 36. Like all fish soups, the seafood doesn't improve once cooked. But you can still enjoy it for a day or two.

Note: Epazote is a Mexican herb that is available in Mexican markets and some farmers' markets. Do not substitute dried epazote for the fresh. ❖ serves 6 generously

2	pounds plum tomatoes
1	large onion, cut in half
4	large garlic cloves, unpeeled
4	small or 2 to 3 larger dried chipotle chilies, or 2 canned chipotles, rinsed and seeded
1	fresh jalapeño pepper
1	strip of Mexican cinnamon, or ½ teaspoon ground cinnamon
6	whole black peppercorns
2	toasted corn tortillas (see page 391), ground in a spice mill
2	tablespoons olive oil
	Salt (2 to 3 teaspoons)
1	large sprig of fresh epazote—about 2 tablespoons chopped—or ¼ cup chopped fresh cilantro
1½	pounds medium shrimp (shelled and deveined), crabmeat, or fish fillets cut in 1-inch pieces
2	or 3 corn tortillas, cut in wedges and toasted, for serving (optional)
	Limes to taste

heat the broiler. Line a baking sheet with foil. Place the tomatoes and onion on the baking sheet and set under the broiler, 2 to 3 inches from the heat. When the tomatoes are charred on the top, after 2 to 5 minutes, turn them over and broil until charred on the other side. Transfer the tomatoes to a bowl to allow to cool. The onion will take about 5 minutes longer than the tomatoes to roast and should be turned several times. It should be browned on the edges and in spots, and slightly softened. Remove from the heat, chop coarsely, and transfer to a blender. Peel the tomatoes and transfer to the blender, along with any juice that may have accumulated in the bowl.

Meanwhile, place a griddle or heavy-bottomed frying pan over medium heat. Toast the garlic and fresh jalapeño, turning often until softened and brown in several spots. Remove from the heat and allow to cool. Skin the garlic, stem the jalapeño, and add to the blender with the tomatoes and onion. Open the dried chilies out flat and remove the seeds and veins (use plastic gloves as they are extremely picante), and toast on the griddle, pressing down with a spatula for a few seconds, just until you see the chili blister and puff, then turn and repeat on the other side. Add to the blender. If using canned chipotle chilies, just add to the blender after rinsing and seeding. Toast the cinnamon strip and peppercorns for a few seconds, just until the strip of cinnamon browns slightly and the peppercorns begin to smell a bit toasty. Grind the cinnamon and peppercorns in a spice grinder and add to the blender. Blend the ingredients together until smooth, and strain into a bowl. Combine 1 cup of water with the ground toasted tortillas in the blender and blend together for a few seconds, then add to the purée. Stir well.

advance preparation
The broth can be prepared through this step hours ahead of serving. It will keep for a few days in the refrigerator and can be frozen for a couple of months.

Heat the oil over medium-high heat in a large, heavy soup pot or Dutch oven. Drizzle in a small amount of the purée and if it sizzles loudly, add the rest (wait a few minutes if it doesn't). Stir the mixture, and turn the heat to medium. If it splutters all over your stove, cover partially. Cook, stirring often, for 10 to 15 minutes, until the mixture is thick. Add 2 quarts water to the tomato mixture, stir well, and bring to a simmer. Add salt (be generous). Simmer for 15 minutes, stirring occasionally, and remove from the heat. Taste and adjust the salt.

Ten minutes before serving, bring the broth to a boil and add the epazote and the seafood. Simmer the shrimp and crabmeat for 5 minutes, fish for 5 to 10 minutes, until opaque. If using cilantro, stir in now. Taste and adjust the seasonings. Serve with tortillas and cut limes.

veracruzana crab or fish soup

This soup has been the star attraction of many a dinner party in my house. It's based on my Veracruz-style Crab Soup from Mexican Light *(Bantam Books, 1996), but because I can't always get terrific crabmeat, I sometimes use the same soup base for fish. Crab is always my first option, but halibut, mahimahi, snapper, and shark all make a fine soup with an intriguing depth of flavor resulting from the combination of pickled capers, pickled jalapeños (don't substitute fresh for canned here), and olives.* ❖ **serves 6 generously**

1	tablespoon olive oil
2	medium onions, chopped
3	large garlic cloves, minced or put through a press
2	(28-ounce) cans tomatoes, drained and chopped
	Salt
1½	pounds (5 to 6 medium) waxy potatoes, scrubbed and diced
1	pound winter squash or zucchini, peeled and diced (about 2 cups diced)
2	medium-size canned jalapeño chiles (en escabeche), seeded and chopped (about 3 tablespoons chopped)
¼	cup chopped green olives
	Scant ¼ cup capers, drained, rinsed, and chopped
2	sprigs of fresh cilantro, plus ½ cup chopped
1	sprig of fresh mint
½	teaspoon dried oregano
2	bay leaves
1½	pounds fresh crabmeat, or 1½ pounds fish fillets, such as snapper, halibut, mahimahi, or shark (can use a combination), cut in 1-inch pieces
3	limes, cut in wedges, for serving

advance preparation
The soup can be prepared through
this step a day or two ahead and
refrigerated.

heat the oil over medium heat in a large, heavy soup pot or Dutch oven and add the onions. Cook, stirring, for 5 to 10 minutes, until tender. Add the garlic and cook for another minute or two, until the garlic begins to color. Add the tomatoes and about ½ teaspoon salt and cook, stirring, for about 15 minutes, until the tomatoes are somewhat cooked down and the mixture smells fragrant. Add the potatoes, winter squash, jalapeños, olives, capers, sprigs of cilantro and mint, the oregano, and the bay leaves and stir together for 5 minutes. Add 2 quarts water and salt to taste, and bring to a simmer. Simmer for 30 minutes, until the potatoes and squash are tender and the broth tastes marvelous. Adjust the seasonings, adding more salt and/or garlic if you wish. Remove from the heat if not serving right away.

advance preparation
Like all fish soups, this is best served
on the day the fish is cooked in it.
But the base will be good for 3 or
4 days if you want to get the real
work out of the way.

Bring the soup back to a simmer and stir in the fish (if using crab, bring to just below a simmer). Simmer the fish for 5 to 10 minutes, until just cooked through, and remove from the heat (for crab, stir in and heat through, stirring and being careful not to let the soup boil or he crabmeat, which is already cooked, will become too rubbery). Just before serving, remove the bay leaves and stir in the chopped cilantro. Serve, with lime wedges on the side.

peruvian seafood chowder

This is a comforting soup, thick with potatoes and corn, creamy even though it contains no cream and very little milk. I was surprised that my four-year-old gobbled it up, asking about halfway through, "Mommy, is this a little hot?" Just a little. ❖ serves 6

½ pound shrimp, peeled and deveined (reserve shells)

Salt

2 tablespoons vegetable or canola oil

1 large onion, chopped

2 to 4 large garlic cloves (to taste), minced or pressed

1 to 2 dried red or yellow chilies (to taste), preferably Peruvian or Mexican, seeded and chopped or crumbled, or ¼ to ½ teaspoon cayenne pepper

2 large tomatoes (1 pound), peeled, seeded, and chopped

1 pound Yukon gold or russet potatoes, peeled and diced

⅓ cup rice

2 ears of corn, kernels removed (1½ cups kernels)

Freshly ground black pepper

1 pound white-fleshed fish, such as sea bass, snapper, halibut, or mahimahi, cut in 1-inch pieces

2 eggs, beaten

1½ cups milk

place the shrimp in a bowl and salt lightly. Refrigerate if not using right away. Combine the shells with 5 cups water in a big saucepan or soup pot and bring to a boil. Reduce the heat, cover partially, and simmer for 30 minutes. Drain through a strainer lined with cheesecloth set over a bowl. Measure and add water if necessary to make 4½ cups.

Heat the oil over medium heat in a large, heavy soup pot or Dutch oven and add the onion. Cook, stirring often, until tender, about 5 minutes, then stir in the garlic and chili. Cook, stirring, until fragrant, 30 seconds to a minute, then add the tomatoes and a generous pinch of salt. Cook, stirring often, for 10 to 15 minutes, until the tomatoes cook down and smell fragrant. Add the potatoes, rice, corn, shrimp shell stock, salt (about 1¼ teaspoons), and pepper, and bring to a boil. Reduce the heat and simmer for 20 minutes, or until the potatoes and rice are tender. Taste and adjust the salt.

Add the shrimp and fish to the soup, cover, and simmer for 5 minutes, or until the shrimp is pink and the fish opaque. Stir the beaten eggs into the soup and add the milk. Heat just to a simmer. Taste, adjust the salt and pepper, and serve.

leftovers This is best eaten the day it's made, but we didn't mind eating the leftovers for dinner the next day. If the soup becomes very thick and you don't have a lot of it left, warm some corn tortillas and use it for quesadillas.

shrimp gumbo

I was very excited when I found a recipe for seafood gumbo in Saveur magazine's July 2002 issue, in an article about okra, that did not call for a roux. The okra and the long cooking of the stew base result in a gumbo with a satiny texture. Inspired by that recipe, I have come up with the following one, and it should satisfy any gumbo lover, at far less the caloric expense. Shrimp may be the main feature of this dish, but the flavors are deeply vegetal, the result of a 2-hour simmer of a stock filled with onions and scallions, celery and bell peppers, okra and tomatoes. ❖ serves 6 to 8

2 pounds shrimp, peeled and deveined (reserve shells)

Salt

4 cups chicken stock (page 378)

2 (28-ounce) cans tomatoes, chopped, with juice

4 bay leaves

Freshly ground black pepper

2 tablespoons unsalted butter

2 onions, chopped

4 celery stalks, chopped

2 green bell peppers, seeded and chopped

1 red bell pepper, seeded and chopped

2 bunches of scallions, trimmed and cut in ½-inch slices

3 large garlic cloves, minced or pressed

1 pound okra, trimmed and sliced

6 ounces Cajun andouille sausage, cut in ¼-inch slices or crumbled

½ cup chopped fresh flat-leaf parsley, divided

¼ scant teaspoon cayenne pepper (or more to taste)

2 to 3 cups rice, cooked (use the smaller amount for 6 people)

put the shrimp in a bowl, salt lightly, cover and refrigerate. Put the shrimp shells in a large saucepan or pot and add 5 cups of water. Bring to a boil, reduce the heat, and simmer, uncovered, for 30 minutes. Strain into a bowl through a strainer lined with cheesecloth. Add enough water to make 4 cups, and pour into a large soup pot or Dutch oven with the chicken stock, tomatoes, bay leaves, and salt and pepper. Bring to a boil, reduce the heat, and simmer, stirring from time to time, for 30 minutes.

advance preparation
The gumbo can be made through this step a day ahead. Refrigerate overnight. Bring back to a simmer before proceeding.

While the stock is simmering, heat the butter in a large, heavy nonstick frying pan over medium heat and add the onions. Cook, stirring, until the onions begin to soften, 3 to 5 minutes, then add the celery, green and red bell peppers, and scallions. Cook, stirring often, until the vegetables are tender, about 10 minutes. Add the garlic and okra and cook, stirring often, until the okra is tender, about 15 minutes. Stir the vegetables into the stock, along with the andouille, half the parsley, and the cayenne. Simmer over medium heat, uncovered, for 2 hours, or until reduced by about half. Taste and adjust the seasonings.

Add the shrimp and remaining parsley to the gumbo. Simmer just until the shrimp is cooked through, about 5 minutes. Taste and adjust the seasonings. Discard the bay leaves.

Divide the rice among 6 to 8 plates or wide soup bowls, spoon on the gumbo, and serve.

leftovers The problem here is that the base gets better and better, but the shrimp do not. Still, it will taste good for a couple of days, and as leftovers dwindle they will make a fine pilaf or jambalaya, with lots of rice.

korean seafood stew

I discovered Korean seafood stews in tofu restaurants in Los Angeles' Koreatown—restaurants that specialize in bubbling-hot, spicy-hot stews served with rice and kimchi. This one, based on the Fiery Seafood Soup recipe in Hi Soo Shin Hepinstall's Growing Up in a Korean Kitchen (but much less fiery), is one of the easiest fish stews I've ever made. What is unique about it, and characteristically Korean, is how the ingredients are boiled rapidly, but for a short time. You can find Korean chili paste at Korean groceries and at some Asian groceries. ❖ **serves 4 to 6**

1	pound littleneck clams, purged (see page 376)
1½	pounds firm white fish fillets, such as halibut, red snapper, or mahimahi, cut in 2-inch pieces
	Salt and freshly ground black pepper
1	tablespoon vegetable or canola oil
5	large garlic cloves, minced or pressed
5	cups chicken stock (page 378) or beef stock
¼	cup Korean rice wine (*ch'ongju*) or dry white vermouth
½	teaspoon freshly squeezed ginger juice (see Note)
¾	pound napa cabbage hearts, cut in 1 by 1 ½-inch pieces
¾	pound Korean radishes or daikon, peeled and cut into 1 by 1½ by ¼-inch dominoes or small dice
¾	pound oyster mushrooms, trimmed and shredded, or white mushrooms, thinly sliced
¾	pound summer squash, sliced ¼ inch thick or diced
½	pound medium-firm tofu, cut into 1 by 1½ by ¼-inch dominoes or diced
1	bunch of scallions, white and light green part only, sliced about ¼ inch thick
1	to 3 teaspoons hot Korean chili powder (*koch'u karu*), to taste
1	to 2 tablespoons Korean hot red pepper paste (*koch'ujang*), to taste
1	hot red Korean chili or ½ red bell pepper, seeded, deveined, and thinly sliced

1 hot green Korean chili or serrano or jalapeño pepper, seeded, deveined, and thinly sliced

¼ pound fresh crabmeat

¼ pound spinach, stemmed, washed, and cut into ribbons

Cooked rice, for serving

combine the clams and 1 cup water in a saucepan or pot and bring to a boil. Cover, reduce the heat, and steam for 4 to 5 minutes, or until the clams open. Remove the clams from the pot and strain the cooking liquid through a strainer lined with cheesecloth set over a bowl. Remove the clams from their shells, rinse briefly to wash off the sand, and coarsely chop. Set aside (in the refrigerator if not finishing the dish for a few hours).

Place the fish in a bowl and season lightly with salt and pepper. Refrigerate if not using within the hour.

advance preparation
The dish can be made through this step and held for a few hours at room temperature, or in the refrigerator overnight. The vegetables won't look as vivid but the flavor of the soup won't suffer. Bring back to a boil and proceed with the recipe.

Heat the oil over medium-high heat in a wide, deep non-stick skillet or Dutch oven and add the garlic. Cook, stirring, for 1 to 2 minutes, until fragrant, and add the clam broth, stock, rice wine, and ginger juice. Add the cabbage, radishes or daikon, the mushrooms, squash, tofu, and half the scallions and bring to a rolling boil. Cover and boil for 7 minutes. Stir in the chili powder, red pepper paste, and the red bell pepper, and stir to dissolve. Taste and adjust the salt.

Add the fish and make sure the fish and vegetables are submerged in the broth. Cover and boil for 3 to 4 minutes, until the fish is opaque. Add the chili pepper(s), clams, and crabmeat, press everything into the broth, cover, and bring back to a boil. Add the spinach and the remaining scallions, cover, and remove from the heat. Let sit for a few seconds, then taste and adjust the salt. Serve in wide bowls, over rice.

Note: To make ginger juice, finely grate the ginger, preferably on a special ginger grater. Put the grated ginger into a garlic press, fine strainer, or cheesecloth bag and press out the juice. Some of the ginger will come out with it, which is fine.

leftovers Though I wouldn't plan to serve leftovers to guests, we've enjoyed this for dinner the next day. I usually fill it out with more rice.

seven

savory tarts, tortes, and pies

Some of the most exciting recipes in this book are in this chapter. Most are vegetarian. It's amazing how much flavor and substance can be packed into a savory crust. Pies are always dramatic—it's something about that tawny pastry—and whether sweet or savory, they're comforting.

There's a great tradition of vegetable pies throughout the Mediterranean. Vegetables would be harvested, sometimes foraged, prepared and set into wide pastry-lined dishes, and taken to the local bakery, where they would be baked in the dying embers of the bread oven.

I don't think I've ever gone to a Mediterranean country and not come home with a new recipe for a savory pie. Throughout the region you find variations on the same vegetable themes: greens of all kinds, winter squash, summer squash, leeks, eggplant, onions. What distinguishes one country's pies from another's are the aromatics—the fresh herbs—the cheeses, and the crusts. A winter squash torte from Provence, earthy with sage and surrounded by a bready olive oil crust, would never be mistaken for a Greek pumpkin torte redolent with mint and leeks, the filling set between layers of crisp filo dough. A Greek spinach or greens pie will be fragrant with dill and packed with feta cheese, whereas its French or Italian cousin will have a moderate amount of Gruyère and/or Parmesan, as well as garlic, thyme, rosemary, and parsley.

Most of these vegetable tortes are big. You can make them in a tart pan or springform pan, as a double-crusted torte, or you can make a galette. The tortes make great party fare, but they're also wonderful for family meals; they're good hot or cold, and leftovers pack easily into a lunch box or picnic basket.

The recipes take time to make, but they are forgiving. The order in which you do things isn't that important; you can make part or all of a filling one day, and the crust another (or vice versa), and put it all together when you're ready. Because they keep so well, they can be made ahead, or frozen. If you do the whole thing, from start to finish, you'll be working for about an hour, but nothing that you have to do is difficult; I love working with the ingredients that go into these. And the yeasted olive oil crust is about the easiest pastry I've ever dealt with.

greek pie crust

This crust, made with baking powder and olive oil, is very easy to work with. It's a crisp pie crust rather than a crumbly one, and the edges are quite hard, though the crust underneath the filling is tender and bready, somewhat like a pizza crust. It works equally well with unbleached white flour, half unbleached and half whole wheat, or whole wheat pastry flour. The whole wheat version has a nuttier flavor. ❖ **makes 2 10-inch crusts**

2¼ cups unbleached white flour, or 1¼ cups unbleached white and 1 cup whole wheat or whole wheat pastry flour, spooned in and leveled

¾ teaspoon salt

2 teaspoons baking powder

3 tablespoons olive oil

¾ cup water

in a bowl or in a food processor fitted with the steel blade, mix together the flour, salt, and baking powder. If using a bowl, make a well in the center and add the olive oil and water, and mix together with a fork. If using a food processor, add the olive oil with the machine running, then the water. The dough should come together in a ball. Do not overwork.

Turn the dough out onto a lightly floured surface and knead just until smooth, not more than a minute. If you have used a food processor, this will entail just a quick shaping of the dough into a ball. Divide the dough in half. Press each half into a circle, about 4 inches in diameter. Dust with unbleached white flour if the dough is sticky. Wrap tightly in plastic and place in a plastic bag. Refrigerate for 15 minutes.

advance preparation | Roll out each piece of dough on a lightly floured surface
The dough will keep for 3 days in the | into a thin 12-inch round, dusting both sides of the
refrigerator and can be frozen for | dough with unbleached white flour as necessary to pre-
several months. | vent it from sticking to the surface or to your rolling pin.

Spray or brush tart or pie pans with olive or vegetable oil. Line the pans with the dough and pinch an attractive edge around the rim. Wrap in plastic wrap and foil (to secure the plastic) and refrigerate or freeze until ready to use.

yeasted olive oil pastry

Yeasted crusts are easier to manipulate than short crusts. Use this Mediterranean crust for double-crusted tortes and galettes, or for any single-crusted savory tart. Remember to roll it thin so that it doesn't become too bready. ❖ **makes enough for 1 10- or 11-inch double-crusted torte or galette, or 2 10-inch tarts**

2 teaspoons active dry yeast

½ cup lukewarm water

½ teaspoon sugar

1 large egg, at room temperature, beaten

¼ cup olive oil

2 to 2½ cups unbleached all-purpose flour, or use half whole wheat flour, spooned in and leveled

¾ teaspoon salt

dissolve the yeast in the water, add the sugar, and allow to sit until the mixture is creamy, about 5 minutes. Beat in the egg and the olive oil. Combine 2 cups of the flour and the salt, and stir into the yeast mixture. You can use a bowl and wooden spoon for this, or a mixer; in the mixer combine the ingredients using the paddle, then switch to the dough hook. Work the dough until it comes together in a coherent mass, adding flour as necessary. Turn out onto a lightly floured surface and knead for a few minutes, adding flour as necessary, until the dough is smooth; do not overwork the dough. Shape into a ball. Place in a lightly oiled bowl, cover the dough tightly with plastic wrap, and allow the dough to rise in a draft-free spot until doubled in size, about 1 hour.

Turn the dough out onto a lightly floured surface, gently knead a couple of times, and cut into 2 equal pieces (or as directed in the recipe). Shape each piece into a ball. Cover the dough loosely with plastic wrap and let rest for 5 minutes. Then roll out into thin rounds, as directed in the recipe, and line the pans. If not using right away, freeze the crusts to prevent them from rising and becoming too bready. The crust can be transferred directly from the freezer to the oven.

classic french pastry
(pâte brisée)

I must admit a weakness for classic French pastry, the buttery kind that has the texture of a cookie. I use this pastry for pies that are bound with eggs, milk, and cheese, as the French quiche is. ❖ **makes enough pastry for 1 10-inch crust, or to cover a pot pie made in a 3-quart gratin dish**

1½ cups unbleached all-purpose flour, spooned in and leveled

½ teaspoon salt

7 tablespoons cold unsalted butter, cut into small pieces

3 to 5 tablespoons ice water

combine the flour and salt in a bowl or in the bowl of a food processor fitted with the steel blade. Add the butter and cut in by rolling the mixture briskly between the palms of your hands to make sure the butter is evenly distributed, or use the pulse action of the food processor. The mixture should have a crumbly, even consistency. Add the water 1 tablespoon at a time. Blend with a fork or your hands until the mixture comes together. If you are using a food processor, turn it on and add the water with the machine running, 1 tablespoon at a time. As soon as the dough comes together on the blades, stop the machine.

Butter your tart pan or pie dish (unless you are using this to top a pot pie). If the dough is quite warm and sticky, press out into a 4- or 5-inch disc, wrap in plastic, and refrigerate for 30 minutes. Otherwise you can roll it out right away on a lightly floured surface. Sprinkle the top lightly with flour to prevent it from sticking to the rolling pin, or cover the dough with a piece of wax paper. Roll out very thin, about ⅛ inch thick. To transfer to the dish, gently fold the dough in half, then lift onto the dish and unfold it. Ease it into the corners of the pan, without stretching the dough or working it, as this causes shrinkage during baking. Pinch an attractive lip around the edge of the dough. Cover with plastic wrap and refrigerate for at least 2 hours, or up to 4 or 5 days, or freeze for up to 3 months.

Note: If using for a pot pie, press into a ½-inch-thick circle, wrap in plastic, and seal in a plastic bag. Refrigerate for several hours or overnight.

greek greens and sweet onion pie

Dill and parsley give this pie its Greek character. Use a mix of greens, or just one type. The crust can be filo dough, Greek Pie Crust (page 263), Yeasted Olive Oil Pastry (page 264), or even commercial puff pastry (less authentic but very easy, and pretty, too). I use chard or beet greens most often for this; the beets go into a salad, the greens into the luscious pie. ❖ **serves 6** ❖

Salt

2 to 2½ pounds greens, such as beet greens, red or green chard, or spinach, stemmed and washed thoroughly

1 tablespoon olive oil, plus more for oiling the pan

2 cups chopped spring onions or 1 large red onion, chopped

2 large garlic cloves, minced or pressed

¼ cup chopped fresh dill

¼ cup chopped fresh flat-leaf parsley

3 large eggs, beaten

¼ pound feta cheese, crumbled

Freshly ground black pepper

For the pastry, either:

    1 recipe Greek Pie Crust (page 263)

    1 recipe Yeasted Olive Oil Pastry (page 264)

    2 sheets commercial puff pastry

    12 sheets filo pastry (with melted butter or olive oil for brushing)

advance preparation
The blanched greens will keep in the refrigerator in a covered bowl for 3 or 4 days.

bring a large pot of water to a rolling boil. Add a tablespoon of salt and the greens. Blanch for 2 minutes, or until just tender. Using a slotted spoon or skimmer, transfer to a bowl of cold water, then drain. Squeeze out any excess water and chop.

advance preparation
This step can be done hours before
you assemble the tart.
Heat the oven to 375°F. Oil or butter a 9- or 10-inch tart pan (preferably) or a ceramic pie pan. Heat the olive oil in a large nonstick skillet over medium heat and add the onions. Cook, stirring often, until tender but not browned, about 5 minutes. Add the garlic and cook, stirring, for another 30 seconds to a minute, until the garlic is fragrant. Stir in the greens and herbs, and stir the mixture for a minute, until the greens are coated with oil. Remove from the heat.

Beat the eggs in a large bowl. Remove 2 tablespoons of the beaten eggs for brushing the crust. Add the feta and greens, mix well, and season with salt and pepper.

Line the pie dish with two thirds of the dough. Fill with the greens mixture. Roll out the other piece of dough and place over the filling. Crimp the bottom and top edges together, then pinch an attractive fluted edge all the way around the rim of the pie. Brush the top with the reserved beaten egg and make a few slashes in the top crust so that steam can escape as the pie bakes. If using filo, line the dish with 7 pieces, brushing each piece with melted butter or olive oil and turning the dish after each piece so the edges of the filo drape evenly over the dish. Fill with the greens. Layer the remaining 5 pieces on top, brushing each and turning the dish. Stuff the edges into the sides of the dish and brush the top well with butter or olive oil.

Bake for 40 to 50 minutes, until the crust is golden. Serve hot, warm, or at room temperature.

leftovers The finished tart keeps for a few days, but you must keep recrisping the filo if using. This is easily done, either in a low oven (250 to 300°F.) for 10 to 20 minutes, or in a hot oven (350 to 400°F.) that has just been turned off, for 5 to 10 minutes.

greens and potato torta or galette

This luscious pie works well with a number of greens—chard, broccoli raab, beet greens, spinach—whatever looks best in the market. It's quite dramatic as a galette, equally delicious put together as a torta. Serve it hot or at room temperature. It's an excellent keeper. ❖ **serves 6**

¾ pound small potatoes such as baby Yukon gold or red-skinned potatoes, peeled if desired

Salt

2 to 2½ pounds greens (chard, beet greens, broccoli raab, spinach), stemmed and cleaned

2 tablespoons olive oil

1 medium or large onion, chopped

2 large garlic cloves, minced

½ cup chopped flat-leaf parsley

2 tablespoons chopped fresh basil

Freshly ground black pepper

1 cup ricotta or low-fat cottage cheese

2 large eggs, beaten

2 tablespoons milk

2 ounces Gruyère cheese, grated (½ cup, tightly packed)

1 ounce Parmesan, grated (¼ cup)

Pinch of freshly grated nutmeg

1 recipe Yeasted Olive Oil Pastry (page 264)

place the potatoes and 2 teaspoons salt in a large pot of water (you'll be cooking the greens in the same water) and bring to a boil. Reduce the heat to medium, cover partially, and boil the potatoes for 20 minutes, or until tender when pierced with a knife. Meanwhile, stem the greens and wash the leaves thoroughly, making sure to remove all sand.

advance preparation
The potatoes and greens can be cooked 3 or 4 days ahead and held in the refrigerator in a covered bowl.

When the potatoes are done, remove from the water with a skimmer, set aside until cool enough to handle, and then cut in ½-inch slices. Bring the water back to a rolling boil and add another teaspoon of salt and the greens. Blanch for about 2 minutes, until just tender.

Remove from the water with a skimmer and transfer immediately to a bowl of cold water. Drain and squeeze dry. Chop coarsely and set aside.

advance preparation
This can be left on the counter for several hours, or in the refrigerator for a day.

Heat the oil over medium heat in a large nonstick skillet. Add the onion and cook, stirring, until tender, about 5 minutes. Add the garlic and cook, stirring, until fragrant, 30 seconds to a minute. Stir in the greens, potatoes, and herbs, and gently toss together. Season to taste with salt and pepper, and transfer to a large bowl.

In a food processor fitted with the steel blade, process the ricotta or cottage cheese until smooth. Scrape down the sides. Set aside 2 tablespoons of the beaten egg, then add the rest to the processor with the milk. Pulse to combine, then scrape into the bowl with the greens. Mix in the other cheeses, more salt and pepper, and the nutmeg.

Heat the oven to 375°F. Gently punch down the dough. If making a galette, roll out into a large, thin circle, about 16 inches in diameter, and transfer to a cookie sheet. Top with the filling, leaving a 2½-inch edge, and fold the edges in over the filling, draping folds all the way around. If you can stretch the dough up to the middle, gather the edges together and shape a little top knot. Otherwise you can leave an opening in the center. If making a torta, oil a 10-inch springform pan or a deep tart pan with a removable rim. Roll out two thirds of the dough into a thin circle, and line the pie dish or pan; ease the dough into the edges. There should be some overhang. Fill with the greens mixture. Roll out the other piece of dough into a circle, and place on top of the filling. Fold the edges of the bottom crust over the top crust, and crimp the dough all the way around the edge. Gently score the top of the dough with a paring knife. Brush the torta or galette with the reserved egg and bake for 45 to 50 minutes, until the top is golden brown.

leftovers : This continues to taste terrific for 3 or 4 days after it's made. It makes handy picnic or lunch fare, and an instant dinner, warmed in the oven or microwave if you wish.

really simple greens pie

This is a standard quiche—a custard made with eggs, milk, and cheese, with onions, greens, and garlic stirred in. It's about the simplest main dish you can do with greens, short of an omelet, which is also great. ❖ serves 4 to 6

Salt

2 bunches of greens (about 1½ pounds), stemmed and washed thoroughly

1 tablespoon olive oil

1 small onion, chopped

1 or 2 garlic cloves (to taste), minced or pressed

Half recipe Yeasted Olive Oil Pastry (page 264) or Classic French Pastry (pages 265)

4 large eggs

¾ cup milk

Freshly ground black pepper

2 ounces Gruyère cheese, grated (½ cup)

1 ounce Parmesan cheese, grated (¼ cup)

advance preparation
The blanched greens will keep in the refrigerator in a covered bowl for 3 or 4 days.

bring a large pot of water to a rolling boil, add a tablespoon of salt, and add the greens. Blanch for 2 minutes, or until just tender. Using a slotted spoon or deep-fry skimmer, transfer to a bowl of cold water, then drain. Squeeze out any excess water and chop. Set aside.

advance preparation
This step can be done hours before you assemble the pie.

Heat the oven to 375°F. Heat the oil in a large, heavy nonstick skillet over medium heat. Add the onion and cook, stirring, until tender, about 5 minutes. Stir in the garlic and cook for about 30 seconds to a minute, just until fragrant. Stir in the greens, toss together, and remove from the heat.

Roll out the pastry and line a 9- or 10-inch pie plate or tart pan. Beat the eggs, brush the crust with a little bit of the beaten egg, and bake the crust for 5 minutes. Remove from the oven and cool on a rack while you finish the filling.

Beat together the eggs, milk, ½ teaspoon salt, and pepper to taste. Stir in the greens and the cheeses. If you're using beet greens from red beets, the mixture will be pink, but it will be much less pink after baking. Pour into the crust. Bake for 30 to 40 minutes, until the filling is firm and the top is just beginning to brown. Serve hot, warm, or at room temperature.

leftovers ⦙ This will be good for at least 3 days after it's baked. It makes a great, easy lunch. I cut it into squares and pack them in my son's lunch box.

spanakopita

This is just one version of the popular Greek spinach pie. Like the other Greek classic, mous-saka, spanakopita has been badly done too many times in too many mediocre Greek restaurants (both here and in Greece). This one is alive with flavors of the Greek countryside—dill, rosemary, thyme, parsley—and it's packed with spinach. ❖ **serves 6**

2¼ pounds spinach, stems removed and leaves washed

2 tablespoons olive oil, plus olive oil for the filo dough

3 large leeks, white and light green parts only, cleaned and thinly sliced

Leaves from 1 bunch of flat-leaf parsley, chopped

2 tablespoons chopped fresh rosemary or 2 teaspoons crumbled dried rosemary

4 tablespoons chopped fresh dill

1½ teaspoons fresh thyme leaves, or ¾ teaspoon dried thyme

3 large eggs, beaten

6 ounces feta cheese, crumbled

Salt and freshly ground black pepper

¼ teaspoon freshly grated nutmeg

12 sheets filo dough

1 egg white, lightly beaten

advance preparation
The wilted spinach will keep for 3 or 4 days, covered, in the refrigerator.

wilt the spinach over medium-high heat in a large nonaluminum frying pan in the water left on the leaves after washing. Transfer to a colander, rinse with cold water, and press out as much water as possible. Then wrap it in a towel and squeeze out more water. Chop fairly fine and set aside.

Heat the oven to 375°F. Heat the olive oil in a large, heavy nonstick skillet over medium heat and add the leeks. Cook for about 10 minutes, stirring often, until soft-ened and just beginning to brown. Add the spinach and stir together until the spinach is coated with oil. Remove from the heat.

advance preparation
You can make the recipe through
this step several hours or a day
ahead. Keep on top of the stove or in
the refrigerator in a covered bowl.

advance preparation
The spanakopita can be assembled a
few hours before you bake it, and
held in or out of the refrigerator.

Combine the parsley with the spinach and leeks in a large bowl, along with the remaining herbs, the beaten eggs, feta, salt, pepper, and nutmeg.

Brush a 10- or 12-inch tart pan with olive oil and layer in 7 sheets of filo dough, turning the pan as you layer so that the edges overlap the sides of the pan all the way around. Brush each sheet with olive oil before adding the next sheet. Top with the spinach mixture. Fold the edges of the dough over the spinach mixture and brush them with olive oil. Layer 5 more sheets of dough over the top, brushing each sheet with olive oil, and crimp the edges into the sides of the pan. Brush the top with beaten egg white. Pierce the top of the pie in several places with a sharp knife. Bake for 45 to 50 minutes, until the top is golden brown. Serve hot or at room temperature.

leftovers The finished tart keeps for a few days, but you must keep recrisping the filo if using. This is easily done, either in a low oven (250 to 300°F.) for 10 to 20 minutes, or in a hot oven (350 to 400°F.) that has just been turned off, for 5 to 10 minutes.

provençal zucchini and greens torte

This is a gorgeous double-crusted savory torte, packed with vegetables, texture, and flavor. The filling could as easily be used for a gratin, if you don't feel like putting it into this easy-to-work-with and satisfying pastry (see the variation that follows). It's important to cut the zucchini into very small dice, about ¼ or ⅓ inch, for the best texture and look. You can use a number of greens for this—spinach, chard, and beet greens are all good choices. You can prepare the filling for this while the dough is rising. ❖ serves 6 to 8

Salt

1 pound greens, such as Swiss chard, beet greens, or spinach, stemmed and washed

2 tablespoons olive oil

1 medium onion, finely chopped

2 pounds zucchini, cut in small dice (¼ to ⅓ inch)

2 to 3 large garlic cloves (to taste), minced or pressed

½ cup chopped fresh flat-leaf parsley

1 teaspoon fresh thyme leaves, or ½ teaspoon dried thyme

1 to 2 teaspoons chopped fresh rosemary, or ½ to 1 teaspoon crumbled dried rosemary (to taste)

Freshly ground black pepper

3 large eggs

½ cup Arborio or medium-grain rice, cooked

2 ounces Gruyère cheese, grated (½ cup, tightly packed)

1 recipe Yeasted Olive Oil Pastry (page 264)

advance preparation
The blanched greens will keep for 3 or 4 days in the refrigerator in a covered bowl.

bring a large pot of water to a rolling boil; add a tablespoon of salt and the greens. Blanch for 2 minutes, or until just tender. Using a slotted spoon or deep-fry skimmer, transfer to a bowl of cold water, then drain. Squeeze out any excess water and chop. Set aside.

advance preparation
The zucchini and greens mixture can
be prepared up to a day ahead and
kept in the refrigerator in a covered
bowl. The zucchini's color will fade.

Heat the oil over medium heat in a large nonstick skillet and add the onion. Cook, stirring, until tender, about 5 minutes, then stir in the zucchini. Season to taste with salt, and cook, stirring, until just tender and still bright green, about 8 minutes. Stir in the garlic and cook until the garlic is fragrant, about 1 or 2 minutes. Stir in the greens, parsley, thyme, and rosemary, toss everything together, and remove from the heat. Taste and season with salt and pepper.

Beat the eggs in a large bowl, and remove 2 tablespoons for brushing the crust. Stir in ¼ to ½ teaspoon salt (depending on your taste), the zucchini mixture, the rice, and the Gruyère. Mix everything together and add lots of pepper.

Heat the oven to 375°F. Oil a 10- or 12-inch tart pan or springform pan. Roll out two thirds of the dough and line the pan, with the edges of the dough overhanging. Fill with the zucchini mixture. Top with the remaining dough, then crimp the edges of the top and bottom together. Cut 4 or 5 small slits in the top crust with a sharp knife, brush with beaten egg, and bake for 40 to 50 minutes, until golden brown. Allow to rest for at least 10 minutes before serving (preferably longer). This can also be served at room temperature.

leftovers The finished tart keeps for a few days in the refrigerator, and it makes a great leftover. Take wedges to work for enviable lunches.

zucchini and greens gratin

variation
Omit the crust. Make the filling as directed and spread in an oiled 2-quart gratin dish. Mix together ¼ cup of bread crumbs with 1 tablespoon olive oil and sprinkle over the top. Bake at 375°F. for 40 to 45 minutes, until the top is nicely browned.

greek winter squash and leek pie

I first ate a Greek savory pumpkin pie, in filo pastry, at a conference on Greek gastronomy organized by Oldways in 1991. The lunches at the conference were prepared by people from all over Greece, brought in from their villages to make local specialties in a market setting. I found myself back at the booth with the vegetable pies over and over again.

If using butternut squash for this, cut in half crosswise, just above the bulbous bottom part, then cut these halves into lengthwise quarters and scrape away the seeds and membranes.

❖ serves 6

2½ pounds winter squash (such as 1 large or 2 smaller butternut squash), seeds and membranes scraped away, cut into large pieces

½ cup chopped fresh flat-leaf parsley

¼ cup chopped fresh mint

¼ teaspoon freshly grated nutmeg

1 cup crumbled feta cheese (about 5 ounces)

½ cup grated Parmesan cheese (2 ounces)

2 tablespoons olive oil, plus additional for brushing the filo

3 large leeks (about 1½ pounds), white and light green parts only, cleaned and chopped

2 large garlic cloves, minced or pressed

3 large eggs

Salt and freshly ground black pepper

12 sheets filo dough

advance preparation
The squash can be cooked and mashed 3 or 4 days ahead, and kept in the refrigerator in a covered bowl. Do not stir in the herbs, nutmeg, and cheese until the day you bake it.

steam the squash for 15 to 20 minutes, until tender, then transfer to a colander and allow to cool and drain for another 15 minutes (butternut squash will not be watery). When the squash has cooled, peel and place in a bowl. Mash with a fork, a large wooden spoon, a potato masher, or a pestle. Stir in the herbs, nutmeg, and cheeses.

advance preparation
The filling will keep for 2 or 3 days in
the refrigerator.
Heat the olive oil over medium heat in a large, heavy
nonstick frying pan and add the leeks. Cook, stirring,
until tender and just beginning to color, 5 to 10 minutes.
Add the garlic and continue to cook for another minute,
until fragrant. Remove from the heat and add to the squash. Beat the eggs and remove
2 tablespoons for brushing the tart, then stir the rest into the squash. Season to taste
with salt and pepper.

Heat the oven to 375°F. Brush a 10- or 12-inch tart pan or cake pan with olive oil and
layer in 7 sheets of filo dough, turning the pan as you layer so that the edges overlap
the sides of the pan all the way around. Brush each sheet with olive oil before adding
the next sheet. Fill with the squash mixture, and fold the edges over. Brush the filo
with olive oil, then layer 5 more sheets of dough over the top, brushing each sheet
with olive oil. Crimp the edges into the sides of the pan. Brush the top with the
reserved beaten egg. Pierce the top of the pie in several places with a sharp knife. Bake
for 40 to 50 minutes, until the top is golden brown. Serve warm or at room temperature. Re-crisp the crust if necessary in a low oven for 10 to 20 minutes.

Note: You can also make this as a galette or a double-crusted tart, using either a Greek
Pie Crust (page 263) or a Yeasted Olive Oil Pastry (page 264).

leftovers | The finished tart keeps for a few days, but you must keep
crisping the filo. This is easily done, either in a low oven (250 to 300°F.) for 10 to 20 minutes, or in a hot oven (350 to 400°F.) that has just been turned off, for 5 to 10 minutes.

provençal winter squash torte

In Provence, many of the vegetable tortes are bound with rice, which both gives them substance and texture, and makes them easy to slice, thus very portable. This wonderful torte is seasoned with sage, one of winter squash's favorite companions. The filling also makes a terrific gratin, without the crust, and it can also be made as a galette (see instructions on page 268). ❖ **serves 6**

2 to 2½ pounds winter squash (such as 1 large or 2 smaller butternut squash), seeds and membranes scraped away, cut into large pieces (see headnote on page 276)

2 tablespoons olive oil, plus more for oiling the pan

1 large onion, chopped

3 large garlic cloves, minced or pressed

½ cup Italian Arborio or medium-grain rice, cooked

2 tablespoons chopped fresh sage

2 tablespoons chopped fresh flat-leaf parsley

2 ounces Gruyère cheese, grated (½ cup)

1 ounce Parmesan cheese, grated (¼ cup)

3 large eggs, beaten

Salt (about ½ teaspoon or more) and freshly ground black pepper

1 recipe Yeasted Olive Oil Pastry (page 264)

advance preparation
The squash can be cooked and mashed 3 or 4 days ahead, and kept in the refrigerator in a covered bowl.

steam the squash for 15 to 20 minutes, until tender, then transfer to a colander and allow to cool and drain for another 15 minutes (butternut squash will not be watery). When the squash has cooled, peel and place in a bowl. Mash with a fork, a large wooden spoon, a potato masher, or a pestle.

advance preparation
The filling will keep for 2 or 3 days in
the refrigerator.
Heat the oil over medium heat in a heavy nonstick skillet and add the onion. Cook, stirring, until tender, about 5 minutes, and stir in the garlic. Cook for another minute or two, until fragrant. Remove from the heat and toss with the squash, rice, sage, parsley, cheeses, all but 2 tablespoons of the eggs, salt, and pepper.

Heat the oven to 375°F. Oil a 10- or 12-inch tart pan or springform pan. Roll out two thirds of the dough and line the pan, with the edges of the dough overhanging. Fill with the squash mixture. Top with the remaining dough, then crimp the edges of the top and bottom together. Cut 4 small slits in the top crust with a sharp knife, brush with the reserved beaten egg, and bake for 45 to 50 minutes, until golden brown. Allow to rest for at least 10 minutes before serving. This can also be served at room temperature.

leftovers The finished tart keeps for a few days in the refrigerator. Serve it warm or at room temperature. It makes a fine leftover, for lunch or dinner.

greek leek and fennel pie

Leeks and fennel, already softened in the pan, sweeten as they bake in this generous Greek pie.
Dill and parsley provide that Greek sparkle to the mix. ❖ **serves 6**

2 tablespoons olive oil, plus additional for the filo

1 medium onion, finely chopped

4 leeks (about 1½ pounds), white and light green parts only

Salt

3 large garlic cloves, minced or pressed

2½ pounds fennel, trimmed, quartered, cored, and chopped

Freshly ground black pepper

3 large eggs

6 ounces feta cheese, crumbled (about 1½ cups)

¼ cup chopped fresh dill

¼ cup chopped fresh flat-leaf parsley

12 sheets filo dough

advance preparation
You can cook the fennel and leeks a day or two ahead and keep them in a covered bowl in the refrigerator.

heat the oil over medium heat in a large nonstick skillet and add the onion. Cook, stirring, until it begins to soften, about 3 minutes. Add the leeks and cook, stirring, until they begin to soften, a couple of minutes, then add a generous pinch of salt. Cook, stirring often, until the onion and leeks are thoroughly tender. Stir in the garlic and the fennel. Cook, stirring often, for 5 to 10 minutes, until the fennel is tender and fragrant. Season to taste with salt and pepper, and remove from the heat.

advance preparation
You can make the filling hours or even a day before assembling the pie, and keep in the refrigerator.

Heat the oven to 375°F. Oil a 10- or 12-inch tart pan or cake pan. Beat the eggs in a large bowl. Crumble in the feta and stir in the cooked vegetables, the dill, and the parsley. Season with salt and pepper.

advance preparation
The pie can be assembled, covered
tightly with plastic, and refrigerated
for a day. The filo is best if the tart is
served not too long after baking.

Layer in 7 sheets of phyllo dough, turning the pan as you layer so that the edges overlap the sides of the pan all the way around. Brush each sheet with olive oil before adding the next sheet. Top with the fennel mixture. Fold the edges of the dough over the filling and brush them with olive oil. Layer 5 more sheets of dough over the top, brushing each sheet with oil. Crimp the edges into the sides of the pan. Brush the top. Pierce the top of the pie in several places with a sharp knife. Bake for 45 to 50 minutes, until the top is golden brown. Serve hot or at room temperature.

leftovers The finished tart keeps for a few days, but you must keep crisping the filo. This is easily done, either in a low oven (250 to 300°F.) for 10 to 20 minutes, or in a hot oven (350 to 400°F.) that has just been turned off, for 5 to 10 minutes.

greek cheese and squash pie

This light summery pie is absolutely heady, with dill, parsley, and mint as the star seasonings.

❖ serves 6

3 pounds zucchini, coarsely shredded or finely chopped

Salt

2 tablespoons olive oil, plus additional for brushing the filo

1 large red onion, finely chopped

Freshly ground black pepper

3 large eggs

½ pound feta cheese (Greek or Bulgarian if possible), crumbled

½ pound ricotta (about 1 cup)

¼ cup Yogurt Cheese (page 387)

¼ cup chopped fresh flat-leaf parsley

¼ cup chopped fresh dill

1 heaped tablespoon chopped fresh mint, or 1 heaped teaspoon dried mint

12 sheets filo dough

toss the zucchini with about ½ teaspoon salt. Let sit in a colander for 15 to 30 minutes, or longer. Then squeeze out the water.

advance preparation
This step can be done a day ahead.
Refrigerate the zucchini in a covered bowl, and drain again the next day if necessary.

Heat the olive oil over medium heat in a large nonstick skillet and add the onion. Cook, stirring often, until tender, about 5 minutes. Stir in the zucchini and cook, stirring often, until tender, 10 to 15 minutes. Season to taste with salt and pepper. There should not be much liquid from the zucchini in the pan, because of the salting, but if there is, transfer the mixture to a colander and allow to drain in the sink for 15 minutes.

Heat the oven to 375°F. Oil a 10-inch tart or cake pan or a 12 by 10-inch baking pan.

Beat the eggs in a large bowl. Add the feta, ricotta, and drained yogurt and mix together well. Stir in the zucchini, parsley, dill, and mint. Add salt and pepper.

advance preparation
You can assemble the pie several hours before you bake it. Cover with plastic and refrigerate.

Line the baking dish or pie pan with the first 7 sheets of filo dough, draping each piece over the side of the pan and brushing each one with olive oil before adding the next, and turning the pan a little bit after adding each sheet so that they fan out around the pan. Top with the filling and spread in an even layer. Fold the edges of the filo over, and top with the remaining 5 sheets of dough, brushing each sheet with olive oil. Tuck the edges into the sides of the pan.

Pierce the dough in a few places with a sharp knife, and place in the oven. Bake for 50 minutes, or until the crust is golden. Remove from the oven and cool on a rack for at least 15 minutes before serving. Serve hot, warm, or at room temperature.

leftovers : This is best served the day it's made, but it will keep for a few days in the refrigerator, and leftovers taste good. But you must keep crisping the filo. This is easily done, either in a low oven (250 to 300°F.) for 10 to 20 minutes, or in a hot oven (350 to 400°F.) that has just been turned off, for 5 to 10 minutes.

deep-dish eggplant torte

This is really a molded eggplant parmigiana in a crust. It slices beautifully and is great for a vegetarian showcase main dish. It's time-consuming, but you can make all or part of it well before you wish to serve it. It looks beautiful on a buffet. ❖ **serves 8**

Salt

3 to 3½ pounds eggplant (3 large), cut in ⅓-inch slices

Olive oil

2 to 3 large garlic cloves, minced or pressed (to taste)

3 pounds tomatoes, quartered, or 2 (28-ounce) cans tomatoes, drained of all but about ½ cup of the juice

⅛ teaspoon sugar

1 tablespoon tomato paste

2 to 3 tablespoons slivered fresh basil leaves

Freshly ground black pepper

1 recipe Yeasted Olive Oil Pastry (page 264) or 2 recipes Classic French Pastry (page 265) (can use half whole wheat flour for the French pastry if desired)

4 large eggs, beaten

6 ounces mozzarella, thinly sliced if fresh, otherwise grated

½ cup fresh bread crumbs

1 heaped cup freshly grated Parmesan

salt the eggplant slices and let stand for 30 minutes. Meanwhile, heat the oven to 450°F. and make the tomato sauce.

advance preparation
The tomato sauce will hold for 3 or 4 days in the refrigerator and can be frozen for a few months.

Heat 1 tablespoon of olive oil over medium heat in a large, heavy nonstick skillet and add the garlic. When the garlic just begins to color, after about 30 seconds, add the tomatoes and their liquid, the sugar, tomato paste, and salt to taste. Cook, stirring often, for 20 to 25 minutes, until the tomatoes are cooked down and fragrant. Remove from the heat and pass through the medium blade of a food mill. Stir in the fresh basil and add a few grinds of the pepper mill. Taste and adjust the seasonings.

Rinse the eggplant slices and blot dry. Generously oil baking sheets with olive oil. Place the eggplant rounds on the baking sheets and brush the tops with olive oil. Bake until lightly browned and tender, 10 to 15 minutes. Remove from the heat. Turn the oven down to 375°F.

Generously butter or oil a 10-inch springform pan or cake pan. Roll out two thirds of the dough to a large, thin round and line the pan, making sure that there is some over-hang all the way around the edge. Beat the eggs and use a bit to brush the bottom and inside of the crust. Make a layer of eggplant over the crust, with the pieces slightly overlapping. Top with a layer of one third of the mozzarella, then a layer of tomato sauce, and a third of the bread crumbs and Parmesan. Repeat the layers two more times, ending with the tomato sauce, bread crumbs, and Parmesan. Pour on all but 2 tablespoons of the beaten eggs; they should sink into the mixture.

advance preparation
The torte can be assembled and refrigerated or frozen for a day before baking. The finished torte will hold for several hours.

Roll out the remaining dough and place it over the top of the torte. Fold over the overhanging edge and pinch an attractive lip around the rim of the pan. Brush the top crust with the reserved beaten egg. Bake for 50 minutes to 1 hour, until golden brown. Remove from the oven and allow to sit for 15 to 30 minutes. Serve hot or at room temperature, in wedges.

leftovers The torte will be good for about 5 days, and although the bottom of the crust will probably get soggy after a while, it will taste fantastic.

flemish leek tart

There are many ways to make this classic French flamiche. Some cooks use a béchamel and lit-tle cheese and egg. But this version is quicker, and it tastes incredibly rich, though it needn't be, especially if you use the drained yogurt instead of cream (this is my method and far from authentic, but it works beautifully). The important thing is to use a quantity of leeks—don't skimp. The tart should be packed with them. ❖ serves 6

2 tablespoons unsalted butter

3 pounds leeks, white and light green parts only, cleaned (see page 375) and chopped

¾ teaspoon salt

Freshly ground black pepper

1 recipe Classic French Pastry (page 265)

3 large eggs

¼ cup Yogurt Cheese (page 387), crème fraîche, milk, or heavy cream

3 ounces imported ham, such as Paris or Parma, chopped (optional)

3 ounces Gruyère cheese, grated (¾ cup)

advance preparation
The leeks can be cooked hours or even a day before you assemble the tart. Keep for up to 3 hours on top of the stove, or refrigerate in a covered bowl. Allow to come to room tem-perature before assembling the tart.

heat the butter over medium-low heat in a large, heavy nonstick skillet and add the leeks. Cook, stirring often, until they begin to soften, 3 to 5 minutes, then add ¼ teaspoon of the salt, cover the pan, and turn the heat to low. Cook, stirring from time to time, for 15 minutes, until very soft but not browned. Add freshly ground pepper and remove from the heat. If there is a lot of liquid in the pan, drain the leeks in a colander.

Heat the oven to 400°F. Roll out the crust and line a buttered 10-inch tart pan. Beat the eggs and brush the crust with a little of the egg, then prebake the crust for 7 minutes.

Beat together the eggs, the remaining ½ teaspoon of salt, and the yogurt, crème fraiche, milk, or cream. Stir in the leeks and ham, if using, and all but ¼ cup of the cheese. Scrape into the pie crust. Sprinkle the remaining cheese on the top.

Bake for 40 to 45 minutes, until the top is nicely browned. Serve warm or at room temperature.

leftovers ⋮ This will keep for 3 or 4 days in the refrigerator. We took our leftovers to the opera and had a lovely supper during intermission.

alsatian cheese, bacon, and onion tart

This is the pizza of Alsace, called tarte flambée *or* flammenküche *in the local dialect, a paper-thin crust topped with bacon, onion, and a creamy white cheese called fromage blanc. It's traditionally baked in a wood-fire oven, but a very hot home oven will do just fine. The trick to a successful tarte flambée is to roll the dough as thin as you can.* ❖ makes 2 12- to 14-inch pies

for the dough

2 teaspoons active dry yeast

1 cup lukewarm water

1 teaspoon salt

2½ to 3 cups unbleached white flour

for the topping

2 tablespoons unsalted butter

2 medium onions, sliced into very thin rounds

1 cup cottage cheese or ricotta (can use low-fat)

1 cup crème fraîche, sour cream, or plain yogurt (can use low-fat or nonfat)

Salt and freshly ground black pepper

8 ounces slab bacon, rind removed, or rindless bacon, cut into slivers

make the dough. Dissolve the yeast in the water and allow to sit for a few minutes, until the mixture is creamy. Combine the salt with half the flour and stir into the dough. Fold in the remaining flour until you can turn the dough out onto a work surface. Flour your work surface, turn out the dough, and knead for 10 minutes, adding flour as necessary. The dough should be elastic and slightly sticky. Clean and oil your bowl, place the dough in it, turn the dough over, and cover the bowl tightly with

advance preparation
You can make the dough, roll it out
(see below), and freeze it in the pans
up to a couple of months before you
use it. Wrap in plastic, then tightly
in foil. Remove from the freezer,
spread with the topping, and bake
without defrosting first.

advance preparation
The filling can be made a few hours
before you make the pies. Refrigerate
if holding for more than an hour.

advance preparation
The tarts can be baked a few hours
ahead and reheated or crisped in a
hot oven.

plastic wrap. Let rise until doubled, about 1½ to 2 hours. Punch down the dough and divide into two pieces. Shape each piece into a ball and cover with a damp towel.

While the dough is rising, make the filling. Heat the butter over medium heat in a large, heavy nonstick skillet and add the onions. Cook, stirring, just until tender, 5 to 8 minutes, and remove from the heat. Blend the cottage cheese or ricotta in a food processor fitted with the steel blade until smooth, scraping down the sides once or twice. Add the crème fraîche, sour cream, or yogurt and blend together. Scrape into a bowl and stir in the onions. Season with salt and pepper.

Heat the oven to 450°F., preferably with a baking stone in it. Roll out one piece of the dough, flouring your work surface and the top of the dough to prevent sticking, into a very thin round, about 12 inches in diameter. Place on a baking sheet or pizza pan. Spread half the cheese mixture over the dough and sprinkle on half the bacon. Season liberally with pepper, and place in the oven (or roll out the other piece of dough, assemble the second tart, and put them both in the oven). Bake until crisp, 20 to 25 minutes. If the second tart isn't already assembled, do so while the first one is baking. These are best eaten hot from the oven, but can be made ahead and recrisped.

eight

rice, stir-fries,
and couscous

It's not surprising that entire books, much bigger than the one you're reading, have been devoted to the subject of rice. Rice is a staple that has traveled around the world and found a different expression wherever it landed. An Asian stir-fry or an Indian pilau could never be confused with a rich, saucy Italian risotto or a spicy Cajun jambalaya. But one thing these dishes do have in common is that they make nourishing and satisfying one-dish meals.

One glance at the contents of this chapter and you'll see that my heart and experience with rice lie in the Mediterranean, and specifically, that I have a weakness for risotto. It can be a vehicle for practically any vegetable, and I find that it's as calming to make as it is to eat; stirring the rice is leisurely for me, and the dinner always tastes extravagant. Ingredients for risotto can always be prepped in advance when it's convenient for you. And I've learned over the years that risottos can also be cooked ahead up to the halfway point, making them viable dinner party entrées. Even though they're served when they're ready, you won't have to finish them until *you* are ready.

Asian stir-fries, whether served with rice or noodles, also make terrific one-dish meals. Unlike many of the recipes in this book, stir-fries are cooked in a matter of minutes and eaten straightaway. But the prep work required can be as unhurried as you wish it to be. You can prepare noodles, vegetables, and aromatics the night before, arrange them in bowls or bags, and make dinner quickly, as soon as you come home from work. Or the chopping and measuring itself can be a relaxing activity in the early evening over a glass of wine. If your children like to help in the kitchen, prep for stir-fries can be fun for them, because they'll see the results of their work so quickly.

Another comforting grainy staple that makes a feast of a meal is couscous. A couscous dinner can be an event; it can also be a simple family meal. Whether simple or elaborate, couscous meals are particularly forgiving—most of them get better with time, some can be done in stages, and the couscous can be reconstituted whenever it's convenient for you, then steamed right before dinner. The vegetable, meat, and fish stews that accompany couscous are from Tunisia and Morocco—cuisines that differ greatly, but have couscous in common.

cauliflower and snow pea pilaf

I probably never would have developed this recipe if my friend John Lyons, gardener par excellence, hadn't brought me a gorgeous huge cauliflower and some snow peas one New Year's Day. Knowing that cauliflower is much loved by Indian cooks, and that peas go well with it, I adapted this recipe from one by Neela Paniz, owner of the Bombay Cafe in Los Angeles. Hers is spicier than mine, which has plenty of Indian flavors but only a slight amount of heat. ❖ **serves 6**

1½ cups basmati rice

2 tablespoons peanut oil

2 teaspoons cumin seeds

1 tablespoon chopped fresh ginger

1 large cauliflower (2 to 2½ pounds), rinsed, trimmed and cut into small florets, the florets sliced if desired

2 teaspoons ground coriander

¼ teaspoon cayenne pepper

¼ teaspoon turmeric

1¼ teaspoons salt

2¾ cups hot water

½ pound snow peas or sugar snap peas, stems and strings removed

2 to 4 tablespoons chopped fresh cilantro (to taste)

place the rice in a bowl and wash in several changes of water until the water runs clear. Cover with water and soak while you prepare the remaining ingredients.

Heat the oil over medium-high heat in a large, lidded nonstick skillet or flameproof casserole. Add the cumin seeds and when they begin to sizzle, add the ginger. Stir-fry for 30 seconds to a minute, until fragrant and just beginning to color. Add the cauliflower to the pan. Cook, stirring, over medium heat until the edges begin to color, about 5 minutes. Add the ground coriander, cayenne, and turmeric, stir together, add ¼ teaspoon of the salt and a couple of tablespoons of the hot water, cover, and simmer over low heat for 5 minutes, or until the cauliflower is crisp-tender.

advance preparation Putting the towel over the rice prevents it from becoming soggy. For this reason, you can make this dish up to a day in advance, but do not add the cilantro until you reheat and serve. Reheat the rice gently in the microwave, or, to reheat the rice in the oven, lightly oil a 3-quart baking dish and spread out the rice in an even layer. Cover with foil and refrigerate. Reheat for 20 minutes in a 325°F. oven. Sprinkle with cilantro and serve.

Stir in the rice, snow peas, and the remaining hot water, bring to a boil, and add the remaining teaspoon of salt. Cover, reduce the heat, and simmer for 15 minutes. Turn off the heat; place a clean dish towel across the top of the pan and replace the lid. Let stand, covered, for 10 minutes. Add the cilantro, fluff the rice, and serve.

leftovers The leftovers will keep for 3 or 4 days. You could use the leftovers for a different sort of pilaf, such as shrimp or chicken. Clean and shell ½ pound shrimp, or cut 2 chicken breasts into slivers. Heat 1 tablespoon oil and sauté the shrimp until pink, about 3 minutes, or the chicken until there is no trace of pink, about 5 minutes. Stir in the rice, heat through, and serve.

how to make risotto

Risotto is one of the world's great dishes. I make it often for impromptu dinner parties. Everybody loves it, and it's very difficult to get a good one in a restaurant, because it's a dish that should go from the pan to your plate immediately.

But this doesn't mean you can't cook risotto ahead, at least partially. I do it all the time; I cook the risotto halfway through, spread the rice out in a thin layer in the pan, then finish the dish just before serving.

The creamy dish is made with round Italian Arborio rice, which yields up its sauce-thickening starch as it slowly cooks, while retaining its chewy texture. Risotto can be embellished with just about any vegetable. Seafood risotto is also a classic; you'll see how good it is when you make the Shrimp Risotto with Peas on page 298.

The stock is important in a risotto, because it seasons the rice as the rice cooks. Chicken stock is the most common type used, but for the Mushroom Risotto on page 308 I use a mushroom stock, and for seafood risottos I like to use a seafood stock of some kind, even if it's as simple as one made by boiling shrimp shells in water or chicken stock, or combining chicken stock with clam juice. Vegetarian stocks include Garlic Broth (page 381) and the Simple Vegetable Stock on page 377. If all I've got on hand is a can of chicken stock and I want to make a risotto, I'll just stretch the stock with some water, and make sure that my risotto is adequately seasoned.

Below are the basic steps in making a risotto. You can feed 4 people generously with 1½ cups Arborio rice and 6 to 7 cups stock.

1. Prepare your ingredients. Put your stock or broth into a saucepan and bring it to a simmer on the stove, with a ladle nearby or in the pot. Make sure that it is well seasoned with salt. It will remain at a simmer the entire time you are making the risotto, and you will add it a ladleful or two at a time to the rice.

2. Heat 2 tablespoons butter or olive oil (more or less, according to the recipe) over medium heat in a wide, heavy nonstick skillet. Add the onion if onion is called for. The onion also seasons the rice. Cook gently until it is just tender.

3. Stir in the rice and if the recipe calls for garlic, add that with the rice. Traditional risottos call for more fat than mine, and the rice absorbs it before you add the other ingredients. In this case you will stir the rice just until the grains become separate, which doesn't take very long.

4. Add ½ cup wine for 1½ cups rice and cook, stirring, until it is absorbed. The wine is important for flavor, as it adds a delicious acidity to the dish. The alcohol boils off. The heat should be moderate; the wine should bubble as soon as you add it to the rice, but

it should not boil off so quickly that the rice doesn't have time to absorb its flavor. A dry white wine such as pinot grigio or fumé blanc is the best wine to use. Don't use chardonnay, which is too oaky and not dry enough.

advance preparation
You can begin up to several hours before serving: Proceed with the recipe and cook halfway through Step 5; that is, for about 15 minutes. The rice should still be hard when you remove it from the heat, and there should not be any liquid in the pan. Spread it in an even layer in the pan and keep it away from the heat until you resume cooking. Fifteen minutes before serving, resume cooking as instructed.

5. Begin adding the simmering stock, a couple of ladlefuls (about ½ cup) at a time. The stock should just cover the rice and should bubble, not too slowly but not too quickly. Stir often; you don't have to stand there and stir constantly, as I used to think you did—you can be preparing other ingredients—but you do have to stir often, to keep the grains separate and distribute their starch throughout the mixture, and also to ascertain when it's time to add the next portion of stock. The rice will be cooked through but still be chewy after 20 to 25 minutes of adding the stock in increments and stirring. When the rice is tender all the way through but still chewy, it is done. Taste now and correct the seasoning.

6. Add another ladleful of stock to the rice. Stir in the Parmesan if called for, and remove from the heat. The mixture should be creamy. Add freshly ground pepper, taste one last time, and adjust the salt. Stir once and serve right away.

leftovers : Risotto will lose that wonderful chewy texture over time, but it will still taste good for 2 or 3 days. One way to stretch leftovers is to stir them into a frittata.

risotto frittata

leftovers variation

Risotto makes a great frittata. Beat 4 to 10 eggs and add salt and 1 to 3 tablespoons milk. Stir in ½ to 2 cups of the risotto. Make the frittata in a heavy, wide nonstick skillet following the directions on page 392.

shrimp risotto
with peas

The shrimp shells are used here to make a subtle shellfish broth for the risotto. The dish, with its beautiful saffron, pink, and green colors, is quite beautiful. Make sure you don't overcook the shrimp; they will only take 4 to 5 minutes to cook, and the contrast of their succulent texture against the chewy rice is most pleasing—but it will be lost if the shrimp become rubbery.

❖ serves 4

1   pound medium shrimp

    Salt

1   quart chicken stock (page 378) or water

2   tablespoons olive oil

1   small sweet red or yellow onion, chopped

1½ cups Arborio rice

2   large garlic cloves, minced or pressed

½   cup dry white wine

2   generous pinches of saffron (optional)

1   cup fresh or thawed frozen peas

2   tablespoons chopped fresh flat-leaf parsley

    Freshly ground black pepper

advance preparation
The broth can be made several hours before you wish to cook the risotto.

shell the shrimp and devein if necessary. Salt them lightly and set aside in a bowl, in the refrigerator if you won't be making and serving the risotto right away. Rinse the shells and combine them with 1 quart of water in a medium saucepan. Bring to a boil, skim off any foam, reduce the heat to low, and simmer, partially covered, for 30 minutes. Strain and add the stock to the chicken stock or water. Taste and add enough salt to make a well-seasoned stock. Place the stock in a saucepan and bring to a simmer.

Heat the oil over medium heat in a large nonstick frying pan and add the onion. Cook, stirring, until the onion softens, 3 to 5 minutes, and add the rice and the garlic. Cook, stirring, until the grains of rice are separate and beginning to crackle.

Stir in the wine and cook over medium heat, stirring constantly. The wine should bubble, but not too quickly. When the wine has just about evaporated, stir in a ladleful or two of the simmering stock, enough to just cover the rice. The stock should bubble slowly. Cook, stirring often, until it is just about absorbed. Add another couple of ladlefuls of the stock. Crush the saffron threads between your fingers and stir in. Continue to cook, stirring often, not too fast and not too slowly, adding more stock when the rice is almost dry, for 20 minutes.

advance preparation
You can begin this dish several hours ahead and finish it when you're ready. See instructions on page 296.

Taste a bit of the rice. It should taste chewy but not hard in the middle. Continue adding more simmering stock and stirring until the rice reaches this al dente stage. Stir in more stock to cover, and add the peas and shrimp.

Cook, stirring, for another 4 to 5 minutes, until the shrimp is pink and cooked through but still moist and the peas are bright. Stir in the parsley and another small ladleful of stock, remove from the heat, add pepper, stir for a few seconds, and serve.

fava bean and green garlic risotto

This is a springtime risotto, a celebration of the young fava beans and tender bulbs of fresh garlic that hit the markets here in Los Angeles from April through June. Substitute a combination of scallions and garlic if green garlic is not to be found. ❖ serves 4

3 pounds fava beans

6 to 7 cups chicken or vegetable stock, as needed

2 tablespoons olive oil

½ cup minced green garlic, or 1 bunch scallions, minced, white and light green parts only, and 2 garlic cloves, minced

1½ cups Arborio rice

½ cup dry white wine

½ teaspoon saffron threads

1 ounce Parmesan cheese, grated (¼ cup)

¼ cup chopped fresh flat-leaf parsley

½ teaspoon grated lemon zest

Salt and freshly ground black pepper

advance preparation
The favas can be blanched and skinned a day or two ahead and refrigerated in a covered bowl.

shell the fava beans while you bring a pot of water to a boil. Drop the beans into the water and boil for 1 minute, then transfer at once to a bowl of ice-cold water. Drain. Slip the favas from their skins by flicking away one end of the husk and gently squeezing out the bean.

Have the stock simmering in a saucepan.

Heat the oil over medium heat in a large nonstick skillet and add the green garlic. Cook, stirring, for about a minute, until it begins to smell fragrant, and add the rice. Cook, stirring, until the grains of rice are separate and beginning to crackle, about 1 minute.

Stir in the wine and cook over medium heat, stirring constantly. The wine should bubble, but not too quickly. When the wine has just about evaporated, stir in a ladleful or two of the simmering stock, enough to just cover the rice. Crush the saffron between your fingers and add. The stock should bubble slowly. Cook, stirring often, until it is just about absorbed. Add another ladleful of the stock and continue to cook in this fashion, not too fast and not too slowly, adding more stock when the rice is almost dry, for about 15 minutes, until the rice is almost cooked through but still a bit hard in the center.

advance preparation
You can begin this dish several hours ahead and finish the rice when you're ready for it. See instructions on page 296.

Stir in the fava beans and another ladleful or two of stock. Continue adding stock and stirring the rice as you have been doing for another 10 minutes, until the rice is cooked al dente.

Add another ladleful of stock to the rice, and stir in the Parmesan, parsley, lemon zest, and salt and pepper. Taste and adjust the salt. The rice should be creamy. Stir for a couple of seconds, and serve.

leftovers Risotto will lose that wonderful chewy texture over time, but it will still taste good for 2 or 3 days. One way to stretch leftovers is to stir them into a frittata (see page 392).

variation
asparagus and fava bean risotto

This is another gorgeous springtime dish. Substitute 1 pound asparagus for 1 pound of the fava beans. Trim the asparagus and cut into 1-inch lengths. Steam for 5 minutes, refresh with cold water, and set aside. Add to the rice with the final ladleful of stock.

sweet pepper risotto

As the peppers sizzle along here, they melt down a bit, their bright color bleeding into the rice, resulting in a very beautiful, as well as sweet and luscious, risotto. ❖ **serves 4**

6 to 7 cups chicken or vegetable stock, as needed

Salt

2 tablespoons unsalted butter or olive oil, or 1 tablespoon of each

½ medium or 1 small onion, minced

1 pound red bell peppers, cored, seeded, and cut into thin 1-inch lengths

1 to 2 garlic cloves, minced or pressed

2 teaspoons fresh thyme leaves

1½ cups Arborio rice

½ cup dry white wine, such as pinot grigio or fumé blanc

Pinch of saffron threads

1 ounce Parmesan cheese, grated (¼ cup; more as desired)

Freshly ground black pepper

in a large saucepan, bring the stock or broth to a simmer over medium-low heat, with a ladle nearby or in the pot. Make sure that it is well seasoned with salt.

advance preparation
You can cook the peppers, then go out for several hours before you finish the dish. Reheat the peppers until they begin to sizzle, and proceed.

Heat the butter or oil in a wide, heavy nonstick skillet over medium heat. Add the onion and cook gently until it is just tender, 3 to 5 minutes. Stir in the peppers, garlic, and thyme, add a little salt, and cook, stirring, until the peppers have wilted slightly, about 5 minutes.

Stir in the rice and stir until the grains become separate and begin to crackle. Add the wine and cook, stirring, until it has just about evaporated and been absorbed by the rice. Stir in a ladleful or two of the simmering stock, enough to just cover the rice. Crumble in the saffron. The stock should bubble slowly. Cook, stirring often, until it is

advance preparation
You can begin this dish several hours ahead and finish it when you're ready for it. See instructions on page 296.

just about absorbed. Add another ladleful of the stock and continue to cook in this fashion, not too fast and not too slowly, adding more stock when the rice is almost dry and stirring often, for about 20 to 25 minutes. When the rice is tender all the way through but still chewy, it is done. Taste and correct the seasoning.

Add another ladleful of stock to the rice. Stir in the Parmesan, and remove from the heat. The mixture should be creamy. Add freshly ground pepper, taste one last time, and adjust the salt. Stir once and serve right away.

leftovers Risotto will lose that wonderful chewy texture over time, but it will still taste good for 2 or 3 days. One way to stretch leftovers is to stir them into a frittata (see page 392).

red risotto with beet greens or red chard

One of the reasons I make this dish often is that throughout the winter I buy beets, with thick bunches of greens attached, and red chard at local farmers' markets. When you use those greens for risotto, the resulting rice is pinkish red, and quite beautiful. In this risotto I use red wine instead of white, to enhance the color. However, if white is all you have on hand, use it. My son is quite a fan of "pink rice." ❖ serves 4 generously

1 bunch (about ¾ to 1 pound) beet greens or red chard, stemmed and washed

6 to 7 cups chicken or vegetable stock, as needed

2 tablespoons unsalted butter or olive oil (or 1 tablespoon of each)

1 small or ½ medium onion, minced

1½ cups Arborio rice

2 garlic cloves, minced or pressed

½ cup red wine

Salt

1 ounce Parmesan cheese, grated (¼ cup)

Freshly ground black pepper

advance preparation
I often blanch greens when I get them home from the market so that they won't wilt or rot in the refrigerator if I don't get around to cooking them right away. If you do this, and want to use them for a risotto, chop the blanched greens and set aside. Add them to the risotto during the last few minutes of cooking, just to heat them through and amalgamate into the dish. The color will not be as red.

wash the greens and cut crosswise into 1-inch-wide strips. Set aside. Have the stock simmering on low heat in a saucepan.

Heat the butter or oil over medium heat in a large non-stick frying pan and add the onion. Cook, stirring, until the onion begins to soften, about 3 minutes, then add the rice and garlic. Cook, stirring, until the grains of rice are separate.

Stir in the wine and cook over medium heat, stirring constantly. The wine should bubble, but not too quickly. When the wine has just about evaporated, stir in a ladleful or two of the simmering stock, enough to just cover the rice. The stock should bubble slowly. Cook, stirring often, until it is just about absorbed. Add another ladleful of the stock and continue to cook in this fashion, not too fast and not too slowly, adding more stock when the rice is almost dry, for 10 minutes.

advance preparation You can begin this dish several hours ahead and finish the rice when you're ready for it. Scatter the greens over the top and remove the risotto and the stock from the heat. See instructions on page 296.

Stir in the greens and continue adding more stock, a ladleful at a time, and stirring, for another 10 to 15 minutes. Taste a bit of the rice. It should taste chewy but not hard in the middle. If it is still hard in the middle, add another ladleful of stock and cook for another 5 minutes or so. Taste for salt and add if necessary.

Add another ladleful of stock to the rice. Stir the Parmesan into the rice and immediately remove from the heat. Add freshly ground pepper, taste one last time, and adjust the salt. The rice should be creamy. Stir once and serve.

leftovers Risotto will lose that wonderful chewy texture over time, but it will still taste good for 2 or 3 days. One way to stretch leftovers is to stir them into a frittata (see page 392).

radicchio risotto

variation

This is a specialty of Venice (well, so is all risotto). The radicchio adds a bitter dimension to the dish. Substitute 1 pound radicchio, sliced like the greens, for the greens, and proceed as directed.

red wine risotto with cauliflower

I'm revisiting an old recipe of mine here, that I used to make in the 1970s with brown rice. It's based on a classic, heavenly Venetian risotto made with Barolo wine. Cauliflower absorbs the color and flavors perfectly. ❖ serves 4 generously

2 cups robust, fruity red wine, such as an Italian Barolo or a Côtes du Rhône

4 to 5 cups chicken stock (page 378), as needed

2 tablespoons olive oil or butter, or 1 tablespoon each

1 small or ½ medium onion, minced

2 large garlic cloves, minced or pressed

1½ cups Arborio rice

1 medium cauliflower, separated into small florets, the florets broken into smaller pieces or sliced ½ inch thick (about 4 heaped cups)

Salt

2 ounces Parmesan cheese, grated (½ cup)

Freshly ground black pepper

combine the wine and stock and bring to a simmer in a medium saucepan.

Heat the oil or butter over medium heat in a large, heavy nonstick frying pan and add the onion. Cook, stirring, until the onion begins to soften, about 3 minutes, then add the garlic and the rice. Cook, stirring, for a couple of minutes, until the grains of rice are separate and beginning to crackle.

advance preparation
You can begin this dish several hours ahead and finish the rice when you're ready for it. See instructions on page 296.

Stir in a ladleful or two of the simmering wine and stock, enough to just cover the rice. The stock should bubble slowly. Cook, stirring often, until it is just about absorbed. Add the cauliflower and another ladleful of the stock and continue to cook in this fashion, not too fast and not too slowly, adding more stock when the rice is almost dry, for 20 to 25 minutes. Taste a bit of the rice. Is it cooked through? If it is still hard in the middle, add another ladleful of stock and cook for another 5 minutes or so. Add salt to taste, remembering that the Parmesan will also contribute saltiness.

Add another small ladleful of stock to the rice. Stir in the Parmesan and immediately remove from the heat. Add freshly ground pepper, taste one last time, and adjust the salt. The rice should be creamy. Stir for a couple of seconds and serve.

leftovers : Risotto will lose that wonderful chewy texture over time, but it will still taste good for 2 or 3 days. One way to stretch leftovers is to stir them into a frittata (see page 392).

mushroom risotto

I have published versions of this dish in many of my cookbooks, but I wouldn't leave it out of this collection. It's one of the most comforting one-dish meals I've ever eaten. Friends E-mail me from all over the country to tell me how good this is. ❖ **serves 4 generously**

1 ounce (about 1 cup) dried mushrooms, preferably porcini

About 4 cups vegetable (page 377) or chicken stock (page 378)

2 tablespoons soy sauce

1 teaspoon salt, plus more to taste

2 tablespoons unsalted butter or olive oil, or 1 tablespoon of each

½ medium or 1 small onion, minced

1 pound button or wild mushrooms, cleaned, trimmed, and sliced thick

2 large garlic cloves, minced or pressed

½ to 1 teaspoon chopped fresh rosemary, or ¼ to ½ teaspoon crumbled dried rosemary, to taste

½ to 1 teaspoon fresh thyme leaves, or ¼ to ½ teaspoon dried thyme, to taste

1½ cups Arborio rice

½ cup dry white wine, such as pinot grigio or fumé blanc

¼ cup chopped fresh flat-leaf parsley

1 ounce Parmesan cheese, grated (¼ cup)

Freshly ground black pepper

place the dried mushrooms in a heatproof bowl or measuring cup and pour on 3 cups boiling water. Let sit for 30 minutes. Line a strainer with cheesecloth or with a double thickness of paper towels, place it over a bowl, and drain the mushrooms. Squeeze the mushrooms over the strainer to extract all the liquid, then rinse them in several changes of water to remove the sand. Chop coarsely and set aside. Combine the mushroom soaking liquid with the additional vegetable or chicken stock to make 7 cups. Add the soy sauce and salt (if the chicken stock is salted, add less salt). Taste and adjust the salt. The liquid should be well seasoned. Transfer to a saucepan and bring to a simmer.

Heat 1 tablespoon of the butter or oil over medium heat in a large nonstick frying pan and add the onion. Cook, stirring, until the onion begins to soften, about 3 minutes, then add the dried and fresh mushrooms. Cook, stirring, until the mushrooms begin to release liquid, and add the garlic, rosemary, and thyme. Cook, stirring, until the mushroom liquid has just about evaporated, and add the remaining tablespoon of butter or oil and the rice. Cook, stirring, until the grains of rice are separate and beginning to crackle.

advance preparation
You can begin this dish several hours ahead and finish the rice when you're ready for it. See instructions on page 296.

Stir in the wine and cook over medium heat, stirring constantly. The wine should bubble, but not too quickly. When the wine has just about evaporated, stir in a ladleful or two of the simmering stock, enough to barely cover the rice. The stock should bubble slowly. Cook, stirring often, until it is almost all absorbed. Add another ladleful of the stock and continue to cook in this fashion, not too fast and not too slowly, adding more stock when the rice is almost dry, for 20 to 25 minutes. Taste a bit of the rice. Is it cooked through? If it is still hard in the middle, add another ladleful of stock and cook for another 5 minutes or so. Now is the time to ascertain if there is enough salt. Add if necessary.

Add another small ladleful of stock to the rice. Stir in the parsley and Parmesan, add freshly ground pepper, taste one last time, and adjust the salt. The rice should be creamy. Serve at once.

leftovers Risotto will lose that wonderful chewy texture over time, but it will still taste good for 2 or 3 days. One way to stretch leftovers is to stir them into a frittata (see page 392).

winter squash risotto

When you cut up winter squash into very small dice, it will partially melt into the rice as this creamy, orange-hued risotto cooks. ❖ **serves 4 generously**

6 to 7 cups chicken stock (page 378), as needed

2 tablespoons olive oil or unsalted butter, or 1 tablespoon of each

1 small or ½ medium onion, minced

1 pound winter squash such as butternut, banana, or hubbard (about ½ of a good-size butternut, for example), peeled, seeded, and finely diced

2 large garlic cloves, minced or pressed

Salt

1½ cups Arborio rice

½ cup dry white wine

1 ounce Parmesan cheese, grated (¼ cup)

Pinch of freshly grated nutmeg

¼ cup chopped fresh flat-leaf parsley

Freshly ground black pepper

have the stock simmering on low heat in a saucepan.

Heat the oil or butter over medium heat in a large, heavy nonstick frying pan and add the onion. Cook, stirring, until the onion begins to soften, about 3 minutes, then add the squash, garlic, and about ¼ teaspoon salt. Cook, stirring, until the squash begins to soften, about 3 minutes, then add the rice. Cook, stirring, until the grains of rice are separate and beginning to crackle.

advance preparation
You can begin this dish several hours ahead and finish the rice when you're ready for it. See instructions on page 296.

Stir in the wine and cook over medium heat, stirring constantly. The wine should bubble, but not too quickly. When the wine has just about evaporated, stir in a ladleful or two of the simmering stock, enough to just cover the rice and squash. The stock should bubble slowly.

Cook, stirring often, until it is just about absorbed. Add another ladleful of the stock and continue to cook in this fashion, not too fast and not too slowly, adding more stock when the rice is almost dry, for 20 to 25 minutes. Taste a bit of the rice. If it is still hard in the middle, add another ladleful of stock and cook for another 5 minutes or so. Add more salt if necessary.

Add another small ladleful of stock to the rice. Stir in the Parmesan, nutmeg, and parsley, and immediately remove from the heat. Add freshly ground pepper, taste one last time, and adjust the salt. The rice should be creamy. Stir for a couple of seconds, and serve.

leftovers : Risotto will lose that wonderful chewy texture over time, but it will still taste good for 2 or 3 days. One way to stretch leftovers is to stir them into a frittata (see page 392).

variation Add 2 teaspoons chopped fresh sage about halfway through the cooking for a savory Mediterranean flavor.

jambalaya with chicken and shrimp

Before refrigeration, this classic Cajun rice dish served as a way to use up leftover seafood. Any number of meats and seafood are found in different versions of jambalaya. What they have in common are the seasonings: onion, scallion, green bell pepper, cayenne, and parsley. In this version I've made the smoked ham optional; it adds one more dimension (smoke), but there's plenty going on without it. ❖ serves 6

¾ pound medium shrimp in the shell

3 cups chicken stock (page 378)

2 tablespoons unsalted butter, canola oil, or vegetable oil

1 (3- to 3½-pound) chicken, cut up and skinned if desired

1 medium onion, chopped

1 bunch of scallions, both white and green parts, chopped

2 large garlic cloves, minced or pressed

1 medium green bell pepper, diced

2 celery stalks, diced

6 ounces andouille or other smoked sausage, such as kielbasa, thinly sliced

4 ounces smoked ham, diced (optional)

1 pound tomatoes, or 1 (14-ounce) can tomatoes, drained, peeled, and diced

¼ to ½ teaspoon cayenne pepper (to taste)

2 cups medium- or long-grain rice

1 teaspoon salt (less if chicken stock is salted, more to taste)

⅛ to ¼ teaspoon freshly ground black pepper (to taste)

½ teaspoon dried thyme

1 bay leaf

½ cup chopped fresh flat-leaf parsley

shell and devein the shrimp and reserve the shells. Combine the shells with 2½ cups water and bring to a boil. Reduce the heat and simmer for 30 minutes. Strain through a cheesecloth-lined strainer set over a bowl. Combine with the chicken stock so that you have 4 cups of liquid, at least half of which is chicken stock. Freeze excess shrimp stock and use for another dish.

advance preparation
You can brown the chicken several hours before cooking the rice. Refrigerate if not cooking within an hour.

Heat the butter or oil over medium-high heat in a large, heavy, lidded nonstick skillet or flameproof casserole, and brown the chicken pieces, in batches, about 5 minutes per side. Transfer the chicken as it's done to a paper towel-lined bowl or plate. Set aside.

advance preparation
The shrimp can be cooked several hours ahead and refrigerated. Bring the stock back to a simmer before proceeding.

Bring the stock to a boil in a saucepan. Add the shrimp and cook for 3 minutes, or until pink. Remove the shrimp from the stock and set aside. Turn the heat to low and keep the stock at a simmer.

Pour off all but a tablespoon of fat from the pan you cooked the chicken in and add the onion. Cook over medium heat, stirring, until translucent, about 3 minutes. Stir in the scallions, garlic, green pepper, celery, sausage, and ham, and continue to cook, stirring, for 2 or 3 minutes, until the vegetables have softened a bit and the mixture smells fragrant. Stir in the tomatoes and cayenne, raise the heat slightly, and cook, stirring, until the tomatoes have cooked down a bit and smell fragrant, about 10 minutes. Stir in the rice and chicken pieces, and mix well to coat the rice.

Add the simmering stock or water and the salt, pepper, thyme, bay leaf, and all but 2 tablespoons of the parsley. Bring back to a boil, cover, reduce the heat to low, and simmer for 30 minutes, or until the chicken is cooked through, the rice tender, and the liquid absorbed. Place a clean kitchen towel between the lid of the pan and the rice and let sit for 10 minutes. Toss with the shrimp and remaining parsley, discard the bay leaf, and serve.

leftovers Although the rice will become a bit soggy, this keeps well for 2 or 3 days. Leftovers can also be frozen for a couple of months.

yangchow fried rice

On a table at a Chinese restaurant, this would be one of many dishes. Here it's the main event, a great dish to make when you have cooked rice on hand. Feel free to add other cooked vegetables and/or meat or seafood to this dish. Although this is a last minute stir-fry, all of the vegetables can be cut up as far ahead as you need to—even a day. Cooked rice keeps for 3 or 4 days in the refrigerator, so you can make this dish when you're ready. ❖ **serves 6 generously**

3 large eggs

Salt

3 tablespoons vegetable or canola oil

2 garlic cloves, minced or pressed

¾ pound medium shrimp, peeled, deveined, and cut in ¾-inch pieces

1 tablespoon dry sherry

1 pound rice, cooked and cooled (about 5 cups cooked rice)

4 scallions, thinly sliced, white and green parts separated

¼ pound cooked ham, preferably honey-cured, diced

¾ cup cooked fresh or thawed frozen peas

2 tablespoons soy sauce

3 tablespoons chicken stock or water

2 tablespoons chopped fresh cilantro

beat 2 of the eggs in a small bowl and salt lightly. Heat 2 teaspoons of the oil over medium-high heat in a medium nonstick frying pan and add the beaten eggs. Swirl the pan to coat evenly like a thin pancake. When the egg is cooked through, roll up and slide onto a plate. Cut in thin strips (you can use a scissors or knife for this). Set aside.

advance preparation
You can cook the shrimp and egg a few hours ahead. Keep in the refrigerator if holding for more than a couple of hours.

Heat a wok or large, heavy nonstick skillet over high heat until a drop of water evaporates upon contact. Add 1 tablespoon of the remaining oil, swirl it around, and add the garlic. As soon as it begins to color (almost immediately), add the shrimp and cook, stirring and tossing with a spatula or wok scoop, until just about cooked through and pink, about 1 minute. Add the sherry, stir together, and when the sizzling stops, remove the shrimp and set aside. Rinse out and dry the wok or pan.

Using a fork or moistened fingers, separate the rice grains. Reheat the wok or skillet over high heat until a drop of water evaporates upon contact. Add the remaining 4 teaspoons oil, swirl it around, and add the white part of the scallions and the remaining egg, beaten, then add the rice. Using a wok scoop or spatula, scoop up the rice with the beaten egg and toss and stir, separating any lumps, until heated through. Stir in the ham and peas, then the shrimp. Stir together and add the soy sauce and stock. Stir in half the egg strips and the green part of the scallions. Transfer to a warm serving platter and sprinkle the remaining egg strips and the cilantro over the top. Serve hot.

leftovers : This dish makes an excellent leftover. Reheat in a wok or nonstick skillet or in the microwave. It will keep for 3 days in the refrigerator. Serve leftovers as a side dish or a main dish, depending on how much you have.

thai combination fried rice *(kao pad)*

Thailand's ubiquitous fried rice dish, kao pad, *is not only one of the country's most popular street foods, but is made in every home. Many foods can accompany the rice in kao pad: pork and eggs, Chinese sausage, shrimp, squid, crabmeat, ham, chicken—whatever the cook has on hand. The most important ingredients are the rice itself, the garlic and the fish sauce. It must be the fish sauce that makes this dish so addictive; whatever it is, it's amazing how much you can eat at one sitting. That's why the portions are so big here. Like Yangchow Fried Rice (page 314), the vegetables, herbs, and rice can be prepared up to a day ahead. You can measure out your seasonings and prepare your garnishes, pork, and shrimp hours ahead. Then cook when ready.* ❖ **serves 3 to 4**

4 tablespoons canola or vegetable oil

8 garlic cloves, minced or pressed

½ pound lean pork, diced

6 ounces shrimp, shelled, deveined, and cut into pieces

4 eggs, beaten and seasoned with salt and pepper

5 to 6 cups cooked rice, preferably Thai jasmine rice

2 tablespoons fish sauce (or more to taste)

2 to 3 teaspoons Thai or Indonesian chili sauce (optional)

1 large tomato, chopped

1 bunch of scallions, both white and green parts, chopped

for garnish

½ cup chopped fresh cilantro

Thinly sliced cucumber

Lime wedges

Scallions, trimmed and sliced

Fish sauce

Minced chilies

have all of your ingredients measured out and in reach. Heat a large, heavy nonstick skillet or wok over medium-high heat until a drop of water evaporates upon contact. Add the oil, swirl, and turn the heat to medium. Add the garlic and cook, stirring, until golden, about 30 seconds. Add the pork and stir-fry until there are no longer any traces of pink. Add the shrimp and cook, stirring, until pink. Push the garlic, pork, and shrimp from the center of the pan and pour in the beaten eggs. Cook, stirring, until just scrambled, and add the rice. Cook the rice, scooping it up, then pressing it into the pan and scooping it up again, for about 2 minutes. Add the fish and chili sauces, the tomato, and scallions and stir together for about 30 seconds. Serve, garnishing each plate with the cilantro and cucumbers and passing lime wedges, scallions, and fish sauce with the chilies. Diners should squeeze lime juice onto their rice as they eat.

leftovers ⦙ This makes a delicious leftover for about 3 days. You could fill a rice wrapper with it, but it's great as it is, reheated and served as a side dish.

stir-fried noodles with pork and greens

This Asian noodle dish is a simple combination of pork and greens seasoned with ginger and garlic. For a vegetarian version you could substitute tofu for the pork. Cook the noodles and blanch the greens ahead, measure out your seasonings, and this is made very quickly. ❖ serves 4

8 ounces Japanese somen noodles, soba, wide egg noodles, or wide rice vermicelli

1 tablespoon Chinese sesame oil

Salt

2 large bunches of greens, such as Swiss chard, beet greens, turnip greens, or kale (about 1½ pounds), stemmed and washed well in several changes of water

2 tablespoons vegetable, canola, or peanut oil

¾ pound lean pork, cut in ¼ by 2-inch strips

2 tablespoons minced or grated fresh ginger

2 large garlic cloves, minced or pressed

2 to 3 tablespoons soy sauce (more to taste)

¾ cup chicken stock (page 378)

advance preparation
The noodles can be cooked a day ahead and kept in the refrigerator.

fill a large pot, if possible one with a pasta insert, with water and bring to a boil. Add the noodles, and stir to separate the strands. Add a couple of tablespoons cold water, just so the water doesn't boil over. Boil somen noodles for 2 minutes, egg noodles and rice vermicelli for 5 to 7 minutes, until tender. Remove the noodles from the water and rinse with cold water. Place in a bowl of cold water, then drain, toss with 2 teaspoons of the sesame oil, and set aside.

advance preparation
The cooked greens will keep for
3 or 4 days in a covered bowl in the
refrigerator.

Bring the water in the pot back to a boil; add 1 tablespoon of salt and the greens. Cook the greens for 1 to 2 minutes, until just tender, and transfer with a slotted spoon or skimmer to a bowl of cold water. Drain and gently squeeze out the water (you don't have to squeeze them completely dry). Chop coarsely.

Heat a large, heavy nonstick skillet or wok over high heat until hot enough to evaporate a drop of water on contact. Add 1 tablespoon of the vegetable oil, swirl to coat the pan, and reduce the heat to medium-high. Add the pork and cook, stirring, for 2 to 3 minutes, until the meat is cooked through and there are no longer any traces of pink.

Add the remaining tablespoon of oil and the ginger and garlic and cook, stirring with a wooden paddle or spoon, until fragrant and beginning to color, 20 to 30 seconds. Stir in the greens, noodles, soy sauce, and stock, heat through, stirring, and remove from the heat. Drizzle on the remaining 2 teaspoons sesame oil and serve.

leftovers : This will keep for about 3 days in the refrigerator, though the greens will fade and won't taste as vivid. You can simply reheat, or add an egg or two to the mixture. Beat the eggs, season with a little salt, and cook in a teaspoon or two of hot oil in a small nonstick skillet, or in the skillet in which you will reheat your noodles. Break up with a wooden spoon when set, then toss with the noodles.

variation vegetarian noodles with tofu and greens

Substitute ¾ pound firm tofu for the pork. Cut the tofu in small dice or dominoes and stir-fry in place of the pork for 3 to 4 minutes, until beginning to color, before proceeding with the recipe.

singapore noodles with shrimp, squid, and garlic

It's amazing how much flavor rice noodles, which are pretty bland on their own, pick up when they're cooked with lots of garlic, fish sauce (I could get addicted to this seasoning), and soy sauce. This big stir-fry recipe is flexible; if you can't find squid, use all shrimp instead. You can prep everything in the morning—including soaking the noodles—and cook the dish when you get home from work. ❖ serves 4

¾ pound dried rice noodles

3 tablespoons peanut, vegetable, or canola oil

4 garlic cloves, minced or pressed

½ pound medium shrimp, shelled, deveined, and cut in half lengthwise

½ pound fresh squid, cleaned and cut into ½-inch rings, plus tentacles

1 red or green serrano chili, thinly sliced

1 tablespoon Thai fish sauce (or more to taste)

1 tablespoon soy sauce (or more to taste)

4 scallions, trimmed, flattened with the side of a cleaver or chef's knife, and cut in ½-inch lengths

1 cup bean sprouts

2 eggs, beaten

½ cup chicken stock (page 378)

Salt (optional)

2 tablespoons chopped fresh cilantro (or more to taste)

Lime wedges, for garnish

advance preparation
The noodles can be soaked and
drained a day ahead.

advance preparation
You can do this step a few hours
ahead. Cover tightly with plastic so
the noodles don't dry out. When you
continue with the recipe, the
noodles will soften (if they've
become a bit hard) when you
simmer them in the stock.

soak the noodles in hot water for 20 minutes, or until soft. Drain and set aside.

Heat a wok or large, heavy nonstick skillet over medium heat and when hot, add 2 tablespoons of the oil and the garlic. Cook, stirring, until the garlic begins to color, 15 to 30 seconds, and add the shrimp, squid, and chili. Cook, stirring, until the shrimp begins to turn bright pink and the squid opaque, 1 to 2 minutes. Add the fish sauce and the soy sauce, toss together, then add the noodles. Stir-fry for a minute, then either push the noodles and seafood up the sides of the wok so they aren't directly over the heat, or transfer to a bowl.

Add the remaining 1 tablespoon oil, the scallions, and the bean sprouts. Stir-fry for about a minute, just until the bean sprouts begin to wilt, and push the sprouts and scallions up the sides of the wok, or transfer to the bowl with the noodles and fish. Add the eggs and stir until lightly scrambled, then stir the previously cooked ingredients back into the pan and toss to distribute the eggs through the noodles. Add the stock, stir together, cover, and simmer for 1 minute. Remove from the heat, taste, and add salt if desired; transfer to a platter, sprinkle on the cilantro, and serve, passing the lime wedges.

leftovers You can reheat this the next day and enjoy it, even though the bean sprouts will have lost some crunch and the cilantro will have faded. You could also cut up the noodles with a scissors, and make a delicious frittata with the leftovers (page 392).

malaysian stir-fried noodles with shrimp

This is based on a classic Malaysian dish, mee goreng. *With origins in North India,* mee goreng *has more than one version. In the authentic dish the tofu is deep-fried, but I opt for less oil and a different texture. This dish is vibrant with contrasting textures and vivid flavors.* ❖ **serves 4**

Salt

½ pound turnip greens or mustard greens, cleaned, thick stem ends discarded

½ pound egg noodles

3 tablespoons plus 1 teaspoon peanut or canola oil

1½ tablespoons soy sauce

¾ teaspoon salt

1½ teaspoons sugar

3 tablespoons ketchup

1½ teaspoons Asian red chili paste or sauce, such as *sambal oelek*

2 large eggs, lightly beaten with a little salt

½ pound firm tofu, sliced about ¼ inch thick

1 medium red onion, chopped

2 large garlic cloves, minced or pressed

¾-inch-long piece of peeled fresh ginger, grated or finely chopped

½ pound tomatoes, diced

½ pound medium shrimp, shelled, cut in half lengthwise, and deveined

½ pound cabbage, cut in ¾-inch cubes

6 ounces bean sprouts (about 2 generous handfuls)

¼ cup fresh cilantro leaves, for serving

1 lime, cut in wedges, for serving

bring 3 or 4 quarts of water to a boil in a large pot
and add about 1 tablespoon of salt and the greens. Cook
for 30 seconds only, and immediately transfer to a bowl
of cold water, using a slotted spoon or skimmer. Drain,
squeeze out any water, and chop coarsely. Set aside.

Bring the water back to a boil and add the noodles. Cook
for 4 to 5 minutes, until just tender to the bite; drain and rinse with cold water. Shake
off the excess water, toss with a tablespoon of the oil, and set aside.

In a small bowl, mix together 1 tablespoon of the soy sauce, the salt, sugar, ketchup,
and chili paste. Stir to dissolve the sugar and salt and set aside.

Heat 1 teaspoon of the oil over medium-high heat in a
medium nonstick frying pan until a drop of egg sizzles
upon contact. Add the eggs. Tilt the pan to distribute
the eggs in an even layer. As soon as they are cooked
through, like a thin pancake, remove from the pan by
tilting the pan and sliding or rolling out of the pan. Roll up and slice thin (you can
use a scissors or a knife for this). Set aside.

Heat a wok or large, heavy nonstick skillet over medium-high heat and add the
remaining 2 tablespoons oil and the tofu. Cook, stirring, until the tofu begins to
brown, 3 to 5 minutes. Sprinkle with the remaining 1½ teaspoons soy sauce. Add the
onion and continue to cook, stirring, until tender, 3 to 5 minutes. Stir in the garlic and
ginger and cook, stirring, for about 30 seconds or until the garlic and ginger are fragrant. Add the tomatoes and increase the heat slightly. Stir until the tomatoes begin to
break down, about 3 minutes. Add the shrimp, cabbage, and blanched greens and cook,
stirring, until the shrimp curl and turn pink and the cabbage is crisp-tender, about
5 minutes. Add the noodles and soy sauce mixture and stir together until the noodles
are heated through and coated with the sauce. Add the shredded egg and the bean
sprouts, toss together quickly, and remove from the heat. Sprinkle on the cilantro and
serve, with lime wedges on the side.

leftovers Leftovers will taste good for a couple of days. Serve at
room temperature, reheat in a microwave, or gently reheat on top of the stove.

stir-fried tofu with red chard and noodles

I love the pink color that the tofu takes on when it's cooked with red chard, and beet greens do the same trick. However, you could make the dish with green chard if red were not available.

❖ serves 4

1 ounce dried shiitake mushrooms

3 tablespoons soy sauce

2 tablespoons chopped or grated fresh ginger

2 teaspoons sugar

¾ to 1 pound firm tofu, cut in 1 by ½-inch pieces

½ pound soba or udon noodles

Salt

2 bunches of red chard (about 1½ pounds), stemmed and thoroughly cleaned (reserve the stems)

2 tablespoons canola or peanut oil

2 large garlic cloves, minced or pressed

put the dried mushrooms in a heatproof bowl or measuring cup and cover with boiling water. Soak for 20 to 30 minutes. Drain through a cheesecloth- or paper-towel-lined strainer set over a bowl. Rinse the mushrooms, squeeze dry, and cut the caps in ¼-inch-thick slivers. Discard the stems. Set aside ¼ cup of the soaking liquid and combine with 1 tablespoon of the soy sauce.

advance preparation
You can marinate the tofu for a day.

Mix together the remaining 2 tablespoons soy sauce, 1 teaspoon of the ginger, and the sugar. Toss with the tofu in a bowl and set aside. Marinate for 15 minutes or longer. Refrigerate if not using right away.

advance preparation
The noodles can be cooked a day
ahead and kept in the refrigerator.
Meanwhile, cook the noodles. Fill a large pot, if possible one with a pasta insert, with water and bring to a boil. Add the noodles, and stir to separate the strands. Add a couple of tablespoons of cold water, just so the water doesn't boil over. Boil udon noodles for 2 to 3 minutes and soba noodles for about 4 minutes, until tender. Remove the noodles from the water with a skimmer, place in a bowl of cold water, then drain again and set aside.

advance preparation
The cooked greens will keep for 3 or
4 days in a covered bowl in the
refrigerator.
Bring the water in the pot back to a boil; add 1 tablespoon of salt and the red chard leaves. Cook the chard for 1 to 2 minutes, until just tender, and transfer with a slotted spoon or skimmer to a bowl of cold water. Drain and gently squeeze out the water (you don't have to squeeze it completely dry). Chop coarsely.

Trim the chard stalks and slice crosswise, about ¼ inch thick. Lift the tofu from the marinade and set aside.

Heat a large, heavy nonstick skillet or wok over high heat until hot enough to evaporate a drop of water on contact. Add 1 tablespoon of the oil, swirl to coat the pan, and reduce the heat to medium-high. Add the chard stalks and cook, stirring, for 1 minute. Add the tofu and sliced mushroom caps to the pan and cook, stirring, for 2 or 3 minutes, until the tofu is lightly browned. Add the remaining tablespoon of oil and the garlic and remaining ginger, and stir together for about 30 seconds to a minute, until fragrant. Stir in the red chard leaves, the noodles, the tofu marinade, and the ¼ cup of mushroom soaking liquid mixed with the tablespoon of soy sauce, and cook, stirring, for another minute or two, until heated through and fragrant. Serve hot.

leftovers ⫶ This will keep for about 3 days in the refrigerator, though the greens will fade and won't taste as vivid. You can simply reheat, or add an egg or two to the mixture. Beat the eggs, season with a little salt, and cook in a teaspoon or two of hot oil in a small nonstick skillet, or in the skillet in which you will reheat your noodles. Break up with a wooden spoon when set, then toss with the noodles.

szechuan braised tofu with pork and broccoli

I've taken a standard Szechuan dish here, mapo doufu, *and added broccoli to the mixture so that you can have your protein and vegetables in one spicy dish. The master dish,* mapo doufu— *tofu braised with pork—is on every Szechuan restaurant menu. It used to drive me crazy when I was a vegetarian, because menus loosely translated the dish as "braised tofu." They didn't mention the pork, which has so much to do with the flavor of the dish. When preparing ingredients for this dish, you can mince the garlic, ginger, and the white part of the scallion together in a food processor or mini-chop, and grind the pork in a food processor. This dish is worh making even if you can't find Szechuan peppercorns—just use regular black peppercorns instead. Serve the dish with rice.* ❖ **serves 4**

Salt

1 bunch of broccoli, broken into florets, the florets sliced about ½ inch thick

¾ pound firm tofu, drained

½ teaspoon sugar

1½ tablespoons rice wine, dry sherry, or dry vermouth

2 tablespoons soy sauce

¾ cup water or chicken stock (page 378)

2 tablespoons peanut, vegetable, or canola oil

4 large garlic cloves, minced or pressed

1 tablespoon minced fresh ginger

2 scallions, white and dark green parts separated, minced

½ pound ground pork butt (or substitute top-round beef)

1 tablespoon Chinese chili sauce (available in Chinese markets; use Thai or Indonesian chili sauce if you can't find the Chinese product)

¼ to ½ teaspoon ground Szechuan peppercorns, to taste

1½ teaspoons cornstarch dissolved in 1½ tablespoons water or chicken stock

Cooked rice, for serving

advance preparation
The blanched broccoli will keep for 2 or 3 days in the refrigerator.

bring a large pot of water to a boil; add a couple of teaspoons of salt and the broccoli. Boil for 1 minute and transfer immediately to a bowl of ice-cold water. Drain and set aside. (If you want the broccoli a little softer, boil for 2 minutes.)

Blot the tofu dry with a clean dish towel or paper towels and cut into ½-inch dice. Place in a sieve while you prepare the other ingredients.

In a small bowl or measuring cup, stir together the sugar, rice wine, soy sauce, and water or chicken stock.

Heat 1 tablespoon of the oil over medium-high heat in a large, heavy nonstick skillet or wok. When a drop of water evaporates upon contact, add the tofu and cook, stirring, for 2 to 3 minutes, until it begins to color. Add the remaining tablespoon of oil and the garlic, ginger, and white part of the scallion, and stir-fry for about 30 seconds, until fragrant. Add the pork and stir-fry for 2 to 3 minutes, until there are no traces of pink and the meat is fragrant. Add the chili sauce and the chicken stock mixture, and bring to a boil. Turn the heat to low, cover, and simmer for 10 minutes, stirring from time to time. Stir in the ground peppercorns and the broccoli. Heat through, stirring. Taste and adjust the seasoning. Add the dissolved cornstarch and stir until the mixture is glazed. Transfer to a warm serving dish, sprinkle the scallion greens over the top, and serve with rice.

leftovers The dish is best served right from the pan, but leftovers will taste good for a couple of days. Reheat them in the microwave or gently on the stove and serve with rice. The dish will become spicier with time. You could also chop the broccoli a bit smaller and use this as a filling for wontons or rice wrappers.

stir-fried beef and peppers

There are so many dimensions to this dish, it's hard to believe how easy it is to throw it together, especially if you've prepped the meat and peppers and measured the seasonings in advance. The beef and peppers look and taste wonderful together, the sweetness of the peppers drawn out even more by the sweet, hot, and salty seasonings. My husband's comment about the dish couldn't have been more complimentary: "You get this kind of dish all the time in Chinese restaurants, only this one is so much better." ❖ **serves 4**

1 pound flank steak or round steak

2 tablespoons soy sauce

1 tablespoon (firmly packed) light brown sugar

1 tablespoon cornstarch

3 tablespoons vegetable, peanut, or canola oil

2 tablespoons Chinese rice wine or dry sherry

2 teaspoons hoisin sauce

1 teaspoon sesame oil

1 red bell pepper, seeded and cut in 1-inch squares

1 green bell pepper, seeded and cut in 1-inch squares

2 large garlic cloves, minced or pressed

1 tablespoon minced fresh ginger

¼ teaspoon red pepper flakes

3 scallions, white and green parts separated, cut on the diagonal into 1-inch lengths

¼ to ½ teaspoon coarse sea salt or kosher salt (more to taste)

Cooked rice or noodles, for serving

trim off all of the fat and tough sinews from the meat. Slice crosswise against the grain into ⅛-inch-thick slices, then cut the slices into 1½-inch-long dominoes.

advance preparation
The meat can be marinated and the
ingredients prepared, the sauce
mixed together, a day ahead of time.

In a medium bowl, mix together 1 tablespoon of the soy sauce, 1 teaspoon of the brown sugar, the cornstarch, and 1 tablespoon of the vegetable oil. Toss with the meat, making sure all of the pieces of meat are coated. Cover with plastic wrap and marinate for at least 30 minutes out of the refrigerator, or for up to a day in the refrigerator. Bring to room temperature before cooking.

In a small bowl, stir together the remaining 1 tablespoon soy sauce and 2 teaspoons brown sugar, the rice wine, hoisin sauce, and sesame oil. Set aside.

Heat a large nonstick skillet or wok over high heat until a drop of water evaporates on contact. Add the remaining 2 tablespoons vegetable oil, turn the heat to medium-high, and add the bell peppers. Stir-fry for a couple of minutes, until the peppers begin to soften, and add the garlic and ginger. Stir-fry for 10 to 20 seconds, until the garlic and ginger begin to smell fragrant, and add the meat (making sure to scrape all the marinade from the bowl into the pan), the red pepper flakes, and the white part of the green onions. Stir-fry until the meat is no longer red, about 2 minutes; sprinkle everything with salt. Give the sauce a stir and add it to the pan. Cover and cook for 3 minutes. Remove the lid, stir the ingredients in the pan, taste and adjust the seasonings, and serve with rice or noodles.

leftovers Stir-fries are cook-and-serve dishes, but that doesn't mean the leftovers can't be enjoyed. When I first tested this recipe I cooked it in the afternoon, and Bill and I ate it for dinner late that night, and it was still fabulous. I just warmed it gently in the pan and scraped it into a serving bowl. Bill had it again for dinner the next night. Still good. It will stay good for 3 days, even though the peppers will lose their crunch. If you only have a small amount, cut the meat into even smaller pieces, cook up a bunch of rice, and mix it all together, then heat it in some oil in a large nonstick pan for a tasty fried rice.

spicy hunan chicken with ginger, scallions, and asparagus

This spicy Chinese chicken stir-fry is based on Barbara Tropp's recipe for Tung-An Chicken in The Modern Art of Chinese Cooking (William Morrow and Co., 1982). Inspired by her menu suggestions, I have incorporated asparagus into the dish. ❖ serves 4

Salt

¾ pound asparagus, trimmed and cut on the diagonal into 1-inch lengths

2 whole chicken breasts, split

4 slices of fresh ginger, plus 2 tablespoons minced or slivered fresh ginger

1 bunch of scallions

4 large or 8 medium Chinese mushrooms

2 teaspoons Szechuan brown peppercorns, twigs removed

½ teaspoon red pepper flakes

1 cup chicken stock (use the poaching broth from the chicken breasts)

¼ cup soy sauce

2 tablespoons Chinese rice wine or dry sherry

1 tablespoon sugar

1 to 2 teaspoons kosher salt, to taste

2 tablespoons peanut, vegetable, or canola oil

1 tablespoon unseasoned rice vinegar (if you only have seasoned vinegar, reduce sugar to 2 teaspoons)

2 teaspoons cornstarch dissolved in 2 tablespoons cold chicken stock or water

1 teaspoon sesame oil

2 teaspoons toasted sesame seeds

bring a large pot of water to a boil. Add 2 teaspoons salt and the asparagus. Boil for 20 seconds and immediately transfer the asparagus with a skimmer to a bowl of ice-cold water. Drain and set aside. Do not drain the hot water.

advance preparation
The asparagus may be blanched and the chicken parboiled a day ahead. Keep the asparagus in a covered bowl and the chicken in a resealable plastic bag or a well-sealed bowl in the refrigerator.

Rinse the chicken under cold water and place in a medium heavy saucepan or flameproof casserole. Smash the ginger slices and 2 of the scallions with the flat side of a cleaver, and cut the scallions into 1-inch lengths. Place in the pot with the chicken breasts. Bring the asparagus water back to a boil and pour over the chicken, making sure that all of the pieces are covered. Bring back to a boil over high heat, then reduce the heat and simmer, partially covered, for 10 minutes. Remove the chicken from the broth with tongs or a skimmer, and allow to cool.

Place the mushrooms in a heatproof bowl and pour on hot or boiling water to cover. Let sit for 30 minutes, or until soft. Cut away the tough stems and rinse the caps under cold water to remove any sand, then cut in slivers.

Place the peppercorns in a dry skillet and toast over medium heat, stirring constantly, until they begin to smell fragrant and smoke, about 1 minute. Remove from the pan at once and crush either in a mortar or in a spice mill. They should be coarsely ground.

Remove the skin from the chicken breasts, and the chicken breasts from the bones in one piece. Pull off any visible clumps of fat and tendon. Cut crosswise, against the grain, into ½-inch-thick slices, and cut the slices into 1½-inch lengths. The meat may still be pink.

Cut the remaining scallions into lengthwise slivers, about ⅛ inch thick and 2 inches long. Combine with the minced ginger and red pepper flakes in a bowl.

Stir together the stock, soy sauce, rice wine, sugar, and kosher salt, stirring until the sugar is dissolved. Set aside.

Heat a large, heavy nonstick skillet or wok over high heat until a drop of water evaporates upon contact. Add the peanut oil and turn the heat to medium-high. Add the coarsely ground peppercorns and let them sizzle for 5 seconds, then turn the heat to medium and add the scallions, ginger, and red pepper flakes. Stir until fragrant, about 20 seconds, and add the mushrooms. Stir together and pour in the stock mixture. Stir together and bring to a simmer. Add the chicken pieces and the asparagus and cook, stirring, until the chicken is white, about 3 minutes. Using a skimmer or a slotted spoon, remove the chicken and asparagus from the liquid and transfer to a warm serving dish.

Add the rice vinegar to the liquid, taste, and adjust the seasonings. It should taste sharp, with a good balance of pungent and sweet. Turn the heat to low. Stir the cornstarch and add to the pot. Stir until the sauce thickens, about 10 seconds, and pour over the chicken and asparagus. Drizzle on the sesame oil and sprinkle on the sesame seeds. Serve with rice or noodles.

leftovers ⋮ The asparagus will lose its bright color because of the acid in the sauce, but this will still taste great for a couple of days. Barbara Tropp recommended using leftovers as a salad topping for mixed greens or shredded carrots, dressed with sesame oil and rice vinegar. I think that's a terrific idea too.

stir-fried chicken and eggplant with asian basil

I have, once again, my friend John Lyons to thank for the inspiration for this dish. I needed to use up a bag of Asian basil he gave me, and some beautiful Asian eggplants. I found a recipe in Naomi Duguid and Jeffrey Alford's Hot Sour Salty Sweet *for Chicken with Asian Basil, and I used that as a springboard for this dish. Even though this is a stir-fry, and stir-fries by definition are "last-minute" dishes, I have to admit that this was just as delicious reheated a few hours after making it. And the leftovers make a great filling for lettuce wraps or spring rolls. Prepare the ingredients for this in the morning, if you wish, and finish after work.* ❖ **serves 4**

5 garlic cloves, peeled

1 tablespoon minced ginger

2 serrano or Thai chilies, stemmed

¼ teaspoon salt

1 tablespoon fish sauce

2 teaspoons soy sauce

1 teaspoon sugar

Freshly ground black pepper

3 tablespoons peanut or vegetable oil

1 pound boneless, skinless chicken breasts, rinsed and dried, cut into small dice

1 pound Asian eggplant, diced

1 cup Asian basil leaves

Cooked rice, for serving

advance preparation
You can make the paste several hours ahead. It will only become more pungent.

place the garlic, ginger, and chilies in a mortar with the salt and pound to a paste. In another small bowl, mix together the fish sauce, soy sauce, sugar, and pepper, and set aside.

advance preparation
The cooked chicken will keep for a
day in the refrigerator.

Heat a large, heavy nonstick skillet or wok over high heat
until a drop of water evaporates immediately upon contact. Add 1 tablespoon of the oil, turn the heat down to
medium-high, and add the garlic paste. Stir-fry for 30
seconds, and add the chicken. Stir-fry for 3 to 4 minutes, until the chicken is cooked
through and no traces of pink remain. Transfer to a bowl.

advance preparation
I have made the dish, refrigerated it
for a few hours, then reheated it and
served it with warm rice, and
I thought it was heavenly.

Heat the remaining 2 tablespoons of oil and add the
eggplant. Cook, stirring, until the eggplant is cooked
through, 10 to 15 minutes. Stir the chicken mixture back
into the pan and add the fish sauce—soy sauce mixture.
Stir together for a minute, then stir in the basil leaves. Stir
once, then remove from the heat. Serve at once, with rice.

leftovers Leftovers will keep for a couple of days in the refrigerator. Make lettuce roll-ups or rice-wrapper spring rolls for a delicious hors d'oeuvre or
starter.

reconstituting and steaming couscous

The recipes that follow will instruct you to mix a certain amount of the broth from the stew with water for reconstituting the couscous.

advance preparation
The couscous can be reconstituted up to a day ahead, then steamed before serving. Place the couscous in a bowl with salt as directed (see recipes). Combine the stock you have set aside with enough warm water to cover the couscous by about ½ inch. Let sit for 20 minutes, until the liquid is absorbed. Stir every 5 minutes with a wooden spoon or rub the couscous between your moistened thumbs and fingers, so that the couscous doesn't clump. The couscous will now be fairly soft; fluff it with a fork or with your hands. Taste the couscous and add salt if necessary.

Have the stew at a simmer, or you can steam the couscous over a small amount of water in a large pot, or in the oven or microwave (see below). To steam above the stew or boiling water, place the couscous in a colander, sieve, or the top part of a *couscoussière* and set it over the stew or boiling water, making sure that the bottom of the colander does not touch the liquid (remove some of the liquid if it does). Wrap a towel around the edge of the colander and the pot if there is a space, so that steam doesn't escape. Steam for 15 to 20 minutes.

The couscous can also steam in the oven or in the microwave. I use the oven most often when I'm entertaining, partly because it's easy to present the couscous in an attractive earthenware baking dish alongside the stew. To steam in the oven, place the couscous in a lightly oiled baking dish, cover tightly with foil, and place in a 350°F. oven for 20 minutes. To steam in a microwave, transfer to a microwave-safe bowl, cover tightly with plastic wrap, and pierce the plastic a couple of times with a knife. Microwave for 2 minutes at high. Let sit for 1 minute, then carefully remove the plastic and fluff the couscous with a fork.

cauliflower and tomato couscous

This is a thick, hearty Tunisian-inspired tagine that will please guests at any season of the year. There's no fat in it at all, but it tastes as rich as can be. It may be my favorite cauliflower recipe of all time. ❖ **serves 6 to 8**

1 pound (2½ cups) chick peas, soaked in 2 quarts water for 6 hours or overnight

1 medium onion, chopped

2 leeks, white part only, cleaned and sliced

4 large garlic cloves, minced

1 teaspoon coriander seeds, ground

1 teaspoon caraway seeds, ground

2 teaspoons cumin seeds, ground

2 tablespoons harissa (or more to taste; substitute ½ teaspoon ground cayenne pepper or more to taste if harissa is unavailable), plus additional for serving

2 tablespoons tomato paste

1 pound fresh tomatoes, peeled, seeded, and chopped, or 1 (14-ounce) can tomatoes, with liquid

Salt

1 large cauliflower, broken into small florets

½ cup imported black olives, such as kalamatas, pitted and cut in half lengthwise

3 cups couscous

1 cup chopped fresh flat-leaf parsley

1 cup chopped fresh cilantro

drain the chick peas and transfer to a large pot or the bottom part of a *couscoussière*. Add 2½ quarts water. Bring to a boil, reduce the heat, and simmer for 1 hour, while you prepare the remaining ingredients.

advance preparation
The dish can be prepared through this step up to a day ahead and refrigerated. Bring back to a simmer before proceeding.

advance preparation
The entire stew can be prepared through this step a day ahead and refrigerated. Bring back to a simmer and proceed with the recipe.

advance preparation
The couscous can be reconstituted up to a day ahead, then steamed before serving.

Add the onion, leeks, garlic, coriander, caraway, cumin, harissa, tomato paste, tomatoes, and salt (about 2 teaspoons or more) and simmer for another 30 minutes to an hour, until the chick peas are thoroughly tender and the broth is fragrant. Remove ½ cup of the broth and set aside.

Add the cauliflower and olives to the simmering stew and cook, partially covered, for another 15 to 20 minutes, until the cauliflower is tender. Taste and adjust the seasonings, adding salt, garlic, or harissa as desired.

Reconstitute and steam the couscous. Place the couscous in a bowl with 1 teaspoon salt. Combine 3 cups hot water with the ½ cup of strained cooking liquid from the stew and pour it over the couscous. The couscous should be completely submerged, with about ½ inch of water to spare. Follow the directions on page 335.

Bring the stew to a simmer and stir in the parsley and cilantro. Simmer for a couple of minutes, taste, and adjust the seasonings.

Transfer the couscous to a wide serving bowl, such as a pasta bowl, or directly to wide soup plates. Spoon on the stew and serve, passing additional harissa at the table.

leftovers This will keep for 4 or 5 days in the refrigerator. It will become quite thick, and you can thin it out with water if you wish. Leftovers can be eaten as a main dish or side dish, with couscous, rice, or pasta, or as a side dish with meat or fish. It gets better and better.

couscous with chick peas and chard

This thick stew is typical of many Tunisian vegetable stews, fragrant with layers of flavor emanating from spices (caraway, cumin, coriander seeds) and chilies (harissa), and from the beans and vegetables themselves. It makes a perfect vegetarian meal. ❖ **serves 6**

1 pound (2½ cups) chick peas, soaked in 2 quarts water for 6 hours or overnight

1 to 1½ pounds Swiss chard (2 bunches)

2 tablespoons olive oil

1 medium onion, chopped

2 leeks, white part only, cleaned and sliced

4 large garlic cloves, minced

1 teaspoon coriander seeds, ground

1 teaspoon caraway seeds, ground

2 teaspoons cumin seeds, ground

2 tablespoons harissa (or more to taste; substitute ½ teaspoon ground cayenne pepper if harissa is unavailable), plus additional for serving

2 tablespoons tomato paste

Salt

1 large bunch of flat-leaf parsley, stemmed, washed, and chopped

3 cups couscous

drain the chick peas and transfer to a large pot. Add 2 quarts water. Bring to a boil, reduce the heat, and simmer for 1 hour. Meanwhile, prepare the remaining ingredients.

Tear the chard leaves off the stems. Wash the stems and slice crosswise, about ¼ inch thick. Wash the leaves thoroughly and chop coarsely. Set aside.

advance preparation
The dish can be made through this step up to 3 days ahead and refrigerated. Bring back to a simmer and proceed as directed. You may also want to add a cup of water when you reheat. Adjust the seasonings accordingly.

Heat the oil over medium heat in a heavy flameproof casserole or Dutch oven, or if you have one, in the bottom of a *couscoussière*. Add the onion and leeks and cook, stirring, until tender, about 5 minutes. Add the chard stems and stir together for a couple of minutes, until they begin to soften. Stir in the garlic and ground spices, and stir together for 30 seconds to a minute, until the garlic is fragrant. Add the harissa or cayenne and the tomato paste and stir together for another minute or two. Add the chick peas with their cooking liquid, plus another cup of water, stir together, and bring back to a simmer. Add salt (you will need a generous amount, 2 to 3 teaspoons), cover, and simmer for 30 minutes to an hour, until the chick peas are thoroughly tender and the broth is fragrant. Strain off ½ cup of the liquid.

Stir in the chard greens, allowing each handful to cook down a bit before adding the next. Simmer for 10 to 15 minutes, until the greens are tender. Stir in the parsley. Remove from the heat. Taste and adjust the seasonings, adding salt, garlic, or harissa as desired.

advance preparation
The couscous can be reconstituted up to a day ahead, then steamed before serving.

Reconstitute and steam the couscous. Place the couscous in a bowl with 1 teaspoon salt. Combine 3 cups hot water with the ½ cup of strained cooking liquid from the vegetables and pour it over the couscous. The couscous should be completely submerged, with about ½ inch of water to spare. Follow the directions on page 335.

Transfer the couscous to a wide serving bowl, such as a pasta bowl, or directly to wide soup plates. Spoon on the stew and serve, passing additional harissa at the table.

leftovers This keeps well in the refrigerator for 3 or 4 days. However, the chard will lose its bright green color.

couscous with winter squash

This Tunisian-style stew should simmer until the squash begins to fall apart, thickening the mixture. ❖ **serves 4 generously**

1 tablespoon plus 1 teaspoon olive oil

1 large onion, sliced

2 large garlic cloves, minced or pressed

2 teaspoons coriander, ground

¾ teaspoon caraway, ground

¼ teaspoon cayenne pepper

1 tablespoon harissa (or more to taste)

2¼ pounds winter squash, peeled, seeded, and cut in large dice

½ pound waxy potatoes, scrubbed and diced

Salt

1 tablespoon tomato paste

1 (15-ounce) can chick peas, drained and rinsed

½ cup chopped fresh flat-leaf parsley

2 cups couscous

advance preparation
The stew can be made, without the addition of the parsley, a day or two ahead and refrigerated. Bring back to a simmer and add the parsley.

heat the oil in a large, heavy soup pot, Dutch oven, or *couscoussière* over medium heat and add the onion. Cook, stirring, until tender, about 5 minutes, then stir in the garlic, coriander, caraway, and cayenne. Stir together for about 1 minute, then add the harissa, squash, potatoes, and 5 cups of water. Bring to a boil, add a generous amount of salt, reduce the heat, cover, and simmer for 45 minutes, or until the squash is beginning to fall apart. Taste and adjust the salt. Remove 1 cup of broth and set aside. Stir in the chick peas and the parsley. Simmer for another 15 minutes. Taste and adjust the seasonings.

advance preparation
The couscous can be reconstituted
up to a day ahead, then steamed
before serving.

Reconstitute and steam the couscous. Place the couscous in a bowl with 1 teaspoon salt. Combine 1½ cups hot water with the cup of strained cooking liquid from the vegetables and pour it over the couscous. The couscous should be completely submerged, with about ½ inch of water to spare. Follow the directions on page 335.

Transfer the couscous to a wide serving bowl, such as a pasta bowl, or directly to wide soup plates. Spoon on the stew and serve, passing additional harissa at the table.

leftovers The stew will keep for 3 or 4 days in the refrigerator. Serve it with more couscous, or with rice, bulgur, or other grains for a change. Or make a puréed soup, simply by putting it through the medium blade of a food mill or blending it with a hand blender or in a blender.

spring farmers' market couscous

Everything in this vegetable stew came from an early June farmers' market, when spring vegetables are giving way to those of summer, but there are still favas and spring onions to be had. Whatever looked good and sweet, I bought. Use the trimmings from the spring onions, garlic, and carrots to make a light vegetable stock for this. You can simmer it for 20 or 30 minutes while you prepare everything, then use it in the stew. This is a perfect light, vegetarian dinner.

❖ serves 6

1 tablespoon olive oil

1 large sweet onion (red, white, or yellow), chopped

1 bunch of small spring onions, dark green ends separated, bulbs trimmed and cut in half lengthwise

1 head of green garlic, cloves peeled if they have formed, chopped

1 pound tender carrots, thickly sliced

1 bunch of tender turnips, peeled and cut in wedges

1 bunch of small new potatoes, cut in half if bigger than a large marble, quartered if bigger than a golf ball

Salt

5 cups Simple Vegetable Stock (page 377) or water

2 pounds fava beans

3 cups couscous

½ pound green beans, trimmed

Zest of 1 lemon

1 cup chopped fresh cilantro

Harissa, for serving

advance preparation
This step can be done several hours
or even a day ahead. Refrigerate
overnight, or keep on top of the
stove for a few hours.

heat the oil over medium heat in a large, heavy soup pot, Dutch oven, or *coussoussière* and add the onion. Cook, stirring often, until tender, about 5 minutes. Stir in the spring onions and the garlic and cook, stirring, until the spring onions begin to soften and the garlic is fragrant, about 3 minutes. Add the carrots, turnips, potatoes, and salt, toss together, and add the stock or water. Bring to a simmer, reduce the heat, cover, and simmer 20 to 30 minutes, until the vegetables are tender but not mushy and the broth is fragrant. Taste and adjust the seasonings. Remove 1 cup of broth and set aside.

advance preparation
This step can be done a day ahead,
and the vegetables can be held in the
refrigerator.

While the vegetables are simmering, shell the fava beans. Bring a medium-size pot of water to a boil, drop in the shelled beans, and boil for 1 minute. Transfer immediately to a bowl of cold water and drain. Slip off the skins and set aside. Bring the water back to a boil; add a teaspoon of salt and the green beans. Blanch for 3 to 4 minutes, until just tender. Transfer to a bowl of cold water, then drain.

advance preparation
The couscous can be reconstituted
up to a day ahead, then steamed
before serving.

Reconstitute and steam the couscous. Place the couscous in a bowl with 1 teaspoon salt. Combine 2½ cups hot water with the cup of strained cooking liquid from the vegetables and pour it over the couscous. The couscous should be completely submerged, with about ½ inch of water to spare. Follow the directions on page 335.

Add the favas, green beans, lemon zest, and cilantro to the simmering stew. Simmer for 5 minutes, taste, and adjust the seasonings. Transfer the couscous to a wide serving bowl, such as a pasta bowl, or directly to wide soup plates. Spoon on the stew and serve, passing harissa at the table.

leftovers Once the favas and green beans are simmered with the lemon zest in the stew, they will lose their bright green color. But that doesn't mean that this stew won't remain delicious for another 4 days. Keep serving it with couscous, or with rice or pasta.

couscous with chicken, lemon, and olives

This is my amalgamation of two classic Moroccan chicken tagines, one with olives and one with preserved lemon. I love the way the flavors mix, the lemon and the salty preserved lemon and olives, the spices and the herbs. If you can't find preserved lemon at imported food shops, make your own, following the instructions on page 389. ❖ serves 4

1	(3½- to 4½-pound) chicken, cut up and skinned
½	teaspoon ground ginger
½	teaspoon freshly ground black pepper
1	teaspoon cracked coriander seeds
⅛	teaspoon powdered saffron, or a pinch of crushed saffron threads
½	teaspoon ground cumin
½	teaspoon sweet paprika
	Salt
2	large garlic cloves, minced or pressed
2	tablespoons olive oil
½	pound (1 large or 2 medium) leeks, white and light green part only, thinly sliced
	A few sprigs each of flat-leaf parsley and cilantro
2	cups couscous
2½	cups chicken stock (page 378) or water
1	preserved lemon, quartered and cut in thick slices
⅓	cup imported green olives, pitted and cut in half
¼	cup fresh lemon juice (or more to taste)
¼	cup chopped fresh flat-leaf parsley
¼	cup chopped fresh cilantro

combine the chicken, all the spices, ½ teaspoon salt, the garlic, and 1 tablespoon of the olive oil in a large, flameproof casserole or Dutch oven, or in the bottom of a *couscoussière.* Toss together, cover, and let sit for 30 minutes to an hour, stirring from time to time.

advance preparation
The chicken can be simmered a day ahead, then refrigerated in the broth. This will allow you to skim fat from the top of the broth after it has chilled. Bring back to a simmer and proceed with the recipe.

Pour 3 cups water over the chicken and bring to a boil over medium-high heat. Skim off any foam that rises. When you have skimmed away all the foam, add the leeks and parsley and cilantro sprigs to the pot, reduce the heat, cover, and simmer gently for 30 minutes, or until the chicken is just about tender. Do not add much salt, because you'll be reducing this broth and the preserved lemon and olives you'll be adding to it are salty.

advance preparation
The couscous can be reconstituted a day or two ahead and kept in the refrigerator.

While the chicken is simmering, reconstitute the couscous. Stir ½ teaspoon salt into the couscous and cover with 2½ cups chicken stock or water. Follow the directions on page 335.

Add the preserved lemon and the olives to the chicken. Continue to simmer for another 10 to 15 minutes, until the chicken is very tender, almost falling off the bone. Transfer the couscous to a large bowl or serving dish and toss with the remaining 1 tablespoon olive oil. Arrange the chicken pieces and the preserved lemon and olives on top of it. Bring the liquid in the casserole to a boil and reduce by a third. Stir in the lemon juice and the chopped herbs. Taste and adjust the seasonings, adding lemon juice or salt if desired. Pour this over the chicken, and serve.

leftovers This is at its best the day it is made, because the lemon juice and herbs will lose their fresh flavor with time. But don't scoff at the leftovers. They'll taste good for about 3 or 4 days. Eat with couscous or, for a change, with rice.

lemon chicken pilaf

Take whatever chicken remains off the bones. Strain the broth and use for cooking rice, mixing it with water to obtain the needed amount. Cook rice following the directions on page 384, and when ready, toss with the chicken and leftover stew.

couscous with moroccan lamb and prune tagine

Moroccan tagines have more in common with Persian dishes than those from the other North African countries. The dishes are perfumed with sweet and subtle seasonings, such as cinnamon, saffron, and ginger. This one is a sweet and savory combination, lamb embellished with prunes, carrots, and rutabagas, the broth sweetened with sugar and cinnamon. Green beans add a bright touch, and the final sprinkling of toasted sesame seeds is the perfect garnish. ❖ serves 4 to 6

2 tablespoons unsalted butter (or to taste)

2 tablespoons vegetable or canola oil

3 pounds shoulder of lamb, trimmed and cut into 1½- to 2-inch pieces

1 cinnamon stick

1 teaspoon ground cinnamon

Generous pinch of saffron threads, or ½ teaspoon powdered saffron

½ teaspoon freshly ground black pepper

1 teaspoon ground ginger

2 medium onions, minced

Salt

1 pound rutabaga, peeled and cut in wedges or chunks

½ pound green beans, trimmed and broken in half if long

6 ounces pitted prunes

2 large carrots, peeled and cut in thick slices

2 to 3 tablespoons sugar (to taste)

3 cups couscous

2 tablespoons toasted sesame seeds

melt 1 tablespoon of the butter with 1 tablespoon of the oil over medium heat in a large, heavy nonstick skillet. Gently brown the meat in batches for 8 to 10 minutes, transferring it to a bowl as it's done. When all of the meat has been browned, add 1 cup water to the pan and bring to a boil. Scrape the pan with a wooden spoon until all of the bits clinging to the bottom have been loosened, and pour into the bowl with the meat.

Heat the remaining tablespoon each butter and oil over medium heat in a large, heavy flameproof casserole, in a Dutch oven, or in the bottom of a *couscoussière* and add the cinnamon stick, half the ground cinnamon, the saffron, pepper, ginger, and onions. Cook, stirring, until the onions are golden, about 10 minutes, and add the meat with its juices to the casserole. Add 3 cups water, enough to barely cover the meat. Bring to a boil, add salt, reduce the heat, cover, and simmer for 1 hour.

advance preparation
I have cooked the dish through this step, then turned it off and gone about my errands for 2 hours, then come back to it. Bring back to a simmer and proceed.

Bring a medium pot of water to a boil; add 1 teaspoon salt and the rutabaga. Cook for 1 minute, then, using a skimmer, transfer the rutabaga to the pot with the lamb. Bring the water back to a boil, add the beans, and cook for 4 minutes, until just tender. Transfer to a bowl of ice-cold water, then drain. Set aside.

advance preparation
The stew can be made, and benefits from it, a day ahead. Skim the fat off from the chilled broth before reheating. The couscous can be reconstituted a day ahead as well. Keep the beans covered in the refrigerator.

Add the prunes, carrots, the remaining ½ teaspoon cinnamon, and the sugar to the lamb. Continue to simmer for another 30 minutes, or until the prunes have swollen and the meat is very tender. Remove the meat, vegetables, and prunes from the broth and keep warm in a covered dish. Strain off ½ cup of the broth and mix with 3 cups water. Use this to reconstitute the couscous, following the directions on page 335.

Turn up the heat and boil the sauce until it is thick (you can steam the couscous above the boiling sauce if you wish). Taste and adjust the seasonings. Stir the meat, vegetables (including the green beans), and prunes back into the sauce, heat through, and transfer to an attractive, deep serving dish. Scatter the sesame seeds over the top and serve, with the couscous.

leftovers This tagine is a good keeper. It will be tasty for 3 or 4 days and can be frozen. You can serve leftovers with couscous or with rice.

fish couscous

This recipe could have just as easily been placed in Chapter 6, for it is a fisherman's stew served with couscous. This one is Tunisian in character, a tomatoey broth filled with vegetables and spicy with harissa and cayenne. It's nice to use two or three types of fish for this, but nobody will complain about this dish if you just use one. ❖ **serves 8**

2 tablespoons olive oil

1 large onion, chopped

2 leeks, white and light green parts only, sliced

1 large green bell pepper, cored, seeded, and chopped

6 garlic cloves, minced or pressed

1 teaspoon cumin seeds, ground

1 pound tomatoes, peeled, seeded, and chopped, or 1 (28-ounce) can tomatoes, with liquid

Salt and freshly ground black pepper

¼ cup tomato paste dissolved in ½ cup water

¼ to ½ teaspoon cayenne pepper, to taste

1 tablespoon harissa (or more to taste), plus additional for serving

2 quarts Easy Fish Stock (page 380), made without wine, or shrimp shell broth (page 257)

½ pound waxy potatoes or Yukon golds, peeled and quartered

½ pound carrots, peeled, quartered, and cut into 2-inch sticks

½ pound turnips, peeled and quartered

2 medium zucchini, cut in half lengthwise and into 2-inch lengths

3 cups couscous

1 can chick peas, drained and rinsed

2 to 2½ pounds mixed fish fillets, such as gray or striped
mullet, snapper, halibut, grouper, shark, cod, porgy, or
monkfish, cut into 2-inch pieces

1 bunch of flat-leaf parsley or cilantro, chopped

advance preparation
The stew can be made through this
step a day ahead of time. Bring
back to a simmer and proceed
with the recipe.

heat the oil over medium heat in a large, heavy flameproof casserole, in a Dutch oven, or in the bottom of a *coussoussière* and add the onion and leeks. Cook, stirring, until tender, about 5 minutes, and stir in the bell pepper. Cook, stirring, until the pepper is just about tender, about 5 more minutes, and stir in the garlic and ground cumin seeds. Cook together, stirring, until fragrant, about a minute, and add the tomatoes, and salt and pepper to taste. Cook, stirring often, until the tomatoes have cooked down somewhat and the mixture smells very fragrant. Stir in the dissolved tomato paste, the cayenne, harissa, fish stock, potatoes, carrots, turnips, and zucchini, add more salt as desired, and bring to a simmer. Cover and simmer for 15 minutes, or until the vegetables are tender. Taste and adjust the seasonings. Strain off 1 cup of the stock.

Reconstitute and steam the couscous. Place the couscous in a bowl with 1 teaspoon salt. Combine 2½ cups hot water with the cup of strained stock and pour it over the couscous. The couscous should be completely submerged, with about ½ inch of water to spare. Follow the directions on page 335.

advance preparation
The couscous can be reconstituted
up to a day ahead, then steamed
before serving.

Add the chick peas to the simmering stew. Simmer for 10 minutes (if you are steaming the couscous above the stew, do it now), and stir in the fish and the parsley or cilantro. Simmer very gently for 5 to 10 minutes, until the fish is opaque. Taste and adjust the seasonings.

Transfer the couscous to a wide serving bowl, such as a pasta bowl, or directly to wide soup plates. Top the couscous with fish, vegetables, and plenty of broth, and serve, passing harissa at the table.

leftovers Like all fish stews, this doesn't improve overnight. But you can enjoy the leftovers for a day or two. When we have a lot left over, we stir leftover couscous into the broth and serve it up in wide bowls as a marvelous soup.

nine
some comforting desserts

Although the hearty one-dish meals in this book can as easily be followed by a piece of fruit as by a "real dessert," I know you'll be using this book for entertaining as often as you will for family dining. So I've put together a short chapter of desserts that I think are both comforting and easy to make. You don't have to be a pastry chef to make a warming crumble, a chocolate pudding that will delight kids and grown-ups alike, a peach pie, or a delightful chocolate mousse.

In the spirit of the rest of this book, these are desserts that can be done ahead—if not completely, then partially—and that aren't fussy. Most of them are fruit-oriented, because that's the kind of dessert I like to make and the kind I feel good about feeding my family night after night. My son, Liam, has taught me how important dessert can be to a child (he asks nightly what he's going to have for dessert well before he's halfway through his dinner), and he was very happy to be the tester of all of these recipes.

dessert pastry

This is an easy, tender butter pastry that I use for all of my fruit pies and tarts. It freezes well and keeps well for a couple of days in the refrigerator. ❖ makes enough for 2 single 9-inch pies or 1 double-crusted or lattice-crusted pie

2¼ cups unbleached all-purpose flour

1 tablespoon sugar

½ teaspoon salt

12 tablespoons cold unsalted butter (1½ sticks)

About ½ cup ice water, or 1 egg yolk mixed with enough ice water to make ½ cup (reserve the white for brushing the crust)

put the flour, sugar, and salt in the bowl of a food processor and turn on for about 10 seconds to mix. Cut the butter into small pieces and place in the food processor. Cut in, using the pulse action. When the mixture has a crumbly consistency, add the liquid, by tablespoon, either with the machine running or pulsing. When the pieces of dough adhere to each other, or when the dough comes together on the blades of the food processor, you have added enough water. Remove from the processor and gently shape into a ball, then divide into 2 equal pieces for 2 pies, or for a double-crusted or lattice pie divide into 2 pieces with 1 piece slightly larger than the other. Press each piece into a ½-inch-thick disk, and wrap in plastic. Refrigerate for 30 minutes before rolling out.

advance preparation
You can make the dough a few days or even weeks ahead. Roll it out and line your pie dish, then cover with plastic wrap and foil and freeze. Freeze the top crust, and thaw in the refrigerator for a few hours or a day when ready to prepare the pie. You can prebake or fill directly from the freezer.

Sprinkle the work surface lightly with flour and roll out the crust, following the recipe of your choice. Sprinkle flour over the surface of the dough to prevent the rolling pin from sticking to the dough.

crème anglaise
(vanilla custard sauce)

Crème anglaise—vanilla custard sauce—is my ultimate weakness. I could eat it like soup, and I do when I make Floating Island (page 366). I serve it with crumbles, cakes, and baked apples. It can turn a humble dessert into something truly memorable. ❖ **makes 2½ cups**

½ to 1 vanilla bean (to taste)

2 cups milk (whole or reduced-fat)

5 egg yolks

⅓ to ½ cup sugar (to taste)

Small pinch of salt

split the vanilla bean in half lengthwise and, using the tip of a paring knife, scrape the seeds into the milk. Put the bean in the milk and bring to a simmer in a heavy, medium, nonreactive saucepan over medium heat. Do not boil. When the milk comes to a simmer, with small bubbles around the edges of the pan and the surface moving but not breaking, remove from the heat, cover, and let the vanilla bean steep for 15 minutes.

While the milk is steeping, fill a large bowl with ice or ice water and nest a smaller bowl in the ice. Place a strainer over the smaller bowl.

Meanwhile, whisk together the egg yolks, sugar, and salt in a medium bowl until thick and lemon colored. Remove the vanilla bean from the milk and scrape any remaining seeds into the milk. (Rinse the pod and set it aside to dry on paper towels so that you can use it in vanilla sugar; see page 399.) Bring the milk back to a simmer, remove it from the heat, and ladle out ½ cup of the hot milk. Drizzle it slowly into the eggs, whisking all the while. Then whisk this mixture back into the milk. Scrape out the bottom of the bowl with a heatproof rubber scraper.

Place the pan back on the stove and heat over low heat, stirring constantly. Watch very closely. Stir in figure eights, using a heatproof rubber spatula or a wooden spoon and scraping the bottom of the pan constantly. After 2 to 5 minutes the sauce should begin to thicken. Do not let the mixture boil or the eggs will curdle.

When the sauce coats your spatula or spoon like cream and leaves a canal when you run your finger down the middle, remove from the heat. Stir for a few seconds, then strain the sauce into the bowl set in the ice bath. Stir occasionally for the next 10 to 15 minutes. As the sauce cools it will thicken.

Note: If the sauce does curdle, place in a blender or food processor and blend until smooth. Reheat over low heat, stirring as directed above, until the mixture coats a spoon like cream. Remove from the heat and proceed as directed above.

leftovers ⋮ The sauce will keep for up to 2 days in the refrigerator.

chocolate pudding

It never occurred to me to make chocolate pudding until I began working on this book. It was just one of those blissful dessert memories from childhood. I toyed around with a number of recipes before settling on this one. ❖ serves 4

2⅓ cups milk

½ cup plus 1 tablespoon sugar

Pinch of salt

4 tablespoons cocoa

2 tablespoons cornstarch, sifted

1 large egg

2 large egg yolks

2 ounces semisweet chocolate, chopped

½ tablespoon unsalted butter

1 teaspoon pure vanilla extract

Lightly whipped cream or milk, for serving

place 2 cups of the milk, ¼ cup of the sugar, and the salt in a heavy saucepan and bring to a boil over medium heat.

Meanwhile, mix together the remaining 5 tablespoons sugar, the cocoa, and the cornstarch in a medium mixing bowl. Whisk in the remaining ⅓ cup milk, and stir until smooth and free of lumps.

advance preparation If you need to leave the kitchen, you can stop after this step, cover the mixture, and come back in a few hours. Whisk over medium-low heat and bring back to a simmer.

Carefully whisk the hot milk mixture into the bowl; return the mixture to the saucepan. Slowly bring to a boil over medium heat, stirring often. Boil gently, stirring constantly, until the mixture is thick, 2 to 5 minutes.

Whisk the egg and egg yolks together in a small bowl. Making sure that it is not boiling, slowly whisk in 1 cup of the hot cocoa mixture. Whisk the resulting egg mixture back into the saucepan with the hot cocoa mixture, and whisk constantly over medium-low heat, being careful not to allow it to come to a boil (or the eggs will curdle), until the mixture thickens a little more, 3 to 5 minutes. Cool slightly.

Melt the chocolate and butter in a microwave, at 50-percent power for 2 minutes. Whisk into the thickened egg mixture. Stir in the vanilla. Pour into 4 to 6 ramekins, pudding dishes, or glass sundae dishes, and cover with plastic wrap. If you don't want a skin to form on the surface, lay the plastic directly over the surface of the pudding. Chill for 2 to 3 hours or longer, and serve with whipped cream or milk.

leftovers The chocolate pudding will keep for up to 5 days in the refrigerator.

the easiest chocolate
mousse in the world

This is the chocolate mousse that I grew up with. I only recently asked my stepmother for the recipe, which is adapted from Craig Claiborne's Chocolate Mousse I in The New York Times Cookbook *(1961). I couldn't believe that a recipe this simple would work, but it does, and it can be made in minutes. Because it isn't particularly sweet—no sugar is added to the semisweet chocolate—this is more of a grown-up's dessert than a kid's.* ❖ serves 8

4 large eggs, separated

¼ teaspoon cream of tartar

1 cup chocolate chips, or 6 ounces semisweet chocolate, cut into ¼-inch pieces

⅓ cup boiling water

2 tablespoons dark rum or Grand Marnier

beat the egg whites until they begin to foam. Add the cream of tartar and continue to beat until they form stiff but not dry peaks. Set aside.

Place the chocolate chips or chopped chocolate in a food processor fitted with the steel blade and process until the chocolate is pulverized. Scrape down the sides of the bowl. Turn on the food processor and pour in the boiling water. Stop the machine when the chocolate is melted and the mixture is smooth. Scrape down the sides of the processor bowl. Add the egg yolks and rum or Grand Marnier and process for 10 seconds, or until smooth. Scrape into a large bowl.

advance preparation
This can be made the day before you plan to serve it.

Stir a large spoonful of egg whites into the chocolate mixture, then gently fold the chocolate mixture into the egg whites. Spoon into pot-de-crème dishes or ½ cup ramekins, and chill for at least 1 hour, or until set.

leftovers
Because of the uncooked eggs, the chocolate mousse should be eaten within a couple of days of making it. That won't be difficult to do.

crumble topping

❖ makes enough for 1 crumble made in a 2- to 2½-quart baking dish

⅓ cup pecans

1 cup rolled oats

¾ cup unbleached all-purpose flour

⅓ cup plus 1 tablespoon firmly packed light brown sugar
   or unrefined turbinado sugar

¼ teaspoon salt

7 tablespoons cold unsalted butter

heat the pecans in a dry skillet over medium heat, shaking it or stirring the pecans constantly, until they begin to smell toasty. Remove from the skillet at once and chop coarsely. Mix together the oats, flour, sugar, and salt, either in a bowl or in a food processor fitted with the steel blade. Cut in the butter using the pulse action of the food processor, or by taking up the mixture in handfuls and rubbing it briskly between your fingers and thumbs. The mixture should have a crumbly consistency. Stir in the pecans. Freeze in a resealable plastic bag, or sprinkle over your prepared fruit and bake as directed. If freezing, when ready to use, sprinkle the mixture directly over your fruit without thawing and proceed with the recipe.

plum and cherry crumble

I use the sweet-tart Santa Rosa plums that we get in the summer farmers' markets here in California for this, but any juicy plum will do. I love the interplay here between the tart plums, the sweeter cherries, and the sweet crumble topping. ❖ **serves 6 to 8**

3 pounds mixed ripe sweet-tart plums, such as Santa Rosa

½ pound cherries

¼ cup sugar or 3 tablespoons mild honey, such as clover or acacia

3 tablespoons red wine

Seeds from 1 vanilla pod or ½ teaspoon pure vanilla extract

Crumble Topping (page 357)

advance preparation
I like to get ahead on a crumble by preparing all of the fruit hours before assembling the dish. Keep the fruit in a covered bowl, in or out of the refrigerator (depending on how far ahead you're prepping). Measure out your other ingredients, but don't toss with the fruit until ready to assemble the crumble.

advance preparation
This can be baked a few hours ahead, but it's best if not baked too far in advance, to ensure a crisp topping.

leftovers

heat the oven to 375ºF. Butter a 3-quart baking or gratin dish. Cut up the plums by cutting down each side of the pits, as you would cut a mango. Cut the larger pieces in half. Cut the cherries in half using a sharp paring knife, and remove the pits. Place the plums and cherries in a bowl and toss with the sugar or honey, the wine, and the vanilla seeds or extract.

Scrape the fruit into the buttered dish. Spoon the crumble topping over the fruit in an even layer. Bake until bubbling and browned, 40 to 45 minutes. If you wish, finish very briefly under the broiler, being careful not to burn. Serve warm or at room temperature. Serve with Crème Anglaise (page 353), whipped cream, or vanilla ice cream.

Leftovers will keep for a few days in the refrigerator. It won't stay crisp, but it will still be delicious.

peach and nectarine crumble with a few blueberries

One of the reasons I love crumbles is that crumble toppings hold up over time, so leftovers are scrumptious. This is one of those irresistible height-of-summer desserts. ❖ serves 6 to 8

3 pounds peaches and/or nectarines

½ cup blueberries (optional)

3 tablespoons sugar, or 2 tablespoons mild honey, such as clover or acacia

Seeds from 1 vanilla pod or ½ teaspoon pure vanilla extract

½ teaspoon cinnamon

Crumble Topping (page 357)

advance preparation
I like to get ahead on a crumble by preparing all of the fruit hours before assembling the dish. Keep the fruit in a covered bowl, in or out of the refrigerator (depending on how far ahead you're prepping). Measure out your other ingredients, but don't toss with the fruit until ready to assemble the crumble.

advance preparation
This can be baked a few hours ahead, but it's best if not baked too far in advance, to ensure a crisp topping.

heat the oven to 375°F. Butter a 3-quart baking or gratin dish. Slice the peaches and nectarines. If they cling to the pits, slice them by cutting down each side of the pit, as you would cut a mango. Place in a bowl with the blueberries, if using, and toss with the sugar or honey, the vanilla seeds or extract, and the cinnamon.

Scrape the fruit into the buttered dish. Spoon the crumble topping over the fruit in an even layer. Bake until bubbling and browned, 40 to 45 minutes. If you wish, finish very briefly under the broiler, being careful not to burn. Serve warm or at room temperature. Serve with Crème Anglaise (page 353), whipped cream, or vanilla ice cream.

leftovers The underside of the topping will eventually sink into the crumble, but that won't prevent this from being a luscious leftover that I personally love to eat for breakfast, with yogurt. It will keep for a few days in the refrigerator.

pear and ginger crumble

Pears and ginger always marry well, and this is one of my most irresistible desserts. You can make it ahead, then recrisp the top in a warm oven (300°F. for 15 minutes). But in this case, cutting up the pears too far ahead of time might cause them to discolor, so I advise you to make the crumble in one go. ❖ **serves 6 to 8**

2½ to 3 pounds ripe but firm pears (about 5 large), peeled, cored, and sliced

3 tablespoons sugar

2 tablespoons fresh lemon juice

2 tablespoons chopped candied ginger

½ teaspoon pure vanilla extract

2 teaspoons cornstarch

Crumble Topping (page 357)

Whipped cream, Crème Anglaise (page 353), or vanilla ice cream for serving (optional)

heat the oven to 375°F. Butter a 2- to 2½-quart baking or gratin dish. Toss together all the ingredients for the filling and turn into the dish.

advance preparation
This can be baked a few hours ahead, but it's best if not baked too far in advance, to ensure a crisp topping.

Spoon the crumble topping over the fruit in an even layer. Bake until bubbling and browned, 40 to 45 minutes. If you wish, finish very briefly under the broiler, being careful not to burn. Serve warm or at room temperature, topped if you wish with whipped cream or Crème Anglaise (page 353) or accompanied by vanilla ice cream.

leftovers
Like the other crumbles, you can enjoy the leftovers for a few days, even if the top doesn't remain crisp.

peach pie

Peach pie was always my favorite when I was little, and may still be. It's those soft, sweet peaches, transformed by baking into the most luscious treat. ❖ **makes 1 double-crusted or latticed pie, serving 8**

1 recipe Dessert Pastry (page 352)

2½ pounds peaches (or nectarines), sliced

¼ cup sugar

1 teaspoon pure vanilla extract

1 teaspoon ground cinnamon

1 egg white

while the dough is chilling, prepare the filling. Cut up the peaches and toss with the sugar, vanilla, and cinnamon.

Heat the oven to 350°F. with a rack in the lower-third position. Butter a 10-inch pie dish. Dust the work surface with flour and roll out the larger circle of dough. Line the pie dish, with an edge draping over the sides. Place the peach filling on top. Roll out the second disk of dough, and either cut into strips for a lattice crust, or place over the peaches for a double crust. Fold the bottom crust overhang in over the lattices or the top crust, and crimp together. Pinch an attractive edge around the rim of the pie. If using a top crust, make a few slashes in the top with the tip of a sharp knife. Place the pie on a baking sheet.

advance preparation
This is best served the day it's baked. However, the crust stands up to that peach juice remarkably well.

Beat the egg white until a little frothy, and lightly brush the dough.

Bake for 40 to 50 minutes, or until the crust is golden brown and the filling is bubbling. Let cool for at least 30 minutes before tucking in.

leftovers I never met a leftover piece of peach pie I didn't like. It'll keep for a few days out of the refrigerator, though the juice might run out onto the pie dish (eat it with a spoon). Refrigerate after a couple of days.

bill's irish trifle

My husband, Bill, grew up with Irish trifle, a yearly treat and one he never fails to assemble for our Christmas dinners. At one of these dinners, prepared by a number of accomplished cooks, it was voted best dish by the children who attended. Bill admits that the trifle he grew up eating and loving was made with shop cake and boxed custard mix. He also admits that this one, from scratch, is better. I should also note that Bill never measures the sherry; he just adds it until it tastes "right," which is fairly boozy but not over the top. ❖ serves 6 to 8

for the sponge cake

4 eggs, separated

Salt

Scant ¼ teaspoon cream of tartar

⅔ cup superfine sugar

1½ teaspoons pure vanilla extract

1 cup plus 2 tablespoons all-purpose flour, sifted

3 tablespoons warm melted butter (optional)

for the trifle

Raspberry jam (about ¼ cup)

Cream sherry

1 recipe Crème Anglaise (page 353)

1 cup heavy cream

make the sponge cake at least one day ahead. Heat the oven to 350°F. Butter and flour an 8-inch round cake pan and line with parchment.

Beat the egg whites with a clean, dry whisk or electric beaters until they begin to foam. Add a pinch of salt and the cream of tartar. Beat until soft peaks form. Add 1½ tablespoons of the sugar and beat again until stiff peaks form. Set aside.

Beat the egg yolks in another bowl with a whisk or an electric mixer. Add the remaining sugar, 1 tablespoon at a time, and beat until the mixture is pale yellow and leaves a ribbon trail when the whisk is lifted. Beat in the vanilla. Stir in ¼ cup of the beaten egg whites.

Place one-third of the remaining egg whites on top and sift on one fourth of the flour. Gently fold in. Repeat with one third of the remaining egg whites and one fourth of the flour; then with half of the remaining egg whites and flour. Fold in the remaining egg whites and flour, then fold in the warm melted butter, if using.

advance preparation
The cake can be made a few
days ahead and kept at room
temperature, wrapped in foil.
Or you can wrap it in plastic and
foil and freeze for a month.

Pour the batter into the prepared cake pan. Tap once against the work surface to deflate large air bubbles. Bake for 25 to 30 minutes, until firm and a cake tester comes out clean. Remove from the oven and allow to cool in the pan on a rack for 15 minutes, then invert onto another rack, remove the pan, peel off the parchment, and invert again to cool on the rack.

The day before, or the morning of the night you wish to serve this, cut the cake into 2-inch squares. Spread the top of the squares of cake with jam. Line a flat, wide bowl (a trifle dish is a lovely stemmed glass bowl with a flat bottom and straight sides) with the cake, in one layer. Douse the cake with cream sherry. Cover with wax paper or plastic, then set set a plate on top, and a weight, such as a large can of tomatoes, on top of the plate. Cover and refrigerate for 12 hours or longer.

Uncover the cake. Add a little sherry to the crème anglaise and pour over the cake. Chill for an hour or more in the refrigerator.

Beat the cream until it forms soft peaks, and flavor it with cream sherry to taste. Spoon over the trifle, and refrigerate until ready to serve.

leftovers Trifle is one of those leftover desserts you love to keep eating. The sherry will become more pronounced, something we like, and the cake soggier. But in my opinion leftovers, which keep for a couple of days if you're lucky, can be even more comforting than the showcase dessert.

christine's apple cake

I learned this cake from my dear friend Christine Picasso, who is my "French mother" and has taught me many wonderful dishes. It's a moist cake—really more apple than cake—that she makes often in the fall and winter. She sometimes serves it with Crème Anglaise (page 353).

❖ serves 8 to 10

for the cake

½ cup all-purpose flour

1 tablespoon baking powder

⅛ teaspoon salt

2 large eggs

⅓ cup sugar

⅓ cup milk (whole or reduced-fat)

2 tablespoons vegetable oil or canola oil

2 tablespoons light rum or additional milk

1 teaspoon pure vanilla extract

2 pounds apples, such as Gala, Gravenstein, Pippin, or Golden Delicious, peeled, cored, and thinly sliced

for the topping

1 large egg

3 tablespoons butter, melted

¼ cup light brown sugar, packed

make the cake. Heat the oven to 400°F. Butter or pan-spray a 9-inch springform pan.

Sift together the flour, baking powder, and salt into a medium bowl. In another, larger bowl, beat together the eggs and sugar until thick. Beat in the milk, oil, rum, and vanilla. Whisk the dry ingredients into the egg mixture and stir gently to blend. Fold in the apples.

Scrape the batter into the cake pan and place in the middle of the oven. Bake for 40 minutes, or until not quite firm but fairly brown.

Meanwhile, mix together the topping ingredients. Beat the egg, then whisk in the melted butter and the sugar.

Remove the cake from the oven and pour the topping over it. Return to the oven. Bake for another 10 minutes, or until the top is caramelized and the cake is firm when gently pressed.

advance preparation This cake is a good keeper, and will be good for a dinner party if you make it the day before. Remove from the oven and cool in the pan for 10 minutes. Run a knife around the edge of the pan and unmold, but keep the cake on the bottom of the pan. Allow to cool completely on a rack.

Cut into wedges and serve, with Crème Anglaise if desired.

leftovers Keep in the refrigerator after the first day. Serve it until it's gone, for a couple of days.

floating island

What could be more luxurious than little puffs of meringue floating in a sea of crème anglaise? For me this is the ultimate dessert. I seldom see it on menus in the United States, but in France, where it is called oeufs à la neige *("eggs in snow") as well as* île flottante *("floating island"), it's a dessert-trolley standard. Use the egg whites for the meringues, and make the crème anglaise with the yolks and the milk used for poaching the meringues. In my version I've dispensed with the caramel that is traditionally drizzled over the meringues.* ❖ **serves 6**

2 cups milk, plus additional as needed

1 vanilla bean, split

5 large eggs, separated

Pinch of salt

¼ teaspoon cream of tartar

⅔ to 1 cup sugar or Vanilla Sugar (page 399), divided (to taste)

pour the milk into a wide saucepan or skillet. Scrape in the vanilla seeds and add the pods. Heat the milk to a bare simmer. Bubbles should appear around the edge but the surface should not break. Remove from the heat and let sit, covered, while you prepare the meringues.

Place the egg whites in a large bowl or the bowl of an electric mixer and beat until they begin to foam. Add the salt and cream of tartar, and continue beating until they form soft peaks. Slowly beat in half the sugar, a tablespoon at a time, and continue to beat until the meringue is stiff and silky, but not dry.

Using a serving spoon or soup spoon, take up a spoonful of the beaten egg whites. Take another spoon and round off the top of the mound so that the blob of egg whites is shaped like an egg. Gently slide off the spoon onto the milk, using a spatula to help if necessary. Drop as many as will fit on the surface of the milk without crowding the pan. Return the milk to low heat, and when the surface barely begins to quiver, cook the meringue for 2 minutes, never letting the milk break into a boil. Carefully flip the meringues over and cook for another 2 minutes. Lift out with a skimmer and drain on a kitchen towel, then place in a wide bowl and refrigerate.

Turn off the heat. Remove the vanilla bean from the milk and scrape any remaining seeds into the milk. Pour into a measuring cup and add enough milk to make 2 cups. Using the milk and the yolks left over from the floating islands, make Crème Anglaise, following the directions on page 353. Chill the crème anglaise.

advance preparation
This can be assembled as far ahead as the morning of the day you wish to serve.

Fill an attractive bowl, preferably glass, with the Crème Anglaise. Float the meringues on the Crème Anglaise, and serve.

leftovers
You can keep the Crème Anglaise with the meringues in it in the refrigerator for 2 days.

apple pie

There couldn't not be a recipe for apple pie in this book. This one is a classic. I prefer tart apples, but you can also use sweet ❖ serves 6

½ lemon, plus 2 tablespoons fresh lemon juice

10 tart apples (about 2½ pounds) such as Galas, Braeburns, Pippins, McIntosh, or Pink Lady, or 10 sweet apples such as Fujis, Golden Delicious, or Jonathans

½ cup granulated sugar, or use ¼ cup granulated sugar and ¼ cup tightly packed light brown sugar

2 tablespoons cornstarch

1 to 2 teaspoons ground cinnamon, to taste

½ teaspoon freshly grated nutmeg

1 teaspoon pure vanilla extract

1 recipe Dessert Pastry (page 352)

1 egg white (from the egg you used for the dough), optional

fill a large bowl with water and squeeze in the juice of half a lemon, then put the lemon half into the water. Peel, core, and cut the apples into eighths, dropping them into the water as they are cut.

Sift together the sugar, cornstarch, cinnamon, and nutmeg into another bowl. Drain the apples and toss with the 2 tablespoons of lemon juice and the vanilla, then with the sugar mixture.

Heat the oven to 375°F. with a rack in the lower-third position. Butter a 10-inch pie dish. Dust the work surface with flour and roll out the larger circle of dough. Line the pie dish, with an edge draping over the sides. Place the apple filling on top. Roll out the second disk of dough, and either cut into strips for a lattice crust, or place over the apples for a double crust. Fold the bottom crust overhang in over the lattices or the top crust, and crimp together. Pinch an attractive edge around the rim of the pie. If using a top crust, make a few slashes in the top with the tip of a sharp knife.

Beat the egg white until a little frothy, if using, and lightly brush the dough.

Place the pie on a foil-lined baking sheet and bake for 45 to 50 minutes, or until the crust is golden brown and the filling is bubbling. Let cool for at least 30 minutes on a rack. Serve warm or at room temperature, with vanilla ice cream if you wish.

honey-baked apples with crème anglaise

Apples baked to a stage that's almost as soft as applesauce are comforting indeed. This dessert comes right out of a French kitchen. ❖ serves 6

6 large, fairly tart apples, such as Braeburns

½ lemon

¼ cup single-malt whiskey

Ground cinnamon

¼ cup mild honey, such as clover or acacia

1 tablespoon unsalted butter (optional)

1 recipe Crème Anglaise (page 353)

heat the oven to 350°F. Butter a baking dish into which all the apples will fit. Core the apples and squeeze lemon juice over the cut surfaces.

advance preparation The Crème Anglaise can be made a day ahead. The baked apples will hold for several hours at room temperature.

Warm the whiskey over medium heat in a small, heavy saucepan. Before it reaches the simmering point, light it with a match, standing back from the pan. Carefully pour the flaming whiskey over the apples. When the flames die down, sprinkle the apples with cinnamon and drizzle on the honey. Top each apple with a thin pat of butter if you wish. Cover the dish with foil and place in the oven. Bake for 45 minutes to an hour, until the skins have split and the apples are soft. Remove from the oven and allow to cool. Serve warm or at room temperature, topped with Crème Anglaise.

leftovers Keep the apples in the refrigerator for a few days. They won't look good but they'll still taste great.

one-bowl chocolate cake

This is an easy, moist chocolate cake, perfect when you need to whip up a quick birthday cake or chocolate dessert. Ice it with the ganache frosting for a major chocolate hit. ❖ **serves 10 to 12**

2 cups cake flour, sifted

2 teaspoons baking powder

½ teaspoon baking soda

¼ teaspoon salt

½ cup plus 2 tablespoons cocoa

8 tablespoons (1 stick) unsalted butter, at room temperature

1¼ cups granulated sugar

2 large eggs

¾ cup sour cream (can use reduced-fat)

1½ teaspoons pure vanilla extract

⅓ cup strong brewed coffee

ganache frosting

8 ounces bittersweet chocolate, finely chopped

8 tablespoons (1 stick) unsalted butter

½ cup confectioners' sugar

heat the oven to 350°F. with the rack in the middle. Coat two 9-inch cake pans or one 10-inch springform pan with pan spray and line with parchment. Spray the parchment.

advance preparation
You can sift the ingredients together hours or even days in advance. But if you do, sift once more before proceeding with the recipe.

Combine the flour, baking powder, baking soda, salt, and cocoa, and sift together two times. Set aside.

In the bowl of an electric mixer, beat the butter at high speed for 1 minute. Slowly add the sugar and beat at high speed for 5 to 6 minutes, until light and very fluffy.

Scrape down the sides of the bowl with a rubber scraper. Add the eggs, one at a time, and beat until the first egg is incorporated into the butter–sugar mixture before adding the next. When the eggs are mixed in, add the sour cream and vanilla, and mix together well at medium speed.

Slowly beat in the flour mixture and coffee, alternating the dry and wet ingredients. Beat at medium speed for a couple of minutes until well blended.

Pour into the pans and bake for 25 to 30 minutes for 9-inch pans, 40 to 50 minutes for a springform pan, until a cake tester comes out clean and the cakes rebound when gently pressed.

Allow to cool in the pans for 10 minutes before unmolding onto a rack. Cool completely and frost.

advance preparation
This cake will keep for a couple of days if wrapped airtight, and if uniced it will freeze for a couple of weeks. The frosting can be refrigerated for up to 2 days. Beat for 3 to 4 minutes in a standing mixer fitted with the paddle attachment before using.

Make the ganache. Combine the chocolate and butter in a microwave-safe bowl and zap at 50-percent power for 2 minutes. Stir together with a rubber scraper and zap again at 50-percent power for 30 seconds if the chocolate isn't completely melted. (Alternatively, place the bowl over a saucepan filled with simmering water and stir with a rubber scraper until the chocolate is melted.) Sift the confectioners' sugar into the chocolate and stir for several minutes, until the sugar is absorbed and the mixture is smooth. Ice the cake right away, before the ganache stiffens up.

some basic techniques and recipes

In this chapter you'll find techniques and basic recipes that come up often throughout the text of this book. For example, many of the recipes for stews and stir-fries tell you to serve rice as an accompaniment; and here, if you don't have a tried-and-true method of your own, you'll find my methods for cooking rice. Leftovers, in many instances, can be transformed into a polenta gratin, an omelet, or a crêpe, and in these pages you'll find two ways to cook polenta, a recipe for crêpes, and a recipe for a flat omelet, or frittata.

The techniques that are described in these pages by no means comprise an exhaustive list for the beginning cook. They represent just a few tricks that may make following some of the recipes easier for you, as well as techniques that come up often enough to devote a page to them here, rather than lengthen a given recipe. These include purging clams or mussels, cleaning greens and leeks, and peeling favas.

Other basic recipes and techniques are specific to a chapter in the book, such as pie crust recipes and savory cobbler toppings. You'll find those recipes and tips in the relevant chapters.

miscellaneous tips

The following is a somewhat random list of techniques that come up more than once throughout the book.

CRUSHING SPICES

If you don't have an electric spice mill, use a mortar and pestle for crushing. And if you don't have a mortar and pestle (you should), there are a couple of other ways to do it. In France, chefs sometimes put spices on a cutting board, cover them with the bottom of a frying pan, and lean back and forth on the frying pan, rolling them underneath it and crushing them under the weight. You could also do this with a rolling pin, or pound them with the blunt end of a knife.

HOW TO MAKE GARLIC PASTE WITH A KNIFE

The owner of a cooking school in Houston showed me how to do this about thirty years ago, and I must say it is brilliant. Your tools here will be salt, a cutting board, and a knife. It can be a chef's knife, a paring knife, or even a blunt dining knife. Place a clove of garlic on a cutting board with about ⅛ to ¼ teaspoon of salt. Take your knife and, holding the blade perpendicular to the garlic clove, scoop up a little salt and slide the blade down the side of the garlic clove, scraping off a bit of the garlic into the salt. The salt helps to break down the garlic. When you've scraped off most of the clove, and can no longer get a purchase on it, crush the remaining bit of the clove with the flat side of your knife, crushing it into the salt and mashing, until you have a nice paste. It won't taste as strong and pungent as garlic that is pounded, because pounding releases more volatile oils.

CLEANING LEEKS

Even when leeks appear to be clean, they're usually harboring some sand between the layers. Cut off the root ends, and cut the ends off at the point where the leeks begin to go from light to dark green. Cut the leeks in half lengthwise. Place them in a bowl of cold water for 5 minutes (or longer), then run under the faucet, fanning the layers so that the running water can flush out the dirt caught in between. Shake off water before slicing or chopping.

SOAKING RAW ONIONS OR SHALLOTS

If you are going to be serving onions or shallots raw, as a condiment (as in My Pozole, page 130), you'll want to soak them in acidulated water to rid them of some of the strong volatile oils that make your mouth (and breath) taste of raw onion for hours. Cut up the onion as directed. Fill a bowl with cold water and add a teaspoon of cider or wine vinegar. Add the onion. Let sit for at least 5 minutes and as long as 30. Drain and rinse with cold water.

CLEANING GREENS

Many recipes in this book call for greens. Most will tell you what to do to prepare them, but just to make it really clear, here's what I do.

I undo a bunch of greens and put it in one side of my double sink. If I didn't have a double sink, I'd just put the greens in the sink, with a big bowl or the bowl of my salad spinner on the side. Next, I tear the leaves from the stems and discard the stems, unless I need them for the recipe. I put the leaves into a bowl (which is usually the bowl of my salad spinner) or into the other side of my sink, depending on the quantity I'm dealing with. Then I fill the sink or bowl with water and swish the greens around. Because my sink has a pull-out spray attachment, I can apply a lot of water pressure to the greens by spraying water into the bowl and moving the greens around. I then lift the greens out of the sink or bowl; I don't pour them out with the water, because if I did the sand would nestle back into the folds of the greens. Then I pour out the water from the bowl, or drain my sink, and rinse until I can see no more sand. Then I repeat the process. There's always more sand. I wash salad greens the same way.

PEELING FAVA BEANS

Fava beans have to be peeled after you shell them. Some people find this tedious, but I rather enjoy it, and I think it goes pretty quickly. And what you get, when you finish, is so wonderful.

Bring a pot of water to a boil while you shell the favas. When the water is boiling, drop in the beans and boil for 1 minute. Immediately transfer to a bowl of ice-cold water, then drain. Slip the favas out of their skins by slitting one side with your thumbnail and gently squeezing out the beans. I find that the process goes quickly if I pick up a handful of beans, hold one between my thumb and forefinger, and use my other thumbnail to flick off the edge of the bean, squeeze the bean into my thumb and forefinger, and put it into the bowl I've placed on the work surface.

PITTING OLIVES

Until fairly recently I would always recommend an olive pitter for this task. But I found, when I was doing the recipes for this book, that I preferred pitting olives by laying them on a cutting board and leaning on them with the flat side of a knife, then halving the olives with my fingers and pulling out the pits. I could do more than one at a time this way, and it was easier to make sure that the pits didn't get mixed in with the olives.

PURGING MUSSELS AND CLAMS

Mussels and clams usually come with a fair amount of sand inside their tightly closed shells. Brushing and rinsing them under cold water help to get rid of some of the sand, but by taking the steps below, you are actually getting some help from the bivalves. When you put them into extra-salty or vinegary water, they tend to react by expelling the water—and sand—from their shells in the process.

Brush and rinse clams or mussels several times with cold water. Pull out the mussels' beards. Look at each one—clams and mussels—closely, and throw out any with cracked or open shells. They are dead. If the shell is a little bit open, tap on it, and if it moves a little, then the clam or mussel is all right.

Place the picked-over clams or mussels in a bowl of water and add a tablespoon of salt or vinegar to the water. Let sit for 15 minutes. Drain and repeat for another 15 minutes. Drain and rinse again.

simple vegetable stock

This is a very simple stock, in which the vegetables are just thrown into the pot. No need to roast them first, unless you want a darker, more intensely flavored broth. Make sure to include lots of carrots for sweetness and garlic for depth of flavor. ❖ **makes 7 cups**

1 onion, quartered

4 carrots, thickly sliced

1 celery stalk, sliced

4 to 8 garlic cloves, to taste, crushed and peeled

1 leek, white part only, cleaned and sliced

Salt (about 2 teaspoons)

Choice of vegetable trimmings, such as chard stalks, sliced; parsley stems, sliced; leek greens, cleaned and sliced; mushroom stems; or scallion trimmings

combine all of the ingredients with 2 quarts water in a large soup pot, pasta pot, or Dutch oven and bring to a boil. Reduce the heat, cover partially, and simmer gently for 30 minutes or longer. Strain through a fine strainer.

leftovers This is best used within a day of being made, but you can freeze it.

chicken or turkey stock

I'm not too fussy about my chicken stock. If I have a chicken carcass after a roast chicken, or a turkey carcass after Thanksgiving, you can bet I'll make stock sometime over the next few days. It'll be a light stock, made with lots of carrots and onions to sweeten the broth. If I want a richer stock I'll add some chicken wings and backs to the mixture. If I want homemade stock and don't have any in the freezer (this is rare) and don't have the carcass of a bird hanging about, I'll go and buy a chicken, or some chicken pieces, and make the stock. The turkey stock has a much richer flavor, and it is a bigger operation than making stock with the carcass from a roast chicken, simply because the carcass of a turkey is so big.

A confession: I don't always tie together my bay leaf, thyme, and parsley sprigs into a bouquet garni. Why should I? The broth is going to be strained anyway. ❖ **makes 2½ quarts**

Fresh or cooked carcass of a chicken or turkey plus 4 wings if desired; or 1 chicken, cut up; or 3 pounds chicken legs and thighs

4 medium carrots, thickly sliced

2 medium onions, peeled and quartered

1 leek, white and light green part only, cleaned and thickly sliced (optional)

6 garlic cloves, crushed and peeled

Bouquet garni made with 1 bay leaf and a couple of sprigs of fresh thyme and flat-leaf parsley, tied into the dark green outer leek leaf if using a leek, otherwise just tied together with string if desired

1 teaspoon black peppercorns

Salt to taste, if salting (½ to 1 teaspoon per quart of water, to taste)

if you're using a fresh chicken carcass, crack the bones slightly with a hammer. Otherwise, just place the bones or chicken pieces and all of the other ingredients in a big soup pot or Dutch oven and cover by 1 inch with water. Bring to a boil and skim off any foam that rises to the top. Reduce the heat to very low, cover partially, and simmer for 2 to 4 hours.

a note on salting
Most chefs don't salt their chicken stock, because they often reduce it for other dishes and it would become too salty. It's easier to gauge how much salt to use in other dishes if you don't salt your stock; but if you know you're going to be using it for chicken soup or another soup, then go ahead and salt to taste.

Strain through a cheesecloth-lined strainer into a large bowl or pot. Discard everything in the strainer, and place the bowl in the refrigerator, uncovered, for several hours or preferably overnight.

Remove the chilled stock from the refrigerator. Lift off the fat that will be floating on the surface, using either a slotted spatula or a skimmer. Strain the stock again through a fine-mesh strainer or a cheesecloth-lined medium strainer. Chill for up to 3 days, or freeze in 2-cup and 1-quart containers for up to 6 months.

leftovers Chicken and turkey stock freeze well. They'll be good for at least 6 months in the freezer. In the refrigerator they'll be fine for 3 days.

easy fish stock

There are several ways to make a fish stock without much hassle. If your recipe calls for shrimp, you can make a stock with the shells (see the Cioppino on page 248). A classic fish stock is made with fish carcasses and aromatics, but sometimes it isn't easy to find fish bones. Even my local fish store has to be informed beforehand if I want fish heads and bones, because they sell most of their fish off the bone, cut into steaks and fillets. If you can't get bones or heads, then use an inexpensive fish fillet for your stock. Don't use salmon, mackerel, tuna, or swordfish for the stock; they are too strong and fatty. ❖ **makes 4 to 5 cups**

1 pound fish trimmings (heads and bones) from a white-fleshed fish, or a whole white-fleshed fish, gills discarded and rinsed, or 1 pound white-fleshed fish fillets or steaks, rinsed

1 onion, quartered

1 carrot, sliced

1 celery stalk, sliced

1 leek, white and light green part only, cleaned and sliced

2 garlic cloves, crushed

Bouquet garni made with 2 sprigs of fresh flat-leaf parsley, 2 sprigs of fresh thyme, and 1 bay leaf

1 cup dry white wine (optional)

Salt

advance preparation
The stock is best made on the day you wish to make fish soup, but you can make it a day ahead and keep it in the refrigerator.

combine the fish trimmings or fish, the onion, carrot, celery, leek, garlic, and bouquet garni with 1 quart of water in a large soup pot or pasta pot. Bring to a boil, skim off all foam, reduce the heat, and simmer for 15 minutes. Add the wine, if using, and simmer for another 15 minutes. Remove from the heat and strain into a bowl through a fine sieve or a strainer lined with cheesecloth or paper towel. Discard the fish bones and vegetables. Taste and add salt as desired.

a really simple anchovy broth

If you have access to dried fish, such as the dried anchovies that are sold in Korean markets, you can make a very simple broth by tying about ½ ounce of the dried anchovies into a cheesecloth pouch, combining with 1 quart of water in a saucepan, and bringing to a boil. Decrease the heat to medium-low and boil gently for 10 minutes. Strain. This too should be used soon after making.

garlic broth

This vegetarian stock is the closest you can get to chicken stock, if you want a richly flavored broth without any meat. The garlic is mollified by the cooking, and the resulting broth is sweet, with a deep rich flavor. ❖ **makes 7 cups**

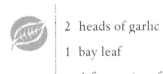

2 heads of garlic

1 bay leaf

   A few sprigs of fresh thyme

   A few sprigs of fresh flat-leaf parsley

2 teaspoons salt, or to taste

6 peppercorns

1 tablespoon olive oil

separate the garlic cloves, crush them with the flat side of a knife (place 1 or 2 cloves under the flat side of the knife and lean on the knife), and remove their skins.

Combine all the ingredients with 2 quarts water in a large soup pot, pasta pot, or Dutch oven and bring to a boil. Reduce the heat to very low, cover, and simmer for 1 to 2 hours. Strain and discard the garlic and herbs. Taste and adjust the salt.

leftovers ⦙ This will keep for a day in the refrigerator and freezes well.

japanese dashis

In Japan, one of the measures of a cook is the quality of his dashi, the kelp broth that is at the heart of many soups. Japanese chefs use kelp and bonito flakes, and the good ones have just the right touch when it comes to quantities and timing. These broths are less tricky, because the Japanese home cook uses a dashi bag, a packet like a tea bag, made primarily from bonito flakes, with seaweed and salt. You can use these Japanese broths for the Japanese noodle meals on pages 29–31. They're easy to put together, and they certainly give those soups an authentic flavor. You can get the ingredients at any Japanese market.

plain dashi

1 dashi bag

1 teaspoon soy sauce, or more to taste

½ to 1 teaspoon sugar, to taste

following the instructions on the dashi bag package, combine the dashi bag with 3 to 6 cups water in a medium saucepan and bring to a simmer. The package will tell you how long to simmer the bag. Discard the bag and add soy sauce and sugar to taste.

dashi with mirin

For a sweeter, richer dashi, add 1 to 3 tablespoons Japanese mirin or sweet sherry to the above, and increase the amount of soy sauce to 2 to 3 teaspoons.

mushroom dashi

Before combining the dashi bag with water, make a mushroom broth by steeping 10 dried shiitake mushrooms in 5 to 6 cups boiling water for 30 minutes. Strain and use the broth in place of water for your dashi.

béchamel

A béchamel is a "cream" sauce, though there is rarely cream in it. What causes it to be creamy and rich is the suspension of a flour and butter (or oil) paste, or roux, in a liquid, which is milk in a classic béchamel, but can also be stock. In this collection of recipes a béchamel is most often called for in gratins, lasagnes (which are really a kind of gratin), and pot pies. Sometimes the ingredients and procedure for the béchamel will be in the recipe, because of variations in quantity needed and ingredients. But this is the basic. ❖ **makes 2 cups**

2 tablespoons unsalted butter

2 cups milk (regular, low-fat, or nonfat)

2 tablespoons flour (3 tablespoons for a thicker sauce)

Salt and freshly ground white or black pepper

advance preparation
You can make a béchamel up to a day ahead of using it and keep it in the refrigerator. If you lay a sheet of plastic or wax paper directly on the top, there is less chance that a skin will form. But even if it does, you can get rid of it by whisking vigorously when you reheat the béchamel. Then the sauce should be as smooth as it was when you made it.

melt the butter over medium-low heat in a heavy medium saucepan, and heat the milk in another saucepan or in the microwave (2 minutes at 100-percent power works well in mine; I just heat it in a heatproof glass measuring cup). Add the flour to the butter and cook, stirring, for about 3 minutes, until smooth and bubbling but not browned. Whisk in the milk and bring to a simmer. Simmer, stirring, for 5 to 10 minutes, until the sauce has thickened and lost its raw flour taste. Season with salt and pepper.

variation

olive oil béchamel

In traditional Provençal cooking, béchamel was usually made with olive oil, which works beautifully and makes a sauce that is especially appropriate for lusty Provençal gratins, like the Spinach and Fish Gratin on page 212. Just substitute olive oil, tablespoon for tablespoon, for the butter. Heat over medium heat, then add the flour and proceed as directed above.

how i cook rice

You'll notice I'm not calling these recipes "How *to* Cook Rice," because there is more than one way to achieve a good pot of rice, and many people feel very strongly that their way of cooking it is the only way. The methods described below work well for me. Using a towel is the key to achieving rice that is fluffy, with separate grains. When the water has evaporated, turn off the heat, put a clean dish towel (or a couple of layers of paper towel) over the pot, replace the lid, and let it sit undisturbed for 10 to 15 minutes. The towel will absorb excess moisture.

steamed long-grain or basmati rice

This is how my package of Trader Joe's White Basmati Rice from India says to cook the rice. They don't tell you about the towel, though. ❖ serves 4

1 cup long-grain or basmati rice

1¼ to 2 cups water

½ to ¾ teaspoon salt, to taste

if using basmati or Thai jasmine rice, place the rice in a bowl and rinse in several changes of water until the water runs clear. Regular Carolina-style white rice doesn't need rinsing. Drain the rice and combine in a heavy saucepan with 1¼ cups water for firm rice or 1¾ to 2 cups water for softer rice (use 2 cups for Carolina rice). Bring to a boil, add the salt, cover, and turn the heat to low. Simmer for 12 to 20 minutes, until the water is absorbed (the less water you have, the less time it will take). I test by sticking the end of a chopstick down to the bottom of the pan. The rice should be just sticking to the bottom.

Remove from the heat, uncover, and place a clean dish towel or a few layers of paper towel over the top of the pan. Cover again and lift the edges of the towel up over the lid. Let it sit, undisturbed, for 10 to 15 minutes or longer.

pilaf-style rice

This is a slightly richer rice, and some insist this method is the best way to achieve a wonderfully fluffy result. Use long-grain or basmati rice. Don't use converted rice. ❖ serves 4

1　cup long-grain or basmati rice

1　tablespoon unsalted butter or oil (to taste)

2　cups warm water or chicken stock (page 378)

½　to ¾ teaspoon salt, to taste

if using basmati rice, place the rice in a bowl and rinse in several changes of water, until the water runs clear. If there is time, soak the rice for 30 minutes. Drain.

advance preparation
The towel allows you to cook rice ahead and not worry about the rice going soggy. You can leave it on a warm stovetop for an hour and it will be fine. Just don't disturb it. If you've cooked for a crowd, it's best to spread the rice out in a lightly oiled baking dish after it's sat under the towel for 10 to 15 minutes. Allow to cool completely, then cover with foil. Reheat in a 325°F. oven for 20 minutes.

Melt the butter or heat the oil over medium heat in a 2-quart, heavy saucepan. Add the rice and cook, stirring, for 2 to 3 minutes, until it absorbs the butter or oil and just begins to crackle. Add the water or stock and the salt and raise the heat to high. Bring to a boil, then reduce the heat to low, cover tightly, and cook for 12 to 15 minutes, until the liquid is absorbed. Check by sticking the end of a wooden spoon or a chopstick down to the bottom of the pot. The rice should be just starting to stick.

Remove from the heat, uncover, and place a clean dish towel or a few layers of paper towel over the top of the pan. Cover again and lift the edges of the towel up over the lid. Let sit, undisturbed, for 10 to 15 minutes or longer.

leftovers Cooked rice will keep for 4 or 5 days in the refrigerator, and it's great to have on hand for quick stir-fries, pilafs, and salads.

iranian rice *(chelo)*

Iranian rice is the pride as well as staple of Persian cuisine. As the rice steams gently in a generous amount of butter, a golden crust forms on the bottom of the pan. Called a tah-dig, the crust is served on the side, and is considered the measure of a cook. When I first tested this recipe, 3 cups of rice seemed like too much to me, but when I served it up to six people there was very little left over. Similarly, tested again, 2 cups of rice was not too much for four people, and my husband and I polished off 1 cup with no effort.

If you don't want to make such a large quantity of rice, use 2 cups rice and 6 cups water. Use the same quantities of butter, saffron, and yogurt as listed below. ❖ **serves 6 generously**

3 cups basmati rice

1½ teaspoons salt

4 tablespoons (½ stick) unsalted butter, melted

¼ to ½ teaspoon ground saffron, dissolved in 2 tablespoons hot water

2 tablespoons plain low-fat yogurt

pick over the rice, place in a bowl, and wash in several changes of cold water, until the water runs clean.

Bring 2 quarts water to a boil in a large, heavy pot (I recommend either enameled cast iron or nonstick). Add the salt, then add the rice. Boil for 5 to 10 minutes, stirring once or twice to make sure the rice doesn't stick to the bottom of the pan, until just tender but still firm. Drain in a colander and rinse.

Heat 3 tablespoons of the butter over medium heat in the nonstick pot. Stir in 2 table-spoons hot water, a teaspoon of the dissolved saffron, and the yogurt. Now take one spoonful of rice at a time and carefully mound it into the pot, heaping it in the center. Using the handle of a long wooden spoon, poke holes in the rice in several places, down to the bottom of the pot. Mix the remaining melted butter with 2 tablespoons hot water and pour over the pyramid. Cover the pot with a clean dish towel and cover tightly with a lid. Fold the edges of the towel up over the lid so that they do not make contact with the flame or burner. Cook for 10 minutes over medium heat, then turn the heat very low and cook for 40 to 50 minutes. Remove from the heat and place the

advance preparation
This rice can sit in the pot, with the towel and lid on, for an hour before you serve it.

pot on a damp towel. Allow to cool for 5 minutes without opening. Remove 4 tablespoons of the rice and mix with the remaining saffron in a dish. Set this aside.

Carefully mound the rice, a spoonful or spatula at a time, into a pyramid on a large oval or round serving platter. Do not disturb the crust on the bottom of the pot. Sprinkle the saffron rice over the top. Detach the crust on the bottom of the pan using a wooden or plastic spatula. Serve the rice with the bits of crust on the side.

leftovers : Cooked rice will keep for 4 or 5 days in the refrigerator. Use leftovers for pilafs, stir-fries, and salads.

yogurt cheese

I use yogurt cheese for toppings, spreads, sauces, and dips. It is yogurt that has been drained in a cheesecloth strainer (or in a convenient yogurt drainer that's worth having if you make this often). The yogurt loses half of its water content and thickens to a spreadable consistency.
❖ makes 1 cup

 2 cups yogurt (regular, low-fat, or nonfat)

line a strainer with a double thickness of cheesecloth and set it over a bowl. Or you can use a large coffee filter in a Melitta holder, as long as your Melitta doesn't smell too much of coffee. Place the yogurt in the strainer or filter and refrigerate for at least 1 hour and preferably 4 hours or longer. Discard the drained liquid. Transfer the thickened yogurt cheese to a covered container and refrigerate.

leftovers : This will last through the sell-by date on your yogurt. It will continue to give up water in the container, which you can simply pour off.

harissa

It's not too difficult to find harissa, the hot, spicy chili paste that is ubiquitous in Tunisian cooking. It's sold in tubes in most imported-foods markets. But homemade harissa is much better, and you can keep it for months in the refrigerator, as long as you keep it covered with olive oil. This harissa is based on the recipe given to me by my friend and colleague Clifford Wright.

❖ makes 1½ cups

2	ounces dried guajillo chili peppers, or a combination of guajillos and other hot dried peppers
2	ounces dried anaheim or pasilla peppers
	Boiling water
5	garlic cloves, peeled
1½	teaspoons salt
¾	teaspoon caraway seeds, ground
½	teaspoon coriander seeds, ground
4	to 5 tablespoons olive oil

wear rubber gloves to seed the chilies. Take the stems off and remove the seeds. The easiest way to do this is to open the chilies and knock the seeds out before you soak them. Place the chilies in a bowl and pour on boiling water to cover. Place a small plate or lid over the chilies so they'll stay submerged, and soak for 1 hour. Drain.

Crush the garlic to a paste in a mortar and pestle, or with the flat side of a knife with some of the salt. Place the drained chilies, the caraway, coriander, and salt in a food processor fitted with the steel blade and process until everything is chopped. Stop the machine and scrape down the sides. Add the garlic paste, turn on the food processor again, and with the machine running, add 2 tablespoons water and 3 tablespoons of the olive oil. Process until the mixture is smooth, stopping to stir down the sides if necessary. Transfer to a jar. Wipe the inside edges of the jar with a paper towel, then pour on a film of olive oil to cover the harissa. Top with a lid and refrigerate.

leftovers ⋮ Harissa is a condiment for the refrigerator. It will keep for months if covered with olive oil, so each time you use it, wipe down the insides of the jar carefully and pour on a little oil.

preserved lemons

Lemons preserved in a salt brine are a staple ingredient in North African cooking. They are used as both a condiment and an ingredient in tagines (stews) and salads. Thin-skinned lemons are best for preserving; Meyer lemons, the sweet-tasting light orange-hued lemons from California, are particularly well suited. Because a little preserved lemon goes a long way, you needn't pickle too many at a time, but you need enough to tightly pack the jar you are using. I've seen many different recipes for preserved lemons and tried several of them. They all seem to work. This is how I do it. ❖ **makes 6 to 12 lemons**

6 to 12 organic lemons or Meyer lemons (enough to fill a wide-mouth 1-pint or 1-quart jar), scrubbed

Sea salt or kosher salt

Fresh lemon juice, as needed

sterilize a jar by submerging it and its lid in boiling water for a minute. Very carefully lift the jar and lid out of the water using tongs. Tip the water in the jar out of the jar into the pot as you remove it, so that you don't get scalded. Set the jar on a clean dish towel, open side down, to drain.

Quarter each lemon lengthwise from the pointed end down to within about ½ inch of the bottom, making sure to keep the lemon intact. Pack the cut lemons with salt, filling each cut with salt. Place the lemons in the jar, packing as many salted lemons as will fit. Add additional lemon juice to completely cover the lemons, and cover tightly. Set in a cool place or in the refrigerator (that's where I keep mine) for at least 3 weeks. The lemons are ready when they have softened. To use, simply remove from the jar, rinse, and slice or chop as directed.

leftovers | These will keep for at least 6 months. If a film develops, just rinse it off.

rouille *(spicy garlic mayonnaise)*

Rouille is a spicy, saffrony garlic mayonnaise. The spice comes from ground cayenne, or a dried hot red pepper that is pounded with the garlic. I can make my rouille in a mortar and pestle, as many cooks do in Provence, because I have a big heavy marble one, which works much better than my wooden one. But a food processor works fine, and the food processor version is fluffier.

❖ **makes about 1¼ cups**

2 to 4 large garlic cloves, peeled, cut in half, and green shoot removed (to taste)

¼ teaspoon salt (or more to taste)

2 generous pinches of saffron

¼ teaspoon ground cayenne, or 1 dried hot red pepper, seeded

2 egg yolks

1 cup extra-virgin olive oil

whether or not you are using a mortar and pestle for the mayonnaise, begin by mashing the garlic, salt, saffron, and cayenne together in a mortar and pestle. Blend to a smooth paste.

advance preparation
This should not be made too many hours ahead, because the garlic will become too strong. However, you can always make the mayonnaise base (which is, after all, the time-consuming element in this recipe) several hours or even a day ahead. Make the garlic paste shortly before serving, then work it into the mayonnaise.

Using the mortar and pestle: Add the egg yolks to the mortar and pestle and beat with the pestle until smooth. Gradually drizzle in the olive oil, a spoonful at a time, and continue to stir constantly in one direction. As the mayonnaise begins to emulsify you can begin adding the olive oil in a steady stream, but stir constantly. When all of the oil has been added and the mayonnaise is thick, taste and adjust the salt.

Using the food processor: Make the garlic paste as directed above in the mortar and pestle. Place the egg yolks in the food processor fitted with the steel blade.

Turn on, and begin drizzling in the oil in a thin stream. When all of the oil has been added, stop the processor and scrape in the garlic paste. Process for a few seconds, until well mixed into the mixture. Taste and adjust the salt.

aïoli

This is a simpler garlic mayonnaise and is made just like the rouille, but without the saffron or cayenne. ❖ makes about 1¼ cups

follow the directions for rouille on page 390, but omit the saffron and cayenne.

leftovers ⋮ Mayonnaise with lots of garlic in it doesn't keep well because it becomes very pungent. Try to use it up the next day, by mixing it into a salad dressing or using in place of regular mayonnaise for a potato salad or a tuna or egg salad.

microwave-toasted tortillas

This is a marvelous way to make crispy low-fat tortilla chips. The microwave pulls all the moisture out of the tortillas, resulting in a dry, crisp chip.

place whole or cut-up tortillas in a single layer on a plate in the microwave. Zap at full power for 1 minute. Turn the wedges or whole tortillas over and zap again. Turn over, if they are not brown and crisp, and zap again. Cooking times vary from one microwave to another, but in mine it usually takes 2½ minutes. Remove when brown and crisp and let cool in a basket or bowl.

leftovers ⋮ After a day, these will lose their crispness.

frittata

A flat omelet, or frittata, is one of my favorite vehicles for leftovers. You can transform many of the ragouts, especially, into new meals by stirring them into eggs and making an omelet for as many people as you have eggs and leftovers for. For a one-person frittata use an 8-inch omelet pan; for a frittata that will serve 4 to 6 you can use a 10-inch pan; and for big frittatas use a 12-inch. You'll really appreciate your nonstick cookware when you make these.

2 to 10 large eggs

Salt and freshly ground black pepper

1 to 3 tablespoons low-fat milk

Filling of your choice

1 tablespoon olive oil

beat the eggs in a large bowl. Stir in the salt, pepper, milk, and the filling.

Heat the olive oil over medium-high heat in a heavy nonstick skillet. Hold your hand above it; it should feel hot. Drop a bit of egg into the pan and if it sizzles and cooks at once, the pan is ready. The reason it must be hot is that you want the eggs to form a cooked surface on the bottom of the pan immediately. You will be lifting this gently with a spatula and tilting the pan, so that the uncooked eggs run underneath and the omelet cooks layer by layer. Pour in the egg mixture. Swirl the pan to distribute the eggs and filling evenly over the surface. Shake the pan gently, tilting it slightly with one hand while lifting up the edges of the omelet with the spatula, in your other hand, to let the eggs run underneath during the first few minutes of cooking.

A 2-egg omelet will be done quickly, with just the tilting of the pan and letting the eggs run underneath until it is no longer moist on the top. A larger omelet must be covered and cooked over low heat. Turn the heat down to low, cover (use a pizza pan if you don't have a lid that will fit your skillet), and cook for 5 to 10 minutes, depending on the number of eggs, shaking the pan gently every once in a while. From time to time remove the lid and loosen the bottom of the omelet with a wooden or heatproof plastic spatula, tilting the pan so that the bottom doesn't burn. It will, however, turn a deep golden brown. This is fine. The eggs should be just about set; cook a few minutes longer if they're not.

A small 1- or 2-person frittata can be slid from the pan to a plate and served at once. A larger frittata may require finishing underneath the broiler and allowing to cool in the pan before serving.

advance preparation
Frittatas can be made a few hours ahead and served at room temperature.

For a large frittata: Heat the broiler. Finish the omelet under the broiler for 2 to 3 minutes, watching very carefully to make sure the top doesn't burn (it should brown slightly, and it will puff under the broiler). Remove from the heat, shake the pan to make sure the omelet isn't sticking (it will slide around a bit in the nonstick pan), and allow it to cool for at least 5 minutes and up to 15. Loosen the edges with a wooden or plastic spatula. Carefully slide from the pan onto a large round platter. Cut in wedges and serve.

leftovers Frittatas are good cold, and make great picnic or lunch-box fare. If serving the next day, allow to cool to room temperature, cover with plastic, then foil, and refrigerate. They'll keep for about 3 days in the refrigerator.

crêpes

Crêpes used to be a hot menu item, many years ago. Then we sort of forgot about them. But these paper-thin pancakes make a great vehicle for leftovers from many of the dishes in this collection, so I'm including both buckwheat crêpes and regular wheat crêpes in this chapter. Buckwheat crêpes have a very earthy, rustic flavor, whereas the wheat crêpes are more delicate.

❖ makes 12 to 14 crêpes

classic crêpes

¾ cup milk

½ cup water

2 large eggs

½ teaspoon salt

¾ cup plus 2 tablespoons unbleached all-purpose flour

3 tablespoons unsalted butter, melted, plus butter for the pan

buckwheat crêpes

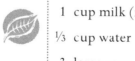

1 cup milk (regular, reduced-fat, or low-fat)

⅓ cup water

3 large eggs

½ teaspoon salt

⅔ cup buckwheat flour

½ cup unbleached white flour

2 tablespoons unsalted butter, melted, plus additional for cooking

place the milk, water, eggs, and salt in a blender or food processor fitted with the steel blade. Turn on and with the motor running add the flour(s), then the melted butter, and blend at high speed for 1 minute. Transfer to a bowl, cover, and refrigerate for 1 to 2 hours before making the crêpes. Whisk again before making the crepes.

Heat a 6- to 7-inch seasoned crêpe pan or nonstick skillet over medium heat and brush lightly with butter. When the pan just begins to smoke, remove from the heat and pour in or ladle in about 3 tablespoons batter per crêpe, enough to thinly coat the bottom of the pan. Tilt or swirl the pan to distribute the batter in an even layer. Return the pan to the heat and cook the crêpe for about 1 minute, or until it is easy to loosen the edges with a thin spatula or butter knife. The bottom of the crêpe should be nicely browned and should not stick to the pan. Flip the crêpe over and cook for 30 seconds on the other side, until it is speckled. Turn out onto a plate.

Cook all of the crêpes like this, whisking the batter from time to time, until all of the batter is used up. If not using right away, stack between pieces of wax paper. Seal in a plastic bag and refrigerate, or wrap in foil, then seal in a bag, and freeze.

Filling crêpes: Crêpes can be folded in half like an omelet, rolled like an enchilada, or folded into quarters. The nature of the filling and whether or not you're going to reheat the crêpes will help you determine how to fill the crêpe. If it is a substantial filling with some bulk, then folding or rolling the crêpe is the best way to fill it. If it is spreadable, or a simple filling like grated cheese, then the crêpe can be quartered and served right away. To quarter a crêpe, spread or sprinkle the filling over the crêpe, fold it in half, then fold in half again. To roll it, spread the filling on the crêpe and roll up like an enchilada. To fold, put the filling in the middle or on one side and fold the warm crêpe over it.

leftovers : Crêpes keep well in the refrigerator for a couple of days and can be frozen for a couple of months. They thaw in minutes.

two ways to make polenta

Polenta makes a fantastic setting for leftover stews and ragouts. Spread them over the top, warm them in the oven, maybe add a little cheese and brown the top, and you have a second meal made out of the first one. The traditional way to make polenta is to add it ever so slowly to a pot of simmering water, or for a rich polenta, milk, and to stir with a long-handled spoon until the mixture is thick and creamy (which usually coincides with getting a blister on the inside of your thumb, if you want a handy hint for timing). Polenta made this way is undoubtedly creamier than the polenta made the easy way. But we are, after all, talking about making an easy and delicious dinner out of leftovers, so I invariably choose the easy way. But here are both options. The polenta I get comes in a medium or coarse grind. Either works fine. However, do not substitute regular corn-meal, which can be too powdery.

easy polenta
❖ serves 6 to 8

2 cups coarse or medium polenta

8 cups water

2½ teaspoons salt

1 to 2 tablespoons butter, to taste

heat the oven to 350°F. Combine all the ingredients in a 3- to 4-quart baking dish. Stir together and place in the oven. Bake for 1 hour and 20 minutes. Remove from the oven, stir, and return to the oven for 10 more minutes. Remove from the oven, let sit for 5 minutes, and serve with the topping of your choice, or as a side dish with a vegetable gratin.

advance preparation
If you are serving the polenta hot with a topping, it's best to serve it when it comes out of the oven, though it can sit for more than the required 5 minutes.

Note: This recipe can be halved. But when making only 1 cup of polenta, bake for 1 hour only, not 1 hour and 20 minutes. Then stir the polenta and return to the oven for 10 minutes as in the above recipe.

classic polenta

❖ serves 4

4 cups water

1 teaspoon salt

½ pound (about 1⅓ cups) coarse or medium polenta

have a kettle of water at a simmer, in case you need to add more water to the polenta. Bring the 4 cups of water to a boil in a large (at least 3-quart) saucepan or pot. Meanwhile, prepare your platter or cutting board by brushing it with butter or olive oil. Add the salt to the water and reduce the heat to low. The water should be just boiling, with bubbles breaking through from time to time. Using a long-handled spoon, stir the water in one direction only while you add the polenta in a very slow stream. The easiest way to do this is to pick up handfuls of cornmeal and let it slip between your fingers into the water.

Once all of the cornmeal has been added, continue to stir in one direction for 30 minutes, or until the polenta is thick and comes away from the sides of the pot. If it becomes too thick to stir, add a little simmering water. The polenta should have a creamy consistency when done, and a spoon should stand up when stuck in the middle.

When the polenta is done, immediately pour it onto the platter or cutting board. Serve right away, or allow to cool and then slice it to serve with a topping.

leftovers ┊ Polenta will keep, once cooked, for several days in the refrigerator, and it is delicious cut into pieces and grilled, toasted, or broiled.

polenta made with milk

variation

Some very rich Northern Italian polenta dishes call for milk instead of water. You can use regular, low-fat, or skim. If you'll be adding a lot of cheese or butter to the polenta, I recommend using skim.

vinaigrette to keep in the refrigerator

I like to make this sharp vinaigrette regularly so that salads only take as long to make as it takes to wash lettuce. Not that it takes a long time to make a vinaigrette. But with this on hand, you'll be inspired to turn some leftovers into wonderful salads. I keep this in a squeeze bottle.

❖ **makes 1½ cups**

¼ cup sherry vinegar or wine vinegar

1 tablespoon balsamic vinegar

Salt

1 tablespoon Dijon mustard

1 cup extra-virgin olive oil (more to taste)

1 medium or large garlic clove

whisk together the vinegars, salt, and Dijon mustard. Whisk in the olive oil. Cut the garlic clove into thin slices and place either in a jar or a squeeze bottle. If using a jar, impale the garlic slices on a toothpick, leaving space between the slices. Pour the dressing over the garlic and let sit for an hour out of the refrigerator, or up to a week or longer in the refrigerator. Use as needed, shaking well before each use.

leftovers The dressing doesn't deteriorate much over time, because the sliced garlic flavors the mixture slowly, without making it too pungent. You can make it as far ahead as you wish. It will keep well for a week or 10 days. If the olive oil hardens in the refrigerator, simply bring the dressing to room temperature and shake the jar well before using.

vanilla sugar

Vanilla sugar is just what the words say: vanilla-scented sugar. In France it's a staple.

❖ makes 2 cups

 To make vanilla sugar, reserve the pods from vanilla beans you have used in another recipe. Rinse them and allow them to dry completely on a paper towel. Submerge the pods in 2 cups of sugar and store in a jar or covered container. Whenever a recipe calls for vanilla beans, add the pods to the sugar (if they're simmered, dry them first). Within a couple of weeks your sugar will be beautifully scented.

index

CONVERSION CHART

American cooks use standard containers, the 8-ounce cup and a tablespoon that takes exactly 16 level fillings to fill that cup level. Measuring by cup makes it very difficult to give weight equivalents, as a cup of densely packed butter will weigh considerably more than a cup of flour. The easiest way therefore to deal with cup measurements in recipes is to take the amount by volume rather than by weight. Thus the equation reads:

1 cup = 240 ml = 8 fl. oz.   ½ cup = 120 ml = 4 fl. oz.

It is possible to buy a set of American cup measures in major stores around the world.

In the States, butter is often measured in sticks. One stick is the equivalent of 8 tablespoons. One tablespoon of butter is therefore the equivalent to ½ ounce/15 grams.

LIQUID MEASURES

Fluid Ounces	U.S.	Imperial	Milliliters
	1 teaspoon	1 teaspoon	5
¼	2 teaspoons	1 dessertspoon	10
½	1 tablespoon	1 tablespoon	14
1	2 tablespoons	2 tablespoons	28
2	¼ cup	4 tablespoons	56
4	½ cup		110
5		¼ pint or 1 gill	140
6	¾ cup		170
8	1 cup		225
9			250, ¼ liter
10	1¼ cups	½ pint	280
12	1½ cups		340
15		¾ pint	420
16	2 cups		450
18	2¼ cups		500, ½ liter
20	2½ cups	1 pint	560
24	3 cups		675
25		1¼ pints	700
27	3½ cups		750
30	3¾ cups	1½ pints	840
32	4 cups or 1 quart		900
35		1¾ pints	980
36	4½ cups		1000, 1 liter
40	5 cups	2 pints or 1 quart	1120

SOLID MEASURES

U.S. and Imperial Measures		Metric Measures	
Ounces	Pounds	Grams	Kilos
1		28	
2		56	
3½		100	
4	¼	112	
5		140	
6		168	
8	½	225	
9		250	¼
12	¾	340	
16	1	450	
18		500	½
20	1¼	560	
24	1½	675	
27		750	¾
28	1¾	780	
32	2	900	
36	2¼	1000	1
40	2½	1100	
48	3	1350	
54		1500	1½

OVEN TEMPERATURE EQUIVALENTS

Fahrenheit	Celsius	Gas Mark	Description
225	110	¼	Cool
250	130	½	
275	140	1	Very Slow
300	150	2	
325	170	3	Slow
350	180	4	Moderate
375	190	5	
400	200	6	Moderately Hot
425	220	7	Fairly Hot
450	230	8	Hot
475	240	9	Very Hot
500	250	10	Extremely Hot

Any broiling recipes can be used with the grill of the oven, but beware of high-temperature grills.

EQUIVALENTS FOR INGREDIENTS

all-purpose flour—plain flour
baking sheet—oven tray
buttermilk—ordinary milk
cheesecloth—muslin
coarse salt—kitchen salt
cornstarch—cornflour
eggplant—aubergine

granulated sugar—caster sugar
half and half—12% fat milk
heavy cream—double cream
light cream—single cream
parchment paper—greaseproof paper
plastic wrap—cling film
scallion—spring onion

shortening—white fat
unbleached flour—strong, white flour
zest—rind
zucchini—courgettes or marrow